国家出版基金项目
NATIONAL PUBLICATION FOUNDATION

THE CHINESE PATH

REGIONAL ECONOMIC DEVELOPMENT IN CHINA

WEI HOUKAI

Translated by
ZHANG AIMIN

中国财经出版传媒集团
经济科学出版社
Economic Science Press
·北 京·

图书在版编目（CIP）数据

中国区域经济发展 = Regional Economic
Development in China：英文 / 魏后凯著；章爱民译.
北京：经济科学出版社，2025.5.--（《中国道路》丛
书：英文版）.-- ISBN 978-7-5218-6081-8

Ⅰ.F127

中国国家版本馆 CIP 数据核字第 20241C9E25 号

责任编辑：李　宝
责任校对：易　超
责任印制：张佳裕

中国区域经济发展

ZHONGGUO QUYU JINGJI FAZHAN

Regional Economic Development in China

魏后凯　著

章爱民　译

经济科学出版社出版、发行　新华书店经销
社址：北京市海淀区阜成路甲 28 号　邮编：100142
总编部电话：010-88191217　发行部电话：010-88191522
网址：www.esp.com.cn
电子邮箱：esp@esp.com.cn
天猫网店：经济科学出版社旗舰店
网址：http://jjkxcbs.tmall.com
北京季蜂印刷有限公司印装
787×1092　16 开　18.75 印张　530000 字
2025 年 5 月第 1 版　2025 年 5 月第 1 次印刷
ISBN 978-7-5218-6081-8　定价：88.00 元
（图书出现印装问题，本社负责调换。电话：010-88191545）
（版权所有　侵权必究　打击盗版　举报热线：010-88191661
QQ：2242791300　营销中心电话：010-88191537
电子邮箱：dbts@esp.com.cn）

Preface

The Chinese path refers to the path of socialism with distinctive Chinese characteristics. As Chinese President Xi Jinping points out, it is not an easy path. We are able to embark on this path thanks to the great endeavors of the reform and opening up over the past 30 years and more, and the continuous quest made in the 60-plus years since the founding of the People's Republic of China (PRC). It is based on a thorough review of the evolution of the Chinese nation over more than 170 years since modern times and carrying forward the 5,000-year-long Chinese civilization. This path is deeply rooted in history and broadly based on China's present realities.

A right path leads to a bright future. The Chinese path is not only access to China's development and prosperity, but also a path of hope and promise to the rejuvenation of the Chinese nation. Only by forging the confidence in the path, theory, institution and culture can we advance along this path of socialism with Chinese characteristics. With this focus, *The Chinese Path Series* presents to readers an overview in practice, achievements and experiences as well as the past, present and future of the Chinese path.

The Chinese Path Series is divided into ten volumes with one hundred books on different topics. The main topics of the volumes are as follows: economic development, political advancement, cultural progress, social development, ecological conservation, national defense and armed forces building, diplomacy and international policies, the Party's leadership and building, localization of Marxism in China and views from other countries on the Chinese path. Each volume on a particular topic consists of several books which respectively throw light on exploration in practice, reform process, achievements, experiences and theoretical innovations of the Chinese path. Focusing on the practice in the reform and opening up with the continuous exploration since the founding of the PRC, these books summarize on the development and inheritance of China's glorious civilization, which not only display a strong sense of the times, but also have profound historical appeal and future-oriented impact.

1

The series is conceived in its entirety and assigned to different authors. In terms of the writing, special attention has been paid to the combination of history and reality, as well as theory and practice at home and abroad. It gives a realistic and innovative interpretation of the practice, experience, process and theory of the Chinese path. Efforts are made on the distinctive and convincing expression in a global context. It helps to cast light on the "Chinese wisdom" and the "Chinese approach" that the Chinese path has contributed to the modernization of developing countries and solutions to human problems.

On the basis of the great achievements in China's development since the founding of the PRC, particularly since the reform and opening up, the Chinese nation, which had endured so much and for so long since the modern times, has achieved tremendous growth—it has stood up, become prosperous and grown in strength. The socialism with distinctive Chinese characteristics has shown great vitality and entered a new stage. This path has been expanded and is now at a new historical starting point. At this vital stage of development, the Economic Science Press of China Finance & Economy Media Group has designed and organized the compilation of *The Chinese Path Series*, which is of great significance in theory and practice.

The program of *The Chinese Path Series* was launched in 2015, and the first publications came out in 2017. The series was listed in a couple of national key publication programs, the "90 kinds of selected publications in celebration of the 19th CPC National Congress", and National Publication Foundation.

Editorial Board of *The Chinese Path Series*

Contents

Chapter 1
General Introduction

The central government of China has consistently aimed to leverage regional strengths and stimulate regional economic vitality under a new development pattern of regional economies. This pattern allows each region to focus on economic activities that align with their unique features, leading to a rational division of labor, coordinated development, and common prosperity. Since the founding of the People's Republic of China (PRC) in 1949, China has witnessed significant strategic shifts in its regional economic development. Initially, the emphasis was on achieving balanced development across different regions, which later shifted towards unbalanced development. Currently, the priority is on coordinated regional development. Through long-term and continuous efforts, the Chinese government has made steady progress in improving strategies for regional coordination and implementing differentiated regional policies, ultimately establishing a distinctively Chinese approach to coordinated regional development.

1.1   Zoning and characteristics of China's economic regions

China, a vast developing country with significant regional variations, faces a substantial imbalance in its economic development across different regions. During the initial stages of the reform and opening up, the Chinese government employed the conventional "dichotomy" to illustrate the disparities between coastal and inland areas in its Sixth Five-year Plan.[1] During the Seventh Five-year Plan period, the Chinese government continued the "dichotomy" approach and divided the whole country into three major economic regions: the eastern region, the central region, and the western region (see Table 1-1). This division was based on variations in geographical location

---

[1] As early as the First Five-year Plan period (1952-1957), China adopted the "dichotomy" that divided the whole country into coastal and inland areas. In 1956, Mao Zedong discussed in detail the relationship between coastal and inland areas in his book *On the Ten Major Relationships*. See Mao Zedong, *On the Ten Major Relationships*, Beijing: People's Publishing House, 1976.

and levels of economic development, and served a foundation for determining economic development priorities and optimizing productivity layout. Although somewhat simplified and generalized, this method of division did have an important influence on China's regional statistics and policy making. The central region and the western regions here actually referred to "inland area" mentioned previously, which are commonly referred to collectively as the central & western region. Therefore, in the Eighth Five-year Plan, the Chinese government resumed the approach of dichotomy between coastal and inland areas. In the Ninth Five-year Plan, however, these regions were expressed as the eastern region and the central & western region. It should be noted that in the Ninth Five-year Plan, although the Chinese government proposed to establish seven inter-province (autonomous regions, municipalities) economic regions directly under the Central Government with their own characteristics, this idea was not effectively implemented. The main reason for that was the need for further study on rationality of such divisions, and more importantly, the lack of clarity regarding the purpose of such zoning. This method was clearly influenced by the Soviet Union's practice of zoning comprehensive economic regions. However, with China's transition from a planned economy to a market economy, the central government had actually lost its capacity of developing comprehensive economic regions.

Table 1-1   China's zoning of economic regions since the
reform and opening up

National Plan	Period	Zoning Results
The Sixth Five-year Plan	1981-1985	Coastal area and inland area
The Seventh Five-year Plan	1986-1990	Eastern coastal region, central region, western region
The Eighth Five-year Plan	1991-1995	Coastal area and inland area
The Ninth Five-year Plan	1996-2000	(1) The Yangtze River Delta and the areas along the Yangtze River, the Bohai Rim region, the southeast coastal region, some provinces in southwest and south China, the northeastern region, the five provinces in central China, and the northwest region; (2) eastern region, and central and western region
The 10th Five-year Plan	2001-2005	Western region, eastern region, central region
The 11th Five-year Plan	2006-2010	(1) Western region, northeastern region, central region and eastern region; (2) old revolutionary base areas, areas with large ethnic minority populations and border areas; (3) four types of functional zones—development zones to be optimized, key development zones, restricted development zones and prohibited development zones

(continued)

National Plan	Period	Zoning Results
The 12th Five-year Plan	2011-2015	(1) Western region, northeastern region, central region and eastern region; (2) old revolutionary base areas, areas with large ethnic minority populations, border areas, and impoverished areas; (3) functional zones
The 13th Five-year Plan	2016-2020	(1) The western region, the northeastern region, the central region and the eastern region; (2) Beijing-Tianjin-Hebei region and Yangtze River Economic Belt; (3) old revolutionary base areas, areas with large ethnic minority populations, border areas and impoverished areas; (4) functional areas

Source: Sorted according to the Outline of the Five-Year Plan for National Economic and Social Development of the People's Republic of China over the years.

In order to facilitate coordinated regional development, a national strategy for the large-scale development of the western region was launched in 1999. Apart from the 10 western provinces as identified in the Seventh Five-year Plan, two other autonomous regions—Guangxi (previously included in the eastern region) and Inner Mongolia (previously included in the central region) —were added into its coverage. Thus, from the perspective of provincial administrative units, the "Extended Western Region" concept of "10+2" (the strategy also covered Yanbian Korean Autonomous Prefecture in Jilin Province, Enshi Tujia and Miao Autonomous Prefecture in Hubei Province, and Xiangxi Tujia and Miao Autonomous Prefecture in Hunan Province) and the new three-zone pattern in the context of the developing west China have been formed. After that, national strategies of revitalizing old industrial bases in northeast China and stimulating the rise of the central region were successively implemented, thus forming a new pattern of the four major regions of east, central, west and northeast China. Later, this four-major-region zoning method was adopted in the outlines of the 11th Five-year Plan to 13th Five-year Plan. Liaoning (originally belonged to the eastern region), Jilin and Heilongjiang provinces (originally belonged to the central region) were thus zoned as the northeastern region. In this case, there are only 10 provinces left in the eastern region, and six provinces in the central region (see Figure 1-1). In reality, judging from economic ties and integration level, the central region is currently not complete or independent enough to be taken as an economic region. And further, there are significant internal disparities between the eastern and the western regions. For example, within the western region, the southwest and the northwest differ much in development level; within the eastern region, great differences also exist among the Yangtze River Delta,

Pearl River Delta, Shandong Peninsula, and Beijing-Tianjin-Hebei region.[1] In this sense, only the northeastern region can be roughly regarded as a relatively independent economic region.

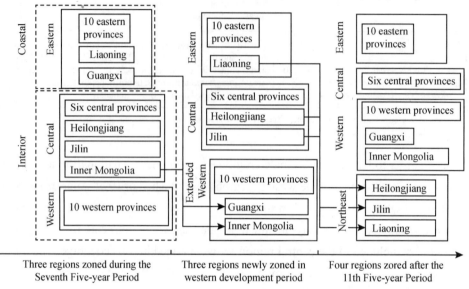

Figure 1-1   Changes in China's three major economic zonings in recent years

Note: The 10 eastern provinces include Beijing, Tianjin, Hebei, Shandong, Jiangsu, Shanghai, Zhejiang, Fujian, Guangdong, and Hainan. The six central provinces refer to Shanxi, Henan, Anhui, Hubei, Hunan, and Jiangxi. The 10 western provinces include Sichuan, Chongqing, Shaanxi, Guizhou, Yunnan, Tibet, Gansu, Ningxia, Qinghai, and Xinjiang.

Source: Wei Houkai et al., Research on the Adjustment of China's Industrial Layout, Institute of Industrial Economics, Chinese Academy of Social Sciences, December 2005.

Unless otherwise stated, this book adopts the four-major-region zoning method used in China's 11th Five-year Plan, by which the whole country is zoned into four major regions. Specifically, the eastern region comprises 10 provinces: Hebei, Beijing, Tianjin, Shandong, Shanghai, Jiangsu, Zhejiang, Fujian, Guangdong, and Hainan; the northeastern region covers Liaoning, Jilin, and Heilongjiang provinces; the central region includes Shanxi, Henan, Anhui, Hubei, Hunan, and Jiangxi provinces; and the western region encompasses 12 provinces: Inner Mongolia, Guangxi, Shaanxi, Gansu, Ningxia, Qinghai, Xinjiang, Chongqing, Sichuan, Guizhou, Yunnan, and Tibet.

---

[1] The concept of Bohai Rim Economic Zone used to be mentioned in academia. But in fact, the Bohai Rim region consists of Shandong Peninsula, Liaodong Peninsula and Beijing-Tianjin-Hebei region, which enjoy different characteristics, are independent of each other and are not closely linked economically. In the near future, it is difficult for the Bohai Rim region to form a relatively complete economic region.

Table 1-2 shows that in 2016, despite accounting for only 38.4 percent of the national population, the eastern region achieved significant results in several aspects. Its gross regional product (GRP) accounted for 52.3 percent; industrial added value, 53.7 percent; value added of the tertiary industry, 56.1 percent; local general public budgetary revenues, 57.3 percent; total retail sales of consumer goods, 51.6 percent; and value of exports, 84.4 percent, of the entire country. In contrast, the total economic output of the central and western regions was significantly lower than their respective population shares. This mismatch between economic performance and population distribution has resulted in imbalances and substantial gaps in China's regional economic development.

In 2016, the GRP per capita in the eastern region reached US$11,479, while in the northeast, central, and western regions, it stood at only US$7,218, US$6,526, and US$6,299, respectively. At the provincial level, Tianjin boasted the highest GRP per capita in the year, was 4.19 that times of Gansu, the lowest-ranking province. Despite the significant reduction in the ratio of the maximum to minimum value since the reform and opening up, it remains substantial when compared to developed countries. Even at the level of prefecture-level cities, counties, or towns, the gap remains substantial. Arguably, China is still one of the countries with the largest regional development disparities in the world.

Table 1-2　　　Proportion of the main indicators of China's four
major regions to the whole country in 2016　　　　Unit: %

Main indicators	Whole country[a]	Eastern region	Central region	Western region	Northeastern region
Total population	100	38.4	26.6	27.1	7.9
Gross regional product	100	52.3	20.6	20.3	6.8
Added value of the secondary industry	100	53.7	21.9	18.6	5.8
Added value of the tertiary industry	100	56.1	18.6	18.5	6.8
Local general public budget revenues	100	57.3	17.6	19.8	5.3
Total investment in fixed assets	100	42.1	26.6	26.1	5.2
Total retail sales of consumer goods	100	51.6	21.1	18.5	8.8
Export volume[b]	100	84.4	7.0	6.0	2.6

Note: [a] The proportion of the indicators of four major regions to those of the whole country is calculated based on taking the total of all regions of the country as 100. [b] The export volume is sorted by domestic origin of the exports.

Source: Calculated in accordance with *China Statistical Yearbook* (*2017*) and *China Statistical Abstract* (*2017*).

1.2 Transformation of regional development strategy since the reform and opening up

Since the reform and opening up in 1978, China's regional economy has experienced a strategic transformation from unbalanced to coordinated development. Generally speaking, this strategic change can be roughly divided into three stages, namely, the unbalanced development favoring the eastern region (1979-1990), the launching of regional coordinated development strategies with the focus transferred to the central and western regions (1991-1998), and the full implementation of regional coordinated development strategies (after 1999) (Wei Houkai et al., 2011). In March 1991, the Chinese government formally proposed for the first time in the Eighth Five-year Plan to promote coordinated regional economic development, indicating that the coordinated regional development would be elevated to the level of national strategy. The national strategy for the large-scale development of the western region, strategy of revitalizing the old industrial bases in the northeast, and strategy of promoting the rise of the central region were officially announced in September 1999, October 2003, and January 2004 respectively, which marked that China's regional coordinated development strategy entered the third stage of full implementation.

1.2.1 Stage Ⅰ (1979-1990): pursuit of east-favored unbalanced development

During the 1979-1990 period, China's regional development strategy was primarily influenced by the then trend of unbalanced development. The state-level investment layout and regional policies centered around the objective of enhancing efficiency, favoring coastal regions with better conditions, while also providing support to economically disadvantaged and underdeveloped areas, as well as areas with large ethnic minority populations. As the economic development strategy and system transitioned, China's regional policy tools have become increasingly diverse.

1.2.1.1 Changes in the guidelines for regional economic development

Starting from the Sixth Five-year Plan, the guidelines for China's productivity layout and regional economic development have gradually shifted towards improving economic benefits and favoring coastal areas, rather than preparing for war and reducing regional disparities as before. The Sixth Five-Year Plan for National Economic and Social Development stated the intention to leverage the favorable conditions of coastal areas, "giving full play to their unique features and promoting further development of

China's interior economy". At the same time, we should "strive to develop China's interior economy" and "continue to actively support and effectively help the areas with large ethnic minority populations to develop a productive and prosperous economy". The Seventh Five-Year Plan for National Economic and Social Development went further by dividing the country into three major economic zones: the eastern, the central, and the western regions. It proposed "to accelerate the development of the coastal eastern region, to build the central region into the source of energy and raw materials, and at the same time, make active preparations for further developing the western region". In 1988, the Central Committee of the Communist Party of China (CPC) and the State Council of the PRC introduced the economic development strategy of coastal areas with coastal township enterprises as the main driving force and "integrating both ends of the production process (raw material the supply and product marketing) into global market and engaging in large-scale import and export activities" as the main content.

1.2.1.2   Gradual shift of national investment focus towards the east

During the Sixth Five-year Plan period, China's productivity layout largely focused on improving economic benefits and favoring regions with certain advantages. Statistically, 47.7 percent of China's investment in capital construction went to the coastal areas, rising from 42.2 percent in the Fifth Five-year Plan period, while that to the inland areas decreased from 50 percent to 46.5 percent. During this period, 51.5 percent of China's investment in technical updates and transformation went to the coastal areas, but only 45.8 percent to the inland. By the early period of the Seventh Five-year Plan, China's productivity layout had further inclined towards coastal areas. Between 1985 and 1988, China witnessed an increase in the proportion of investment in capital construction towards coastal areas, rising from 48.4 percent to 53.2 percent. Conversely, investment in inland areas experienced a decline, dropping from 45.0 percent to 39.9 percent. As a result, the ratio of investment between coastal and inland areas grew from 1.07 : 1 to 1.36 : 1. During the three-year rectification period (1988-1990), the state increased the proportion of its investment in the inland areas, in a bid to support the development of key industries such as energy and raw materials. In 1990, in China's investment in capital construction, the proportion to coastal areas reached 50.9 percent, with only 40.1 percent to the inland areas, and the ratio of coastal and inland investment dropped to 1.27 : 1. However, in the whole Seventh Five-year Plan period, the ratio of coastal and inland infrastructure investment was still as high as 1.29 : 1, much higher than 1.03 : 1 in the Sixth Five-year Plan period and 0.84 : 1 in the Fifth Five-year Plan period.

1.2.1.3 Implementation of coastal open-door policy

In 1978, China developed a strategic policy of opening to the outside world and invigorating the internal economy.

To accelerate the pace of opening to the outside world, in July 1979, the CPC Central Committee and the State Council formally approved Guangdong and Fujian provinces to implement special policies and flexible measures in their foreign economic activities. Since 1980, China has successively established five Special Economic Zones, namely Shenzhen, Zhuhai, Shantou, Xiamen, and Hainan, which have since implemented special economic policies and management systems. In 1984, the central government decided to further open 14 Coastal Open Cities (Dalian, Qinhuangdao, Tianjin, Yantai, Qingdao, Lianyungang, Nantong, Shanghai, Ningbo, Wenzhou, Fuzhou, Guangzhou, Zhanjiang, and Beihai), allowing them to set up economic and technological development zones and enjoy favorable policies similar to those for the Special Economic Zones. After that, the state successively opened up the Yangtze River Delta, the Pearl River Delta, the Xiamen-Zhangzhou-Quanzhou Delta in southern Fujian, the Liaodong Peninsula, and the Jiaodong Peninsula as coastal economic open zones, and established Investment zones for businessmen from Taiwan region in Fujian. In June 1990, the CPC Central Committee and the State Council sanctioned the development and opening of Pudong New Area in Shanghai, along with the implementation of several preferential policies akin to those for special economic zones. Consequently, these initiatives resulted in the establishment of a coastal open zone that stretches from the southern to the northern regions along the coastline.

1.2.1.4 State-led poverty alleviation and development policies

In the early 1980s, the Chinese government began to conceive plans to tackle problems in impoverished areas. In 1982 and in cooperation with the World Bank, China carried out its pilot projects for poverty alleviation first in the Hexi Corridor and the arid Dingxi of Gansu, and the Xihaigu area of Ningxia. In 1984, the central government promised to help lift the people in poverty-stricken areas out of poverty first, with focus on more than a dozen contiguous areas of extreme poverty. In 1986, the State Council Leading Group of Poverty Alleviation and Development was established to identify the poverty-stricken counties, to develop the standards for supporting them, and also, as stated in the Seventh Five-year Plan, to help develop old revolutionary base areas, areas with large ethnic minority populations, border areas, and impoverished areas to get rid of economic and cultural backwardness as soon as possible. After that, the Central government put forward a two-step idea to eliminate poverty in China: the first step is to ensure that the whole population would have adequate food and clothing, that is, by 1990, to ensure the food and clothing for more than 90 percent of poor households in poverty-stricken counties in normal years; the second step is to ensure the people a moderately prosperous life, that is, on the basis of ensuring food and clothing and through regional economic development, to make poor areas capable of developing on their own and gradually becoming prosperous. To boost the development in poverty-stricken regions, the government has augmented its investments in poverty alleviation, adopted a work-for-relief approach, and established policies to ease the burden on these areas and foster local economic growth.

1.2.1.5   Further improved policies for areas with large ethnic minority populations

Since 1979, despite the primary focus of investment layout and policy support on coastal areas, the state has also ensured adequate support to areas with large ethnic minority populations in terms of manpower, finance, materials, and technology. Additionally, several specific preferential policies have been implemented, which include the following measures: (1) the national policy that some economically developed provinces and municipalities have been designated to support areas with large ethnic minority populations from 1979 till now; (2) financial subsidy policies for autonomous regions and provinces treated as autonomous regions; (3) various special subsidies allocated by the central government, such as ethnic mobility funds, subsidies for areas with large ethnic minority populations, special funds for infrastructure construction in border areas, and subsidies for border construction; (4) low-interest loans and retained profits to ethnic trade enterprises in remote mountainous areas and pastoral areas; and (5) preferential treatment in terms of foreign exchange retention and tax relief.

1.2.2   Stage Ⅱ (1991-1998): initiation of regional coordinated development strategy

As the reform and opening up have deepened and China's national strength has increased, the Chinese government has elevated "promoting coordinated regional economic development" as a vital national strategy since the early 1990s. This strategy aims to address the expanding gap in regional development, particularly between the eastern and western regions. It has also established guidelines for coordinated development of regional economies and other measures, including, opening cities along the Yangtze River and inland border port cities and provincial capitals successively, making decisions to speed up the development of township enterprises in the central and western regions, and implementing the Priority Poverty Alleviation Program (1994-2000). This marked a fundamental shift in China's regional development strategy from unbalanced to coordinated development.

1.2.2.1 Formulation of general guideline for coordinated regional economic development

In March 1991, the then Premier Li Peng put forward for the first time in his Report on the Ten-Year Plan for National Economic and Social Development and the Outline of the Eighth Five-Year Plan that, we should "promote the rational division of labor and coordinated development of regional economy", and that "the rational distribution of productive forces and coordinated development of regional economy is an extremely important issue in China's economic construction and social development". The Ten-Year Plan for National Economic and Social Development and the Outline of the Eighth Five-Year Plan further pointed out clearly that it is necessary to "promote the regional economy to advance in the direction of rational division of labor, developing its strengths, complementing each other's advantages and coordinating development". In September 1995, the Fifth Plenary Session of the 14th CPC Central Committee approved the Proposal of the CPC Central Committee on Formulating the Ninth Five-year Plan for National Economic and Social Development and the Long-Term Goals for 2010, in which "adhering to the coordinated development of regional economy and gradually narrowing the regional development gap" was clearly regarded as one of the important policies that must be implemented during the next 15 years, and "starting from the Ninth Five-year Plan, we should pay more attention to supporting the development of the inland, implement policies conducive to alleviating the widening gap, and gradually intensify our work to actively work in the direction of narrowing the gap" was stated. In September 1997, the then President Jiang Zemin stressed in his report to the 15th CPC National Congress that "All-round efforts should be made to gradually narrow the regional development gap" and "promote the rational distribution and coordinated development of regional economy".

1.2.2.2 Implementation of all-round policy of opening up

As early as January 1988, the State Council approved the Minutes of Discussing Xinjiang's Opening-up Work, granting a range of preferential policies to expand opening up to Xinjiang. In 1991, the State Council issued the document titled Opinions on Actively Developing Border Trade and Economic Cooperation to Promote Prosperity and Stability in Border Areas, which outlined the guiding principles and preferential policies for border trade. Especially, after Deng Xiaoping's South Tour Speeches in 1992,

China obviously accelerated the pace of opening up in the central and western regions, while also consolidating the achievements of coastal areas' opening up to the outside world. On the one hand, the government expanded the coastal economic open areas by establishing some new state-level economic and technological development zones and 15 bonded zones (including Shanghai Waigaoqiao, Tianjin Port, and Shenzhen Futian) in coastal areas. On the other hand, the country successively opened up several cities along the land border, the Yangtze River, and inland provincial capitals. This was achieved by setting up the Three Gorges Economic Open Zone and establishing a number of state-level economic and technological development zones in the central and western regions. The government also delegated the approval authority to inland provinces, autonomous regions, and specifically designated cities in the state plan to attract foreign direct investment. Additionally, it encouraged foreign-invested enterprises in the eastern region to reinvest in the central and western regions. These efforts have resulted in the formation of a multi-level, all-round pattern of opening up, facilitating further international connections of regions along the coast, rivers, and border areas as well as inland provincial capitals.

1.2.2.3   Adjustment of policies on national investment and industrial layout

In order to speed up the economic development of the central and western regions, the central government has directed a higher proportion of investment to the central and western regions, and actively promoted the gradual transfer and relocation of some coastal processing and manufacturing industries to resource-rich areas in the central and western regions. The specific measures are as follows: (1) National investment distribution has gradually shifted its focus to the central and western regions. During the Eighth Five-year Plan period, the state proposed to give equal priority to the western region in developing and utilizing resources and building large-and medium-sized construction projects, and also to increase the proportion of investment in the western region. During the Ninth Five-year Plan period, in order to speed up the construction of energy and raw material industrial bases in the central and western regions, the state further increased investment in key construction projects in the central and western regions. (2) The township enterprises in the central and western regions were supported in terms of funds and policies through setting up a number of relevant demonstration zones under the Demonstration Project of East-West Cooperation of Township Enterprises. (3) Coastal areas and central cities were guided to gradually transfer their capacity of cotton spinning primary processing to cotton-producing areas in the central and western regions through combining technical upgrading on pressing spindles. The government would provide policy and financial support to facilitate the relocation of local industries from Beijing, Tianjin, Shanghai, and Guangdong to Xinjiang.

1.2.2.4 Improvement of national policies on impoverished areas and areas with large ethnic minority populations

In order to eliminate poverty as soon as possible, in April 1994, the State Council launched the Priority Poverty Alleviation Program (1994-2000), China's first ever national poverty alleviation program, which committed to ensuring that the basic needs of 80 million impoverished rural residents would be met in the seven years from 1994 to 2000. In October 1996, the CPC Central Committee and the State Council issued the Decision on Ensuring the Basic Needs for the Impoverished Rural Residents as Soon as Possible, calling for the whole Party and the whole society to help the poor and needy, highlighting key points and concentrating on providing enough food and clothing for the impoverished rural residents. The Ninth Five-year Plan also set the goal of basically eliminating poverty. To promote poverty alleviation efforts, China further increased its financial support and encouraged collaboration through the "pairing assistance" program. In 1998, the central government allocated a total of RMB18.3 billion for poverty alleviation. Simultaneously, various policies and measures have been implemented to boost development and achieve prosperity in areas with large ethnic minority populations. For instance, in 1992, the central government set up special funds for the development of areas with large ethnic minority populations.

1.2.3 Stage III (after 1999): full implementation of regional coordinated development strategy

Since 1999, to promote the coordinated development of regional economy, China has successively formulated and implemented the strategies of the large-scale development of the western region, revitalizing the old industrial bases in the northeast, and promoting the rise of the central region, thus forming a sound overall strategy for regional development, and then the strategies of national functional zoning, coordinated development of the Beijing-Tianjin-Hebei region, Yangtze River Economic Belt, and the Belt and Road, indicating that China has reached a new stage of fully implementing regional coordinated development strategy. As the Outline of the 13th Five-Year Plan for National Economic and Social Development stated, "Based on the master strategy for regional development and using, as guidance, the Belt and Road Initiative, coordinated development of Beijing-Tianjin-Hebei region, and the Yangtze River Economic Belt, we will promote the formation of north-south and east-west intersecting economic belts primarily along the coastline, the Yangtze River, and major transportation routes as well as a pattern of coordinated development between regions that ensures the mobile and well-ordered flow of factors of production, effective functional zoning, equitable access to basic public services, and development that is within the carrying capacity of the environment and natural resources." The report to the 19th National Congress of the CPC proposed to "implement the coordinated regional development strategy" and listed it as one of the seven strategies to secure a decisive victory in finishing the building of a moderately prosperous society in all respects.

1.2.3.1   The master strategy for regional development

In September 1999, the Fourth Plenary Session of the 15th CPC Central Committee approved the strategy for the large-scale development of the western region. After the State Council issued the Notice on Several Policies and Measures for Implementing the Western Development in October 2000, relevant departments formulated and implemented a series of policies and measures to support the western development and increase capital investment in the western region. In October 2003, the CPC Central Committee and the State Council decided to accelerate the revitalization of old industrial bases in the northeast[1] and jointly issued Several Opinions on Implementing the Revitalization Strategy of Old Industrial Bases in the Northeast and Other Parts of the Country. Relevant departments formulated and implemented a series of specific policies and measures on project investment, fiscal and taxation reform, finance, reform of SOEs, pilot program of social security, pilot transformation of resource-based cities, opening up to the outside world, and infrastructure construction (Wang Luolin & Wei Houkai, 2005a). In January 2004, the Central Conference on Economic Work proposed to "promote the rise of the central region" and in April 2006 issued Several Opinions of the CPC Central Committee and the State Council on Promoting the Rise of the Central Region. Thus, on the basis of encouraging the eastern region to take the lead in development since the reform and opening up, China successfully developed a complete overall strategy for regional development. As the Outline of the 11th Five-Year Plan adopted in March 2006 stated, we should "adhere to the overall regional development strategy of promoting the large-scale development of the western region, revitalizing the old industrial bases in the northeastern region and other parts of the country,

---

[1] In fact, "old industrial bases" are not only limited to the northeast; they also exist in other regions. For the sake of convenience, the phrase "and other parts of the country" has, in most cases, been omitted in the text that follows. —*Tr.*

promoting the rise of the central region, and encouraging the eastern region to take the lead in development". The Outline of the 12th Five-Year Plan further clarified to "implement a master strategy for regional development". This entails giving priority to the large-scale development of the western region, while fully revitalizing old industrial bases in the northeast and other parts of China, promoting the rise of the central region, and encouraging the eastern region to take the lead in development. As stated in the Outline of the 13th Five-Year Plan, "We will implement the master strategy for regional development so as to develop the western region, revitalize northeast China, fuel the rise of the central region, and support the eastern region as it leads the country. We will also make innovations to policies and improve mechanisms for regional development, promote coordinated, collaborative, and common development between regions, and strive to narrow the gaps in regional development." In summary, the master strategy for regional development forms the cornerstone of China's current approach to regional coordinated development.

1.2.3.2　The functional zoning strategy

The system of functional zoning is a typical and innovative Chinese approach to regional development. In 2006, the Outline of the 11th Five-Year Plan stated that "Taking into full account China's population and economic distribution, territorial utilization, and urbanization pattern in the future, the Outline groups territorial space into four types of functional zones—development zones to be optimized, key development zones, restricted development zones and prohibited development zones—based on carrying capacity of resources and environment, current intensity of development, and development potential. The zoning result will be taken as a basis in adjusting and improving national policies, and evaluate regional performance." In order to push forward the planning and building of functional zones, the State Council issued Opinions on the Preparation of the National Plan for Functional Zones in July 2007. In June 2010, the executive meeting of the State Council reviewed and approved in principle the National Plan for Functional Zones, which defined the scope, goals, directions, and principles for the development of the four functional zones. In March 2014, the National Development and Reform Commission (NDRC) and the Ministry of Environmental Protection jointly issued the Notice on Effectively Conducting the Pilot and Demonstration Work for the Development of National Functional Zones, and decided to take the national key ecological function zone's as the main body and select some cities and counties to carry out the pilot and demonstration work to develop national functional zones. At the same time, the central government has also increased transfer payments, and established an ecological compensation mechanism in forests, grasslands, wetlands, water flows and other fields as well as key ecologically functional zones. From 2008 to 2015, the central government allocated a total of RMB251.3 billion in transfer payments for ecological compensation. Out of this amount, RMB98.6 billion was allocated for forest ecological benefit compensation from 2001 to 2015; RMB77.3 billion, for grassland rewards and subsidies from 2011 to 2015; and RMB1 billion, for wetland ecological benefit compensation pilot funds from 2014 to 2015.

1.2.3.3   The support the development of areas with special features

Since the reform and opening up, the central government has always intensified its policy support for the development of old revolutionary base areas, areas with large ethnic minority populations, border areas, and poverty-stricken areas[1] As to policies for old revolutionary base areas, the central government began to made transfer payments to old revolutionary base areas since 2001 to subsidize contiguous old districts and counties that had made significant contributions but are currently suffering from financial difficulty. Since 2005, the National Development and Reform Commission has setup special funds within the national budget to support the infrastructure construction of key "red tourism" sites[2]. The Ministry of Agriculture has also offered some support to the agricultural development of old revolutionary districts and counties. Since 2012, the State Council has also approved several Revitalization Plans for old revolutionary base areas, like Shaanxi-Gansu-Ningxia Old Revolutionary Base Area, the Former Central Soviet Area in Jiangxi, Fujian and Guangdong, the Old Revolutionary Base Area by Zuojiang River and Youjiang River in Guangxi, Dabie Mountain Old Revolutionary Base Area, and Sichuan-Shaanxi Old Revolutionary Base Area, so as to provide policy support for local development. From 2001 to 2015, the central government has made total transfer payments of RMB41.2 billion to the old revolutionary base areas, of which the amount reached RMB7.8 billion in 2015. As to policies for areas with large ethnic minority populations, since 2007, the State Council has successively issued Opinions on promoting the economic and social development of Xinjiang, Ningxia, Guangxi, and Inner Mongolia as well as Tibet and areas with large Tibetan populations in Qinghai and other provinces, further intensifying its support for areas with large ethnic minority populations. Based on the original support to Tibet, in 2010, the central government

---

[1] These four types of challenging areas were collectively termed as "areas with special features".

[2] "Red tourism" features visits to sites with significance of revolutionary history. —*Tr.*

made major strategic arrangements for national paring assistance to areas with large Tibetan populations in Qinghai province and Xinjiang Uygur autonomous region. As to policies for border areas, the central government increased capital inputs and policy support by beginning to make transfer payments to border areas and to grant subsidies to 250 counties and cities along the land border and coastal areas since 2001, and by formulating and implementing action plans for prospering border areas and enriching locals from the 11th Five-year Plan to the 13th Five-year Plan including the completion of a batch of key projects. From 2001 to 2015, the central government has made a total transfer payment of RMB72.3 billion to border areas, of which the amount reached RMB13.6 billion in 2015. In terms of poverty alleviation policies, the government successively released and enacted the Outline for Development-Oriented Poverty Alleviation for China's Rural Areas (2001-2010) and the Outline for Development-Oriented Poverty Alleviation for China's Rural Areas (2011-2020), further increasing financial and policy support. And the rural poverty line standards were also raised in both 2008 and 2011. From 2011 to 2015, the central government allocated a total of RMB189.8 billion in special funds for poverty alleviation, with the funds for 2015 amounting to RMB46.7 billion. By 2017, the central and local governments provided over RMB140 billion in poverty relief funds to support local poverty reduction efforts. Out of this amount, RMB86.095 billion was contributed by the central government, while the remaining RMB54 billion was provided by 28 provinces responsible for poverty alleviation.

1.2.3.4　The vitality of regional economic development

To give full play to regional advantages and mobilize local enthusiasm, under the framework of four major regions, the state went further in recent years to work out a series of plans and measures for regional development of some provinces, autonomous regions, and municipalities as well as some important economic regions, economic zones, city clusters, and economically functional zones. These mainly plans and measures fall into three types: (1) the opinions issued by the State Council to promote regional economic growth, social development, openness to the outside world, and comprehensive reform; (2) regional development plans approved by the State Council at different spatial levels; (3) various economically functional zones approved by the State Council and relevant departments. At present, China has approved and established 219 state-level economic and technological development zones, 156 state-level high-tech industrial development zones, 63 export processing zones, 12 bonded zones, 65 comprehensive bonded zones, 14 bonded ports, 17 border economic cooperation zones,

19 state-level new areas, 12 national comprehensive reform pilot zones, 11 free trade pilot zones, 17 national independent innovation demonstration zones, 14 overseas industrial parks, and more than 30 other national development zones including China national tourist resorts, bonded logistics parks, border trade zones, science and technology industrial parks, cross-border industrial zones, finance and trade zones, economic development zones, circular economy pilot zones, and overseas Chinese high-tech venture parks, etc. At the same time, based on the overall strategy for regional development, China has rolled out a series of State-level regional development strategies including the Belt and Road Initiative, the Beijing-Tianjin-Hebei Integration Plan, and the Yangtze River Economic Belt. To ensure regional coordinated development, the Guidelines for Coordinated Development of the Beijing-Tianjin-Hebei Region was released on April 30, 2015; the decision to build Xiong'an New Area was made on April 1, 2017; the Guideline of Developing the Yangtze River Economic Belt Based on the Golden Waterway and the Regulations on Comprehensive Three-dimensional Traffic Corridor of the Yangtze River Economic Belt (2014-2020) were issued in September 2014; the Guidelines for Development Along the Yangtze River Economic Belt was approved on March 25, 2016. This series of measures has greatly stimulated the vitality and introduced new momentum to regional economic development.

1.3 Effects of coordinated development of China's regional economy

Since the early 1990s, the Chinese government has formulated the overall guideline to promote the coordinated development of regional economy. However, throughout the 1990s, the focus of national investment layout and policy support remained primarily centered on coastal areas. It wasn't until 1999 that the focus gradually shifted to the central, western, and northeastern regions, with the implementation of strategies for the large-scale development of the western region, revitalization of old industrial bases in the northeast, and the rise of the central region. With strong support of national policies, coordinated regional development has achieved remarkable results: the proportion of investment in the central and western regions has steadily increased, driving a relatively balanced growth pattern in the regional economy; the development gap between the eastern and the western regions has shifted from widening to narrowing; and poverty alleviation efforts in rural areas have made steady progress. Nevertheless, it is important to acknowledge that China's rural poverty line is still rather low, and the gap in regional development persists. Thus, there is still much work to be done in order to attain the objective of coordinated regional development.

1.3.1 Ever-larger share of investment in the central and western regions

To promote economic growth and enhance resource allocation efficiency, China has progressively redirected investment and policy support towards the eastern coastal region with greater potentials since the reform and opening up. Thus from 1985 to 1995, the eastern region' share of total investment in fixed assets increased rapidly from 43.0% to 57.5%, an increase of 14.5 percentage points. In contrast, other three regions witnessed a decline: the central region, from 20.5% to 15.6%; the western region, from 19.2% to 15.2%; and the northeastern region, from 12.3% to 8.5%, down 4.9, 4.0, and 3.8 percentage points respectively (see Figure 1-2). During this period, the investment ratio between the eastern and both the central and western regions increased from 1.08 to 1.87. Since the late 1990s, the total investment in fixed assets in the central and western, and northeastern regions has been growing at an accelerating rate due to the implementation of the coordinated regional development strategy and significant fiscal support from the Chinese government; furthermore, the share of investment in each of these regions has been getting ever-larger. Consequently, by 2012, the eastern region's share of total investment in fixed asset had declined to 40.5%, whereas in the central, western, and northeastern regions, the share had risen to 23.1%, 23.8%, and 11.0% respectively; and the investment ratio between the eastern region and central and western region had decreased to 0.87. Notably, with the rapid decline in both growth rate and scale of total investment in fixed assets, the northeastern region's share of investment has sharply decreased, reaching only 5.2% in 2016, whereas the share in the eastern, central, and western regions has increased to 41.7%, 26.3% and 25.9% respectively since 2012. Throughout this period, the investment ratio between the eastern region and central and western region remained largely stable, fluctuating between 0.80 and 0.83.

According to the changes in the distribution pattern of total investment in fixed assets in the four major regions of China, we calculated the average growth rate of investment in each region in the following three periods since the reform and opening up. From 1986 to 1995, the average annual growth rate of total investment in fixed assets in the eastern region was 26.5%, which was higher by 6.9, 6.4, and 8.0 percentage points compared to the central, western, and northeastern regions respectively (see Table 1-3). However, since the mid-1990s, with the support of national policies, this pattern of investment growth of "high growth rate in the east and low in the west" has been fundamentally reversed. From 1996 to 2010, the total investment in fixed assets in the central, western, and northeastern regions increased by an average of 22.2%, 22.2%, and 21.3% respectively, higher than the 19.2% for national average and the 16.6% in the eastern region. This demonstrates that, thanks to the strategies for the large-scale development of the western region, the revitalization of old industrial bases in the northeast and the rise of the central region, the investment growth rate in these three regions has obviously accelerated. It is worth noting that with China's economy entering a "new normal" and the eastern region undergoing industrial transformation and upgrading, the investment growth rate across the country was declining in recent years. However, this decline was significantly slower in the eastern region compared to the central and western regions. Meanwhile, the northeastern region has experienced a substantial decline, with an average annual growth rate of only 0.3% from 2011 to 2016, a decrease of 21.0 percentage points compared to the 1996-2010 period. Specifically, the total investment in fixed assets in the northeast witnessed a year-on-year decrease of 1.4% in 2014, 11.1% in 2015, and 23.4% in 2016.

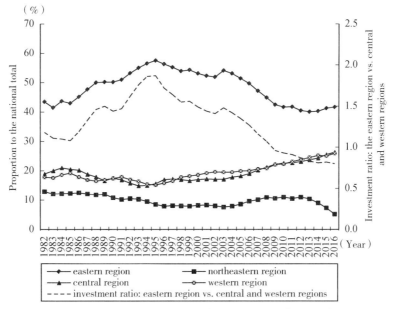

Figure 1-2   Proportion of total investment in fixed assets in China's four major regions

Note: As a result of cross-regional investments, the combined share of investment in the four major regions falls below 100%.

Source: Calculated based on the relevant data in *Comprehensive Statistical Data and Materials on 50 Years of New China* and the series of *China Statistical Abstract* over years.

Table 1-3   Growth rate of total investment in fix assets
in four regions by period   Unit: %

Region	1983-1995	1986-1995	1996-2010	2011-2016
Whole country	23.9	22.9	19.2	13.9
Eastern region	26.6	26.5	16.6	13.9
Northeastern region	20.1	18.5	21.3	0.3
Central region	22.1	19.6	22.2	16.8
Western region	22.4	20.1	22.2	16.8
Cross-region	16.8	17.8	17.0	−3.7

Note: The data in this table was calculated at current prices.

Source: Calculated based on the relevant data in *Comprehensive Statistical Data and Materials on 50 Years of New China* and the series of *China Statistical Abstract* over years.

At the early stage of the reform and opening up, the majority of foreign investment was directed towards the southeast coastal region centered around the Pearl River Delta. With the expanding of opening up since the 1990s, the foreign investment was encouraged to expand their presence in China by transferring from the Pearl River Delta to the Yangtze River Delta and then to the Bohai Rim and the northeastern region and by moving from the eastern coast to the central and western regions. From 1999 to 2004, the proportion of paid-in foreign investment took place changes in different regions. It decreased from 83.9% to 79.0% in the eastern region, and despite a 4.5%-2.6% decline in the western region, the proportion increased from 7.5% to 9.3% in the central region and from 4.1% to 9.0% in the northeastern region (Wei Houkai et al., 2011). During this period, foreign direct investment in China primarily shifted from the eastern region to the central and northeastern regions. Subsequently, it shifted towards the western region at a significantly accelerated pace. To the total of foreign capital actually utilized in all regions, the proportion of foreign capital actually utilized in the western region increased rapidly from 3.22% in 2005 to 9.97% in 2011. In recent years, the proportion of foreign capital actually utilized in the western region has decreased, reaching 7.88% in 2015. However, this figure is still significantly higher than that in the early 21st century. As of 2015, the total amount of foreign capital actually utilized in this region amounted to US$109.315 billion, which accounted for 6.66% of the total utilized in all regions (see Table 1-4).

Table 1-4   Actual utilization of foreign capital in China's three major regions

Year	Foreign capital actually utilized (billion US dollars)				Proportion (%)			
	Total	Eastern	Central	Western	Total	Eastern	Central	Western
2005	60.325	53.558	4.826	1.941	100	88.78	8.00	3.22

(continued)

Year	Foreign capital actually utilized (billion US dollars)				Proportion (%)			
	Total	Eastern	Central	Western	Total	Eastern	Central	Western
2006	65.821	59.542	3.979	2.300	100	90.46	6.05	3.49
2007	74.769	65.638	5.450	3.681	100	87.79	7.29	4.92
2008	92.394	78.340	7.436	6.618	100	84.79	8.05	7.16
2009	90.033	77.588	5.335	7.110	100	86.18	5.93	7.90
2010	105.735	89.855	6.858	9.022	100	84.98	6.49	8.53
2011	116.011	96.604	7.836	11.571	100	83.27	6.75	9.97
2012	111.716	92.513	9.287	9.916	100	82.81	8.31	8.88
2013	117.586	96.878	10.103	10.605	100	82.39	8.59	9.02
2014	119.562	97.922	10.861	10.779	100	81.90	9.08	9.02
2015	126.267	105.868	10.444	9.955	100	83.84	8.27	7.88
Total by 2015	1,642.319	1,399.119	133.885	109.315	100	85.19	8.15	6.66

Note: The eastern region includes Beijing, Tianjin, Hebei, Liaoning, Shanghai, Jiangsu, Zhejiang, Fujian, Shandong, Guangdong, and Hainan; The central region includes Shanxi, Jilin, Heilongjiang, Anhui, Jiangxi, Henan, Hubei, and Hunan. The western region includes Inner Mongolia, Guangxi, Sichuan, Chongqing, Guizhou, Yunnan, Shaanxi, Gansu, Qinghai, Ningxia, Xinjiang, and Tibet.

Source: Foreign Investment Management Department of Ministry of Commerce, *China Foreign Investment Report*, 2005-2016.

1.3.2 Relatively balanced growth of the regional economy

Since the reform and opening up, China has experienced an uneven regional economic growth, with the eastern region growing fast while other three regions lagging behind. During 1980-2006 period, the average annual growth rate of GDP in the eastern region reached 12.1%, compared to only 9.2%, 10.3%, and 9.9% in the northeast, central, and western regions respectively. The eastern region outperformed the northeast, central, and western regions by 2.9, 1.8, and 2.2 percentage points (see Table 1-5). Over the span of 27 years, the eastern region achieved the highest economic growth rate in 21 out of those years, whereas the northeast, central and western regions experienced only two, three, and one year(s) of such success respectively. Later, with the successive implementation of strategies, such as the large-scale development of the western region, the revitalization of old industrial bases in the northeast region, and the promotion of the rise of the central region, the central and northeastern regions gradually gained significant momentum in accelerating economic growth. These efforts were further bolstered by robust national policies. As a result, China's regional economic growth began to exhibit a relatively balanced pattern, with slow growth in the eastern region and rapid growth in the northeast, central, and western regions.

Just as between 2007 and 2012, the average annual growth rate of GRP in the eastern region stood at 11.5%, whereas the northeastern, central, and western regions achieved higher growth rates of 12.8%, 12.7%, and 13.7% respectively. Over the course of these six years, the western region experienced the highest growth rate in five years, with the northeastern region leading in one year (2008). This indicates a shift in China's regional economy from an unbalanced to relatively balanced pattern of growth. By "relatively balanced", it is meant that the less-developed areas experienced accelerated growth, surpassing that of the more-developed areas.[1] However, in recent years, the northeast once again faced challenges and fell into a predicament of slow economic growth due to various factors, including the national economic slowdown and severe industrial overcapacity. From 2013 to 2016, the average annual growth rate of GDP of 31 provinces, autonomous regions and municipalities in China was 8.3%. This growth rate can be broken down into 8.2% in the eastern region, 8.7% in the central region, 9.1% in the western region, and the lowest 5.3% in the northeastern region. In particular, the growth rate of GRP in the northeastern region was only 5.9% in 2014, 4.5% in 2015, and further dropped to 2.5% in 2016. These figures clearly indicated a significant decline in growth. Notably, during this period, the central and western regions continued to enjoy higher economic growth rate compared to the eastern region, highlighting a relatively balanced growth pattern across different regions.

Table 1-5   Changes in GRP growth rate of different regions
since the reform and opening up   Unit: %

Period	Regional average	Eastern	Northeastern	Central	Western
1980-2006	10.9	12.1	9.2	10.3	9.9
2007-2012	12.2	11.5	12.8	12.7	13.7
2013-2016	8.3	8.2	5.3	8.7	9.1
1980-2016	10.9	11.6	9.4	10.5	10.4

Note: The GRP growth rate of the four major regions was calculated in accordance with the actual GRP and growth rate of each province, autonomous region and municipality.

Source: Calculated in accordance with *China's Regional Economy in the Seventeen Years of Reform and Opening up* compiled by the National Bureau of Statistics, relevant annual data of *China Statistical Yearbook* and *China Statistical Abstract* (*2017*).

[1] The aggregated GRP in different regions of China is not comparable with the national GDP data released by the National Bureau of Statistics. Therefore, when comparing the GRP growth rates of different regions, the GRP growth rates of different regions cannot be directly compared with the national GDP growth rate, but should be compared with the aggregated GRP growth rates of each region. For more details, see Wei Houkai (2009a).

1.3.3   Industrial layout from concentration to diffusion

The changes in growth pattern of regional economy led to a gradual shift and diffusion of China's national industrial layout from its previous concentration in the eastern region to the central and western regions. For a relatively long period since the reform and opening up, the unbalanced growth of China's regional economy resulted in the continuous concentration of national economic activities in the eastern region. From 1980 to 2006, the proportion of the eastern region's GRP to the total GRP across all regions in China increased from 43.6% to 55.7%, a growth of 12.1 percentage points. However, during the same period, the proportion decreased from 13.7% to 8.5%, from 22.3% to 18.7%, and from 20.4% to 17.1% in the northeastern, central, and eastern regions, down 5.2, 3.6, and 3.3 percentage points, respectively (see Figure 1-3). Research shows that, from 1985 to 2003, except tobacco processing industry, the production capacity of steel, petrochemical, electronic information, textile and other manufacturing industries was concentrated in the eastern region (Wang Yeqiang & Wei Houkai, 2006). This shows that since the reform and opening up, the active market forces has made China's economic activities gradually shift and gather to the economically prosperous eastern region. This concentration comes from China's economic transformation, which manifests itself mainly in the concentration of various factors of production and industries, especially

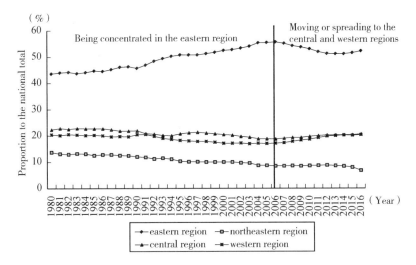

Figure 1-3   Proportion of GRP in four regions of China from 1980 to 2016

Source: Calculated according to data from *China's Regional Economy in Seventeen Years of Reform and Opening up* compiled by the National Bureau of Statistics, *China Statistical Yearbook* (over the years), and *China Statistical Abstract* (*2017*).

manufacturing industries, in the eastern region. This centralization will, to some extent, help to improve the overall efficiency of resource allocation, but it will also aggravate the widening gap in regional economy, which is not conducive to the coordinated development of regional economy.

With the changes in development stages and regional policies since the 21st century, coastal businesses have gained more momentum to move to the central and western regions, especially to the latter. Taking Jiangxi, a province in the central region, as an example, the investment it received from Guangdong, Fujian, Jiangsu, Zhejiang and Shanghai totaled RMB13.939 billion in 2001 and RMB142.606 billion in 2010, with an average annual growth rate of 29 percent. In the case of Zhejiang's entrepreneurs, it is evident that their economic activities were increasingly decentralized as they rapidly expanded their investments in the central and western regions. According to data released in 2006 by the Economic Cooperation Office of Zhejiang Provincial Government and *Zhe Shang Magazine*, the total investment by Zhejiang's enterprises in various parts of China had exceeded RMB1.3 trillion. Specifically, investments in the central, western, and northeastern regions exceeded RMB275.2 billion, RMB299 billion, and RMB93 billion, respectively. These figures accounted for 20.9 percent, 22.7 percent, and 7.0 percent of Zhejiang businesses' investments outside the province (Shen Haixiong & Hu Zuohua, 2006). In 2010, more than 6.4 million people from Zhejiang started 264,000 enterprises outside the province, and also invested a total of RMB3.89 trillion, an increase of 6.3 times over the survey results in 2005. Among Zhejiang businessmen going out of the province, most (1.9 million people) went to the west, where they founded most enterprises (63, 000); and 1.1 million Zhejiang businessmen founded 61, 000 enterprises in the central region, their second largest destination (Xu Yiping, 2011). As is shown in Figure 1-3, the proportion of GRP in the eastern region in the total of all regions in China has gradually decreased since 2006, while the proportion in the central and western regions was just the opposite. By 2013 and compared with 2006, that proportion in the eastern region had dropped to 51.2 percent, down 4.5 percentage points; in the central and western regions, increased to 20.2 percent and 20.0 percent, up 1.5 and 2.9 percentage points respectively; and in the northeastern region, fluctuated between 8.5 percent and 8.8 percent. This shows that, with the accelerated economic growth in the central and western regions, the nationwide economic activities are constantly transferring and spreading to the central and western regions. It should be pointed out that, in recent years, with the gradual slowdown of national economic growth, regions differ much in the decline of economic growth rate. Due to the sharp decline in economic growth rate in northeast China, its proportion of GRP in the total amount of all regions in China dropped sharply, from 8.6 percent in 2013 to 6.8 percent in 2016, down 1.8 percentage points. In the same period, the eastern region increased by 1.1 percentage points, and the central and western regions, by 0.4 and 0.3 percentage points respectively.

1.3.4 The east-west gap: from widening to narrowing

During a relatively long period of time since the reform and opening up, the development gap between the eastern and western regions continued to widen as a result of unbalanced economic growth and concentration of economic activities in the eastern region. Although the widening of this kind did not begin after the reform and opening up, it was undoubtedly fueled by the policy of supporting the east implemented since 1978, the high concentration of foreign investment and exports in a few areas in the east, and the transition of China's economy to a market economy. From 1980 to 2003, the relative GRP per capita in the other three regions tended to decline except the eastern region, where the relative GRP per capita continued to rise. During this period, the relative GRP per capita in the eastern region (taking the average as 100) increased from 128.7 to 159.8, while in the northeastern region, the central region, and the western region, it decreased from 150.8 to 109.3, 78.6 to 65.7, and 71.2 to 59.2, respectively. Since 2004, fundamental changes took place: the relative GRP per capita in the eastern region has begun to decline, while in the central and western regions it has shown an upward trend. By 2014, the relative GRP per capita in the eastern region had dropped to 133.6, while that in the central and western regions had increased to 76.1 and 74.6 respectively. From 2006 to 2012, the GRP per capita in the northeast steadily increased from 101.9 to 107.5. However, recent years have witnessed significant changes in this scenario due to the acceleration of economic transformation and upgrading in the eastern region, as well as the sluggish economic growth in the northeastern region. As a result, the GRP per capita has experienced substantial growth in the eastern region, yet a sharp decline in the northeast. By 2016, the GRP per capita in the northeast plummeted to 85.7, significantly lower than the national average. Meanwhile, GRP per capita in the central region still kept on rising, with slight fluctuations observed in the western region.

It should be pointed out that, apart from the acceleration of economic growth, another important reason for the rise in recent years of the relative GRP per capita in the central and western regions lies in the changes in demographic caliber and the impact of population migration. The population of various regions in China used to be counted based on household registration. Since 2005, each region adopted the method of sample survey of 1% population and thus took full consideration of the floating population, that is, the demographic census was conducted based on permanent residency, with population migration being considered. From 2005 to 2015, the proportion of permanent residents in the eastern region in the total population of all regions of the country increased from 36.1% to 38.3%, among which, Guangdong, Shanghai, Beijing, Tianjin and Zhejiang saw a significant increase; However, it decreased from 8.4% to 8.0% in the northeastern region, from 27.4% to 26.6% in the central, and from 28.0% to 27.1% in the west. Henan, Sichuan, Anhui, Guizhou, Hubei and Heilongjiang saw a large decline in this number. This shows that in recent years, the population in the central, western and the northeastern region are migrating to the east.

In a word, since the reform and opening up, the relative gap of GRP per capita between the eastern region and central and western regions of China has changed from widening in the past to gradually narrowing, during the process of which the year of 2003 was an important turning point. This inverted U-shaped change can be clearly seen in Figure 1-4.[1] Before 2003, except for a few years, the relative gap coefficient of GRP per capita between the eastern region and the central and western regions showed a widening trend. From 1980 to 2003, the coefficient between the eastern and western regions increased from 44.7% to 63.0%, while that between the eastern and central regions increased from 38.9% to 58.9%, up 18.7 and 20.0 percentage points respectively. During this period, although the coefficient of variation of GRP per capita in the four regions fluctuated many times, the overall trend was also increasing, from 0.334 in 1985 to 0.465 in 2003.[2] The gap between the east and the west widened obviously mainly in the four periods of 1986-1989, 1991-1994, 1997-1999, and 2001-2003. After 2004, although the absolute gap of GRP per capita between the eastern region and central and western regions was still widening, its relative gap coefficient begun to shrink year by year. By 2014, the relative gap coefficient had dropped to 44.1% between the eastern region and western region, and to 43.0% between the eastern region and central region, and the coefficient of variation of GRP per capita in these four major regions had dropped to 0.287. It should be noted that, firstly, the gap coefficient from 2001 to 2008 has been revised according to the economic census data, and its calculation result was

---

[1] For a detailed discussion of this inverted U-shaped change in China's regional disparities, see Zhang Yan & Wei Houkai (2012).

[2] Coefficient of variation, an important index to measure regional disparity, is the ratio of standard deviation to average value. The greater its value, the greater the regional disparity.

larger than before the revision. As a result, the gap coefficient in 2001 increased significantly when compared to the previous year,[1] but it showed nearly similar fluctuations. Secondly, since the 1960s, China's east-west gap has been widening, even during the period of "Third Front" Construction (1964-1980). Arguably, the widening east-west gap since the reform and opening up could be seen as a continuation of the past historical period. Since 2015, the GRP per capita gap between the eastern region and central and western regions of China, especially between the eastern region and western region, has slightly widened, which is supposedly only a short-term fluctuation and will not change the long-term narrowing trend. The short-term fluctuation of this kind, however, deserves our great attention and further adjustment of regulatory policy.

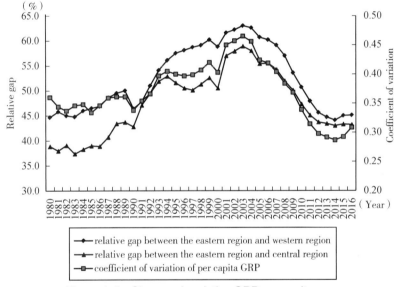

Figure 1-4　Changes in relative GRP per capita gap
in four regions of China from 1980 to 2016

Note: The relative gap coefficient between the eastern region and central and western region= (eastern index value-central and western index value)/eastern index value×10%.

Source: Calculated in accordance with *China's Regional Economy in the Seventeen Years after Reform and Opening up* compiled by the National Bureau of Statistics, relevant annual data of *China Statistical Yearbook* and *China Statistical Abstract (2017)*.

---

[1]　Before the revision based on the economic census data, the coefficients of variation of GRP per capita in the four major regions from 2001 to 2004 were 0.431, 0.440, 0.451, and 0.446, respectively. After the revision, the coefficients of variation rose to 0.450, 0.457, 0.465, and 0.456 respectively, up about 2% to 5%.

1.3.5 Great achievements in poverty alleviation in rural areas

Since the reform and opening up, the Chinese government has always attached great importance to poverty alleviation in rural areas, and invested a lot of manpower, physical and financial resources every year to lift the poor out of poverty and become better off and to support the economic growth and social development in poverty-stricken areas. After unremitting efforts, China has achieved remarkable results in rural poverty alleviation and development. According to the poverty line in 2010 (RMB2, 300 per person per year, 2010 constant prices), China had reduced its impoverished population in rural areas from 770.39 million in 1978 to 43.35 million in 2016, with a total reduction of 727.04 million and an average annual reduction of 19.13 million, and the incidence of poverty decreased from 97.5%to 4.5%. China's efforts in rural poverty alleviation have yielded remarkable achievements, making an important contribution to the cause of global poverty alleviation. It is estimated that, at the international poverty line of US$1.9 per person per day in 2011 purchasing power parity (PPP) terms, 1.1 billion people around the world, including 790 million in China (accounting for 71.82%), were lifted out of poverty from 1981 to 2012 (Li Peilin & Wei Houkai, 2016). Meanwhile, thanks to intensified efforts on promoting development-oriented poverty alleviation, poverty-stricken counties achieved accelerated economic growth and social development, resulting in a gradual reduction of the disparity between these regions and others. Between 2001 and 2010, the GRP per capita of "key poor" counties for alleviation increased from 52.86% to 59.18%, while the Net Income Per Capita of farmers in these counties rose from 58.78% to 62.71% (Li Peilin & Wei Houkai, 2016).

In order to build a moderately prosperous society in all respects, it is imperative to ensure that all rural residents living below the current poverty line have been lifted out of poverty, and poverty is eliminated in all poor counties and regions. In October 2015, the Fifth Plenary Session of the 18th CPC Central Committee set such a goal to be achieved by the year 2020, which followed that before 2020 and on average, China would have to lift more than 10 million people out of poverty per year, or nearly one million people per month. Judging from the experience, at current scale of lifting people out of poverty as defined by the existing standard, the goal of overall poverty elimination would be achieved as scheduled on condition that China could lift 9.33 million people in 1979-1990, 19.63 million in 1991-2000, 29.66 million in 2001-2010, 21.98 million in 2011-2015, and 12.4 million in 2016. However, it should be noted that as poverty alleviation and development entered the sprint stage of tackling key problems, the poverty reduction effect of economic development would decline, making poverty alleviation through development much more difficult than before. In particular, the most of rural poor people live in mountainous and remote areas with poor natural conditions, extremely inconvenient transportation, and frequent natural disasters, especially areas with large ethnic minority populations and border areas in the central and western regions. Across the country in 2016, there were still 26.54 million poor people living in impoverished areas with a poverty incidence of 10.1%; 22.19 million poor people living in "key poor" counties with a poverty incidence of 10.5%. There were still five provinces and autonomous regions with poverty incidence exceeding 10%, namely Tibet (13.2%), Xinjiang (12.8%), Gansu (12.6%), Guizhou (11.6%), and Yunnan (10.1%); There were more than three million poor people in six provinces, namely Guizhou (4.02 million), Yunnan (3.73 million), Henan (3.71 million), Hunan (3.43 million), Guangxi (3.41 million), and Sichuan (3.06 million). Many regions were also faced with the dual tasks of protecting ecology and accelerating development. This showed that the task of poverty alleviation in rural China was still quite arduous. At the end of 2020, China achieved the goal of eliminating extreme poverty-a key goal for the new era of building socialism with Chinese characteristics. The 98.99 million people in rural areas who were living below the current poverty threshold all shook off poverty; all the 128,000 impoverished villages and 832 designated poor counties got rid of poverty. China has eliminated poverty over entire regions and eradicated extreme poverty.

1.4 Thoughts on Chinese path to coordinated regional development

Since the reform and opening up, China has implemented a series of strategies to promote regional development. The focus was initially on encouraging the eastern region to lead in development, then shifting to the large-scale development of the western region, the revitalization of old industrial bases in the northeast, and the rise of the central region. As a result, China has gradually formulated a comprehensive and well-rounded strategy for regional development. Considerable efforts were also made in terms of capital investment and supportive policies to expedite the development of areas with special features. These endeavors have effectively facilitated the coordinated growth of regional economies. Through four decades of hard work, China has successfully embarked on a diversified and progressive path with Chinese characteristics towards coordinated regional development. This achievement has established a solid groundwork for achieving prosperity across all regions and has offered valuable lessons for developing countries aspiring to foster coordinated regional development.

1.4.1   Top-level design to guide regional development

To counteract the notion of balanced development and the practice of equal distribution regardless of individual effort (commonly known as the "communal pot" phenomenon) prior to the initiation of the reform and opening up, Deng Xiaoping made a clear statement in December 1978 during the concluding session of the Central Conference on Economic Work that, "I am of the view that we should allow some regions, some enterprises, some workers and farmers, who because of hard work and good results achieved, to be better rewarded and improve on their livelihood. If some people get better first, they will engender powerful demonstrative effects on their neighbors and lead people in other regions, work units to follow their examples. In this way, the national economy will wave-like, surge forward, with all the people becoming relatively well-off." "But we must admit that, in the northwest, southwest and other regions, production activities and people's lives are still very challenging and tough. The state should offer help in all aspects, especially material support."[1] This is the origin of Deng Xiaoping's famous idea of "those who get rich first help and drive others to get rich later, so that common prosperity can be achieved". In the late 1980s, Deng Xiaoping further proposed the strategic thought of Two Overall Situations: one was that the eastern coastal regions should make full use of local favorable conditions, speed up opening up to the outside world, and develop quickly first, and the central and western regions should take into account this overall situation; the other was that when the development reaches a certain phase, the when the goal of a markedly improved life for the people has become a basic reality by the end of the 20th century, more efforts will be made to help the central and western regions accelerate their development, and the eastern coastal regions will also take into account this overall situation.[2] This strategic thought is a further deepening and concretization of the idea mentioned above.

---

[1] The Research Office of the Secretariat of the CPC Central Committee, the Literature Research Office of the CPC Central Committee, *Insisting on Reform, Opening Up, and Invigorating the Economy: Excerpts from Relevant Important Documents since the Third Plenary Session of the 11th CPC Central Committee*, Beijing: People's Publishing House, 1987, p. 13.

[2] The strategic thought of Two Overall Situations was first put forward by Deng Xiaoping when he heard a report on the price and wage reform plan in September 1988, and it was later called the "Perspective of Two Overall Situations".

Since the reform and opening up, the development of China's regional economy has basically been promoted in an orderly manner and in accordance with Deng Xiaoping's thought. Before 1990, the state focused on supporting the eastern region with better conditions to take the lead in development; although the state put forward the general policy for coordinated regional development in 1991, it did not formulate and implement effective specific policies and measures; After 1999, China has successively implemented strategies for the large-scale development of the western region, the revitalization of old industrial bases in the northeast, and the rise of the central region; devoted more energy to speeding up the development of old revolutionary base areas, areas with large ethnic minority populations, border areas, and impoverished areas, thus changing the long-standing widening regional gap in China, especially the east-west gap, and promoting regional economy began to shift to coordinated development.

It can be said that the idea of "those who get rich first help and drive others to get rich later, so that common prosperity can be achieved" is an important theoretical basis for the distinctively Chinese path to coordinated regional development. From the perspective of regional economic development, the basic core of Deng's idea and thought is to make the long-term development goal of "common prosperity" come true in all regions through an uneven growth approach of "allowing some to get rich first and then help others to get rich". As Deng Xiaoping pointed out, "to build socialism, it is necessary to develop the productive forces. Poverty is not socialism."[1] "If the rich get richer and the poor get poorer, polarization will occur, and the socialist system should and can avoid polarization."[2] In 1995, the author put forth the concept of "uneven yet coordinated development" as an alternative approach to challenge the conventional theories of balanced development and unbalanced development. The central idea of this concept is to achieve long-term regional economic coordination through uneven growth (Wei Houkai, 1995), which is basically consistent with the concepts of "growth with equity" and "inclusive growth" proposed by some foreign scholars.

Clearly, as development concepts evolve, there has been a deeper comprehension of coordinated regional development. Initially, individuals used to perceive it through

---

[1] The Research Office of the Secretariat of the CPC Central Committee, the Literature Research Office of the CPC Central Committee, *Insisting on Reform, Opening Up, and Invigorating the Economy: Excerpts from Relevant Important Documents since the Third Plenary Session of the 11th CPC Central Committee*, Beijing: People's Publishing House, 1987, p.411.

[2] *Selected Works of Deng Xiaoping* (Vol. 3). Beijing: People's Publishing House, 1993, p. 374.

the lens of balanced development or spatial equilibrium. The issues, like balanced distribution, balanced growth, and the narrowing of regional gap in economic development, especially the gap in GRP per capita, have been highly concerned by academia and government agencies. However, this kind of understanding confines itself to just considering issues from the perspective of production or output. As a matter of fact, under a market economy, of economic production and industrial activities tend to be spatially unbalanced. In view of this, people gradually expanded their focus to social, ecological, and all-round development of human beings, emphasizing the pursuit of narrowing the gap in residents' income, consumption level, accessibility of public service, and quality of life. At present, China's regional development has entered a stage of pursuing high-quality development. In light of the new people-oriented development concept, coordinated regional development goes beyond simply narrowing the economic gap. It should encompass the overall coordinated development of both the economy and society, aiming for sustainability and striking a balance between current and long-term interests, as well as between economic development and ecological preservation. Following this logic, besides the coordinated economic development emphasized in the past, more emphasis should be placed on the coordinated development of society and culture, the improvement of the quality and sustainability of development, and the all-round development of human beings.

In the new situation, to judge whether regional development is coordinated or not, one should start from the rich connotation of the concept, and comprehensively examine various indicators such as economy, society, and ecological environment, instead of only looking at a single indicator such as economic growth or per capita income. This cognitive shift has led to a change in the evaluation criteria for coordinated regional development from relying on a single indicator to considering a comprehensive set of indicators. Given the current situation in China, the evaluation should primarily emphasize the following criteria: (1) each region can bring into full and effective play of its own advantages and form its distinctive industrial structure with reasonable division of labor; (2) each region has gradually formed a pattern characteristic of high integration of economic development and ecological preservation, and harmonious coexistence between man and nature; (3) the regional gap in per capita income has gradually narrowed and remained within a reasonable and psychologically bearable range; (4) residents in each region can enjoy equitable access to basic public services and equivalent quality of life; (5) the coordinated development of population, economy, resources, and environment can be achieved across regions. For one thing, it is important to coordinate regional population and economic layout in order to promote the synergy and agglomeration of both population and industries; and for the other, it is necessary to coordinate regional population and economy on the one hand and resources and environment on the other hand in a way that ensures that distribution of population and economic activities within a region aligns with the capacity of the region's resources and the environment. From a broader perspective, coordinated regional development also necessitates a moderate balance in the spatial distribution of national economy. This involves avoiding excessive concentration or inadequate dispersion of economic activities in a certain region, as well as preventing certain regions from experiencing decline or becoming marginalized. Among these criteria, the most vital ones include reducing income disparities between different regions and ensuring equitable access to basic public services.

1.4.2 A multi-level regional development strategy system

In order to promote coordinated regional development, since the reform and opening up, China has successively formulated and implemented regional development strategy with "four-region" as geographical units and each with its own emphasis, that is, the master regional development strategy to develop the western region, revitalize the northeastern region, promote the rise of the central region, and enable the eastern region to spearhead development. The effective implementation and continuous improvement of the master strategy have effectively promoted the formation of a coordinated development pattern of China's regional economy. On the basis of the master strategy, China has further launched three initiatives for regional development in recent years, namely coordinated development of Beijing-Tianjin-Hebei region, the development of Yangtze River Economic Belt, and the Belt and Road Initiative, thus forming a regional development strategic system of "three initiatives + four-region". In this system, the "four-region" strategy covers the whole country and serves as the foundation of the system in that it is the state-level, overall planning for the coordinated development of all regions in China. From the perspective of global and national governance, the "three initiatives" play the role of leading, supporting and connecting role for they take building a community of shared future as the core and focus on international and domestic cooperation and coordinated development. The combined strategic system is an important move to build a moderately prosperous society in all respects and realize the Chinese Dream of national rejuvenation, and it is also an inevitable option to realize the comprehensive, coordinated, and sustainable development of all regions.

First of all, the combination of the "four-region" strategy and the "three initiatives" will produce superposition effects. They are different types of regional development strategies, covering different regions. From the perspective of spatial scope, the former is a kind of zone-based development strategy, while the latter covers different spatial scope: Beijing-Tianjin-Hebei region belonging to the east, the Yangtze River Economic Belt spanning the eastern, central, and western regions, and the Belt and Road initiative running through Asia, Europe, and Africa. From the perspective of strategic types, the former is an overall development strategy that covers the whole country and aims at coordinating all regions; the latter is a kind of strategy mix for developing axis belts (metropolitan areas) to drive the national economic development, with much emphasis on breaking traditional boundaries, removing administrative barriers, and strengthening international and inter-regional connections. In conclusion, implementing a coordinated approach to the strategic system has the potential to harness the synergistic effect of various strategies at different levels. This approach can facilitate the establishment of a multi-center network-like development pattern, which effectively balances efficiency and equity. Moreover, it stimulates the developmental vigor of each region and fosters new momentum in the process of "developing individual areas and then linking them up over time to cover the whole region".

Secondly, the combination of the "four-region" strategy and the "three initiatives" will produce synergistic effects. At present, there is still a huge development gap among China's four regions, with the development disparities between the east and the west far from being fundamentally solved. The north-south difference in economic growth has begun to become prominent, and the spatial differentiation within each region is also increasing. Under the new situation, coordinating regional development remains a formidable task. In this case, we should, guided by the overall strategy for regional development, pursue the coordinated implementation of the "three initiatives" and the "four-region" strategy to form north-south and east-west intersecting economic belts along the coastline, the Yangtze River, and major transportation routes, which will produce the "1+1>2" regional synergy effect and enable regions to complement each other with their respective strengths, have a rational division of work, and gain accelerated integration of regional economy. The regional synergy effect is realized through resource sharing, division of work, and mutual cooperation and coordination within and between regions. It is not only reflected in industrial division of labor and economic integration, but also in the coordinated development of society and the coordinated governance of ecological environment.

Thirdly, the combination of the "four-region" strategy and the "three initiatives" will also produce fusion effects. The four regions were previously isolated from one another as specific development strategy for each was relatively independent. Thus, there was also a lack of strategic connectivity between them. The Yangtze River Economic Belt covers 11 provinces from east to west. The Belt and Road Initiative connects China with Asia, Europe, and Africa, and covers all provinces in China, while Beijing-Tianjin-Hebei region is an important hub connecting the four regions. Therefore, on the basis of the overall strategy for regional development, promoting the implementation of the "three initiatives" will open up the links between the four regions as well as between them and foreign countries, facilitate the flow of factors at home and abroad, the economic cooperation and exchange in the fields of science, technology, and culture, and promote the integration and interaction of economic and social development, thus helping to reduce costs, improve efficiency, and stimulate innovation. This fusion effect plays a significant role in facilitating regional integration.

In conclusion, the multiple effects arising from the combination of the "four-region" strategy and the "three initiatives" will stimulate the endogenous vitality of regional development and cultivate new growth points, poles, and belts, thereby expanding new space for economic development and raising the potential growth rate of China's economy. On the basis of "three initiatives + four-region", the report to the 19th CPC National Congress proposed to implement coordinated regional development strategy, to devote more energy to speeding up the development of old revolutionary base areas, areas with large ethnic minority populations, border areas, and impoverished areas, to give more support to resource-depleted areas in their economic transformation, to create networks of cities and towns based on city clusters to enable the coordinated development of cities of different sizes and small towns, and to pursue coordinated land and marine development. In the Outline of National Territorial Planning (2016-2030) approved by the State Council in January 2017, it was also stated that, by 2030, China will basically establish a new pattern of multi-center network-based land space development with "four vertical and four horizontal" as the zoning boundary, among which, "four vertical" refers to four vertical (on the map) axes, namely the coastal axis belt, Beijing-Harbin and Beijing-Guangzhou axis belt, Beijing-Kowloon axis belt, and Baotou-Kunming axis belt, and "four horizontal" refers to four horizontal axes, namely Lanzhou-Lianyungang and Lanzhou-Xinjiang axis belt, Yangtze River economic axis belt, Shanghai-Kunming axis belt, and Beijing-Lanzhou axis belt. Obviously, the formation of this new pattern will effectively promote the comprehensive and coordinated development of China's regional economy.

1.4.3   Differentiated regional policies under classified management

With its vast territory, China exhibits significant regional disparities in terms of natural conditions and socio-economic characteristics. To effectively carry out macro-adjustment and control or implement regional policies, it is crucial to acknowledge these variations. Merely adopting a uniform or "one size fits all" approach, regardless of the policy's quality, would impede the attainment of optimal outcomes. In order to avoid that phenomenon and improve the effectiveness, accuracy and sustainability of policies, China has gradually explored a series of differentiated regional policies to provide differential treatment to economically functional areas, functional zones, and areas with special features in its over-40-year reform and opening-up practice. The differentiated regional policies were launched in accordance with the principle of "differential treatment and classified guidance", which was conducive to improving their effectiveness.

The first is the preferential policies for economically functional areas. Since the reform and opening up, to promote openness and development and deepen reform, China has set up a large number of economically functional zones of different types, the early types including Special Economic Zones, Coastal Economic Open Zones, Economic and Technological Development Zones, Export Processing Zones, and High-tech Industrial Development Zones, and the subsequent types including Border Economic Cooperation Zones, Bonded (Ports) Zones, New Areas, Comprehensive Supporting Reform Pilot Zones, Independent Innovation Demonstration zones, and Free Trade Pilot Zones. To each type of these economically functional areas, the government has offered corresponding preferential policies on the basis of clearly defining its function, so as to allow it to speed up the opening to the outside world and development, and comprehensively deepen reform.

The second is the regulation policy for functional zones. Since 2005, the Chinese government has actively promoted the planning and construction of functional zones. In December 2010, the State Council promulgated and implemented the National Plan for Developing Functional Zones, which grouped China's territorial space into four types of functional zones—development zones to be optimized, key development zones, restricted development zones and prohibited development zones—based on carrying capacity of resources and environment, current intensity of development, and development potential, so as to standardize the spatial development order, optimize the spatial structure, and promote the harmonious development between man and nature.

For each type of functional zone, the state has clearly defined its main function and development orientation, and requires implementing regional policies under classified management in finance, investment, industry, land, agriculture, population, ethnic groups, environment and other aspects, to establish differentiated performance evaluation methods with different emphases, and to promote the formation of a land and space development pattern in which population, economy, resources and environment are coordinated.

The third is the aid policy for areas with special features. Based on international practices, the majority of regional policies in different countries target various problematic areas, such as underdeveloped regions, economically depressed areas, and regions experiencing excessive growth (Zhang Keyun, 2005). Since the founding of the People's Republic of China in 1949, especially since the reform and opening up, China has implemented a series of aid policies on revitalizing and developing old revolutionary base areas, areas with large ethnic minority populations, border areas, and impoverished areas, which were termed as "areas with special features" and targeted as key support regions in the Outline of the 13th Five-Year Plan referred. The report to the 19th CPC National Congress stated that "we will devote more energy to speeding up the development of old revolutionary base areas, areas with large ethnic minority populations, border areas, and poor areas", and "support will be given to resource-depleted areas in their economic transformation". Although the old revolutionary base areas and areas with large ethnic minority populations are not typical problem areas in the strict sense, their designation as "areas with special features" does imply a recognition of their unique challenges to some extent.

From the perspective of development, with the changes in development stage and economic situation, the central regional policy should be adjusted and optimized accordingly. First of all, with the improvement of the level of economic development and the formation of an all-round opening pattern, economically functional areas should be encouraged to innovate their systems and mechanisms and share reform dividends, instead of keeping on enjoying preferential policies. Secondly, aid policy should be targeted for key problem areas, instead of for areas with special features as before. During China's ongoing economic and social development and transformation, several key problem regions have emerged in recent years. These include underdeveloped regions plagued by poverty, old industrial bases experiencing relative recession, cities with a single industrial structure heavily reliant on depleted resources, major grain-producing areas burdened with financial difficulties, border regions with multiple conflicts, regions prone to natural disasters, and over-expanded metropolitan areas (Wei Houkai et al., 2011). These regions facing many problems are in urgent need of strong support from the central government in terms of funds and policies. When the central government determines whether to provide aid policies for these regions, it should mainly consider such two criteria: (1) the region must belong to problem areas and the problems it faces are more serious than elsewhere; (2) the problems cannot be solved by local governments themselves, and they really need assistance from the central government. In the future, the central government's regional aid policy should be mainly aimed at key problem areas, so as to effectively help various problem areas solve the difficulties they face in development and enhance their capacity for self-development and sustainable development. Equal priority should be given to old revolutionary base areas and areas with large ethnic minority populations.

Therefore, under the principle of differential treatment and classified guidance, the current "four-region" strategy should be adjusted accordingly as the four regions belong to the regional units of strategic planning, and the policies originally specific to them should be carried out based on the region type. Actually, that was the case in recent years. For example, the support policy originally for the old industrial bases in the northeast began to be applicable to 26 old industrial base cities in the central region, and after the release of the National Plan for Adjustment and Transformation of Old Industrial Bases (2013-2022), it became applicable to some old industrial base cities (districts) in the western and eastern region. Similarly, other 69 resource-exhausted cities across the country could also enjoy the pilot policy for the economic transformation of resource-exhausted cities in northeast China; nine county-level units in Greater and Lesser Khingan Mountains Forest Area could enjoy the fiscal transfer payment policy equivalent to that for resource-exhausted cities; 243 counties (cities, districts) in the central region could enjoy the policy for the large-scale development of the western region. In the future, we should continue to integrate the "four-region" strategy in line with the philosophy of classified guidance, so as to gradually form a differentiated regional policy system under classified management.

Chapter 2
China's Regional Economic Development Before the Reform and Opening Up

For a considerable period of time after the founding of the PRC in 1949, there was a prevailing belief in achieving balanced development. During this period, the guidelines for allocating productive forces nationwide and developing regional economies focused primarily on reducing regional disparities and meeting national defense needs. Consequently, there emerged two major waves of state investment shifting from coastal regions to the interior, which meant two major dispersals in industrial distribution and resulted in low economic benefits. Moreover, under the conditions of weak national strength and backward development at that time, the large-scale westward shifts of state investment did not facilitate the full utilization of the old coastal industrial bases. Additionally, it failed to effectively curb the widening development gap between the eastern region and western region. This chapter explores China's regional economic development prior to the launch of the reform and opening up, focusing on four key perspectives: the balanced development strategy, centralization and decentralization, regional economic growth, and regional disparity changes. By delving into these aspects, it offers some necessary background information for a comprehensive understanding of China's regional economic development since 1978.

2.1   The balanced development strategy and its influence

Before 1978, China formulated its strategies and policies for regional development based primarily on the belief in achieving balanced development. Their fundamental objectives were to attain equal development, ensure a balanced layout, and reduce disparities across regions. However, those strategies and policies were mainly centered on the allocation of state investments and key projects, owing to the limitations imposed by the traditional system.

2.1.1　The formation of the idea of achieving balanced development

From the 1950s to the 1970s, the belief in achieving balanced development significantly impacted and controlled the regional distribution of state investment and economic development in China. This belief solely prioritized balanced regional development, placing excessive emphasis on equalizing the distribution of productive forces and reducing regional disparities. It advocated for the state to concentrate its investments on underdeveloped regions, occasionally even adopting an egalitarian approach in resource allocation and policy provision to all regions (Wei Houkai, 1995). As a result, the aforementioned two large-scale westward shifts occurred, the first during the First Five-year Plan period (1953-1957) and the second during the "Third Front" Construction period (1964-1980). This can be clearly observed from Figure 2-1.

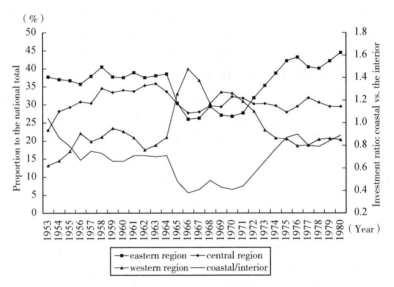

Figure 2-1　Proportion of infrastructure investment in the three
major zones in China from 1953 to 1980

Note: The eastern region covered Liaoning, Beijing, Tianjin, Hebei, Shandong, Shanghai, Jiangsu, Zhejiang, Fujian, Guangdong, Guangxi, and Hainan. The central region included Jilin, Heilongjiang, Inner Mongolia, Shanxi, Henan, Anhui, Hubei, Hunan, and Jiangxi. The western region covered Chongqing, Sichuan, Guizhou, Yunnan, Tibet, Shaanxi, Gansu, Ningxia, Qinghai, and Xinjiang. The eastern region was regarded as the coastal region. The central and western regions were referred to as the inland region ("the interior" for short).

Source: Calculated according to the relevant data in *Statistics on China's Investment in Fixed Assets 1950-1985* compiled by the National Bureau of Statistics.

2.1.1.1　The foundation of productivity layout before 1949

At the beginning of the founding of the PRC, the economic foundation left over from the past was extremely weak. The distribution of productive forces was quite distorted, with industrial activities heavily concentrated in the eastern coastal region, which accounted for less than 12% of the national territory but contributed over 77% of the total industrial output value. In contrast, the vast regions of southwest China, northwest China, and Inner Mongolia had almost no modern industries (Chen Dongsheng, 1993). Under such circumstances, the Chinese people had a subjective desire to change the extremely unreasonable productivity layout as soon as possible. At the same time, it was of objective necessity to gradually develop industry in the interior in a focused manner and locate industry close to the sources of raw materials and fuel supplies as well as to markets, so as to promote industrialization in the interior and the rational allocation of productive forces.

2.1.1.2   Changes in international political and economic situations

On June 25, 1950, the Korean War broke out; later the United States rallied other countries to impose blockades and embargoes on China. Given the tense international situation, it became crucial to prioritize China's national defense and security when allocating industrial projects and determining plant locations. As a result, the majority of industrial enterprises established during the First Five-year Plan period were strategically positioned in rear areas. This was particularly true for national defense industry enterprises. With the exception of shipyards, which required proximity to the coast, none of these enterprises were located in coastal regions vulnerable to enemy aerial attacks.

In 1964, the United States deployed troops to Vietnam, and almost simultaneously, the tensions escalated between China and the Soviet Union. In response to the challenging situation and the imminent threat of war, China proposed expediting the construction in the "Third-Front" regions as the strategic rear area, actively preparing for potential conflicts and bolstering its readiness for war. In April 1965, the CPC Central Committee issued the Instructions on Strengthening Preparations against War, calling for swift concentration of efforts on enhancing the construction of strategic rear areas in various provinces across the country. In line with the instructions from the CPC Central Committee and Mao Zedong, both China's Third and Fourth Five-year plans economic activities were shifted towards prioritizing war preparedness for and the construction of the "Third Front" regions.

2.1.1.3   Theoretical origin of the belief in achieving balanced development

There are two theoretical roots for the formation of the belief in achieving balanced development. The first was the former Soviet Union's theory on productivity allocation.

Some Soviet scholars initially put forward that "the even allocation of productivity throughout the country" was the main principle and law of the socialist distribution of productive forces. This early view was mechanically introduced into China and raised to the position with top priority. In fact, through later discussions, the Soviet Union basically abandoned this view of even or balanced allocation and took the law of economic effect resulting from productivity distribution as the most important law (Saushkin, 1995). The second was the exposition of classical Marxist writers. When analyzing the drawbacks of the capitalist distribution of productive forces at that time, Engels once said, "the abolition of the separation of town and country is therefore not utopian, also, in so far as it is conditioned on the most equal distribution possible of modern industry over the whole country".[1] Lenin also stated positively that, "uneven economic and political development is an absolute law of capitalism".[2] The above exposition by classical writers, served actually as the theoretical basis for balanced development theorists.

The influence of the Soviet theory on productivity allocation, along with the mechanical, dogmatic understanding of balanced development discourse by classical Marxist writers, led to the long-standing dominance of the belief in achieving balanced development in China. At that time, there was a popular belief that the imbalance of regional economic development was a uniquely capitalist phenomenon, and it was necessary and possible for socialist society to eliminate it as soon as possible. Based on this understanding, the academia had for a long period of time held that it was a primary principle for socialist countries to allocate productive forces in a balanced and planned way and to eliminate *de facto* economic inequalities or economic differences between regions, between urban and rural areas and between people of different ethnic groups in their distribution of productive forces. Some scholars even explicitly put forward that "the interior should be taken as the focus of industrialization so as to distribute production to all regions in an even way" (Sha Mo, 1956).

2.1.2 Guidelines and policies for the distribution of productive forces

To rectify the unreasonable distribution of productivity, China has consistently pursued a planned and rational distribution of industries nationwide since 1949. This involves locating industries in proximity to areas supplying raw materials or fuel or

---

[1] *The Complete Works of Marx and Engels* (Vol. 20). Beijing: People's Publishing House, 1979, p. 312.
[2] *Selected Works of Lenin* (Vol. 2). Beijing: People's Publishing House, 1972, p. 709.

consuming products, so as to bolster economic development in underdeveloped areas while also contributing to national defense. This principle and direction of adjusting productivity distribution have been incorporated into successive national plans for economic development.

2.1.2.1　The first large-scale westward shift of productive forces

During the recovery period of national economy (from October 1949 to the end of 1952), in order to resume and develop production rapidly, China first focused its economic construction on the northeastern region with Liaoning as the center by launching a number of key projects such as coal, electricity, steel, aluminum smelting and machinery. At that time, among the 156 projects aided by the Soviet Union, 17 were started from 1950 to 1952, of which 13 located in northeast China. As planned, 51.66% of the national infrastructure investment went to northeast China in 1950, while only 48.34% to other areas. In terms of industrial infrastructure investment, more than half of the total completed in China from 1950 to 1952 was invested in northeast China (Wang Haibo, 1994). At the same time, some light industrial enterprises were moved to the northern part of northeast China, northwest China, north China, and east China to make them close to the sources of raw materials and vast markets.

During the First Five-year Plan period, China began its large-scale infrastructure construction with a focus on heavy industry. In the First Five-Year Plan for National Economic and Social Development of the People's Republic of China, China drew up the guideline of distributing industry in a planned and balanced way throughout the country, and clearly pointed out that "to change the unreasonable layout gradually, we should properly distribute industrial productivity in all regions of the country and locate industry close to the sources of raw materials and fuel supplies as well as to markets, thus making it helpful to consolidate national defense and promote the economic development in backward areas". Under this guideline, China placed great importance on the development of underdeveloped areas in the central and western regions, which significantly influenced the national productivity layout due to national defense considerations.

During this period, as China's first target region for construction and a traditional heavy industry base, the northeastern region absorbed 1/4 of the national infrastructure investment, whereby large-scale expansion and new construction centered on metallurgy, coal, and machinery industries were carried out on the original basis and rapidly shaped itself into a major supply base for means of production to support the then and subsequent national economic development. In addition to northeast China, the state also concentrated effort to build industrial bases in Wuhan, Baotou, Lanzhou, Xi'an, Taiyuan, Zhengzhou, Luoyang, and Chengdu. Of the 694 industrial construction projects above the quota started within these five years, 472 were distributed in the interior, accounting for 68% of the total; 222 were distributed in coastal regions, accounting for 32% (Chen Dongsheng, 1993). China allocated 36.9% and 46.8% of its total investment in infrastructure construction to the coastal regions and the interior, respectively, resulting in a ratio of 0.79 : 1 (see Table 2-1).

Table 2-1   Ratio of infrastructure investment in coastal regions to
that in the interior from 1953 to 1980   Unit: %

Region	The First Five-year Plan period (1953-1957)	The Second Five-year Plan period (1958-1962)	1963-1965	The Third Five-year Plan period (1966-1970)	The Fourth Five-year Plan period (1971-1975)	The Fifth Five-year Plan period (1976-1980)
Coastal	36.9	38.4	34.9	26.9	35.5	42.2
Interior	46.8	56.0	58.3	64.7	54.4	50.0
Coastal/ Interior	0.79	0.69	0.60	0.42	0.65	0.84

Note: As national investment in items like rolling stock, ships, and airplanes, which were purchased uniformly by the state, was not allocated or included to a specific region, the sum of the ratio of investment to the coastal regions to that to the interior was less than 100%.

Source: Calculated based on the relevant data in *China's Fixed Assets Investment Statistics 1950-1985* compiled by the National Bureau of Statistics.

2.1.2.2   Balanced layout and local economic system during the Great Leap Forward period

During the First Five-year Plan period, there was a tendency to overlook the industrial development in coastal regions in terms of national productivity layout. In response, Mao Zedong elaborated upon the relationship between the coastal regions and the interior in his speech On the Ten Major Relationships in 1956, emphasizing that, to even out the distribution of industry as it develops, we must make good use of the old industries in the coastal regions and develop their capacities, and at the same time, strive to promote and support industry in the interior. Therefore, the Second Five-year Plan proposed to make good use of the old industries in the coastal regions and developing their capacities. The Proposal on the Second Five-Year Plan for the Development of the National Economy (1958-1962) adopted by the Eighth CPC National Congress pointed out that while carrying out large-scale industrial construction in the interior, it was also necessary to actively and fully utilize and appropriately develop the existing industries in coastal regions. At that time, the national plan was deployed as follows: continue to develop the industrial bases in northeast China; make full use of and develop the industry in north China, east China and the coastal cities in central and south China; in the interior, actively build new bases centered on iron and steel, non-ferrous metals, and large hydropower stations in the southwest, northwest and around Sanmenxia region while continuing to build new iron and steel bases in Wuhan and Baotou; continue to develop oil and non-ferrous metal industries in Xinjiang (Chen Dongsheng, 1989).

However, the Great Leap Forward[1] campaign that began in 1958 disrupted this deployment. It was envisaged at that time that industrial production would realize a significant leap forward primarily through the development of local industries. During this period, China's policy on productivity layout mainly focused on these two aspects. First, it was expected to achieve a balanced distribution of industry across the country. The state investment shifted its focus further to the interior, and the ratio of infrastructure investment in the coastal regions and the interior dropped from 0.75 : 1 in 1957 to 0.66 : 1 in 1960, and to 0.69 : 1 throughout the Second Five-year Plan period. Second, it was expected that all cooperative regions and provinces could establish a relatively independent and complete economic system of their own. In order to speed up the development of local industry, Mao Zedong proposed that the local government (including cooperative regions and provinces) should establish independent industrial systems. In March 1958, the state introduced the policy of concurrently developing industries under the central and local government. According to the requirements of the central government, a mass campaign to develop industries on a large scale began in the first half of 1958. Regardless of the availability of resources and practical possibilities, each region sought to establish its own industrial system just like playing its own game, with large-, medium-, and small-sized projects blooming everywhere.

In accordance with the policy for "adjusting, consolidating, enriching and improving" the national economy, the first adjustment was made during the period of 1963-1965. As a result, most ill-distributed small-and medium-sized enterprises (mainly the local industries) were transformed, restructured, or even shut down; ill-located projects under construction were suspended; retained enterprises and projects were better laid out through fixing the sources of raw materials, other materials, fuels, power

---

[1] The Great Leap Forward refers to an economic and social campaign launched in China during the early years of the Second Five-year Plan, primarily spanning from 1958 to 1960. While the Second Five-year Plan was scheduled to run from 1958 to 1962, the term "Great Leap Forward" is generally limited to the first three years of this period.

sources, and external cooperative relations (Chen Dongsheng, 1989). In terms of regional layout, the country not only enriched and developed the heavy industry in east China, but also intensified its efforts on industrial construction in the interior. During this period, the proportion of investment in infrastructure in the interior to the national total further increased to 58.3%, and the ratio of investment in coastal regions and the interior decreased to 0.60 : 1.

2.1.2.3 The second large-scale westward shift during the "Third Front" Construction period

The "Third Front" Construction program was mainly carried out during the Third and Fourth Five-year Plan periods. In consideration of national defense, the central government zoned the national territory into three types of regions, known as the first, second, and third front, based on their strategic positions. The first front represented the actual strategic forefront, while the third front served as the strategic rear of the entire country. Within the first- and second-front regions, certain areas were designated as the third-front regions based on local conditions. These regions were traditionally referred to as the "Major Third Front" and "Minor Third Front" respectively.

During the Third Five-year Plan period, the state determined that the investment focus should be shifted to the "Third Front" regions that were neither coastal nor close to the north. The emphasis was placed on strengthening the development of the southwestern region. In terms of project layout, several important railways were built to connect the parts in the southwestern region, including Sichuan-Guizhou, Chengdu-Kunming, Guiyang-Kunming, Xiangyang-Chongqing, and Hunan-Guizhou; five iron and steel bases were built in Panzhihua, Jiuquan, Wuhan, Baotou, and Taiyuan; a large number of coal, electric power, petroleum, machinery, chemical and national defense industry projects were built, renewed, or relocated. Over these five years, RMB63.121 billion (64.7% of the national total) went to the interior to support local construction, with RMB48.243 billion (52.7% of the national total) to 11 provinces as the third-front regions (Wang Haibo, 1986). In this process, a significant number of established enterprises in the coastal regions were systematically relocated to the third-front regions. In August 1965, the State Infrastructure Commission[1] held a conference on nationwide relocation, proposing to construct a few cutting-edge national defense projects under the principle of "locating them near to mountains in a scattered and concealed way", and

---

[1] The State Infrastructure Commission, first established in November 1958 and abolished in January 1961, was re-established in March 1965 and finally abolished in 1982, when the State Council reformed its institutions.

some might even be located inside mountains. This principle exerted great influence on the subsequent economic construction.

During the Fourth Five-year Plan period, while actively constructing the great southwestern region, "Third Front" Construction shifted its focus to the western regions in provinces of Henan, Hubei, and Hunan. During this period, according to the economic development and the requirements of preparations against war, the whole country was zoned into 10 economic cooperation regions, namely southwest, northwest, central plains, south China, east China, north China, northeast, Shandong, Fujian and Jiangxi, and Xinjiang. Each cooperation zone was required to establish an industrial system at different levels, each developing in its own way and vigorously cooperating with each other(for Shandong, Fujian and Jiangxi, and Xinjiang, a "small but complete" economic system was required instead); each province was required to achieve self-sufficiency in complete sets of machinery and equipment and light industrial products as soon as possible, to establish local industry to support agriculture, and to establish its own "small third front" regions; instead of being located in big cities, the industry in the interior should be developed in a more scattered than concentrated way, and factories were required to be located near to mountains in a scattered and concealed way, and some might even be built inside mountains. In these five years, the proportion of infrastructure investment in the interior declined slightly and totaled RMB95.934 billion (54.4% of the national total). Among them, RMB69.098 billion went to 11 provinces as the third-front regions (41.1% of the national total) (Wang Haibo, 1986).

From the late period of the Fourth Five-year Plan to the early period of the Fifth Five-year Plan, there was a gradual shift in the focus of state investment towards the eastern region. Of the 22 large-scale complete sets of equipment projects introduced nationwide in 1978, 10 were set up in the coastal regions, including Baosteel, Ethylene Projects in Nanjing and Shandong (Qilu), and Yizheng Chemical Fiber Factory. With foreign exchange totaling US$13 billion[1] required, the whole investment in these projects amounted to more than RMB60 billion, including the investment in domestic supporting projects (Chen Dongsheng, 1989). In view of the large scale of infrastructure construction, the central government proposed the policy of "readjusting, restructuring, consolidating and improving" to comprehensively reform China's economy in April 1979, marking the beginning of China's second round of national economic adjustment.

---

[1] The exchange rate of the US dollar to the RMB was about 3.77 in 1989. —*Tr.*

2.1.3 Evaluation of implementation effect of the policy before the reform and opening up

Before the reform and opening up, the large-scale westward shift in the focus of state investment played a crucial role in driving industrialization and economic development in the interior. Especially during the First Five-year Plan period and the "Third Front" Construction period, China invested hundreds of billions of yuan in the interior, establishing a large number of state-owned large and medium-sized backbone enterprises and scientific research institutions, and forming dozens of nationally important industrial bases. This laid the foundation for the industrialization of the interior regions. With the strong policy support, the proportion of industrial output from the interior in the whole country continuously increased from 30.6%in 1952 to 39.1%in 1978. Specifically, the proportion of light industrial output in the whole country increased from 28.5% to 35.5%, and the proportion of heavy industrial output in the whole country increased from 34.5% to 41.8% (see Table 2-2), basically changing the extremely unbalanced industrial distribution.

Table 2-2   Gross industrial outputs of coastal regions and the interior from 1952 to 1980

Unit: %

Year	Gross industrial output value		Light industry		Heavy industry	
	Coastal	Interior	Coastal	Interior	Coastal	Interior
1952	69.4	30.6	71.5	28.5	65.5	34.5
1957	65.9	34.1	66.3	33.7	65.6	34.4
1962	63.8	36.2	66.6	33.4	61.3	38.7
1965	63.1	36.9	67.3	32.7	58.8	41.2
1970	63.1	36.9	68.2	31.8	59.3	40.7
1975	61.0	39.0	64.1	35.9	58.6	41.4
1978	60.9	39.1	64.5	35.5	58.2	41.8
1980	61.5	38.5	65.2	34.8	58.2	41.8

Source: Office of the Leading Group for National Industrial Census of the State Council and Statistics Department of Industrial Transportation Materials of the National Bureau of Statistics, *Statistics on China's Industrial Economy* (1986), Beijing: China Statistics Press, 1987.

Before 1978, however, due to an overestimation of the international tension and the threat of war, coupled with a popular desire for quick success, the guidelines for China's productivity layout went wrong in some aspects, such as excessive emphasis on national defense needs and interregional balance, an aggressive pursuit of highly self-contained regional economies, and a push for large-scale decentralization in industrial distribution. As a result, China's productivity layout underwent two large-scale shifts from coastal to interior regions during periods of the First Five-year Plan and the "Third Front" Construction, and two smaller-scale similar shifts during the Great Leap Forward period and after the downfall of the Gang of Four. Moreover, during the periods of Great Leap Forward and the "Third Front" Construction, there were two instances of excessive decentralization in the industrial layout. The intent was to establish a self-contained industrial system in each region. However, this approach resulted in severe disconnection from the actual conditions. Consequently, three specific consequences have emerged.

First, the old industrial bases in the coastal regions failed to play the leading role. During the First Five-year Plan period, the state shifted its investment westward too fast, and neglected the industrial development in the coastal region. With limited state investment in industrial transformation, expansion, and construction, old industrial bases in Shanghai and north China were unable to fully utilize their potential and fulfill their intended role. Consequently, the industrial production in coastal regions has not achieved the expected development. In 1955, the industrial growth rate in the coastal regions was only 4.5%, and even dropped by 4.4%compared with 1954 in Shanghai (Chen Dongsheng, 1989). After that, the focus of the national investment layout was further pushed forward to the interior. Especially during the Third Five-year Plan period, due to the high concentration in the less-developed third front regions, the national investment to the coastal regions accounted only 42% of that to the interior, which seriously hampered the coastal economic potential and hindered the growth of coastal economy.

Second, the westward shift of investment failed to bridge the widening gap between east and west China. The population-weighted coefficient of variation is an important measure of regional disparities and its value is greater than or equal to 0. The greater the value, the greater the regional differences. In the early days of the founding of the PRC, with the support of national policies, the national income per capita gap among the three major regions of China, especially between the coastal regions and the interior, was narrowed down to a certain extent. From 1953 to 1957, the weighted coefficient of variation (WCV) of national income per capita among the three regions decreased from 0.218 to 0.195 (Liu Shucheng et al., 1994). The decline indicated that the gap among the three major regions was narrowing during this period. After that, during the periods of the First Five-year Plan and the "Third Front" Construction, despite further shift of national investment to the interior on a large scale, the widening gap between the east and the west was not prevented due to the deviation of the guidelines for the productivity layout. The WCV of national income per capita among the three major regions rose sharply from 0.195 in 1957 to 0.282 in 1960. From 1965 to 1976, it increased rapidly from 0.209 to 0.390 (Liu Shucheng et al., 1994). Similarly, the ratio of national income per capita between the coastal regions and the interior dropped from 1.38 in 1952 to 1.29 in 1965, and then gradually increased to 1.60 in 1980 (Wei Houkai, 1995). This showed that the mere pursuit of large-scale westward shift of state investment without stressing the investment effect could not achieve the expected effect of narrowing the east-west gap, but hurt the coastal economic growth.

Third, both the macro- and micro-economic benefits fell short of expectations. The unbalanced development between China's coastal regions and the interior was inherited from the past and was a phenomenon shared by many countries in their industrialization. To promote industrialization, it is crucial to properly handle the relationship between old industrial bases and emerging industrial areas, considering the significant regional disparities in investment outcomes between the coastal regions and the interior. In the initial stage of industrialization, if the national investment was shifted westward too fast, new industrial zones were established in a too scattered way, and the transformation of old coastal industrial bases was neglected, it would naturally affect the national economic growth and macro-economic benefits. According to estimates, only RMB250 billion out of the RMB400 billion of fixed assets created nationwide between 1953 and 1980 were truly effective. And even within this RMB250 billion, a portion remained underutilized for a prolonged period due to inadequate external supply conditions and location-related problems (Lu Dadao, Xue Fengxuan et al., 1997).

When viewed in a phased manner, the First Five-year Plan period demonstrated a desirable overall investment effect as a result of the emphasis on scientific argumentation in project layout, despite the slightly rapid westward shift of state investment. Then during the periods of Great Leap Forward and the "Third Front" Construction, the national investment kept further shifting its focus to the west on a large scale, and too much emphasis was placed on the establishment of an independent and complete local industrial system and construction projects were highly dispersed, which led to a sharp decline in the effect of infrastructure investment in the whole country, particularly in the western region. According to relevant estimation, the Great Leap Forward (1958-1960) and the "locating industry everywhere yet yielding no benefits" reduced China's national income by about RMB150 billion (Chen Dongsheng, 1989). During the "Third

Front" Construction period, due to the over-emphasis on the needs of national defense, factories were required to be located near to mountains in a scattered and concealed way, and some might even be built inside mountains, thus artificially cutting off the organic connection of production, resulting in relatively low macro-and micro-economic benefits. During this period, the national capital-output rate was only 0.217, which was greatly reduced from 0.338 in the First Five-year Plan period (Gao Chunde, 1989). Some projects fell into permanent hidden dangers due to unreasonable layout or too-hidden location, so that the industrial layout for the "Third Front" Construction had to be adjusted. During the Seventh Five-year Plan period, China invested a total of RMB3 billion to transform, restructure, relocate or even shut down 121 "Third Front" Construction projects (Wei Houkai, 1995).

2.2 From centralization to decentralization

Since its founding in 1949, the PRC has adjusted the economic administrative authority between the central and local governments from centralization to decentralization for many times. Before 1978, all previous economic reforms focused on adjusting the administrative authority between "tiao-tiao" (literally, the lines of control from the central government) and "kuai-kuai" (literally, jurisdictions of the local governments), either under the direct administration of the central government (i.e., being highly centralized at the government level) or under the direct administration of local government (i.e., being excessively decentralized at the local level). Therefore, all previous decentralization from the central to local governments basically focused on decentralization to the latter. In fact, this was a kind of administrative decentralization, different from the two-way decentralization implemented since 1978, that is, the decentralization from the central to local governments and the power expansion to enterprises were carried out simultaneously, with the latter as the main work.[1]

2.2.1 The formation of highly centralized administrative system

A highly centralized administrative system gradually came into being immediately after the founding of the PRC. This was done to meet the requirements of national

---

[1] Strictly speaking, governments at all levels allowed enterprises to enjoy autonomy, which was not delegating or expanding power, but returning power to them, because these micro-administration decision-making powers, originally belonging to enterprises, had been taken away by governments in the past, but now they were just "returning them to their original owners".

economic development, to consolidate the country's financial resources, materials, and technical capabilities, and to guarantee the successful implementation of key construction projects. As early as March 1950, to overcome the financial and economic difficulties at that time, and stabilize prices and financial markets, the central government began to unify the national fiscal revenue and expenditure, internal and external trade, and monetary finance through implementing the Decision on Unifying National Fiscal and Economic Work and other relevant decisions, thus paving the way to a highly centralized administrative system. During the First Five-year Plan period, the degree of centralization was further strengthened for reasons of the completion of the socialist transformation of the ownership of the means of production, the large-scale industrial construction, and the influence of the Soviet economic system. By the end of this period, a highly centralized administrative system had been largely shaped.

Under this system, from the perspective of the relationship between the state and enterprises, such as the planning, infrastructure, finance, materials, labor wages of enterprises were under centralized and unified administration at the level of the central government. And from the perspective of the relationship between the central and the local governments, all administrative authority was highly concentrated in the central government. Local governments and enterprises had little autonomy over their decisions and activities. For example, in the case of the centralized administration over industrial enterprises, unified leadership and hierarchical administration were exercised during the recovery period. At that time, apart from a portion of state-owned industrial enterprises in north China that were directly managed by the central government, industrial enterprises in other major administrative regions were essentially managed directly by their respective local governments. In 1954, after the abolition of the major administrative regions, major industrial enterprises were gradually brought under the direct administration of various industrial departments under the central government. The number of enterprises under the direct leadership of the central government increased from more than 2,800 in 1953 to more than 9,300 in 1957, accounting for about 16% of the total number of state-owned industrial enterprises in that year, and their industrial output was close to half of the total state-owned industrial output (Wang Haibo, 1986).

In terms of fiscal revenue, after the unification of national finance and economy in 1950, China established a highly centralized fiscal system that unified revenue and expenditure. At that time, both the authority to formulate fiscal policies and systems and the state's financial resources were highly concentrated in the central government; all financial revenues and expenditures, except for local surcharges, were included in the unified national budget, leaving little room for operation to local financial departments. From 1951 to 1952 and during the First Five-year Plan period, in order to bring the initiative of the local governments into play, part of the administrative authority was appropriately delegated and a system of separating revenue and expenditure under hierarchical administration was implemented. Thus, the local governments got fixed sources of income and a certain degree of financial flexibility, but the national financial resources and administrative authority were still highly concentrated in the hands of the central government. During the First Five-year Plan period, the financial resources dominated by the central government accounted for an average of 75% of the national budget, while the financial resources dominated by the local governments accounted for an average of 25% (Tian Yinong et al., 1988).

In terms of material authority, the Central Financial and Economic Committee began to plan and allocate eight important materials, including coal, steel, wood, cement, soda ash, miscellaneous copper, machine tools and sacks, among the greater administrative areas from 1950. In 1952, the types of materials for planned allocation expanded to 55. Since 1953, a planned distribution system has been implemented nationwide. Important materials related to the national economy and livelihood were distributed by the State Planning Commission[1] in a balanced way, while relatively less important materials and special materials were distributed by different administrative departments in a balanced way. In the latter years, more types of materials were included for planned allocation, reaching 532 types by 1957, of which 231 types were allocated in a unified way (by the State Planning Commission) and 301 kinds were managed by administrative departments. The types of materials controlled by the local authorities were on decrease year by year.

In terms of planning administration, direct planning, or mandatory planning, began to be implemented for state-owned enterprises (SOEs) during the recovery period. By 1953, there were 115 types of products that were directly included in planning targets and were under unified administration by the State Planning Commission. In 1956, it soared to more than 380, with the output accounting for about 60% of the total industrial output. In the administration of infrastructure projects, during the First Five-year Plan period, the vast majority of investment in infrastructure was directly made by the central government, accounting for 79% of the total investment budget, while the project

---

[1] The State Planning Commission was established in 1952, renamed the State Development Planning Commission in 1998, and reorganized into the National Development and Reform Commission in 2003.

investment directly administrated by local governments accounted for only 21% (Wang Haibo, 1986). The approval powers for infrastructure projects were also highly concentrated in the central government level, and the local governments only had authority for project less than RMB3 million. Throughout the First Five-year Plan period, local investment in projects accounted for only 18.2% in the investment in infrastructure, and projects directly under central administration accounted for 81.8%. In addition, in terms of labor wages and price stability, the central government had also strengthened centralized and unified administration.

The highly centralized administrative system was formed mainly out of the context as follows: (1) The natural economy had undergone the feudal society for thousands of years. (2) Apart from the wartime communist supply system, the self-sufficient and fragmented administrative system had been formed in the encircled and divided rural areas of revolutionary bases and liberated areas for more than 20 years before the founding of the PRC. (3) Under the influence of the Soviet economic system, particularly in the absence of experience in socialist construction, China essentially adopted the industrial economic management system implemented during the Stalin era of the Soviet Union. (4) Most importantly, this system met the needs of the development of the national economy at that time, especially the need to concentrate efforts on developing heavy industry during the First Five-year Plan period. This highly centralized system had a great advantage in pooling the limited capital, materials, and technical strength of the entire country for the construction of key projects essential to social stability and people's wellbeing and the development of economically weaker sectors and backward regions within the national economy, so as to liberate and develop new productive forces quickly, bridge the development gap among different sectors and regions, and promote the rapid and proportionable development of national economy. It should be said that China's great economic achievements during the First Five-year Plan period owed much to this centralized administrative system.

However, this system has some inherent drawbacks. First of all, the excessive concentration and overwhelming unification deprived enterprises of the vitality they should have, and local governments, the initiative and enthusiasm for developing the economy. In particular, this kind of system fundamentally denied the role of independent market players of enterprises in production and operation, which was not recognized until 1978. It was precisely because of this deviation in ideological understanding that all previous reforms on economic systems in China before 1978 focused on adjusting the relationship between the lines of control from the central government and jurisdictions of the local governments. Secondly, all kinds of economic administrative authority were highly concentrated in the central authorities, which was likely to cause departmental barriers and form divisions, thus cutting off the economic ties between enterprises belonging to different industrial sectors in the same region, hindering the extensive specialization of labor and collaboration in the region, and making the production capacity of each enterprise unable to be fully and rationally utilized.

2.2.2   Administrative decentralization before 1978

As early as 1951, in response to the shortcomings of excessive centralization and unification in some aspects at that time, the central government proposed to hand over some functions and authority suitable for local government administration to local governments under the principle of continuing to maintain unified leadership, unified planning and unified administration of national financial and economic work. However, during the First Five-year Plan period, with the gradual development of industrial construction especially after abolishing the greater administrative areas in 1954, administrative authority at different levels became more and more vested in the central government, resulting in "depriving the localities of their necessary independence"[1]. By the end of the First Five-year Plan period, the highly centralized administrative system had begun to unfold its various malpractices clearly.

In response to this situation, Mao Zedong elaborated upon the relationship between the central and local governments in his speech On the Ten Major Relationships delivered in 1956, and proposed to bring full play to the initiative of both the central and the local governments. As he said, "our attention should now be focused on how to enlarge the powers of the local governments to some extent, give them greater independence and let them do more, all on the premise that the unified leadership of the central government is to be strengthened".[2] "It would be detrimental to our socialist construction if the powers of the local governments were too limited."[3] According to Mao's instructions, the central government decided in 1957 to carry out economic system reform, delegating part of the power of industrial administration, commercial management and financial management to local administrations, factories, mines and

---

[1] *Selected Works of Mao Zedong* (Vol. 5), Beijing: People's Publishing House, 1977, p. 275.

[2] Ibid.

[3] This was a quotation from On the Ten Major Relationships, a speech delivered by Mao Zedong at the enlarged meeting of the Political Bureau of the CPC and the Supreme State Conference. Re-quoted from Bo Yibo, *Review of Some Major Decisions and Events* (Vol. I), Beijing: Central Party School Press, 1991, p. 488.

other enterprises. However, the Great Leap Forward, which began in 1958, disrupted this deployment. In order to achieve local industrial Great Leap Forward and establish an independent industrial system in each province, autonomous region, or municipality, this decentralization was basically centered on enlarging the powers of the local governments, but it went too far and resulted in significant delegation of power. In a short period of time, the vast majority of centrally-administered state-owned enterprises (SOEs) and public institutions were delegated to local administration, and at the same time, the powers of local governments in planning administration, approval of infrastructure projects, fiscal and taxation policy, and labor management were inappropriately expanded. Compared with 1957, the number of enterprises under direct leadership of the central government had decreased to 1,075 by the end of 1958, down 88.4%; the types of materials allocated by the state and those administrated by ministries decreased to 132 in the first quarter of 1959, a decrease of 75%. The proportion of investment in local projects in capital construction increased sharply from 22.1% in 1957 to 63.8% in 1958. Since this significant delegation of power aimed at developing local industry to be self-contained and achieving the so-called Great Leap Forward of "surpassing the UK and catching up with the USA", coupled with other factors as the excessive, hasty, and speedy decentralization, and the legging behind of macro-administration, the whole national economy was thrown into the chaos, resulting in blind location and construction of factories, repeated construction, divided market, regional blockade, and many other problems.

The chaotic situation formed after the excessive decentralization of powers to the local governments compelled the central government to re-emphasize the centralization and unification of the central government and withdraw the powers delegated to the local governments. In June 1959, Mao Zedong pointed out when he was in Lushan Mountain, "there is now some semi-anarchism. The 'four types of powers' (referring to the powers to handle human resources, financial affairs, commercial operations, and industrial development) were decentralized too much and too fast in the past, causing chaos. We now should emphasize unified leadership and centralization and withdraw the powers delegated out properly."[1] Therefore, starting from the second half of 1959, the central government began to resume some authority for the administration of enterprises and materials. After 1961, powers over-delegated out during the Great Leap

---

[1] Zhou Taihe, *Historical Experience of China's Economic System Reform*, Beijing: People's Publishing House, 1983, p. 86.

Forward period were regained by the central government one after another. By 1965, the number of enterprises directly controlled by the central government amounted to 10,533, with the output accounting for 42.3% of the total industrial output of the country;[1] The types of materials allocated by the state and those administrated by ministries reached 592, of which 370 fell into the former category. At the same time, a material administration system and a business operation network were established under vertical leadership from the central government to the local governments. The proportion of investment in projects under the direct leadership of the central government in the total investment in infrastructure also increased from 36.2% in 1958 to 65%. In short, after several years of adjustment, the centralization and unification were intensified again. In some aspects, such as administration on industrial enterprises and materials, the degree of centralization was even higher than that at the end of the First Five-year Plan period, thus re-exposing some drawbacks of the highly centralized administrative system.

In March 1966, Mao Zedong proposed that the central government should focus on formulating general policies and guidelines while exercising little or even no control over specific issues and affairs.[2] He criticized that the central government had over-withdrawn administrative authority over factories that had been delegated to the local government. And he demanded that anyone who had overdone it go out of the central government immediately and to the local government.[3] This thus led to China's significant delegation of power for the second time after 1970.[4] At that time, the role of the central government was denied. Indiscriminately, the administrative powers for almost all enterprises directly under the central government, including Angang Steel, Daqing Oilfield, First Automobile Works and other large backbone enterprises, were delegated to provinces, autonomous regions and municipalities, and many enterprises directly under the province-level administration were further delegated to prefectures and counties. At the same time, the administrative powers of local governments in terms

---

[1] In 1957, the industrial output of enterprises under the direct leadership of the central government accounted for 39.7% of the total industrial output, and in 1958, it was 13.8% (Zhou Taihe, 1983).

[2] Wang Haibo, *Industrial Economic History of the New China*, Beijing: Economy & Management Publishing House, 1986, p. 367.

[3] Ibid.

[4] The Outline of the Fourth Five-year Plan, which was formulated under the guidance of preparations against war in 1970, set high targets including "doubling the national industrial outputs" while blindly pursuing local self-sufficiency and self-sufficiency. In order to realize this unrealistic plan, the hope was pinned on bringing the initiative of the local governments into play. Therefore, reforming the economic system, decentralizing enterprises, and expanding various local governments were once again required.

of material administration, plan administration, fiscal revenue, capital construction and labor wages were expanded through the local responsibility system in terms of materials, fiscal revenue and expenditure, and infrastructure investment. By 1976, the number of enterprises directly under the central government had decreased to 1,674, of which the number of central industrial enterprises for civilian use had decreased to about 700. The output of enterprises directly under the central government accounted for only 6% of the total industrial output. The types of materials controlled by the state had also decreased from 579 in 1966 to 217 in 1972. The aimless decentralization of state-owned key enterprises and administrative authority prompted region to pursue self-sufficiency, blind production and repeated construction, thus aggravating the dispersion and chaos as well as the anarchy and semi-anarchy of economic activities to such extent that the decentralized enterprises and administrative authority had to be withdrawn to strengthen the centralization and unification of the central government.

Thus, in China before 1978, the administrative authority between the central and local government had undergone two and a half cycles of "centralization-decentralization": from the centralization during the recovery period and the First Five-year Plan period to the decentralization during the Great Leap Forward period, then from the centralization during the adjustment period to the decentralization after 1970, and to the subsequent centralization. As both decentralizations made the macro-economy out of control, the state had to carry out overall national economic adjustment and withdraw the decentralized authority. In this way, the national economy has fallen into a vicious cycle of "centralization-decentralization": once delegating power to the local government leads to market disorder, the central government will tighten its control, which in turn often leads to economic stagnation or chaos, and then the central government will have to decentralize again. Generally, this situation was caused by such factors as follows:

First, both of these two decentralizations were aimed at establishing local self-contained industrial systems and at the same time, encouraging local governments to take a proactive role in boosting economy by decentralizing enterprises and by expanding local administrative authority, so as to actualize the too ambitious plans formulated at that time. In this sense, both of these two power delegations were merely temporary measures, reflecting an inherent impatience for immediate success in practice. For example, some large backbone enterprises, essential for social stability and public welfare, were decentralized, despite the fact that they should not have been. Additionally, various forms of administrative authority were also decentralized. Consequently, the previous cooperative relationship was disrupted; the planning power, personnel power, financial power, and administrative power were disconnected with each other; enterprises were placed under multiple leadership and confronted with various contradictions; and, after the local governments took over the administration of these enterprises, many regions became trapped in a cycle of blind production and repeated construction in a pursuit of their own self-contained industrial systems.

Second, the decentralizations were primarily implemented through political mobilization, driven by excessively urgent and hasty demands for a quick resolution. For instance, the central government issued a notice on June 2, 1958 requiring that by June 15, the decentralization procedures of more than 880 units in nine departments be completed in less than half a month. On July 20, another notice was issued, requiring 203 institutions of higher education to be delegated to local government in less than a month before August 15(Zhou Taihe, 1983). Due to the rapid decentralization, local administration could not keep up with it in time, and the central government relaxed its control and guidance on macro-economy, which inevitably led to macro-economic chaos.

Third, both of the two decentralizations went to extremes, resulting in significant delegation of power. Particularly in 1970, the decentralization went more thorough. The result was the transition from a high degree of centralization at the level of the central government to excessive decentralization at the level of local government. In this way, regional blockade was thus formed. All regions were devoted to developing a comprehensive and self-contained industrial system, and enterprises in all regions were trying to develop themselves toward being either "large and complete" or "small but complete", making the regional industrial structure and enterprise organizational structure even more unreasonable.

Fourth, there existed ambiguity in the power boundaries between the state and enterprises, as well as between the central and local government. Additionally, both the centralization and decentralization lacked a solid theoretical foundation. In fact, each time the power was withdrawn or decentralized was only based on the leadership's intention, rather than a reasonable definition of power between the central and local governments as stipulated by the law. Therefore, the centralization and decentralization were usually implemented according to leaders' empirical judgment of the actual economic operations, which was inevitably subjective and arbitrary.

Fifth, the practices attempted to replace market with mandatory plans, which excluded the decisive role of market mechanism and law of value. In this way, the decentralization from the central to the local government could just change the direct central control into the direct local control, and lead to intensified market division and regional blockade.

Sixth, and more importantly, the prevailing circumstances at that time resulted in a lack of recognition that SOEs were relatively independent producers and operators, and that the primary goal of economic system reforms was to boost business vitality. Therefore, previous economic system reforms unexceptionally focused on the adjustment of the relationship between the central and local governments, which was fundamentally responsible for China's failure to get out of the cycle of "centralization-decentralization" for a long time before 1978. As stated in the Decision of the CPC Central Committee on Restructuring the Economic System adopted by the Third Plenary Session of the 12th CPC Central Committee, in the past, "decentralization has been implemented many times, only aiming at balancing the administrative authority between the central and local governments as well as between the lines of control from the central government and jurisdictions of the local governments. The vital matter of granting autonomy to enterprises was overlooked, thereby preventing it from breaking away from the existing framework."[1]

2.3 Regional economic growth pattern before the reform and opening up

Before 1978, China's regional economy exhibited an overall pattern of balanced growth, despite significant fluctuations. In general, the concept of balanced growth defies a single interpretation. From the perspective of balanced growth, it entails the gradual reduction or convergence of regional disparities in economic growth rate over a specific timeframe. This implies that the economic growth rates of different regions gradually approach the national growth rate. When considering the catching up of underdeveloped regions, balanced growth denotes a scenario where the economic growth of these regions surpasses that of developed regions within a specific timespan, thereby narrowing the developmental gap between underdeveloped and developed regions. The balanced growth strategy implemented in China before 1978 aimed to reduce regional disparities by promoting the development of inland regions.

---

[1] The Decision was included in *Upholding Reform, Opening Up, and Invigorating the Economy: Selected Extracts from Relevant Important Documents since the Third Plenary Session of the 11th CPC Central Committee*, Beijing: People's Publishing House, 1987, p. 233.

2.3.1   Growth trends in the coastal regions and the interior

In order to shake off poverty and backwardness as soon as possible, the PRC has started the process of large-scale industrialization since its foundation. With the rapid advancement of industrialization from the coastal regions to the interior, the industry in the interior gained rapid development, and great changes has taken place in the unreasonable situation that industry use to be concentrated in the eastern coastal regions. From 1952 to 1978, the gross industrial output of the whole country increased by 11.32 times, among which, that of the coastal regions increased by 9.82 times, and that of the interior increased by 14.74 times, much higher than the average growth rate in the former two cases   (see Table 2-3). For the interior during this period, the output value of machinery industry increased by 45.41 times; of light industry, 9.18 times; and the output of raw coal increased by 10.35 times; of electricity, by 46.22 times; of steel, 60.91 times; of cement, by 54.11 times; and of yarn, by 7.22 times, all of which were much higher than the growth rate of the coastal regions. It should be pointed out that, due to the poor original foundation in the interior and the mistakes in production layout during the "Third Front" Construction period, the elasticity coefficient of industrial investment in the interior was low and the economic benefits left much to be desired. If the ratio of the growth rate of gross industrial output value to the growth rate of industrial fixed assets' original value is taken as a substitute indicator for investment elasticity coefficient, it can be observed that during this period, the national industrial investment elasticity coefficient was 0.55. Coastal regions had a coefficient of 0.81, while the interior only had 0.35. This demonstrated that prior to the reform and opening up, investment growth in the interior played a significantly lesser role in stimulating industrial growth compared to that in coastal regions.

Table 2-3   Industrial economic growth in the coastal regions
and the interior from 1952 to 1978

Indicator	National total			Coastal regions			Interior regions		
	1952	1978	N-fold	1952	1978	N-fold	1952	1978	N-fold
Gross industrial output value (RMB bn)	34.33	423.08	11.32	23.81	257.53	9.82	10.52	165.55	14.74
Output value of machinery industry (RMB bn)	3.90	115.55	28.63	2.96	71.92	23.30	0.94	43.63	45.41
Gross output value of light industry (RMB bn)	22.11	180.57	7.17	15.81	116.46	6.37	6.30	64.11	9.18
Original value of industrial fixed assets (RMB bn)	14.88	319.34	20.46	10.71	140.05	12.08	4.17	179.29	42.00

(continued)

Indicator	National total			Coastal regions			Interior regions		
	1952	1978	N-fold	1952	1978	N-fold	1952	1978	N-fold
Output of raw coal (bn metric tons)	0.066	0.618	8.36	0.029	0.198	5.83	0.037	0.42	10.35
Power generation (bn kWh)	7.26	256.55	34.34	4.62	131.88	27.55	2.64	124.67	46.22
Output of steel (ten thousand metric tons)	134.9	3, 178.0	22.56	115.8	1,995.6	16.23	19.1	1,182.4	60.91
Output of chemical fertilizer (ten thousand metric tons)	3.87	869.3	223.63	3.87	425.3	109.90	0	444.0	—
Output of cement (ten thousand metric tons)	286.1	5, 623.6	18.66	226.9	3,261.1	13.37	59.2	3,262.5	54.11
Output of yarn (ten thousand metric tons)	65.6	238.2	2.63	53.8	141.2	1.62	11.8	97.0	7.22

Note: The data pertaining to industrial fixed assets was sourced from independent-accounting industrial enterprises owned by the whole people. The gross industrial output value in 1952 and 1978 was calculated at the constant price in 1952 and 1970, respectively.

Source: Statistics Department of Industrial Transportation Materials, National Bureau of Statistics, *Statistical Data on China's Industrial Economy (1949-1984)*, Beijing: China Statistics Press, 1985.

In different periods, economic growth rate varied much between the coastal regions and the interior. On the basis of the difference in industrial growth rate, the process of the industrial growth in the coastal and interior regions could be divided into three stages. The first stage was from 1953 to 1965, during which, the industrialization in the interior was greatly accelerated as a large number of large and medium-sized industrial enterprises and industrial bases had emerged there, and the industrial development had gained a momentum of rapid growth, with growth rate higher than that in the coastal regions. Especially during the First Five-year Plan period, the average annual growth rate of the gross industrial output value in the interior reached 20.5%, 3.7 percentage points higher than that in the coastal regions. Among them, the gross output value of light industry grew by 16.7%, 5.6 percentage points higher than that in coastal regions (see Table 2-4). During the Second Five-Year Plan period, under the influence of the Great Leap Forward, the growth rate of the national industrial economy dropped sharply, but the growth rate of the gross industrial output value in the interior was still higher than that in the coastal regions. Notably, too fast westward shift of the focus of industrial development and insufficient national investment at this stage had seriously affected the original production capacity and the industrial growth of the old coastal industrial bases.

The second stage spanned from 1966 to 1970, during which the large-scale "Third-

Front" Construction program was initiated in the interior. However, due to excessive focus on national defense needs, the industrial layout for the Construction failed to yield the expected satisfactory results, and the huge increase in national investment went nowhere in promoting faster economic growth of the interior, thus making industries in the coastal regions and the interior generally show a constant or balanced growth trend. However, if calculated by light and heavy industries respectively, the average annual growth rate of the gross output value of light industry and heavy industry in the interior is 0.9 and 0.4 percentage points lower than that in coastal regions.

Table 2-4   Average annual growth of gross industrial output of the coastal regions and the interior from 1953 to 1980   Unit: %

Stage	Period	All industries			Light industry			Heavy industry		
		National	Coastal	Interior	National	Coastal	Interior	National	Coastal	Interior
1	1953-1957	18.0	16.8	20.5	12.8	11.1	16.7	25.4	25.5	25.4
	1958-1962	3.8	2.9	4.2						
	1963-1965	17.9	17.5	18.7	21.1	21.5	20.3	15.0	13.4	17.4
2	1966-1970	11.7	11.7	11.6	8.4	8.7	7.8	14.7	14.8	14.4
3	1972-1975	7.7	8.0	7.3						
	1976-1980	9.2	9.4	8.9	11.0	11.4	10.3	7.7	7.6	7.9

Note: Figures in 1953-1957 were calculated at 1952 constant price; in 1958-1962, 1963-1965, and 1966-1970, calculated at 1957 constant price; and in 1972-1975 and 1976-1980, calculated at 1970 constant price.

Source: Office of the Leading Group for National Industrial Census of the State Council and Department of Industrial Transportation and Materials Statistics of the National Bureau of Statistics, *Statistics on China's Industrial Economy* (*1986*), Beijing: China Statistics Press, 1987.

The third stage occurred after 1970. In general, starting from the 1970s, as the national investment focus shifted gradually towards the coastal regions, the economic growth rate in those areas started to accelerate and gradually exceeded that of the interior. From 1972 to 1975 and 1976 to 1980, the gross industrial output value in the coastal regions gained an annual increase of 8.0% and 9.4%, 0.7 and 0.5 percentage points higher than that in the interior respectively. From 1976 to 1980, however, the growth rate of light industry in the interior was lower than that in the coastal regions, while the growth rate of heavy industry, slightly higher.

2.3.2   Growth pattern of provincial economy

Before the reform and opening up, influenced by the national macro policies, China's economic growth fluctuated in a sawtooth shape. From 1953 to 1978, the growth rate of GDP or GRP fluctuated greatly in both the whole country and provinces, autonomous regions and municipalities, and the change trend was generally the same. In this period, although the national GDP growth rate exceeded 10% in 10 years, showing high-speed growth, among which the average annual growth rate in 1953, 1958, 1964-1965 and 1969-1970 exceeded 15%, due to the negative growth of the national economy in six years, the average growth rate of the national GDP during this period was only 6.14%. In terms of provinces, the growth rate of GRP varies greatly from region to region during this period, with the highest average growth rate of 11.23% in Beijing and the lowest average growth rate of 3.51% in Anhui, which means the former is 3.2 times of the latter. If we define a growth rate higher than 8% as high-speed growth, 6.5%-8% as medium-high-speed growth, 5%-6.5% as medium-low-speed growth, and less than 5% as low-speed growth, we can observe that the GRP growth rates of Beijing, Ningxia, Shanghai, and Qinghai exceeds 8%, showing a trend of high-speed growth; Liaoning, Tianjin, Shaanxi, and Guangxi showed medium-high-speed growth; Heilongjiang, Shanxi, Tibet, Shandong and other 14 provinces showed medium-low-speed growth. However, Henan, Jiangxi and Anhui showed a low-speed growth trend (see Table 2-5). It can be seen that during this period, most provinces in China were in the range of medium-low-speed or even low-speed growth.

Similar to the national economic growth trend, China's regional economic growth in during this period was not stable enough and exhibited significant fluctuations. The stability of regional economic growth over a specific duration can be assessed using the instability coefficient (IC), while the fluctuation range of growth can be measured through the coefficient of fluctuation (CF). Both IC and CF values range from 0 and above, with higher values indicating poorer stability and larger fluctuations in regional economic growth. Conversely, lower values suggest greater stability and smaller fluctuations. Analysis revealed that the IC of China's GDP growth rate from 1953 to 1978 was 1.52, with a CF of 7.27. This implied that the absolute range of economic growth fluctuations was 7.27 times the average growth rate. Compared to the national average, 23 out of those 29 provinces exhibited higher IC and CF of economic growth and only five—Zhejiang, Ningxia, Guangdong, Jiangsu, and Guangxi—exhibited lower IC and CF, indicating that, compared to the fluctuations of national macroeconomic growth, regional economic growth had greater volatility and less instability. It can be said that economic growth before the reform and opening up was unstable with significant fluctuations, which was a prevalent feature of China's regional economic growth.

Table 2 –5   GRP growth rate of provinces from 1953 to 1978

Category	Provinces	Average annual growth rate (%)	Fluctuation coefficient	Instability coefficient
	National	6.14	7.27	1.52
High-speed growth	Beijing	11.23	12.28	2.09
	Ningxia	8.98	6.78	1.45
	Shanghai	8.76	7.42	1.62
	Qinghai	8.47	8.17	1.57
Medium-high-speed growth	Liaoning	7.56	10.42	1.91
	Tianjin	7.27	8.25	1.76
	Shaanxi	6.80	9.63	2.04
	Guangxi	6.62	5.87	1.21
Low-medium-speed growth	Heilongjiang	6.34	11.30	1.77
	Shanxi	6.26	9.82	1.96
	Tibet	6.14	8.04	1.45
	Shandong	6.10	7.59	1.67
	Yunnan	6.05	8.31	1.79
	Gansu	6.03	8.98	2.04
	Inner Mongolia	5.98	10.4	2.06
Low-speed-medium growth	Fujian	5.97	8.05	1.67
	Xinjiang	5.87	7.93	1.81
	Hebei	5.79	9.50	1.88
	Jilin	5.74	9.20	1.83
	Zhejiang	5.67	7.22	1.47
	Hubei	5.47	9.34	2.14
	Hunan	5.37	9.11	1.84
	Sichuan*	5.24	6.77	1.82
	Guangdong	5.21	6.69	1.44
	Jiangsu	5.18	6.47	1.47
	Guizhou	5.13	11.37	2.46
Low-speed growth	Henan	4.40	13.86	2.40
	Jiangxi	4.32	8.38	1.77
	Anhui	3.51	13.48	2.73

Note: (1) Instability coefficient $(IC) = \dfrac{\sqrt{\dfrac{1}{N}\sum_{i=1}^{N}(g_n - \bar{g})^2}}{\bar{g}}$; Coefficient of Fluctuation $(CF) = (g_{max} - g_{min})\sqrt{g}$, where, g is the regional economic growth rate in year n; $\bar{g}$ is the average regional economic growth rate in N years; g_{max} and g_{min} are the maximum and minimum regional economic growth rates in N years, and N is the number of sample years. (2) Chongqing was separated from Sichuan Province in 1997 and became China's fourth municipality directly under the central government; Hainan Province was separated from Guangdong Province in 1988. Therefore, Chongqing is excluded in the data for Sichuan; Hainan is excluded in the data for Guangdong. In the case of Chongqing, the average annual growth rate from 1953 to 1978 GRP was 4.75%, the coefficient of fluctuation was 10.02, and the instability coefficient was 2.19; and the data for Hainan is not found.

Source: Calculated based on the relevant data in *China Compendium of Statistics 1949-2008*, compiled by Department of Comprehensive Statistics of Bureau of Statistics. Beijing: China Statistics Press, 2010.

2.4 Changes in development gap between regions before the reform and opening up

In the 1950s, American economist Williamson (1965) suggested an inverted U-shaped relationship between regional disparities and economic development (per capita income level). According to this theory, during the early stage of economic development, the regional gap tends to widen as development progresses. However, as economic growth reaches a mature stage, the gap tends to narrow. This concept, known as Williamson's convergence hypothesis, has not been fully confirmed (Wei Houkai, 2011). However, examining the experiences of some developed countries, it can be observed that during the initial and middle stages of industrialization, the regional gap generally expands to a certain extent due to rapid national economic growth. China has witnessed a widening development gap between its regions as industrialization continues since 1949. This phenomenon can be attributed to the original foundation and development stage of China's economy.

2.4.1 The gap between coastal regions and the interior

The absolute gap in national income per capita between the coastal regions and the interior has been widening since 1949. The national income per capita in the coastal regions and in the interior were RMB118 and RMB85 in 1952; the absolute gap amounted to RMB33, which expanded to RMB48 in 1965 and RMB153 in 1978. However, from the perspective of relative gap as, national income per capita between the coastal regions and the interior had a tendency to narrow due to the westward shift of the focus of national investment, the relative gap was gradually reduced, from 28.0% in 1952 down to 25.4% in 1957 and further down to 22.5% in 1965. However, since the mid-1960s, the development gap between the coastal regions and the interior has begun to widen, with the relative gap in national income per capita between the coastal regions and the interior widened to 37.9% by 1978, up 15.4 percentage points over 1965 (see Table 2-6). This shows that although the large-scale "Third Front" Construction was launched in the interior during this period, due to the excessive emphasis on the national defense needs in China's productivity layout and the undesirable effects from investment, the westward shift of the focus of national investment failed to effectively prevent the widening development gap between the coastal regions and the interior. In general, the gap in national income per capita among China's three major regions has been consistently widening, albeit with some minor fluctuations during its progression.

Table 2-6   Gaps in national income per capita between coastal
regions and the interior from 1952 to 1980

Indicator	1952	1957	1965	1970	1975	1978	1980
Per capita national income in coastal regions (RMB)	118	169	213	258	325	404	497
Per capita national income in the interior (RMB)	85	126	165	187	211	251	310
Absolute gap between coastal regions and the interior (RMB)	33	43	48	71	114	153	187
Relative gap between coastal regions and the interior (%)	28.0	25.4	22.5	27.5	35.1	37.9	37.6

Note: Data in this table was calculated at current prices. Relative gap= (absolute gap/coastal national income per capita) ×100%.

Sources: Wei Houkai, "On the Coordinated Development Strategy of China's Regional Economy", *New Horizons from Tianfu*, 1994(3); Wei Houkai, *Theory and Policy of Regional Economy*, Beijing: China Social Sciences Press, 2006.

Overall, except for a few years, the gap of national income per capita in China's three major regions continued to widen before 1978, even during the "Third Front" Construction period when a balanced development strategy was adopted (Liu Shucheng et al., 1994). From 1952 to 1978, the weighted coefficient of variation of national income per capita among the three regions increased from 0.197 to 0.361, an increase of 83.2%. This shows that the development gap among the three major regions had started to widen before the introduction of reform and opening up policy, being just a continuation of the past trend. Of course, it should be noted that, there emerged some fluctuations in the changes of the gap among the three major regions before the reform and opening up. For example, the periods of 1954-1955, 1961-1963, 1970, and 1977-1978, all witnessed the decline with varying degrees in the weighted coefficient of variation of national income per capita among the three major regions, which, however, did not change the overall expanding trend of regional disparities.

2.4.2   Inter-provincial development gap

In line with the changing pattern of the development gap among the three major regions, the inter-provincial development gap in China was also widening before the reform and opening up. Figure 2-2 reflects the changes in the coefficient of variation, weighted coefficient of variation, and extreme rate of national income per capita (or GRP per capita) across China's provinces, autonomous regions and municipalities from 1952 to 1980. As can be seen from it, whether index of national income (NI) per capita or GRP per capita is adopted, the changes in the coefficient of variation or the weighted coefficient of variation are highly consistent, except that the coefficient of variation of the GRP per capita is the smallest, that of the national income per capita is the largest, and the weighted coefficient of variation of the national income per capita is in the middle. From 1952 to 1978, the coefficient of variation of national income per capita of provinces, autonomous regions and municipalities increased from 0.793 to 1.346, the weighted coefficient of variation of national income per capita increased from 0.627 to 1.174, and the coefficient of variation of GRP per capita increased from 0.591 to 0.972, increasing by 69.7%, 87.2% and 64.5% respectively. Specifically, between 1954 and 1955, there was a temporary narrowing of the gap in national income per capita or GRP per capita among different regions, which could be attributed to the gradual shift of China's industrial focus from the coastal regions to the interior and the notable acceleration of industrialization in the interior, particularly in some underdeveloped areas during the progressive implementation of China's First Five-year Plan. Similarly, the period between 1961 and 1962 witnessed a decrease in China's inter-provincial gap in national income per capita and GRP per capita, which resulted from the policy for national economic adjustment. However, it should be pointed out that the initiation of

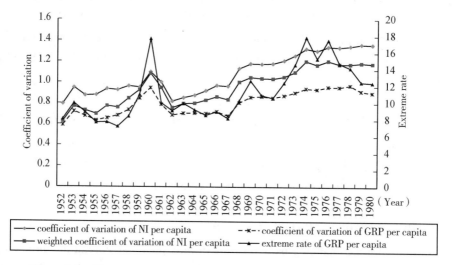

Figure 2-2   Changes in development gap among provinces, autonomous regions and municipalities from 1952 to 1980

Note: The coefficient of variation and extreme rate of GRP per capita are calculated based on the separation of Chongqing from Sichuan. Coefficient of variation is the ratio of standard deviation to average value of sample data. The value of the coefficient is greater than or equal to 0, and the larger the value, the greater the regional gap.

Source: Calculated according to the data in Liu Shucheng et al., *China's Regional Economic Development*, China Statistics Publishing House, 1994; and *China Compendium of Statistics 1949-2008.*

China's "Third Front" Construction program in 1965, which focused on war preparedness, led to a significant investment of funds in the "Third Front" regions. Despite this massive national investment, the inter-provincial gaps in national income per capita and GRP per capita continued to widen due to the misleading guidelines and the turbulent period of the Cultural Revolution.

The extreme rate, which is defined as the ratio of the maximum value to the minimum value of an economic index, represents the maximum relative amplitude of regional disparities. Figure 2-2 illustrates that between 1952 and 1980, the extreme rate of GRP per capita in different provinces, autonomous regions, and municipalities in China exhibited significant fluctuations, which did not align with the coefficient of variation. Before the reform and opening up, the extreme rate of GRP per capita in provinces, autonomous regions and municipalities was lowest at 7.2 in 1957, when the GRP per capita was highest in Shanghai and lowest in Guizhou, the highest being 7.2 times that of the lowest. It should be pointed out that, the extreme rates of GRP per capita in 1960, 1974, and 1976 all exceeded 17, thus forming three peaks, which were mainly caused by the rapid increase of GRP per capita in Shanghai (the highest) but the sharp decline in the lowest Guizhou or Sichuan (excluding Chongqing). For instance, the extreme rate of GRP per capita soared to 17.69 in 1960 because the GRP per capita in Shanghai increased by 1.18 times from 1958 to 1960, but that in Sichuan decreased by 17.6% from 1959 to 1960, making its GRP per capita the lowest across the country. The peaks of extreme rates in 1974 and 1976 were primarily caused by the sharp decline in the GRP per capita in Guizhou: a decrease of 23.0% between 1972 and 1974, and an additional 12.2% in 1976. In contrast, Shanghai experienced an increase of 24.6% and 1.0% during the same periods, respectively.

2.4.3   Urbanization and urban-rural gap

Before the reform and opening up, China's urbanization was slow and wavy due to changes in public policies. During this period, China's urbanization process could be roughly divided into six different stages (see Figure 2-3): (1) the recovery and steady advancement stage from 1950 to 1953, during which the national urbanization level increased from 10.64% in 1949 to 13.31%, with an average annual increase of 0.67 percentage points; (2) the stagnation stage from 1954 to 1955, during which the urbanization level hovered around 13.5%; (3) the "great rash advance" stage of urbanization from 1956 to 1960, dominated by the Great Leap Forward thought, the national urbanization level expanded rapidly from 13.48% in 1955 to 19.75%, with an average annual increase of 1.25 percentage points, which exceeded the affordability of the national economy at that time; (4) the anti-urbanization stage from 1961 to 1963, over which the national urbanization level decreased by 2.91 percentage points, with an average annual decrease of 0.97 percentage points; (5) the growth-recovery stage in 1964, when the urbanization level increased sharply by 1.53 percentage points; and (6) the stagnation and recession period from 1965 to 1977, during which the national urbanization level remained around 17.5% due to the influence of the Cultural Revolution, showing a slight downward trend (Wei Houkai, 2014). During the 28 years before the reform and opening up, the urbanization rate in China experienced an average growth of only 0.25 percentage points per year, leading to an average annual addition of 3.89 million individuals to the urban population.

Overall, before the reform and opening up, China went through a slow process of urbanization, full of twists and turns as well as ups and downs as follows: (1) short yet steady development during the three-year recovery period and the First Five-year Plan period; (2) vigorous development during the three-year Great Leap Forward period and subsequent national economic adjustment period; (3) stagnant development during the Cultural Revolution, and the "Major Third Front" and "Minor Third Front" Construction periods. Under the influence of a series of factors, China's urbanization before the reform and opening up was mainly characterized with ups and downs (Zhou Yixing, 1995; Liu Yong, 2011). It should be noted that, the tortuous and wiggly urbanization during this period could be attributed to numerous factors, including the weak foundation of China's economic and social development, the unstable domestic and international development environment, the mechanical replication of the Soviet model, an excessive focus on heavy chemical industry development, neglect of industrialization strategies for non-productive construction, blind implementation of the Great Leap Forward policy driven by a desire for immediate success, overestimation of international tension, and scattered development of industries without considering the pivotal role of major cities. Furthermore, natural disasters, deteriorating Sino-Soviet relations, and other factors also contributed much to it (Wei Houkai, 2014). Under the mixed influence of a variety of internal and external factors, China implemented policies and measures to shape its urbanization process. These included establishing household registration systems, regulating population mobility, promoting decentralization-driven "Third Front" Construction, controlling the growth of major cities, developing small towns, and stopping urban planning. Collectively, these efforts set the tone for China's subsequent urbanization (Zhou Yixing, 1995).

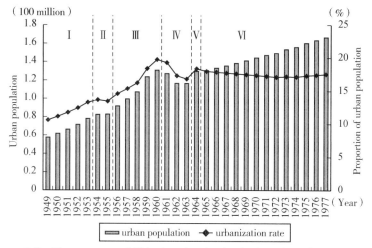

Figure 2-3   The process of China's urbanization before the reform and opening up

Source: Drawn according to Wei Houkai, *A New Road to Urbanization with Chinese Characteristics*, Beijing: Social Sciences Academic Press (China), 2014.

With urbanization developing in a wave-like manner, the changes in China's urban-rural gap also fluctuated greatly before the reform and opening up. Generally speaking, the ratio of consumption level between urban and rural residents reflects the consumption gap between urban and rural residents, which generally changed in wave-like way before the reform and opening up. Leaving some small fluctuations aside, we may divide the changes in the consumption gap between China's urban and rural residents during this period roughly into three stages: (1) The rapid expansion stage before 1960, the ratio of consumption level between urban and rural residents increased rapidly from 2.37 in 1952 to 3.23 in 1960. (2) The rapid decline stage from 1960 to 1967, during which the ratio dropped rapidly to 2.33 in 1967, lower than that in 1952. (3) The gradual expansion stage after 1967. By 1977, the ratio had gradually expanded to 3.0, second only to the level from 1959 to 1960. Further, from the perspective of the income gap between urban and rural residents, official data on per capita disposable income of urban households and Net Income Per Capita of rural households were only available for a few years such as 1957, 1965, and 1978. In 1957, the per capita disposable income of urban households was RMB235.44, while the Net Income Per Capita for rural households was RMB72.92, resulting in a ratio of 3.23∶1. In 1965, the per capita disposable income of urban households decreased to RMB227.04, while the Net Income Per Capita for rural households rose to RMB107.2, making the urban-rural income ratio down to 2.12 : 1. However, the income gap started to widen afterwards. In 1978, the per capita disposable income of rural households surged to RMB316.0 and the Net Income Per Capita of rural households reached RMB133.57. As a result, the urban-rural income ratio increased to 2.37 : 1, significantly higher than that in 1965.

Chapter 3
Changes in China's Regional Economic Development Gap

Since 1978, China has undergone a transformation in its regional economic development strategy, transitioning from unbalanced development to coordinated development. In line with this strategic shift, China has progressively implemented and enhanced its master strategy and some more specific strategies for regional development, including the strategy for coordinated development of the Beijing-Tianjin-Hebei region, the strategy for development of the Yangtze River Economic Belt, and the Belt and Road Initiative. Additionally, differentiated regional policies have been introduced for functional zones and areas with special features. With the strong support of state-level strategies and policies, China's regional development gap, particularly the gap between the eastern and western regions, has turned from continuous expansion to gradual narrowing. This narrowing gap is indicative of the remarkable accomplishments of China's strategy for coordinated regional development since the initiation of the reform and opening up. It can be asserted that ensuring coordinated development of regional economies and then shared prosperity is at the core of China's approach to coordinated regional development since the reform and opening up.

3.1 Changes in China's regional development gap

The changes in China's regional development gap after the reform and opening up are closely related to regional units. The changes in development gaps between different regional units often present different patterns, sometimes even completely opposite. Here we will explore the disparities among four major regions, the inter-provincial disparities, the disparities among urban areas, and that among rural areas through using indicators of GRP per capita and per capita income of urban and rural residents.

3.1.1　Disparities among four major regions

The central government has always prioritized narrowing the development gap among the four major regions, particularly between the eastern and western regions. In 1978, the northeastern region had the highest GRP per capita among the four major regions. It was followed by the eastern region, while the central and western regions had the lowest GRP per capita. Until 1990, the GRP per capita in the northeastern region was higher than that in the eastern region, where the GRP per capita began to overtake that in northeast China in 1991, and since then, the absolute gap between them continued to grow each year, exceeding RMB10,000 in 2007 and reaching RMB28,300 in 2016. With the sustained and rapid economic growth after the reform and opening up, despite the ever-expanding development base of each region, the absolute gap of GRP per capita between the central and western regions and the eastern region has been widening all the time, and that gap between the central and western regions and the northeastern region has been expanding until 2013, and then began to narrow. If calculated at current prices of that year, from 2014 to 2016, the absolute gap in per capita disposable income between the central and western regions and the eastern region would expand by more than 7% each year, while the absolute gap between the northeastern region and the eastern region will expand by more than 10% each year. Due to the difference in development bases and rising price, therefore, it will not be easy to narrow the absolute regional gap in GRP per capita or per capita income.

In contrast to the changes in the absolute gap, when measured using GRP per capita, the gap between China's four major regions and the relative gap between the central and western regions and the eastern region followed an inverted U-shape after the reform and opening up which suggested that the gap consistently widened before 2003 and subsequently began to narrow. This point has been extensively discussed in Chapter 1 and will not be further discussed here. It should be pointed out that since 2014, due to the remarkable economic slowdown in the northeast, central and western regions, the coefficient of variation of GRP per capita in the four major regions and the relative gap coefficient of GRP per capita between the eastern region and central and western regions have all slightly expanded. However, if measured with the per capita disposable income of residents, the gap between China's four major regions and the relative gap between the eastern region and central and western regions have continued to narrow steadily in recent years. From 2013 to 2016, the relative gap coefficient of per capita disposable income decreased from 35.5% to 34.7% between the eastern and central regions and from 41.2% to 40.0% between the eastern and western regions, and the coefficient of variation of per capita disposable income of residents in the four major regions decreased from 0.244 to 0.238. The relative gap of GRP per capita between the northeast and the eastern region has been shrinking from 2004 to 2012, but has been expanding in recent years. In 2013, the per capita disposable income of residents in the northeastern region was 75.6% of that in the eastern region, and by 2016, the ratio had dropped to 72.9%.

3.1.2   Inter-provincial disparities

Since the reform and opening up, China's inter-provincial gap in GRP per capita has generally experienced a continuous narrowing. From a broader historical perspective, this gap could be roughly visualized as an inverted U-shape after the founding of the PRC in 1949, with the coefficient of variation peaking in 1978. Figure 3-1 illustrates the changes in the extreme rate, coefficient of variation, and weighted coefficient of variation of China's inter-provincial GRP per capita from 1978 to 2016. As shown in Figure 3-1, the gap in inter-provincial GRP per capita has experienced three distinct stages of evolution since 1978 as follows:

Firstly, in the initial period of the reform and opening up, China's inter-provincial gap in GRP per capita has obviously narrowed. This could be attributed to two key factors. On the one hand, certain high-income regions such as the northeast and north China experienced an economic downturn, along with the decline of old industrial bases in Shanghai, Liaoning, and other parts of the country. On the other hand, there was rapid economic growth in low- and middle-income areas such as Guangdong, Zhejiang, and Fujian. From 1978 to 1990, the extreme rate of inter-provincial GRP per capita dropped from 14.2 : 1 to 7.3 : 1, while the weighted coefficient of variation and the coefficient of variation decreased by 38.1%(from 0.972 to 0.602)and 39.0%(from 0.753 to 0.459) respectively.

Secondly, since the 1990s, the inter-provincial gap in GRP per capita has begun to expand slowly, primarily driven by the sustained and rapid economic growth in coastal provinces and cities. By 2003, the extreme rate of inter-provincial GRP per capita had reached 10.8 : 1, while the coefficient of variation and weighted coefficient of variation had risen to 0.713 and 0.565 respectively, marking an increase of 18.4% and 23.1% compared to 1990.

Thirdly, since 2003, however, China has witnessed a continuous narrowing of its inter-provincial gap in GRP per capita. In 2014, the extreme rate of China's inter-provincial GRP per capita dropped to 3.98 : 1, while the coefficient of variation and weighted coefficient of variation also declined by 39.0% and 33.7% respectively, compared to 2003.

Despite a slight increase again in recent years, the coefficient of variation and weighted coefficient of variation of China's inter-provincial GRP per capita in 2016 were 54.0% and 48.5% lower than those in 1978, respectively. Furthermore, research on the convergence of regional economic growth revealed that from 1978 to 1995, the growth of China's inter-provincial GRP per capita tended to converge, with the gap between high-income and low-income regions narrowing at an annual rate of approximately 2%. At this pace, it would require around 36 years to narrow this gap by half, marking the half-cycle convergence between the two types of regions (Wei Houkai, 1997a). In fact, it took China 38 years, from 1978 to 2016, to halve the gap.

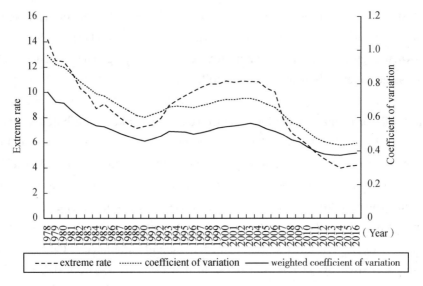

Figure 3-1　Changes in China's inter-provincial gap in GRP per capita

Source: Calculated in accordance with the relevant data in *China Compendium of Statistics 1949-2008*, and *China Statistical Abstract* (2010, 2016, and 2017), compiled by the National Bureau of Statistics.

3.1.3　Urban-rural income gap

With the progress of economic development and urbanization, the income gap between urban and rural areas tends to follow an inverted U-shape, initially expanding and eventually narrowing down (Dong Min & Guo Fei, 2011; Yu Xiuyan, 2013). For instance, in the United States, the income ratio between urban and rural residents increased from 1.7 : 1 in the early 19th century to 3.0 : 1 in 1930, followed by a decrease to 1.4∶1 in 1970. In Japan, this ratio expanded from 1.19∶1 in 1950 to 1.44∶1 in 1960, but subsequently dropped to 0.91∶1 in 1975. Similarly, in the Republic of Korea, the ratio rose from 0.997∶1 in 1960 to 1.49∶1 in 1970, before decreasing to 0.96∶1 in 1980 (Yu Xiuyan, 2013).

Since the reform and opening up, there have been two major expansions in the income gap between urban and rural residents in China. The first occurred from 1984 to 1994, and the second, from 1998 to 2003. Since 1978, due to the gradual reform on rural economic system and the rise of agricultural product prices, the income gap between urban and rural residents in China has been narrowing year by year. By 1983, the ratio of per capita disposable income of urban residents to Net Income Per Capita of rural residents in China had dropped from 2.57∶1 in 1978 to 1.82∶1 (see Figure 3-2). However, since 1984, as the focus of economic system reform has gradually shifted from rural to urban areas, both wage and non-wage income of urban residents have grown rapidly, coupled with the price rise of industrial products and the limited rural potential productivity released out of institutional reform. Under such circumstances, the income gap between urban and rural residents in China has begun to widen again. By 1994, the ratio of per capita disposable income of urban residents to Net Income Per Capita of rural residents had increased to 2.86∶1, much higher than the income gap between urban and rural areas in the early days of the reform and opening up. This situation did not change until 1995. In 1997, the ratio dropped to 2.47∶1, roughly equivalent to the level in the early 1990s. However, the income gap between urban and rural residents has begun to widen on and on since 1997. The ratio of per capita disposable income of urban residents to Net Income Per Capita of rural people has increased to 3.23∶1 by 2003.

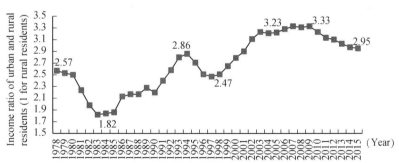

Figure 3-2   Changes in income gap between urban and rural residents in China since the reform and opening up

Note: The income ratio of urban and rural residents is the ratio of per capita disposable income of urban residents to Net Income Per Capita of rural residents.

Source: Calculated according to relevant data in *China Statistical Abstract* (*2016*).

The income gap between urban and rural residents in China has begun to decline steadily since 2009.From 2009 to 2015, the ratio of per capita disposable income of urban residents to Net Income Per Capita of rural people in China decreased from 3.3 to 2.95, an average annual decrease of 0.06. If calculated in accordance with the per capita disposable income of urban and rural residents, the income ratio has declined from 2.81 in 2013 to 2.72 in 2016. The decline was less pronounced when compared to the two declines that occurred during the periods of 1979-1983 and 1995-1997. The main reason for this situation is that with the costs of agricultural production continuously increasing and the prices of agricultural products approaching a "ceiling", the on-going urbanization made it increasingly challenging for rural residents to increase their income, as their primary sources of income growth were work wages and transfer income.

Currently in China, the income gap between urban and rural residents remains at a high level, significantly surpassing the lowest level recorded in 1983 since the launch of the reform and opening up, and even exceeding that observed in many developed countries. However, we can assert that as China has entered a new normal in economic development, the narrowing of the income gap between urban and rural areas in recent years will evolve into a consistent and enduring trend, instead of a temporary fluctuation as witnessed in the past two instances. It can be stated that China's urban-rural income gap has currently surpassed the turning point of the inverted U-shape and transitioned into a phase of consistent reduction. Obviously, this change can be precisely attributed to the characteristics of the current stage of China's economic development. First of all, as industrialization reaches its later stage, the driving force of city-oriented industry for economic growth has been on a decline, and the huge potential of small towns and rural areas is increasingly emerging, opening up new ways for sustained medium- to high-speed growth under the new normal. Secondly, the permanent urban population in China has now exceeded that in rural areas. In recent years, the population transferred from agriculture has migrated to cities on a large scale, which not only creates favorable conditions for developing agriculture on a fairly large scale, but also becomes an important means to increase rural people's income. Finally, with the improvement of development level and economic strength, the government has been able to invest more public resources in the fields relating to agriculture, rural areas, and rural people, so as to promote agricultural efficiency, increase rural people' income, and achieve rural prosperity. In the new period, the continuous narrowing of the income gap between urban and rural areas has become an important prerequisite to ensure medium- and high-speed growth on the long run.

3.1.4   Disparities among urban areas

There was minimal income disparity among urban residents in different regions since 1949. This can be attributed to the longstanding egalitarian distribution policy called the "communal pot" for employees of SOEs in urban areas, as well as the reliance on wages as the primary source of income for urban households. After 1978, there was a gradual widening of the wage gap among workers from different regions, industries, and positions, coupled with a significant increase in the proportion of non-wage income in total income. These changes were a result of progressive adoption of the principle of distribution according to work and capital starting from the reforms targeting labor wages, prices, and the social security system in SOEs. The income gap experienced a sharp surge during some specific period, notably between the mid-1980s and the mid-1990s (see Figure 3-3), which could also be attributed to the concentration of foreign-invested enterprises in coastal regions and some inland cities with well-established transportation infrastructure as their high wage offerings further exacerbated the income gap among urban workers. In terms of per capita disposable income of urban households among provinces in China, from 1986 to 1995, the extreme rate increased from 1.80 to 2.60, while the coefficient of variation rose rapidly from 0.150 to the peak of 0.271 in 1994, an increase of 80.7%; from 1995 to 2006, the coefficient of variation increased

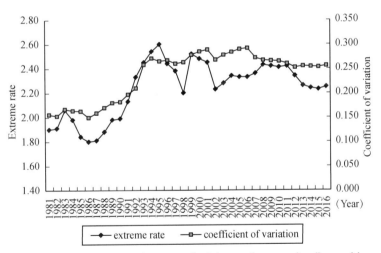

Figure 3-3   Changes in inter-provincial gap of per capita disposable
income of urban residents in China

Note: Due to lack of data, Hainan Province was not included in the 1984 data.

Source: Calculated in accordance with the relevant data in *China Compendium of Statistics 1949-2008*, and the series of *China Statistical Yearbook*, compiled by the National Bureau of Statistics.

slightly from 0.265 to 0.292, an increase of 10.2%; after that, the coefficient of variation began to drop slowly, and the extreme rate also tended to decline in fluctuation after 1995. It should be pointed out that from 2013 to 2016, although the coefficient of variation of per capita disposable income of urban residents among the four major regions remained relatively stable, the gap between the eastern and northeastern regions continued to widen due to the relatively slow growth of urban residents' income in the northeastern region, and the relative gap coefficient of per capita disposable income of urban residents increased from 24.5% to 26.7%. In conclusion, although there was once a significant expansion after the reform and opening up, the current income gap among urban residents in various regions of China should not be deemed excessively large. In fact, there has emerged an encouraging trend towards gradual reduction in recent years.

3.1.5 Disparities among rural areas

Rural people hold the key to developing rural areas. In 2016, there were still 690 million individuals residing in rural areas, despite China's urbanization rate of permanent residence hitting 57.35%. When considering the household registered population, the rural registered population stood at a staggering 810 million, accounting for 58.8% of China's total population. Therefore, the changes in per capita income gap between rural areas will be more revealing. Since the reform and opening up, the rapid development of township enterprises in the suburbs of large- and medium-sized cities and coastal regions have pushed the Net Income Per Capita gap of rural residents between regions in China to widen further. In 1980, Shanghai had the highest Net Income Per Capita among rural residents in China, while Shaanxi had the lowest. The former was 2.82 times that of the latter. However, by 1996, this gap had significantly widened to 4.97 times, marking the peak since the reform and opening up. Since then, the extreme rate of Net Income Per Capita of rural residents among provinces has shown a gradual decrease (see Figure 3-4). As to the Net Income Per Capita of rural residents among provinces in China, the coefficient of variation changed nearly the same way. Before 1993, the coefficient of variation continued to expand, and then gradually decreased, but it rose slightly after 1998. By 2003, the coefficient of variation has amounted 0.469, second only to the peak in 1993, and then gradually decreased. According to the research on Gini coefficient rural areas, over the years after 1993, the Gini coefficient in the rural areas of the four major regions changed in relatively smooth way, but also showed a pattern of rising first and then falling from around 2000 (Ren Yuan & Tai Xiujun, 2016). It should be noted that in recent years, due to the relatively slow growth of rural residents' income in the northeastern region, the income gap between residents in the eastern and northeastern regions has been widening, and the relative gap coefficient of per capita disposable income of rural residents between the eastern region and northeastern region has increased from 17.7% in 2013 to 19.6% in 2016. In summary, despite a substantial expansion in the early stages of China's reform and opening up, the per capita income gap among rural residents has gradually been narrowing in recent years after undergoing fluctuations between 1993 and 2006.

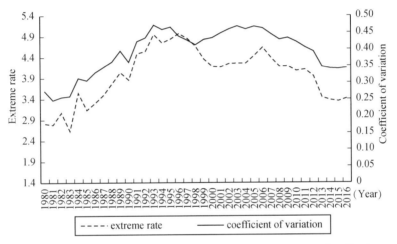

Figure 3-4　Changes in inter-provincial gap of Net Income Per Capita
and disposable income of rural residents in China

Note: Hainan was not included in the data before 1987. Data for 2012 and before were calculated in accordance with Net Income Per Capita and that after 2012, on the basis of per capita disposable income.

Source: Calculated according to the relevant data in *China Statistical Yearbook* over the years.

3.1.6　Intra-provincial regional disparities

In terms of geographical area and population, each province in China overtakes a host of European countries. Hence, it holds great significance to delve deeper into the changes in China's intra-provincial regional disparities since the reform and opening up. According to Yang Dali (1995), from 1985 to 1990, the gap in per capita rural social output value between counties in most provinces of China was widening. The average coefficient of variation at the provincial level rose from 0.484 in 1985 to 0.677 in 1990, an increase of 39.3%. Among the 28 provincial-level units examined, the coefficient of variation in 19 (68% of the total) has increased by more than double digits, especially in Inner Mongolia, Xinjiang, and Sichuan. If all county-level units in China are examined as a whole, the coefficient of variation will increase even more, from 0.869 in 1985 to 1.325 in 1990, an increase of 52.4%. This shows that in the 1980s, although the inter-provincial gap in GRP per capita in China was narrowing, the intra-provincial gap between regions was significantly widening and continued until the early 21st century. In fact, the composite data used in analyzing inter-provincial disparities did conceal the fact that the regional disparities within a province are intensifying. Studies have shown that the largest source of China's total regional disparities after 2000 was the intra-provincial gap, with a contribution of approximately 60% (Feng Changchun et al., 2015). However, it should be noted that since the 11th Five-year Plan period, the widening trend of intra-provincial regional disparities in China has been fundamentally reversed. As can be seen from Figure 3-5, the intra-provincial regional gap in GRP per capita in China changed from expanding to narrowing in 2005 and 2006 in terms of both the coefficient of variation and the extreme rate. The average coefficient of variation of GRP per capita within each province decreased from 0.534 in 2015 to 0.473 in 2015, a decrease of 11.4%; the average extreme rate of GRP per capita in each province decreased from 6.78 : 1 in 2006 to 5.29 : 1 in 2015, a decrease of 22.0%. This indicates that the intra-provincial regional disparities have been steadily shrinking in recent years.

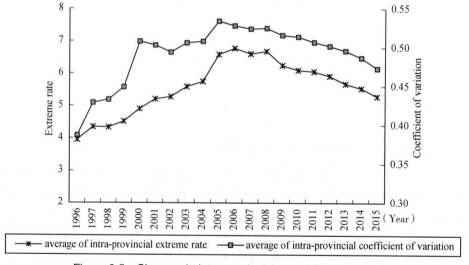

Figure 3-5   Changes in intra-provincial gap of GRP per capita

Note: The intra-provincial gap was calculated in accordance with the GRP per capita of prefecture-level cities, excluding municipalities directly under the central government. Tibet and Qinghai were not included in the data.

Source: Calculated in accordance with relevant data from the local statistical yearbooks and the *China City Statistical Yearbook* over the years.

3.2   Decomposing China's regional development gap

Since 2003, China has made steady progress in reducing the regional disparities in the six aforementioned aspects, albeit with varying turning points. To unveil the primary factors contributing to the changes in regional development gaps, it is imperative to employ quantitative methods to analyze and break down the components and causes of such gaps. Depending on specific research objectives, regional disparities can typically be decomposed based on industrial structure, regional composition, the contribution of growth factors, etc. In this study, we focus on decomposing from the perspective of regional composition.

3.2.1   Decomposing the disparities among regions

After the reform and opening up, the research on regional disparities in China started from examining the changes in gaps among different regional units, such as zones, major regions, and provincial regions, by employing different economic indicators. And in the 1990s, some scholars began to delve into implications of these gaps on overall regional gap using alternative research methods. Among them, for example, Cui Qiyuan analyzed the impact of inter-provincial, intra-provincial and urban-rural gaps on China's regional gap by selecting indicators of per capita gross industrial and agricultural output value, infant mortality, illiteracy and semi-illiteracy rate in 1987 (Cui Qiyuan, 1994; Tsui, 1993). Using Theil index method, Wei Houkai (1996) examined the impact of disparities among three major regions as well as inter-provincial disparities within each region over the period of 1985-1995 on the income gap among residents across regions of China. According to Wei's study, the income gap among residents across regions during this period mainly manifested itself as the gap between the east-western regions, the urban-rural gap, and the gap among rural areas. The widening gap in these three aspects was the primary factor leading to the widening of China's overall regional gap. Hence, he suggested that "while promoting the coordinated development of regional economy, the central government should prioritize policy support aimed at gradually narrowing the gap between the eastern and western regions, particularly the gap among rural areas and the urban-rural gap" (Wei Houkai, 1996).

In the 1960s, Henri Theil (1967) pioneered the application of information theory to create an inequality index which is additively decomposable. This index satisfies the requirements of the Dalton-Pigou principle of transfers, as well as population replication and mean independence (Shorrocks, 1980). Theil index takes many forms, among which the Theil L index (Shorrocks & Wan, 2005) is the most suitable for decomposing regional disparity, and is calculated as follows:

$$TL = \sum_{i=1}^{N} p_i \log \frac{p_i}{y_i} \tag{3-1}$$

Where N is the number of units; p_i is the proportion of the population of the i-th unit in the whole population of the country; y_i is the proportion of income or GRP of the i-th unit in that of the whole country. If all units are divided into g groups with a certain method, the Theil L index can be decomposed as follows (Schwarze, 1996):

$$TL = \sum_{g=1}^{G} p_g \log = \frac{p_g}{v_g} + \sum_{g=1}^{G} p_g TL_g \tag{3-2}$$

The first item in Formula (3-2) represents the income or GRP gap between units in each group. Here, it can be used to measure the inter-provincial gap between the eastern, central, western and northeastern regions. The second item represents the income or GRP gap between groups, that is, between the four major regions. In Formula (3-2), v_g represents the proportion of Group g's income or GDP in total income or GDP; p_g represents the proportion of group g population in the total population. Therefore, the overall regional disparity can be decomposed into the sum of intra-regional disparities and inter-regional disparities between the four regions. Using the above decomposition method, the importance of the intra-regional and inter-regional disparities of the four regions in the overall disparities can be calculated.

Decomposition of the Theil L index based on the four major regions reveals that, on average, the gap among the four major regions and the intra-provincial gap within each major region contributed 63.0% and 37.0% respectively to the overall gap in GRP per capita between 1978 and 2016. Specifically, the inter-provincial gap within the eastern region and the western region contributed only 24.4% and 8.8% respectively; and in contrast, the smaller inter-provincial gap within the central and northeastern regions contributed to only 2.1% and 1.7% respectively. This demonstrates that, overall, the regional development gap in China since the reform and opening up mainly presented itself in the gaps among the four major regions, as well as the inter-provincial gap within the eastern region. The large inter-provincial gap within the eastern region primarily stems from the fact that economically developed provinces and municipalities, such as Shanghai, Beijing, Tianjin, and Jiangsu had much higher GRP per capita than other provinces, particularly Hebei and Hainan.

Judging from the changing dynamics, the contribution rate of the inter-provincial gap within the eastern region to the overall gap was gradually decreasing despite an uptick after 2008. Conversely, surging from 3.7% in 1982 to 19.2% in 2011, that rate in the western region was on a continuous rise after the reform and opening up, and did not decline until recent years. In contrast, that rate in the central and northeastern regions remained relatively stable. Unlike the inter-provincial gap within each region, the gap among the four major regions followed a clear inverted U-shaped change pattern. From 1978 to 1995, the contribution rate of the gap among the four major regions to the overall gap increased from 40.1% to 74.2%. This rate remained relatively stable at around 74% from 1996 to 2004, but experienced a noticeable decline thereafter. By 2014, the contribution rate of the gap among the four major regions to the overall disparities had dropped to 57.9%. Meanwhile, the contribution rates of the inter-provincial gap within the eastern and western regions were 20.1% and 16.6% respectively (see Figure 3-6). As of 2016, except that the inter-provincial gap within the western region continued to decline, the contribution rate of the gaps among the four major regions, within the eastern region, and within the central region to the overall gap slightly rose to 59.5%, 22.4% and 3.4% respectively. These findings highlighted the necessity of addressing intra-regional disparities, even though the gap among the four regions still contributed much to the overall regional gap in China.

Judging from the overall changes, China's overall regional gap has gone through three evolving stages. In the first stage, from 1978 to 1990, the overall regional gap in China was narrowing, with the Theil L index of GRP per capita dropping from 0.1097 to 0.0728, down 33.6%. During this period, 95.4% of the overall regional gap in China was caused by the narrowing of the inter-provincial gap within the eastern region, while the gap among the four major regions widened by 2.7%. The second stage was from 1990 to 2003, the overall regional gap was expanding rapidly. By 2003, the Theil L index of GRP per capita had increased to 0.1233, 69.4% higher than that in 1990, and the gap coefficient among the four major regions had increased by 101.8%. During this period, 91.1% of the overall regional disparities in China were caused by the widening of the disparities among the four major regions, and 11.1% were caused by the widening of the inter-provincial disparities within the western region. In the third stage, from 2003 to 2014, the overall regional gap in China gradually narrowed. By 2014, the Theil L index of GRP per capita had narrowed to 0.0646, 47.6% lower than that in 2003, and the 59.0% decline of the gap coefficient among the four major regions contributed 91.7% of the decline in the overall regional gap coefficient in China. It can be seen that since 1990, both the widening and narrowing of the overall regional gap were mainly caused by the widening and narrowing of the gap among the four major regions.

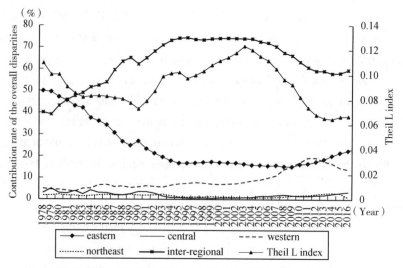

Figure 3-6   Composition of Theil L index of China's GRP per capita

Source: Calculated in accordance with the relevant data in *China Compendium of Statistics 1949-2008* and *China Statistical Abstract* (2010, 2016, and 2017), compiled by the National Bureau of Statistics.

3.2.2   Decomposing the urban-rural income gap

Obviously, the above decomposition does not take into account the urban-rural gap in China. In fact, China is one of the countries with the largest urban-rural gap in the world. From the perspective of urban and rural areas, we can divide the national residents into two groups: urban residents and rural residents. Each group includes 31 provinces. Thus, with the aforementioned Theil index as well as the indicators of per capita disposable income of urban residents and Net Income Per Capita of rural residents, the overall income gap between urban and rural residents can be decomposed into urban-rural income gap, inter-provincial gap within urban areas, and inter-provincial gap within rural areas. The results are shown in Figure 3-7.

The income gap between urban and rural residents in China has been widening since 1981, with only a few exceptions. It was not until 2006 that this situation began to change. From 1981 to 2006, the Theil L index of per capita income of urban and rural residents increased rapidly from 0.0475 to 0.2188, an increase of 3.6 times, among which the urban-rural gap widened by 3.4 times and the inter-provincial gap within urban areas widened by 7.6 times. During this period, 80.1% of the widening of the overall income gap between urban and rural residents in China resulted from the widening of the income gap between urban and rural residents, and 12.3% from the widening of the inter-provincial income gap within rural areas. However, it has gradually declined in recent years since the Theil L index of per capita income of urban and rural residents in China reached its peak in 2006. By 2016, the coefficient value has dropped to 0.1345, down 38.5% from 2006. Among them, the urban-rural gap coefficient dropped by 37.8%, and the inter-provincial gap coefficient within rural areas rose by 57.8%. During this period, 79.4% of the overall income gap between urban and rural residents in China came from the narrowing of the income gap between urban and rural residents, and 18.5% from the narrowing of the inter-provincial income gap within rural areas.

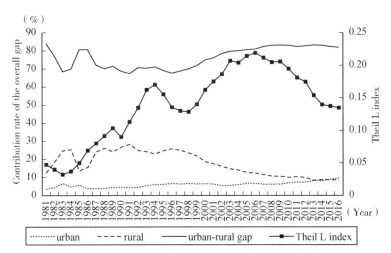

Figure 3-7   Composition of Theil L index of per capita income of
urban and rural residents in China

Note: The urban and rural population data used in the calculation are based on the resident population after 2005. Due to the lack of urban and rural population data of Hebei, Zhejiang, Fujian and Shaanxi before 1990, and Chongqing and Sichuan before 1997, these provinces were not included in the calculation of corresponding years. Since 2013, the urban and rural income data has been based on the survey of urban-rural integrated households, which is different from the previous practice.

Source: Calculated in accordance with the relevant data in *China Compendium of Statistics 1949-2008* and *China Statistical Abstract* (2010, 2016, and 2017), compiled by the National Bureau of Statistics.

To the overall urban-rural income gap from 1981 to 2016, on average, the income gap between urban and rural residents and the inter-provincial income gap within rural areas contributed around 76.3% and 17.6% respectively, while the inter-provincial income gap within urban areas only contributed around 6.0%. Notably, the contribution rate of inter-provincial income gap within rural areas to such an overall income gap was declining, decreasing from 12.5% in 1981 to 8.5% in 2016. The contribution rate of inter-provincial income gap within urban areas was growing, rising from 3.5% in 1981 to 9.6% in 2016, surpassing the former indicator. Furthermore, the contribution rate of the income gap between urban and rural residents increased sharply from 68.5% in 1983 to 83.1% in 2009, and then stabilized at 81.9% in 2016. These finding indicate that the urban-rural income gap has always consistently been the most significant factor contributing to the overall urban-rural income gap. Since the reform and opening up, with government's support for agricultural development and rural well-being, China's inter-provincial income gap of rural residents has obviously narrowed, and currently stands at the same level as the inter-provincial income gap among urban residents.

3.3 Factors influencing the changes in China's regional gap

Overall, after the reform and opening up, China's regional development gap, especially the east-west gap, experienced a general change from widening to narrowing despite some fluctuations during this period, and the gap coefficients calculated in accordance with different indicators, methods, and regional units bear certain differences, and their inflection points also occurred in a different way. On the whole, however, both the widening gap in the early and middle stages of the period of the reform and opening up and the narrowing gap in recent years are the result of the comprehensive action of historical, natural, economic, and social factors, which can generally be listed as follows.

3.3.1 Location and infrastructure

Although the advance of science and technology and the rapid development of transportation have greatly reduced the constraints of natural conditions on economic development, in general, geographical location is still one of the important factors affecting regional economic development. From a global perspective, due to the influence of geographical location, human economic activities are still mainly concentrated in coastal regions and those metropolitan areas with well-developed transportation facilities. China's opening to the outside world is also gradually advancing from the coastal regions to the central and western regions. This opening has further strengthened the original location advantages of the coastal regions, enabling the coastal regions to take the lead in achieving sustained and rapid development by virtue of their location advantages and good foundation. Meanwhile, extensive research reveals that robust infrastructure serves as a crucial prerequisite and cornerstone for the accelerated growth of regional economy. According to Sun (1997), who conducted an empirical research through using China's data from 1985 to 1994, there exists a close relationship between infrastructure improvement and regional development. Using the data in 1999, Wei Houkai (2011b) also made an empirical analysis and found that infrastructure construction is one of the important factors that determine the difference in regional manufacturing development. For a region, infrastructure and manufacturing are mutually causal and mutually reinforcing. The relationship between them goes beyond simple causality, but a two-way interaction. In other words, enhancing regional infrastructure will bolster the growth of local manufacturing sector, which in turn will spur the need for investment in infrastructure. Using the data of China from 1985 to 1998, 1987 to 2007 and 2004 to 2014 respectively, Demurger (2001), Liu Shenglong and Hu Angang (2010), Wang Fei and Li Shantong (2016) further confirmed that transportation infrastructure has a positive effect on regional development. Zhang Xueliang (2012) also found that although the spatial spillover effect of transportation infrastructure is significantly positive on the whole, it may also have a negative impact on regional development in the short term, because the improvement of transportation accelerates the outflow of manpower and factors from underdeveloped areas.

3.3.2   Market-orientedness and factor flows

Thanks to the ongoing reform and opening up, China's economy has become increasingly market-oriented. The lesson from developed market economies shows that market forces will widen rather than narrow the gap between regions, especially in the early and middle stages of economic development. Under the influence of market forces, coupled with the preferential policy for giving superior support to regions with advantages in the early days, domestic and foreign production factors such as capital, labor force and talents are continuously concentrated in coastal regions and large- and medium-sized cities with advantages, thus aggravating the unbalanced growth of regional economy and further strengthening the trend of widening regional disparities. By the end of 2015, 85.19% of the inward foreign direct investment actually utilized was concentrated in the eastern region of China, while only 8.15% and 6.66% were in the central and western regions respectively. A large amount of foreign direct investment flowed into the coastal regions, which plays a very important role in making up for its funding gap, expanding exports, and promoting industrial upgrading and technological innovation. At the same time, since the reform and opening up, a considerable amount of funds has flowed out of the central and western regions to coastal regions, especially special economic zones and open port cities, in various forms such as bank deposit-loan difference, horizontal investment and stock trading. In addition, for a long period of time in the past, a large number of people with expertise, especially senior professionals, flowed from the central and western regions to coastal regions, where benefited much from the "brain gain". Obviously, the large-scale flow of capital, professionals, and labor at home and abroad to coastal regions played a very important role in promoting the rapid economic development of coastal regions.

Theoretically, labor mobility can contribute to the reduction or even elimination of regional disparities. According to the study by Taylor and Williamson (1994) on 17 countries with large-scale immigration inflows or outflows from 1870 to 1910, the contribution of large-scale immigration to the convergence of real wages, GDP per capita and GDP per labor in these 17 countries reached 168%, 50%, and 73% respectively, thus verifying the decisive effect of population movement on economic convergence. Just for this reason, some Chinese scholars hold that removing barriers to labor mobility between regions will effectively narrow the gap between the east and the west (Cai Fang et al., 2001), and some even advocate large-scale migration to the eastern region to bridge the gap between the east and the west. However, the experience of the United States and other countries shows that in the early and middle stages of industrialization, the removal of barriers to inter-regional labor mobility did not play a very important role in narrowing the regional gap. From 1880 to 1950, the whole regional structural transformation contributed 80.9% of the regional wage convergence in the United States, while the elimination of barriers to inter-regional factor flow contributed only 19.1% of the narrowing of the regional wage gap (Caselli & Coleman Ⅱ, 2001). In China, due to great restrictions in the past, labor mobility did not play an important role in narrowing the regional gap. From 1985 to 1990, China's inter-provincial GRP per capita gap was narrowing, and the labor mobility contributed approximately 12%of the narrowing of regional gap during this period, far from being the main factor leading to the narrowing the regional gap during this period (Yao Zhizhong & Zhou Sufang, 2003). Recent empirical research shows that the migration of high-skilled labor brings stronger factor agglomeration than that of low-skilled labor, and the eastward flow of high-skilled labor in China expands regional differences (Zhao Wei & Li Fen, 2007; Peng Guohua, 2015). Although all the above studies show that labor mobility has not effectively narrowed the per capita output gap between regions in China, but due to large-scale remittance out of labor in China, labor mobility can still narrow the gaps of per capita income and consumption level between regions (Xu Zhaoyuan & Li Shantong, 2008). Therefore, it can be argued that eliminating barriers to labor mobility would prove advantageous in narrowing regional gap, but its impact should not be overestimated.

3.3.3   Changes of industrial structure

From the 1980s to the 1990s, the growing disparity among regions in China, particularly between the eastern and western regions, was largely attributed to the widening gap in rural areas. This disparity was primarily caused by the uneven progress of township enterprises and rural industrialization. Zhang Ping (1992, 1994) and Rozelle (1994) analyzed the source of income gap of rural residents of China by decomposing Gini coefficient. The results show that the income gap of rural residents of China was mainly caused by the imbalance of rural industrialization or township industry development. Wei Houkai (1997b) analyzed the data from 1978 to 1993, finding that about 40%-50% of the rural people's Net Income Per Capita gap between the eastern region and central and western regions originated from the work wage gap of township enterprises. Moreover, between the eastern and central regions, the contribution rate of the per capita work wage gap from township enterprises to the Net Income Per Capita gap of rural families generally remained at approximately 40%, while between the eastern and western regions, this rate kept rising. In 1980, only 27.9% of the Net Income Per Capita gap of rural families between the eastern and western regions came from the wage income gap of township enterprises, and in 1993, the proportion increased to 54.2%. Wan Guanghua (1998) used 1984-1996 data to conduct a study, which also shows that although wage income only amounted to 17%-24% of the total net income of rural residents, its contribution rate to Gini coefficient was between 40%-55%. This demonstrates that the structural effect could potentially be one of the fundamental causes for the changes in income gap among rural areas in China.

The uneven industrialization across regions also played an important role in widening the regional gap in China. According to Wei Houkai et al. (1997), the primary factor contributing to the overall gap in GRP per capita among regions in China was the secondary industry, the average contribution rate of which stood at 61.4% between 1978 and 1985 and subsequently declined to 41.6% between 1986 and 1994. In comparison, the tertiary industry made a significantly smaller contribution to the overall gap, despite its consistent growth in contribution rate. Specifically, its contribution rate rose from 3.9% in 1978 to 15.8% in 1994. After dividing the industries into agriculture, industry, construction, transportation, and commerce, the analysis would reveal that during the period of 1952-1992, more than 50% of the inter-provincial gap in national income in

China could be attributed to variations in industrial growth. According to studies by Fan Jianyong and Zhu Guolin (2002) and Fan Jianyong (2008), China's regional gap was closely intertwined with the uneven allocation of the secondary industry and its disproportionately large share of the output value. From 1978 to 1999, the secondary industry played a dominant role in driving the Gini coefficient, surpassing other industries in terms of impact on regional gap.

Since the beginning of the 21st century, with the implementation of strategies for the large-scale development of the western region and the rise of the central region, along with the rapid industrialization in the central and western regions, the impact of industrial structure differences on the regional development gap has started to change. The narrowing of the industrialization gap has become a key factor reducing the disparities in GRP per capita and residents' income across regions. According to Sun Tieshan et al. (2015), the growth of the secondary industry has resulted in an increased economic share for the central and western regions, particularly the central provinces, thus leading to a more coordinated development of regional economies. For one thing, the competitive advantage previously enjoyed by the eastern provinces in the secondary industry was gradually shifting to the central and western regions; and for another, the developed provinces in the east, such as Beijing, Shanghai, and Guangdong, have begun to prioritize the development of the service industry. If the difference in the development level of the tertiary industry is also taken into account to examine the impact of the difference in the non-agricultural level of the whole industry, it is estimated that the contribution of the difference in non-agricultural level of the whole industry to the regional difference in the central and western regions exceeds the contribution of material capital, human capital, population growth and technological progress factors (Yan Chengliang, 2016).

3.3.4   Technological and institutional innovation

Innovation serves as the fundamental driving force behind promoting economic development and social progress. Since 1978, China has implemented numerous reform and opening-up measures, initially piloting them in the coastal regions before gradually extending them to the central and western regions in a comprehensive manner. This is particularly evident in the policy of opening up to the outside world, which has undergone a step-by-step progression from the coastal regions to the interior and ultimately to border areas. Throughout this regional advancement, the coastal regions have taken the lead nationwide in terms of technological and institutional innovation, allowing them to reap greater benefits resulting from such innovation. In reality, this disparity in technological and institutional innovation has played a significant role in widening the regional gap in China during the 1980s and 1990s. According to a study by Hu Angang and Xiong Yizhi (2000) on the differences in economic growth in 30 provinces in China from 1978 to 1995, the growth factor of material capital could only explain 19%of the economic growth differences among various regions, while the remaining 80% is attributed to intangible factors included in total factor productivity. This intangible factor can be divided into such two categories as structural effect and knowledge effect. The structural effect refers to the effect of promoting the flow of factors and improving the efficiency of resource allocation, while the knowledge effect is the knowledge and technical factor that plays a long-term decisive role in economic growth. Since the start of the 21st century, there has been a narrowing of inter-provincial disparities in China, and there has been a convergence in inter-provincial total factor productivity (Yu Yongze, 2015). However, based on the calculations made by Zhu Ziyun (2015), the contribution rate of total factor productivity to these inter-provincial differences remained remarkably high, reaching approximately 60% between 2005 and 2012.

By incorporating the institutional factor into the economic growth function, Wu Lixue (2004) examined the impact of institutional changes on regional gap in China and revealed the crucial role of institutional changes since 1978 in driving China's economy. In his analysis, these changes bolstered the contribution rate of total factor productivity, effectively acting as a catalyst for economic growth during China's transition period; and the institutional differences among different regions played a decisive role in causing disparities in capital accumulation and growth rates, as the discrepancies in institutional efficiency and change trajectories had resulted in substantial disparities in both the rate and quality of growth across different regions. In other institutional fields, particularly in the fiscal system, China's fiscal decentralization from 1997 to 2012 allowed provincial governments to vie for "excellence" in improving production infrastructure, intensifying support for research and development, and facilitating talent recruitment, and also to promote the convergence of inter-provincial total factor productivity (Yu Yongze, 2015). Additionally, China's regional innovation system, an institutional mechanism for allocating research resources, is currently shifting its focus from universities and other research institutions to enterprises as the primary driver of research and development. However, the inter-provincial gap in innovation performance of enterprises is greater than that of the former, and this continuously widening gap will hinder the narrowing of regional disparities (Li Xibao, 2007).

3.3.5 Regional economic development strategy

China initiated its opening-up policy from the coastal regions, the preferred destination of the majority of inward FDI owing to the advantageous geographical location, well-established infrastructure, and robust economic and technological foundations. The large-scale entry of FDI will promote the rapid economic development of coastal regions by increasing capital formation, expanding exports, and creating jobs. In turn, the rapid economic growth in coastal regions will raise the income of local residents, expand the market capacity, and help to improve external conditions and generate agglomeration economic benefits, thus further expanding the entry of foreign direct investment. In this way, a regional circular cumulative causal effect is formed between inward FDI and regional economic growth. This cyclic cumulative causal effect formed by the joint action of export and foreign capital is quite different from the traditional cyclic cumulative causal effect produced by export-oriented growth. Empirical research shows that from the perspective of capital formation, foreign investment has a very important impact on the early economic growth of the developed eastern regions, while the impact on the backward western regions is not so significant. From 1985 to 1999, about 90% of the gap in GRP growth rate between the developed eastern regions and the backward western regions was caused by the difference in foreign investment (Wei Houkai, 2002). According to Sun Haishun (1998), inward FDI is the most significant factor that led to the economic growth disparity and income inequality between the eastern and western regions during the initial stages of China's reform and opening up. FDI is more effective in promoting provinces with strong economic strength, which may be a manifestation of the so-called "minimum requirements" (Wang Chengqi et al., 2002). According to Chen Jianxun (1992), out of China's three major economic zones, only the eastern region's exports had a notable influence on regional economic growth. As a result, during the initial phase of the reform and opening up, the coastal regions' adoption of an export-oriented economic development strategy, which prioritized foreign investment attraction and export expansion, played a crucial role in stimulating coastal economic growth.

Based on relevant research, China's opening-up policy had a relatively weaker effect on regional income gap than on the gap in regional economic growth. According to Wan Guanghua et al. (2005), from 1987 to 2001, the differences in levels of FDI utilization and foreign trade contributed around 20% of the income gap among the three major regions, surpassing the differences in such factors as physical capital, demographic structure, education level, and level of market orientation. In contrast, Gao Lianshui (2011), who used the same control variables but slightly different methods as Wan Guanghua et al. (2005) did, concluded that this rate was much lower from 1987 to 2005, with an average of about 10%. Xie Shenxiang and Wang Xiaosong (2011) found that from 1989 to 2009, the difference in FDI utilization level made negative contribution to inter-regional income gap, while the difference in foreign trade level contributed as high as 48.6% to that gap, still lower than the estimated contribution rate of opening-up policy to the gap in regional economic growth. Controversy still remains in academia over the influence of the opening-up on the income gap between urban and rural areas. Some studies found that from 1978 to 2008, the opening-up widened the urban-rural income gap across the country (Sun Yongqiang & Wan Yulin, 2011). Others held that the opening-up might widen or narrow the gap, depending on specific periods or regions, and the influence was no longer significant in late 2002 (Wei Hao & Zhao Chunming, 2012); Yuan Dongmei et al. (2011) concluded that from 1995 to 2007, foreign trade was conducive to narrowing the urban-rural income gap.

Unlike the coastal regions, which have embraced an export-oriented approach to economic development, certain inland provinces, such as Shanxi, Gansu, and Heilongjiang, have chosen to pursue a resource-based strategy for their economic growth. Some scholars argued that, the phenomenon of "resource curse" encountered by China's resource-rich regions in pursuit of regional economic development by relying on resource endowments was also a cause for China's regional disparities. The heavy dependence of resource-rich areas on resources in their economic development, brought on four main consequences, that is, shrinking share of manufacturing sector, insufficient cultivation of human capital, backward property right system, and serious damage to urban environment, thus making the growth rate of regional GDP significantly lower than that of coastal provinces such as Jiangsu, Zhejiang and Fujian (Xu Kangning & Han Jian, 2005). Other scholars argued that since the 1990s, the "resource curse" effect arising from the energy development in the western region has hindered regional economic growth (Shao Shuai & Qi Zhongying, 2008). However, some recent studies revealed that it was "resource blessing" rather than "resource curse" in the case of China, and the abundance of natural resources would help promote regional economic growth (Yao Yuchun et al., 2014; Liang Bin & Jiang Tao, 2016). Evidently, the abundance in natural resources is an important part of regional comparative advantages. There was nothing wrong for areas rich in natural resources to implement the resource-oriented strategy based on their comparative advantages, but the problem lay in the unthorough implementation, accompanied by the dominant position of primary raw material industries, short industrial chains, low level of resource processing, and low degree of comprehensive utilization of resources. All these reduced the industrial competitiveness and the tolerance for market fluctuations, posing severe challenges for regional economic growth.

3.3.6 Effects of central policies

Central policies, or policies formulated by the Chinese central government, have a two-way impact on changes in regional disparities. On the one hand, the central government provided support to the central and western regions and the areas with special features in many aspects such as capital, technology, talents, which has effectively promoted the development of these regions and helped to narrow regional gap; On the other hand, in the 1980s and 1990s, in order to pursue higher efficiency and achieve growth goals, the central government implemented preferential policies for some coastal regions in terms of investment, taxation, fiscal and financial services, which in turn aggravated the regional disparities. On the whole, the central policies had more of the effect of widening regional gaps over a long period after the reform and opening up. Research shows that, the central government's fiscal transfer payment system ran against its fundamental goal and played a role in widening the regional gap instead: for the heavy average tax burden, the western region enjoyed a high proportion of tax refunds from the central government through transfer payments, while in the transitional period, when an egalitarian approach was adopted, the proportion went relatively low (Ma Shuanyou, 2003). This situation did not change fundamentally until the beginning of the 21st century. With the successive implementation of strategies such as the large-scale development of the western region, the revitalization of old industrial bases in the northeast, and the promotion of the rise of the central region, coupled with the central government's increasing support for developing old revolutionary base areas, areas with large ethnic minority populations, border areas, and so on, China's regional policy has gradually shifted its focus from excessive pursuit of high efficiency and growth goals in the past to the objective of ensuring fairness, that is, from "icing on the cake" to "offering timely help". With the strong support of central policies, China's regional gap, especially the gap between the east and the west, has changed from expanding to narrowing in an inverted U-shaped pattern. Specifically, all of the following gaps have been gradually narrowing. Since 2003, the gap in GRP per capita, per capita general budget revenue and expenditure, inter-provincial GRP per capita, and

Net Income Per Capita gap of rural people among the four major regions, especially between the eastern and western regions. Since 2005, the inter-provincial gap in GRP per capita among regions. Since 2006, the per capita consumption level of residents and the per capita disposable income gap of urban residents among the four major regions, especially between the eastern and western regions. Since 2009, the income gap between urban and rural residents.[1] This shows that China has entered a new period in which the regional gap continued to narrow in an all-round way.

Clearly, by virtue of its enhanced ability to regulate and direct regional development as well as its intensified efforts to support underdeveloped areas in the central and western regions, the central government has played a very important role in facilitating the regional gap's inverted U-shaped transformation. Empirical studies show that the central government's improved macro-control ability has contributed to reducing the development gap among regions, and its efforts in this regard have proved to be highly effective (Zhang Qi, 2001). Additionally, Liu Shenglong and Hu Angang (2010) have highlighted the substantial influence of state investments in transportation infrastructure in the western region, which has contributed to bridging the gap between the central and eastern regions. Furthermore, the Belt and Road initiative and border opening policy formulated by the central government have also effectively promoted the rapid development of the central and western regions. In particular, the Belt and initiative will enhance the openness of the central and western regions, provide the eastern and western regions with new impetus to open up, and ensure the central region's position as the hub for gathering raw materials and technologies, thus ultimately promoting the formation of a new and open pattern of China's regional economic development, a pattern featuring "coordination of the coastal and inland regions and mutual aid between the eastern and western regions" (An Shuwei, 2015). Admittedly, due to the variations in regional development stages and industrial structure characteristics, the strict policies on energy conservation, emission reduction, and environmental protection implemented by the central government under the philosophy of green development had short-term adverse effects on underdeveloped areas in the central and western regions. According to Li Fangyi and Liu Weidong (2014), the implementation of stringent energy-saving policies may deter underdeveloped regions from undertaking industrial relocation, yet imposing fewer constraints on the growth of eastern cities that

---

[1] For a detailed discussion on the turning points of this inverted U-shaped change in China's regional disparities, see Wei Houkai et al. (2012), Zhang Yan and Wei Houkai (2012), as well as the discussion in the second section of this chapter.

heavily rely on consumer services as well as certain central or western provinces with lower level of industrial energy consumption. In this sense, China's national policies on energy conservation and environmental protection should thoroughly consider emission reduction efficiency and regional fairness.

Chapter 4
Effectiveness of Supporting
the Eastern Region in Spearheading
Development

Since the launch of the reform and opening up, China has taken the initiative to support the eastern region in leading the way towards development, in response to the limitations of the previously adopted balanced development strategy. Thanks to this initiative, the eastern region has experienced sustained and rapid economic growth for over four decades, owing to its favorable geographical location and inherent advantages. As a result, it has made significant contributions to China's overall economic development and prosperity. China's practical experience clearly demonstrates that the eastern region's spearheading role is indispensable in ensuring the rapid and sustained growth of the country's economy, as well as its global economic ascent. Hence, it is evident that China's initiative to support the eastern region in leading development has been highly successful, yielding remarkable outcomes.

4.1 The implementation of the initiative for supporting the eastern region in spearheading development

Supporting the eastern region to take the lead in pursuing development is a crucial component of the master strategy for China's regional development. It is also a significant strategic choice made by the Chinese government after reviewing the historical experience gained since the implementation of the reform and opening-up policy. In fact, the Chinese government has taken various measures to implement the strategy since the reform and opening up, although the formal proposal came relatively late. Particularly, during the early stages of the reform and opening up, the national investment distribution and regional policies prioritized efficiency, with a strong focus on the eastern region with favorable conditions. This "focusing on the eastern region" policy helped the eastern region to gain momentum in taking the lead in pursuing development. It can be said that supporting the eastern region in taking the lead in pursuing development is a summary of the experience and practices since the reform and opening up.

4.1.1 Evolution of the initiative for supporting the eastern region in taking the lead in pursuing development

A major strategic decision was made at the Third Plenary Session of the 11th CPC Central Committee to shift the focus of work to socialist modernization. With such a strategic shift, the previously adopted strategy of pursuing balanced development at the cost of efficiency was subjected to theoretical criticism. The criticism was based on a review of China's productivity layout since the founding of the PRC, as well as the lessons learned from it. Furthermore, the principles governing socialist productivity layout were re-examined to emphasize efficiency as the guiding principle or objective. Consequently, an idea of attaining balanced development started gaining popularity nationwide, gradually supplanting the balanced development theory formulated shortly after the founding of the PRC. And this idea consistently held a dominant position in China's productivity layout and regional economic policies from the 1980s to the early 1990s.

In terms of government decision-making, as early as December 1978, Deng Xiaoping made a thematic report on "Emancipating the Mind, Seeking Truth from Facts, Uniting as One and Looking to the Future" at the closing meeting of the Central Working Conference, and put forward the famous idea that "when some people and some regions get rich first, others will be brought along, and through this process common prosperity of the entire population will be gradually achieved". This guiding ideology had an important influence on the formulation of China's regional economic policies. In November 1981, the work report of the Fourth Session of the Fifth National Congress stated that "in light of the growing foreign economic and technological exchanges, it is imperative that we fully leverage the potential of coastal cities and regions, among which, Shanghai, Tianjin, Guangzhou, Dalian, Qingdao, Fuzhou, and Xiamen should make more contributions". In November 1982, the Report on the Sixth Five-Year Plan further pointed out that "special attention should be paid to the role of coastal cities in expanding foreign economic and technological exchanges. Apart from Guangdong and Fujian, which should continue with their special policies and adaptable measures, it is crucial to grant greater autonomy to coastal cities like Shanghai and Tianjin. This will enable them to leverage their unique strengths and exhibit heightened initiative and enthusiasm in the areas of technology acquisition, foreign capital utilization, industrial transformation, and international market exploration." In the Sixth Five-Year Plan for National Economic and Social Development, approved at the Fifth CPC National Congress on December 10, 1982, it was clearly pointed out that it was necessary to "actively utilize the existing economic foundation in coastal regions, fully bring their strengths into play, and drive the further development of the mainland economy"; and in interior should "speed up the construction of energy, transportation and raw material industries and support the economic development of coastal regions". The Seventh Five-Year Plan for National Economic and Social Development reiterated that "From this period (1986-1990) to the 1990s, we should accelerate the development of the eastern coastal zone", focusing on speeding up the technological transformation of old industrial cities and old industrial bases such as Shanghai, Tianjin, Shenyang, and Dalian, and making better use of the central preferential and special policies to build and develop special economic zones, coastal open cities and economic open areas in a focused and step-by-step manner. The Ten-Year Plan for National Economic and Social Development and the Outline of the Eighth Five-Year Plan emphasized that "coastal regions should continue to give full play to their strengths in capital, technology and talent, and actively develop high-technology industries and products to be exported in exchange of foreign exchange". In 1988, the CPC Central Committee and the State Council also put forward the economic development strategy of coastal areas with coastal township enterprises as the main force and "put both ends of the production process (the supply of raw materials and the marketing of products) on the world market and carry on the import and export on a large scale" as the main content.

In his Report on the Outline of the 10th Five-Year Plan for National Economic and Social Development delivered at the Fourth Session of the Ninth National People's Congress on March 5, 2001, the then premier Zhu Rongji proposed that "the eastern coastal region should focus on both domestic and international markets. The top priorities include expediting scientific and technological advancements and fostering innovation. In addition, the region should prioritize the development of industries that utilize high and new technology, as well as enhance its internationally-oriented economy to enhance its overall performance and competitiveness in the global market. Wherever possible, regions with favorable conditions should take the lead in modernization efforts". And the "outline" clarified that "the eastern region should continue to take the lead in institutional innovation, scientific and technological innovation, opening up to the outside world and economic development, and strive to basically realize modernization first in areas where conditions permit". This was the initial interpretation of the concept "taking the lead" put forth by the Chinese government, suggesting that the eastern region should "take the lead in basically achieving modernization". The subsequent Outline of the 11th Five-Year Plan clearly proposed to "encourage the eastern region to take the lead in development" and incorporated it into the master strategy for regional development; and specifically, "the eastern region should take the lead in improving its capability of independent innovation, optimizing and upgrading its economic structure and transforming its growth mode, improving the socialist market economic system, and leading the development of the central and western regions in pursing development and carrying out reform". Later, the Outline of the 12th Five-Year Plan changed "encouraging the eastern region to take the lead in development" to "actively supporting the eastern region to take the lead in pursuing development" and made it clear that "the eastern region should play an important leading and supporting role in the national economic development, participate in international cooperation and competition at a higher level, try first in the reform and opening up, and lead the rest of the country in transforming the economic growth model, upgrading economic structure, and enhancing capacity of independent innovation". The Outline of the 13th Five-Year Plan proposed to build a new highland with international influence and a globally advanced manufacturing base through "supporting the eastern region to take the lead in pursuing development" (the word "actively" was removed) and ensuring that the eastern region "take the lead in equalizing access to public services, improving social civilization, as well as enhancing the quality of the ecological environment". In October 2017, Xi Jinping further clarified in his report to the 19th National Congress of the CPC that we will "support the eastern region in taking the lead in pursuing optimal development through innovation".

In summary, the Chinese government's unwavering commitment since the reform and opening up to supporting the eastern region in taking the lead in pursuing development is well-grounded in both theory and practice. In theory, spatial imbalance is absolute since balance is just a relative concept, and the ultimate goal of balanced development can only be attained through an unbalanced approach. For a large developing country like China with huge regional differences, it must take the path of unbalanced and coordinated development, that is, achieve coordinated development through a moderately unbalanced approach (Wei Houkai, 1993; 1995). In practice, for a long period of time since the founding of the RPC, China has implemented a balanced development strategy, which, however, has not fundamentally changed the widening of regional gaps, especially the gap between the east and the west. Moreover, due to the failure to give full play to the advantages and functions of the eastern region, it has also seriously hindered China's economic growth and international competitiveness, resulting in the loss of economic efficiency. Because of the superior traffic location, excellent natural conditions, sound industrial foundation, densified population and towns, a huge talent pool and strong technical forces, the eastern region has the foundation and conditions to take the lead in pursuing development. Practical experience shows that the relationship between eastern region and central and western regions features not only complementary advantages and rational division of labor, but also long-term and short-term integration and mutual support. Maintaining the sustained and rapid development of the eastern region will provide support for the development of the central and western regions in terms of capital, technology, and talents; and in turn, accelerating the development of the central and western regions can ensure resources availability and broad market for the eastern region. At the same time, since the reform and opening up, narrowing two major gaps, namely, the international and the domestic regional gap, is always a problem facing China's economy. To bridge the gap with developed countries, we must rely more on the eastern region; to narrow the gap among domestic regions, the key lies in accelerating the development of the central and western regions, rather than artificially impeding the progress of the eastern region.

4.1.2   Policy support for the eastern region to spearhead development

Since 1978, China has launched and implemented a series of policies and measures to support the eastern region in taking the lead in pursuing development and then showcasing its success as a model for other regions. These policies focused on investment layout, opening up to the global market, systems reform, and industrial transformation and upgrading. In addition to gradually redirecting investment distribution towards the eastern region, China also intensified its efforts to support the eastern region to take the lead in opening up and development, which was achieved primarily through a progressive approach of opening up from east to west, accompanied with a series of corresponding reform measures and preferential policies.

China initiated its policy of opening up from the eastern coastal region. The Third Plenary Session of the 11th CPC Central Committee, held in December 1978, kicked off China's reform and opening-up policy with a strategic initiative of opening to the outside world and invigorating the economy at home. In order to speed up the opening pace, in July 1979, the CPC Central Committee and the State Council granted Guangdong and Fujian provinces special policies and flexible measures in their foreign economic activities. Its main contents are as follows: (1) the fiscal revenue and foreign exchange of the two provinces would be subject to fixed quota; (2) materials and commerce would be subject to market regulation under the guidance of the national plan; (3) enlarge the power of the local governments in planning, pricing, labor wages, enterprise management and foreign economic activities; and (4) establish pilot special economic zones, which were then known as "Export Special Zones"[1]. As a result, China officially established Shenzhen Special Economic Zone in August 1980, followed by Zhuhai, Shantou and Xiamen Special Economic Zones. Special economic policies and special administrative systems were implemented in these special economic zones, where, (1) the economic development would be driven mainly by the absorption and utilization of foreign capital; (2) the economic activities would mainly be regulated by the market; (3) special preferential treatment and convenience in terms of taxation would be provided to inward investors; and (4) an administrative system different from that in the interior would be implemented. In April 1983, the CPC Central Committee and the State Council made the decision to accelerate the development and construction of Hainan[2] by introducing relaxed policies, granting increased autonomy, and implementing measures similar to those applied in special economic zones. Additionally, in April 1988, the National People's Congress resolved to establish Hainan Province and Hainan Special Economic Zone. Similar to the Special Economic Zones, Hainan would benefit from more flexible and open economic policies, as well as greater autonomy.

In addition to the establishment of special economic zones, China made another significant effort to promote the opening up of the eastern coastal region by opening coastal port cities and coastal economic open zones. In May 1984, the CPC Central Committee and the State Council made the decision to expand the opening up of 14 coastal port cities, including Dalian, Qinhuangdao, and Tianjin. These cities implemented certain policies similar to those in special economic zones, including: (1) relaxing administrative power of local governments and opening them wider to the world in terms of economic activities; (2) relaxing controls on and offering preferential treatment to inward foreign investment; and (3) establishing economic and technological development zones with the aim of facilitating the introduction of much-needed cutting-edge technologies. Since September 1984, coastal port cities witnessed the establishment of the first 14 economic and technological development zones, which

---

[1] The concept "Export Special Zone" was first proposed by Deng Xiaoping on April 30, 1979.

[2] In 1984 the island was designated a special zone for foreign investment; and, though it was still part of Guangdong, it was upgraded to the status of a self-governing district, a prelude to its establishment as a province in 1988. — *Tr.*

later expanded rapidly to other areas. Up to this point, a grand total of 98 state-level economic and technological development zones have been established in the eastern region, accounting for 44.7% of the national total. Specifically, 26 are located in Jiangsu, 21 in Zhejiang, and 6 in Shanghai. The combined count of 53 indicates that the Jiangsu-Zhejiang-Shanghai region has emerged as the most densely concentrated area for state-level economic and technological development zones. To further expand openness, the CPC Central Committee and the State Council made the decision in February 1985 to develop the Yangtze River Delta, the Pearl River Delta, and the Xiamen-Zhangzhou-Quanzhou Delta in southern Fujian as coastal economic open zones. This involved delegating the approval authority to local governments for utilizing foreign capital in these zones, granting the right to operate foreign trade exports, and providing certain preferential policies and conveniences to foreign investors. To implement the strategy for the economic development of coastal areas, the State Council expanded the scope of coastal economic open areas in March 1988, designating Liaodong Peninsula, Jiaodong Peninsula, and 140 cities and counties including Shenyang and Nanjing as coastal economic open areas.

Due to their geographical proximity, Guangdong and Fujian in the eastern region have maintained close economic and cultural connections with Hong Kong, Macao, and Taiwan region for an extended period. In order to foster cross-strait cooperation, the State Council approved in May 1989 to establish Investment Zones for businessmen from Taiwan region in the underdeveloped parts of Xiamen Special Economic Zone in Fujian, Xinglin and Haicang regions under the jurisdiction of Xiamen city, and Mawei Economic and Technological Development Zone in Fuzhou. Later, in January 2012, the approval was granted for the establishment of Investment Zones for businessmen from Taiwan region in Quanzhou and Zhangzhou. These zones are entitled to the same policies as those applied to economic and technological development zones or special economic zones. In 1995, the State Council approved the establishment of a cross-strait science and technology industrial park in Nanjing High-tech Industrial Development Zone, focusing on scientific and technological cooperation with Taiwan-funded enterprises and the development of high-tech industries; The Outline of the 12th Five-Year Plan for National Economic and Social Development passed by the National People's Congress in March 2011 stated that "accelerating the opening and development of Pingtan Comprehensive Experimental Zone", and in November of the same year, the State Council officially approved the Master Development Plan of Pingtan Comprehensive Experimental Zone, agreeing to granting Pingtan the island-wide liberalization and more special and preferential policies than those for special economic zones in terms of customs clearance mode, fiscal and tax support, investment access, finance and insurance, cooperation with Taiwan region, land supporting facilities. In order to stabilize and prosper Macao's economy, in December 2003, the State Council approved the establishment of the Zhuhai-Macao Cross-border Industrial Zone, including Macao Park and Zhuhai Park, and implemented bonded zone policies and an export tax rebate policy for export processing zones for Zhuhai Park; In August 2009, the State Council also launched the Master Development Plan of Hengqin, thus including Hengqin Island into the Zhuhai Special Economic Zone, and proposing that after 10-15 years of efforts, Hengqin would be built into an open (connecting Hong Kong and Macao and being under joint construction), dynamic (enjoying prosperity in economy and desirability for life and industry), smart (focusing on knowledge-intensive industries and having great accessibility of information), and eco-friendly (highlighting resources conservation and environment protection) island.

Since 1990, China has established a large number of bonded zones[1], export processing zones, bonded port areas, national experimental zones for integrated, complete reform, and pilot free trade zones in the eastern region in order to promote its comprehensive deepening of the reform and opening up.

As for bonded zones, as early as June 1990, the State Council approved the establishment of Shanghai Waigaoqiao Free Trade Zone, followed by the establishment of Tianjin Port, Ningbo, Xiamen, Fuzhou, Shenzhen Yantian, Shenzhen Futian, Shenzhen Shatoujiao, Guangzhou, Zhuhai, and Shantou Bonded Zones, with a total of 33 comprehensive bonded zones in the eastern region.

With regard to export processing zones, since 2000, the State Council has successively approved the establishment of 43 export processing zones in the eastern region, accounting for 69.8% of the national total. Among them, 17 are in Jiangsu alone.

In terms of bonded port areas, under the approval of the State Council since 2003, the State Council pilot projects including Bonded Zones of Shanghai Waigaoqiao, Qingdao, Ningbo, Zhangjiagang, Xiamen Xiangyu, Shenzhen Yantian, and Tianjin have been successively established to enhance connections between districts and ports. Furthermore, in June 2005, the Shanghai Yangshan Bonded Port Area was established, followed by the subsequent establishment of Tianjin Dongjiang, Haikou, Ningbo, Xiamen, Shenzhen, Qingdao, Guangzhou, Zhangjiagang, Yantai, and Fuzhou Bonded

---

[1] In China, the alternative term used to refer to this concept is "free trade zones" —*Tr.*

Port Areas.

Regarding national experimental zones for integrated, complete reform, since 2005, the State Council has successively approved or agreed to establish such pilot zones in Pudong New Area of Shanghai, Binhai New Area of Tianjin and Shenzhen, and then added Xiamen Comprehensive Supporting Reform Pilot Zone for Deepening Cross-Strait Exchanges and Cooperation and Yiwu Comprehensive International Trade Reform Pilot Zone, allowing these areas to pilot some major measures for the reform and opening up.

With regard to pilot free trade zones, since 2013, the State Council has successively approved the pilot projects of free trade zones in Shanghai, Guangdong, Tianjin, Fujian, and Zhejiang. Later in September 2014, the State Council also approved the proposal to set up the Pilot Zone of Economic and Cultural Cooperation for Overseas Chinese in Shantou Special Economic Zone. In March 2015, it approved the establishment of China (Hangzhou) Cross-border Electronic Commerce Comprehensive Pilot Zone.

The construction of three state-level types of zones, namely, national high-tech industrial development zones, national innovation demonstration zones and state-level new areas, is the key move for promoting the eastern region to take the lead in realizing a new model of innovation-driven economic development. As early as June 1998, the State Council approved the establishment of Beijing New Technology Industry Development Experimental Zone. In March 1991, the State Council further approved 21 high-tech industrial development zones approved by the National Science and Technology Commission[1] (including nine in the eastern region) as national high-tech industrial development zones. At the same time, Shanghai Caohejing Hi-Tech Park, Dalian High-Tech Industrial Zone, Shenzhen Technology Industrial Zone, Xiamen Torch Development Zone for High Technology Industries, and Hainan International Science and Industry Park were designated as national high-tech industrial development zones. Following that, a series of similar zones were approved one after another in the eastern region, resulting in a total of 67 national high-tech industrial development zones in the eastern region, accounting for 42.9% of the entire country. Among them, there are 17 in Jiangsu, 12 in Shandong, and 12 in Guangdong. At the same time, in order to promote innovation and develop high-tech industries, the State Council approved in March 2009 of the construction of a national innovation demonstration zone in Zhongguancun Science

---

[1] The National Science and Technology Commission, established in 1956, was renamed the Ministry of Science and Technology in 1998.

Park. Subsequently, it approved the establishment of 8 national independent innovation demonstration zones in the eastern region (Shanghai Zhangjiang, Shenzhen, Tianjin Binhai, Hangzhou, Fuzhou-Xiamen-Quanzhou, Shandong Peninsula, Pearl River Delta, and Southern Jiangsu). In addition, in order to promote a new round of all-round development and opening up, as early as June 1990, the CPC Central Committee and the State Council approved Shanghai to develop and open Pudong New Area through implementing some preferential policies applied for special economic zones. Since 2005, the State Council has approved the establishment of several State-level new areas, including Tianjin Binhai New Area, Zhoushan Archipelago New Area in Zhejiang, Nansha New District in Guangzhou, West Coast New Area in Qingdao, Jiangbei New Area in Nanjing, Fuzhou New Area in Fujian, and Xiong'an New Area in Hebei, bringing the total number of such areas in the eastern region to eight.

To facilitate the eastern region's advancement in development and invigorate local growth, the State Council has devised and executed an array of guiding documents and plans in recent years. These initiatives have successfully propelled the transformation and progress of the eastern region. The pertinent opinions and plans are outlined below:

(1) Two documents in 2008—Guiding Opinions on Further Promoting the Reform and Opening up and Economic and Social Development of the Yangtze River Delta Region and the Outline of the Reform and Development Plan of the Pearl River Delta Region both of which clearly granted the Pearl River Delta Region greater autonomy in development.

(2) Six in 2009—the Opinions on Accelerating the Development of Modern Service Industry and Advanced Manufacturing Industry in Shanghai, Building an International Financial Center and an International Shipping Center; Several Opinions on Supporting Fujian Province to Accelerate the Construction of the Economic Zone on the West Coast of the Taiwan Straits; Several Opinions on Promoting the Construction and Development of Hainan International Tourism Island; Development Plan for the Coastal Area in Jiangsu Province; Development Plan for Efficient Ecological Economic Zone in Yellow River Delta Region; and Development Plan for Economic Zone on the West Coast of the Taiwan Straits.

(3) Three in 2011—Development Plan for Shandong Peninsula Blue Economic Zone; Development Plan for Hebei Coastal Area; and Plan for Zhejiang Marine Economic Development Demonstration Zone.

(4) One in 2013—Plan for Modernization Demonstration Zone in Southern Jiangsu.

(5) Two in 2014—Several Opinions on Supporting Fujian Province to Further Implement the Strategy of Ecological Province and Accelerate the Construction of

Ecological Civilization Pilot Demonstration Zone and Development Plan for Pearl River-Xijiang River Economic Belt.

(6) Two in 2015—Guidelines for Coordinated Development of the Beijing-Tianjin-Hebei Region (approved by the Political Bureau of the Central Committee of the CPC), and Outline of Cooperative Development in Bohai Rim Region.

(7) Two in 2016—Guidelines for Deepening Regional Cooperation in the Pan-Pearl River Delta; and Development Plan for the Yangtze River Delta Urban Agglomeration.

4.2 The achievements made by the eastern region in taking the lead in development

With the strong backing of national policies, the eastern region has experienced sustained and rapid economic growth since the initiation of the reform and opening up. It has achieved remarkable results in its export-oriented economy, substantial improvement in overall economic strength and international competitiveness, and significant advancements in living standards. These accomplishments serve as a testament to the effectiveness of the national strategy supporting the eastern region in spearheading its development. Having established itself as the primary growth hub propelling sustained and rapid economic progress in other parts of China, the eastern region currently plays a pivotal role in driving the development of other regions. Its leadership and demonstrative efforts are instrumental in realizing a well-rounded prosperous society, attaining modernization, and fostering innovation-driven development and economic transformation.

4.2.1 Sustained and high-speed economic growth

Owing to its location advantages and various favorable conditions as well as the unwavering support of national policies, the eastern region has achieved sustained, stable, and high-speed economic growth for over four decades since the reform and opening up. In general terms, if the economic growth rate remains above 8%, it is regarded high-speed growth, and if it exceeds 10%, it is classified as super-high-speed growth. From 1980 to 2016, the average annual growth rate of GDP in the eastern region reached 11.6%, 0.7 percentage points higher than the average growth rate of various regions, 2.2 percentage points higher than that in the northeastern region, and 1.1 and 1.2 percentage points higher than that in the central and western regions respectively. Among those 37 years, there were 32 years in the eastern region with economic growth rates of 8% and above, and 27 years with economic growth rates of 10% and above. This suffices to explain the sustained, stable and high-speed growth of the eastern region's economy since the reform and opening up. In terms of provinces, during this period, Guangdong achieved the highest average growth rate of 12.7%, followed by Fujian, Jiangsu, and Zhejiang (12% or above), and Shandong (11.5%) (see Table 4-1). These five provinces, known as newly industrialized region for the sustained, high-speed growth rate, have become the second-version leading regions supporting China's sustained and rapid economic growth after the old industrial bases such as the Northeast since the reform and opening up. In contrast, the economic growth rates of Shanghai, Beijing and Hebei were relatively low, lower than the average growth rates of all provinces. In terms of stages, the average growth rate of GRP in the eastern region was 10.2% from 1979 to 1990, 14.7% from 1991 to 1998, and 11.1% from 1999 to 2016, showing a pattern of accelerating first and then decelerating. The only exception in this region was Tianjin, which, as an important old industrial base in China, continued to grow at a high rate in recent years due to the development and opening up of Binhai New Area. From 1999 to 2016, the average annual growth rate of GRP in Tianjin was as high as 13.4%, 1.0 and 5.9 percentage points higher than that in 1991-1998 and in 1979-1990 respectively.

Table 4-1   Comparison of GRP growth rates among eastern
provinces from 1979 to 2016   Unit: %

Period	Beijing	Tianjin	Hebei	Shanghai	Jiangsu	Zhejiang	Fujian	Shandong	Guangdong	Hainan	Eastern region
1979-2016	10.0	11.3	10.3	9.8	12.0	12.0	12.3	11.5	12.7	10.9	11.6
1979-1990	9.2	7.5	9.0	7.4	10.4	11.5	12.0	10.5	13.7	11.0	10.2
1991-1998	11.3	12.4	13.4	13.5	15.2	15.0	15.6	13.7	15.1	12.8	14.7
1999-2016	10.1	13.4	9.9	9.8	11.6	10.9	11.0	11.2	10.9	10.1	11.1

Source: Calculated according to *Historical Data on China's GDP Accounting* (*1952-2004*) and *China Statistical Yearbook* over the years and *China Statistical Abstract* (*2017*).

Due to its own sustained and high-speed economic growth, the eastern region has played a crucial role in supporting the continuous and rapid development of the Chinese economy since the reform and opening up. Between 1979 and 2016, the eastern region accounted for a significant portion of the nominal growth of national GRP, with a contribution rate as high as 52.3%. Specifically, from 1979 to 1990, the eastern region contributed 48.5% to the growth, followed by 55.8% from 1991 to 1998, and 52.1% from 1999 to 2016. This shows that China's initiative for supporting the eastern region to take the lead in pursuing development since 1978 has effectively promoted the sustained and rapid economic growth of the eastern region, which in turn supported the sustained and rapid development of the national economy, thus rapidly improving China's status in global economy, and significantly narrowing the development gap between China and developed countries. China's GDP accounted for only 1.7% of the world total in 1978, but rapidly increased to 9.2% in 2010 and 14.8% in 2015. Notably, over for a long period of time after the reform and opening up, the sustained and high-speed economic growth in the eastern region was mainly driven by large-scale and rapid industrialization. In recent years, however, the eastern region has witnessed a shift in its economic landscape as it approaches the late stage of industrialization. While the manufacturing industry has lost its momentum, there has been a notable acceleration in the transition towards a service-oriented economy. From 2006 to 2016, the contribution rate of the secondary industry to the nominal growth of GRP decreased from 51.9% to 42.3%; within this, the contribution rate of traditional industry declined from 47.1% to 37.4%, but the tertiary industry experienced a significant increase, with its contribution rate rising rapidly from 40.8% to 52.4%. Therefore, in order to ensure sustained and rapid economic growth in the future, it remains crucial for the eastern region to prioritize the development of the real economy, including the manufacturing sector, particularly the high-end manufacturing industry.

4.2.2   Significant improvement in economic development level

During the early stages of the reform and opening up, the eastern region did not boast the highest level of economic development among the four major regions. In 1978, the GRP per capita in the eastern region stood at RMB465.5, surpassing the central and western regions, but falling 16.9% short of the northeastern region. However, with the advent of reform and opening up, and the unwavering support of national policies, the economy of the eastern region has taken a leading role in achieving sustained and rapid growth, significantly enhancing its level of economic development. Since 1991, the eastern region has surpassed the northeastern region and ranked top among the four major ones in terms of GRP per capita, thereby establishing itself as the zone with the highest level of economic development in China. If calculated according to the current average exchange rate of renminbi to US dollar, the GRP per capita in the eastern region was US$366.6 in 1981. It exceeded US$1,000 in 1996, US$5,000 in 2008, and US$10,000 in 2013. By 2016, it had reached US$11,479.0. According to the World Bank, low-income economies are defined as those GNI per capita of US$1,035 or less in 2012; high-income economies are those with GNI per capita of US$12,616 or more; and the middle-income economies fall between these two categories and are further divided into lower middle-income economies and upper middle-income economy, with a boundary set at US$4,086 (World Bank, 2013). After over 30 years of continuous and rapid growth, the eastern region as a whole has nearly reached the lower threshold of high-income economies by 2016. Notably, Tianjin, Beijing, and Shanghai have surpassed US$17,000 and Jiangsu has exceeded US$14,000 in terms of GRP per capita. These regions have steadily emerged as high-income economies and Zhejiang has been on the verge of joining them.

With sustained and rapid economic growth and large-scale industrialization, the eastern region has also significantly improved its urbanization level. In the eastern region in 1978, the urbanization rate of permanent residents was 15.73%, far lower than that in the northeastern region and only slightly higher than that in the central and western regions; by 2016, the urbanization rate has reached 65.94%, 4.27 percentage points higher than that in the northeastern region, 13.17 and 15.74 percentage points higher than that in the central and western regions respectively (see Table 4-2). Among the 10 eastern provinces, Shanghai, Beijing, and Tianjin have steadily entered the advanced urban society with an urbanization rate of more than 80%; Guangdong, Jiangsu, Zhejiang, and Fujian have entered the intermediate urban society with a rate of over 60%.[1] From 1978 to 2010, the urbanization rate in the eastern region increased by an average of 1.37 percentage points per year, much higher than that in the central region (an annual increase of 0.92 percentage points), the western region (an annual increase of 0.86 percentage points) and the northeastern region (an annual increase of 0.64 percentage points). It is worth noting that the on-going urbanization in the eastern region has been slowing down since 2010. The average annual increase in urbanization rate, which was 1.59 percentage points from 2006 to 2010, has dropped to 1.04 percentage points from 2011 to 2016. This rate has already been lower than that in the central and western regions.

---

[1] Here, Wei Houkai's classification for urban society (2013) is adopted, that is, the urbanization rate between 51% and 60% represents a primary urban society, 61%-75%, an intermediate urban society, 76%-90%, an advanced urban society, and, more than 90%, a complete urban society.

Table 4-2   Changes in urbanization rate in four
                            major regions from 1978 to 2016

Year	Urbanization rate (%)				Period	Annual growth rate (percentage points)			
	Eastern	Northeast	Central	Western		Eastern	Northeast	Central	Western
1978	15.73	37.01	14.08	13.78	—	—	—	—	—
1980	17.91	39.08	15.23	15.76	1978-1980	1.09	1.04	0.58	0.99
1985	28.00	45.98	19.57	20.16	1981-1985	2.02	1.38	0.87	0.88
1990	32.44	48.69	22.32	21.96	1986-1990	0.89	0.54	0.55	0.36
1995	39.29	51.37	26.99	25.97	1991-1995	1.37	0.54	0.93	0.80
2000	44.61	52.26	29.82	28.68	1996-2000	1.06	0.18	0.57	0.54
2005	51.78	55.15	36.55	35.36	2001-2005	1.43	0.58	1.35	1.34
2010	59.70	57.62	43.58	41.43	2006-2010	1.59	0.49	1.41	1.21
2013	62.80	60.22	48.49	45.98	2011-2013	1.03	0.87	1.64	1.52
2014	63.64	60.83	49.79	47.37	2014-2016	1.05	0.48	1.43	1.41
2015	64.75	61.35	51.24	48.74	2011-2016	1.04	0.68	1.53	1.46
2016	65.94	61.67	52.77	50.20	—	—	—	—	—

Source: Calculated based on *A New Road to Urbanization with Chinese Characteristics*, Beijing: Social Sciences Academic Press (China), 2014, *China Statistical Yearbook* (2014-2016), and *China Statistical Abstract* (*2017*).

City clusters emerge as urbanization reaches a certain level. In recent years, with the rapid advancement of population urbanization, regional integration and interconnected transport network, a number of city clusters with different sizes, scales and levels of development have emerged in China. As a brand-new regional unit for the country to participate in global competition and international division of labor, these city clusters have become the leading areas leading and supporting China's rapid economic growth and dominate the lifeblood of China's economic development (Yao Shimou et al., 2006; Xiao Jincheng, Yuan Zhu et al., 2009; Fang Chuanglin et al., 2011; Fang Chuanglin et al., 2015). With the rapid rise of city clusters, China has entered a new era of regional competition based on city clusters. City clusters have become the main form of urbanization and the main destination for new urban population in China. In the eastern region, there are currently five mature city clusters, namely, Yangtze River Delta, Pearl River Delta, Beijing-Tianjin-Hebei region, Shandong Peninsula, and the West Coast of the Taiwan Straits. In these five major city clusters in 2015, the urbanization rate reached 69.6%, the degree of economic openness reached 60.7%, the GRP per capita reached US$13,500, and the proportion of non-agricultural industries reached 96.0% (see Table 4-3), which were far higher than the national and eastern average. These city clusters, characterized by their dense population, high-level urbanization, and thriving modern manufacturing and service industries, played a pivotal role in driving the economic development of the eastern region. In 2015, these five city clusters accounted for 73.8% of the permanent population in the eastern region, and contributed 87.1% of the GRP and 96.8% of the total imports and exports to the region. On a national scale, these figures alter into 28.3%, 45.0%, and 80.1%, respectively.

Table 4-3   Main economic indicators of five major city
clusters in eastern region in 2015

Main indicator	City Clusters[a]					
	Yangtze River Delta	Pearl River Delta	Beijing-Tianjin-Hebei	Shandong Peninsula	West Coast of the Taiwan Straits	Total
Number of cities	18	9	10	8	16	61
Number of big cities with total urban population over 1 million[b]	12	7	6	5	5	35
Urbanization rate (%)	72.1	84.4	65.9	63.3	61.5	69.6
The degree of economic openness (%) [c]	64.4	97.5	46.4	31.9	43.2	60.7
Ratio of non-agriculture output (%)	96.9	98.2	95.3	94.4	92.4	96.0
GRP per capita (US dollars/person)	15,622	17,019	11,413	14,024	9,029	13,470
Proportion of permanent population in the eastern total (%)	23.4	11.2	17.2	8.6	13.4	73.8
Proportion of permanent population in the national total (%)	9.0	4.3	6.6	3.3	5.1	28.3
Proportion of GRP in the eastern total (%)	32.1	16.7	17.2	10.5	10.6	87.1
Proportion of GRP in the national total (%)	16.6	8.6	8.9	5.4	5.5	45.0
Proportion of im-export volume in the eastern total (%)	37.8	29.8	14.6	6.1	8.4	96.8
Proportion of im-export volume in the national total (%)	31.3	24.7	12.1	5.1	6.9	80.1

Note: a. For specific cities included in each cluster, see Xiao Jincheng, Yuan Zhu et al. (2009). Since the planning of the city clusters on the Yangtze River Delta and the West Coast of the Taiwan Straits has been approved by the State Council, the scope here is based on the planning. The data of each city cluster calculated in this table does not include cities belonging to the central region. Specifically, the city cluster of the Yangtze River Delta city cluster includes Shanghai, Nanjing, Wuxi, Changzhou, Suzhou, Nantong, Yancheng, Yangzhou, Zhenjiang, Taizhou, Hangzhou, Ningbo, Jiaxing, Huzhou, Shaoxing, Jinhua, Zhoushan, and Taizhou; the city cluster of the Pearl River Delta includes Guangzhou, Shenzhen, Zhuhai, Foshan, Huizhou, Dongguan, Zhongshan, Jiangmen, and Zhaoqing; the city cluster of the Beijing-Tianjin-Hebei region includes Beijing, Tianjin, Shijiazhuang, Chengde, Zhangjiakou, Qinhuangdao, Tangshan, Langfang, Baoding and Cangzhou; the city cluster of the West Coast of the Taiwan Straits include Wenzhou, Quzhou, Lishui, Fuzhou, Xiamen, Putian, Sanming, Quanzhou, Zhangzhou, Nanping, Longyan, Ningde, Shantou, Meizhou, Chaozhou, and Jieyang; the city cluster of the Shandong Peninsula includes Jinan, Qingdao, Zibo, Dongying, Yantai, Weifang, Weihai, and Rizhao.

b. Total urban population includes urban permanent and temporary population.

c. The degree of economic openness is the ratio of the total import and export volume to the GDP of the region, calculated by using the average exchange rate of renminbi against US dollar in 2015.

Source: Calculated in accordance with *China Statistical Yearbook* (2016), *China Urban Construction Statistical Yearbook*, Statistical Yearbook released by the eastern provinces and municipalities and the statistical bulletin of prefecture-level cities in Hebei Province in 2015.

4.2.3   Remarkable results in export-oriented economy

Due to its favorable conditions and national policy support, the eastern region has successfully emerged as a leader in pursuing development. It has achieved remarkable accomplishments in developing its export-oriented economy through effectively utilizing foreign capital, adopting advanced foreign technology, and expanding its exports. From the perspective of foreign investment actually utilized, as of the end of 2016, there had been 400,000 foreign-invested enterprises registered in the eastern region, accounting for 79.2% of the country; the total investment is US$4,004.6 billion, accounting for 78.2% of the whole country; the registered capital is 2,488.3 billion, accounting for 79.6% of the whole country; Among them, the foreign registered capital is US$1,918.1 billion, accounting for 80.2% of the whole country. These foreign-invested enterprises are highly concentrated in the Yangtze River Delta (Jiangsu, Zhejiang and Shanghai), Beijing-Tianjin-Hebei region and Pearl River Delta (Guangdong), especially in a few areas such as Shanghai, Jiangsu, Guangdong, Beijing, and Zhejiang. By the end of 2016, the number, total investment and registered capital of foreign-invested enterprises registered in these three economic core regions accounted for 67.4%, 67.3% and 68.7% of the whole country respectively. In particular, the number, total investment and registered capital of foreign-invested enterprises registered in Shanghai, Jiangsu, and Guangdong accounted for about 50% of the whole country. It is evident that despite the "westward movement" of foreign investment towards the central and western regions since the initiation of the 10th Five-year Plan, overall, foreign investment in China remains predominantly concentrated in select eastern regions.

Export in foreign trade is one of the important indicators reflecting the performance of an export-oriented economy. Since the reform and opening up, the eastern region has played a pivotal role in driving the growth of China's exports. As shown in Table 4-4, despite fluctuations between 2000 and 2016, the region consistently accounted for over 80% of the national export total each year, surpassing its share of population and GRP by a significant margin. In 2016, the proportion remained as high as 84.4% (slightly lower than before), with Guangdong contributing 31.2%, Jiangsu 15.8%, Zhejiang 13.0%, Shanghai 7.9%, Shandong 6.9%, and Fujian 4.2%. These six provinces collectively represented 79.0% of China's total exports, indicating a more pronounced geographical concentration of China's foreign trade exports compared to the regional distribution of foreign investment. This concentration pattern in the eastern region has led to its far higher export dependence compared to the central, western, and northeastern regions.

In recent years, due to the downturn in the international market and China's economic transformation, the export dependence of the eastern region has begun to drop sharply, from 40.8% in 2010 to 29.1% in 2016, but it was still far higher than that of the central and western regions and the northeastern region. Obviously, over the past 40 years of the reform and opening up, the rapid development of export-oriented economy dominated by foreign investment and exports has played a very important role in promoting the sustained and rapid economic growth in the eastern region. However, exports in the eastern region was largely driven by foreign-invested enterprises. In 2016, 44.2% of the total exported goods in the eastern region came from foreign-invested enterprises, including 74.3% in Shanghai, 63.8% in Tianjin and 56.4% in Jiangsu.

Table 4-4   Proportion of total export volumes of goods
                        and export dependence by region   Unit: %

Region	The proportion of total export volume									Export dependence						
	2000	2005	2010	2011	2012	2013	2014	2015	2016	2010	2011	2012	2013	2014	2015	2016
Total	100	100	100	100	100	100	100	100	100	24.4	23.5	22.4	21.6	21.0	19.6	18.1
Eastern	85.8	89.2	88.6	87.2	85.6	85.0	83.6	84.1	84.4	40.8	39.4	37.4	35.8	34.4	31.9	29.1
Northeast	5.8	4.2	3.5	3.5	3.3	3.2	3.2	2.8	2.6	10.1	9.4	8 6	8.1	7.9	6.8	6.9
Central	4.2	3.2	4.1	4.8	5.5	5.9	6.3	7.1	7.0	5.0	5.7	6.1	6.3	6.6	6.8	6.1
Western	4.2	3.4	3.8	4.5	5.6	5.9	6.9	6.0	6.0	4.9	5.5	6.3	6.3	7.2	5.9	5.3

Note: The total export volume of goods is sorted by domestic origin of goods. Export dependence is the ratio of total exports to regional GDP.

Source: Calculated in accordance with *China Statistical Yearbook* and *China Statistical Abstract* (2017).

4.2.4   The formation of a group of national competitive industries

The level of industrial development serves as a crucial indicator for assessing the quality of regional industrial growth. When a region's industrial growth is primarily propelled by industries characterized by elaborately transformed manufacturing, significant value addition, and advanced technical elements, it signifies a high-quality industrial growth in the region. Conversely, it indicates a low-quality industrial growth when those characteristics are lacking. Since the reform and opening up, in the process of large-scale and rapid industrialization, a number of national featured products with international influence and competitiveness have gradually emerged in the eastern region. These outstanding products have played a crucial role in establishing China as a prominent global manufacturing powerhouse and facilitating the remarkable transition of its industry from a humble producer to a formidable force. In order to examine the advantages of industrial products in various regions, we calculated the location quotient of major industrial products in the four major regions in 2016. Location quotient, also known as specialization coefficient, refers to the ratio of the proportion of industrial product output in the whole country to the proportion of industrial added value in the whole country. If the location quotient is greater than 1, it means that the product has certain degree of specialization; on the contrary, if the location quotient is less than 1, it means that the product does not have professional significance. In 2016, the eastern region accounted for 38.4% of the country' total population, yet it contributed impressive 53.7% to the national total of industrial added value, showcasing the formidable industrial strength of the eastern region as a whole. If the location quotient of industrial products in the eastern region is greater than 1, it requires that the output of this product accounts for more than 53.7% of the whole country, and its advantages are more significant. Obviously, the location quotient calculated according to the proportion of industrial added value underestimates the advantage degree of industrial products in the eastern region. If calculated in accordance with the proportion of population, the types and advantages of the specialization of industrial products in the eastern region have obviously increased. As can be seen from Table 4-5, a large number of featured industrial products have been formed in the eastern region at present, with strong industrial processing capacity. Most of its specialized products belong to industrial finished products with higher processing level. In particular, computers, mobile communication equipment, integrated circuits, household appliances, large machine tools and other modern manufacturing industries have a high location quotient in the eastern region, indicating that they have obvious advantages in specialization. In addition to industrial products, with the accelerated transformation to a service-oriented economy in recent years, the service industry in the eastern region also enjoyed obvious advantages in the whole country. For example, in 2015, the wholesale and retail trade sector in the eastern region contributed 59.7% of the country's total value added. Similarly, the financial industry contributed 58.7%, and the software and information technology industry, 76.5%.

Table 4-5　　　　　　Major specialized products and location
quotients by region in 2016

Region	Counted in terms of the proportion of industrial added value	Counted in terms of the proportion of population
Eastern region	Cloth (1.48), machine-made paper and paperboard (1.37), caustic soda (1.00), ethylene (1.22), raw materials for chemical pesticide (1.30), primary form plastics (1.06), chemical fiber (1.69), flat glass (1.06), pig iron (1.04), crude steel (1.06), steel (1.17), metal cutting machine tool (1.17), car (1.01), room air conditioner (1.15), household washing machine (1.20), mobile communication handset (1.18), integrated circuit (1.51), color TV (1.56)	Crude oil (1.03), raw salt (1.27), beer (1.15), cloth (2.08), machine-made paper and paperboard (1.93), caustic soda (1.40), soda ash (1.19), ethylene (1.71), chemical pesticide technology (1.82), primary form plastic (1.48), chemical fiber (2.37), flat glass (1.48), pig iron (1.45), crude steel (1.49), steel (1.64), metal cutting machine tool (1.65), large and medium tractors (1.02), automobile (1.18), cars (1.42), generator set (1.25), household refrigerator (1.30), room air conditioner (1.61), household washing machine (1.68), mobile communication handset (1.66), microcomputer (1.21), integrated circuit (2.13), color TV (2.19), power generation (1.03)
Northeastern region	Crude oil (4.56), beer (2.18), coke (1.20), ethylene (3.43), primary form plastics (1.40), pig iron (1.78), crude steel (1.54), steel (1.09), metal cutting machine tool (2.39), automobile (2.27), cars (3.62), 9 (3.15)	Crude oil (3.35), beer (1.60), ethylene (2.52), primary form plastics (1.03), pig iron (1.30), crude steel (1.14), metal cutting machine tools (1.76), automobile (1.67), car (2.66), generator set (2.31)
Central region	Raw coal (1.50), cigarettes (1.20), coke (1.46), sulfuric acid (1.41), soda ash (1.14), agricultural nitrogen, phosphorus, and potassium fertilizers (1.61), cement (1.26), flat glass (1.03), household refrigerator (2.01), room air conditioner (1.41), household washing machine (1.34)	Raw coal (1.24), coke (1.21), sulfuric acid (1.16), soda ash (1.28), agricultural nitrogen, phosphorus, potassium fertilizer (1.33), cement (1.04), household refrigerator (1.66), room air conditioner (1.18), household washing machine (1.10)
Western region	Raw coal (3.07), crude oil (1.74), natural gas (4.39), raw salt (1.56), finished sugar (4.72), beer (1.25), cigarette (1.96), Coke (1.63), sulfuric acid (2.60), caustic soda (1.58), soda ash (1.48), agricultural nitrogen, phosphorus, and potassium fertilizers (2.45), primary forms of plastics (1.42), Cement (1.84), large and medium tractor (2.03), automobile (2.03), generator set (1.66), microcomputer (2.42), power generation (1.87), hydropower (3.53)	Raw coal (2.11), crude oil (1.19), natural gas (3.01), raw salt (1.07), finished sugar (3.24), cigarettes (1.35), coke (1.12), Sulfuric acid (1.78), caustic soda (1.08), soda ash (1.02), agricultural nitrogen, phosphorus, and potassium fertilizers (1.68), cement (1.26), large and medium tractor (1.39), generator set (1.14), microcomputer (1.66), power generation (1.28), hydropower (2.42)

Source: Calculated in accordance with *China Statistical Yearbook Abstract* (2017).

4.3　The accelerated economic transformation and upgrading in the eastern region

Driven by the national strategy, the eastern region has achieved remarkable results in economic development since the reform and opening up. However, with the economic development level improving and the domestic and international environment changing, the eastern region no longer enjoys those traditional advantages, and instead, begins to encounter such problems as rising labor costs, shortage of land and environmental deterioration. That is, its advantages have been gradually transformed into capital and human capital accumulated in the development process (Pei Changhong & Zheng Wen, 2014). Under such circumstances, the eastern region is in urgent need to shift from taking the lead in pursuing development in the past to taking the lead in pursuing transformation and optimization, and drive a new round of sustained and rapid growth through transformation and upgrading.

4.3.1 Financial crisis in 2008 and economic predicament

Since the reform and opening up, the eastern region has maintained a high-speed growth momentum in its economy. Notably, areas such as the Pearl River Delta and the Yangtze River Delta have emerged as the primary drivers of China's economic development. Between 2003 and 2007, the eastern region witnessed a remarkable annual growth rate of over 13% in GRP, averaging at 14.1%. However, with the large-scale agglomeration and extensive expansion of low-end industries over the years, the rapid economic growth in the eastern region was achieved at the cost of huge consumption of energy, land, raw materials, labor and other resources, and with a large amount of "Three Wastes"[1] as the byproduct, which has resulted in a general increase in the cost of labor, land and other factors, and the deterioration of environment. Under such circumstances, coupled with the shock of the 2008 financial crisis and the appreciation of the renminbi, the eastern region is rather economically challenged, which manifests itself in the continuous decline in foreign trade exports, the sluggish industrial growth, the difficulties faced by small- and medium-sized enterprises (SMEs), and the decline in local fiscal revenue and the heavy employment burden (Wei Houkai, 2009b). For instance, the financial crisis has significantly reduced orders from international markets since the second half of 2008. This has posed a threat to the profitability and even the survival of foreign trade enterprises and export-oriented small- and medium-sized manufacturing enterprises in the eastern region. Especially, in Guangdong, Zhejiang and other places, many SMEs have suspended production or closed down due to cancellation of orders and ineffective capital turnover, and quite a few enterprises earn low margins of profit or even at a loss. At the same time, affected by the decline in demand and orders,

---

[1] Industrial wastewater, waste gases, and residues. — *Tr.*

enterprises in some areas of the Pearl River Delta and Yangtze River Delta have cut or stopped production, downsized staff, or even shut down, leading to an extremely grim job market with decreasing demand for employment and rising rate of unemployment. It is especially true of the export-oriented industries and labor-intensive industries as well as the SMEs.

The economic difficulties faced by the eastern region were a consequence of the interplay of various internal and external factors. In particular, four key external factors can be identified: (1) The financial crisis has led to a decline in demand in both European and American markets. As a result, international orders have significantly decreased, forcing numerous OEM companies to halt production. (2) The renminbi appreciated rapidly against the US dollar, by 15.2% from 2006 to 2008, which severely undermined the profitability of those labor-intensive, export-oriented SMEs. (3) The rising cost of production factors, especially the cost of land, wages and environmental governance in the Pearl River Delta, Yangtze River Delta and other places has threatened the survival of some enterprises with high dependence on resource consumption and low labor costs. (4) The reduction of tax rebates for exports, the implementation of stricter policies for processing trade, and the enhancement of environmental protection standards have also severely affected the labor-intensive and export-oriented SMEs in the eastern region. In reality, numerous small enterprises involved in processing trade heavily relied on tax rebates and other policies to sustain their minimal profits.

Clearly, these external factors are merely superficial. At a more profound level, the fundamental cause can be attributed to the significant flaws within the economic structure of the eastern region. These flaws have resulted in a decline in its industrial competitiveness and sluggish economic growth. For a long time, in eastern regions such as Guangdong and Zhejiang, traditional industries hold a large proportion, in which SMEs and plants specializing in processing trade operate as the main players to provide low value-added, low-technological products. For the lack of independent brands and innovation ability, they gained their competitive edge by virtue of low costs of labor and other resources, but resulted in high resource consumption and "Three Wastes" emission. According to the data from the survey on the 2006 National Industrial Enterprise Innovations, both the growth rate and the proportion of innovation expenditure in the main business income of industrial enterprises in the eastern region are the lowest in the country. Both the labor productivity and the growth rate of all industrial employees in the eastern region are not the lowest in China. In the eastern region, the total industrial labor productivity in 2007 was lower by 22.6%, 12.5%, and 21.0% compared to the northeastern region, central region, and western region, respectively; and similarly, the average annual growth rate of total industrial labor productivity between 2004 and 2007 was lower by 6.8, 14.4, and 13.6 percentage points, respectively.

Industrial clusters were once the driving force behind the rapid economic growth in the eastern region. In the past, specialized towns accounted for nearly 1/3 of Guangdong's total industrial output value, while the "block economies" contributed to 50% of Zhejiang's industrial output value. In Fujian, approximately 52% of the output value was achieved through various "quasi-clusters", and in Jiangsu, the proportion was close to 40% (Wei Houkai et al., 2008). However, due to the structural defects of the cluster at that time and the impact of the international financial crisis in 2008, the eastern industrial cluster was facing a serious risk of recession (Wei Houkai, 2009c). Eastern industrial clusters have a large share in international markets because most of their products are exported, so they are significantly affected by the crisis. In 2008, the export of garments and apparel accessories in Guangdong Province witnessed a decline of 25.3% against the previous year, indicating a generally unfavorable situation for certain clothing industry clusters. At the same time, due to the sharp decrease in orders from international markets, exchange rate changes and the overall rise in factor costs, some SMEs in the cluster are in a state of semi-shutdown or shutdown, and more businesses went broke. According to the data from Guangdong Economic and Trade Commission, in Guangdong, a total of 7,148 enterprises closed down from January to September in 2008, and an additional 8,513 enterprises ceased production in that October.[1] Many SMEs in Zhejiang's "block economy" have also stopped production or closed down due to cancellation of orders and ineffective capital turnover. According to a survey on Wenzhou's 10 key villages and towns, 14% of enterprises in the most-affected villages and towns closed down, and 5% of enterprises in the least affected villages and towns closed down, with an average closing rate of 8%.[2] In addition, due to the lack of land and tight energy supply, the costs of labor, land, raw materials and other factors have risen in an all-round way, resulting in the gradual migration of some enterprises in the eastern industrial cluster to the surrounding and central and western regions. Since the 10th Five-year Plan, many labor-intensive and resource-intensive enterprises in Zhejiang have accelerated their transfer to Jiangxi and other central and western regions.

---

[1] Wang He & Ren Xuan, "Shutting down and transferring 15,000 small- and medium-sized enterprises to survive the cold winter", *Guangzhou Daily*, Dec. 17, 2008.

[2] Liu Wenjie, Xing Mei and Feng Yuan, "People in the city calm and free, people outside the city frightened: A Survey on the Living Conditions of Private Enterprises in Zhejiang", *Economic Information Daily*, Nov. 11, 2008.

Pearl River Delta enterprises have also begun to move to the east and west wings of Guangdong, the mountainous areas of northern Guangdong and the central and western provinces, while Foshan ceramic enterprises have moved to Jiangxi, Hunan, Sichuan, Shandong and other places.

The decline risk faced by the eastern industrial clusters is primarily attributed to their structural deficiencies. These deficiencies are chiefly evident in the following four aspects: (1) The industries are positioned at the lower end of the market. The majority of industrial clusters in the eastern region are primarily focused on labor-intensive traditional industries, which are characterized by low grades, low added value, low technical content, and low prices. The growth of these clusters largely depends on offering low prices in the mass market, indicating that the competitive advantage of the eastern industrial clusters is primarily derived from middle- and low-grade manufacturing at the lower end of the product value chain. (2) There is fragmentation within the supply chain. On a vertical scale, most of these clusters exhibit a diamond-shaped organizational structure. This implies that the product value chain is fragmented, with a focus on strong production and manufacturing capabilities, while the links related to R&D, design, marketing, brand management, and other aspects are relatively weak. On a horizontal level, numerous SMEs within these clusters find themselves trapped in a state of homogeneous over-competition. Consequently, they lack the necessary organic connectivity and specialized division of labor and cooperation. Moreover, the industrial organizations in these clusters are widely dispersed, resulting in a lack of robust support systems. (3) Production heavily relies on OEM branding. In the eastern industrial clusters, numerous enterprises have not yet developed their own brands and primarily engage in OEM production. Consequently, they position themselves as mere "production workshops" for multinational corporations, resulting in meager profit margins from processing activities. (4) There is a prevailing inclination towards technological imitation. Many enterprises within the clusters prioritize imitation over innovation, leading to a significant dearth of innovative products, talented innovators, and inadequate innovation capabilities. As a result of these inherent structural shortcomings, the eastern industrial clusters can solely rely on low cost and low price to maintain their competitive edge. However, the emergence of escalating factor costs due to extensive industrial agglomeration, such as the surging land prices, labor wages, and the expiration of various preferential policies, poses a significant risk of mass exodus for the enterprises within these clusters. Meanwhile, the manufacturing process is plagued by fierce competition as a result of the absence of independent brands and innovations, causing numerous SMEs to face homogeneous challenges. In an effort to gain a competitive edge, these enterprises resort to flooding the market with low-priced products, resulting in dwindling profits and pushing numerous businesses to the brink of low profits or even losses. Additionally, the meager profits provide limited flexibility for pricing risks within the clusters and hinder the implementation of extensive R&D initiatives for these enterprises.

Therefore, the predicament of the eastern economy in recent years cannot solely be attributed to the financial crisis. Prior to the crisis, it is noteworthy that certain regions within the Pearl River Delta and Yangtze River Delta had already experienced a decline in both economic growth and industrial competitiveness. The crisis in 2008 just intensified and exposed the drawbacks formed under the traditional development model. With the changes in development environment at home and abroad, and especially, the overall rise in factor costs, the traditional development model in the eastern region, characterized by huge consumption of resources, high dependence on exports, low position in industrial chain, low price on mass markets, and reliance on low cost and low price to obtain competitive advantages, has been increasingly challenged and has come to an end. It can be said that after entering the 21st century, the economy of the eastern region has reached a new stage of comprehensive transformation and upgrading. In this stage, the eastern region will face two major tasks of economic transformation and industrial upgrading at the same time, rather than just the latter one. Obviously, to fundamentally get rid of the difficulties faced by the eastern economy, the key lies in accelerating the economic transformation and upgrading in the eastern region.

4.3.2   Efforts to expedite the economic transformation of the eastern region

In response to the financial crisis and the economic plight, the eastern provinces have accelerated their economic transformation and upgrading in recent years. Greatly affected by the financial crisis, Zhejiang and Guangdong took the lead in economic transformation. As early as December 2007, the Economic Work Conference of CPC Zhejiang Provincial Committee proposed the major strategic task of accelerating economic transformation and upgrading, which marked the official start of a new round of economic transformation in Zhejiang. Then, in September 2008, Zhejiang Provincial Committee adopted the Decision on Deeply Studying and Practicing the Scientific Outlook on Development, Accelerating the Transformation of Economic Development Mode, and Promoting Economic Transformation and Upgrading, which highlighted the necessity to "promote the shift from Made-in-Zhejiang to Created-in-Zhejiang and the leap from a big provincial economy to a strong provincial economy", and by 2012, "to make significant progress in the transformation of economic development mode and economic transformation and upgrading, and take the lead across the country in this respect". In order to speed up the pace, in 2013, the Zhejiang Provincial Committee and Provincial Government made a major decision to solve the long and heavy reliance of Zhejiang's economy on low-end industries, low-cost labor force, resource consumption, and traditional markets and business models. The decision, a key move to accelerate the economic transformation and upgrading, involves the measures in such two aspects: (1) to phase out the industries and enterprises with high energy-consumption, high emissions but low output, and replace them with high value-added, high-tech, eco-friendly ones; to downsize staff and improve efficiency through substituting machines for workers; to optimize the location of industries and enterprises and utilize land resources in an intensive way; and to innovate and business models through promoting e-commerce; and (2) to make every effort to help the branding of products made and created in Zhejiang, and also to support the development of the enterprises and the entrepreneurs with high goodwill.

Guangdong Province has also made active explorations in accelerating economic transformation. As early as May 2008, in response to the financial crisis, the CPC Guangdong Provincial Committee and the provincial government issued the document Decision on Promoting Industrial and Labor Transfer. The strategy known as "Double Transfer" aimed to optimize the regional industrial layout and achieve coordinated regional development by means of transferring labor-intensive industries from the Pearl River Delta to the adjacent eastern and western areas as well as the mountainous regions in northern Guangdong, and meanwhile, transferring the labor force from these areas to local secondary and tertiary industries as well as the developed Delta area. This strategy has attracted wide attention from all walks of life. In June 2010, the Guangdong Provincial Committee and the provincial government issued Several Opinions on Accelerating the Transformation of Economic Development Mode, which proposed to focus on cultivating top 500 enterprises in the province, namely 100 advanced manufacturing projects, 100 modern service projects, 100 projects of industries with traditional advantages, 100 modern agricultural projects and 100 projects of strategic emerging industries, and phasing out outdated capacity and promote the optimization and upgrading of industrial structure by implementing measures such as differential power pricing and differential sewage charging. In January 2015, the Fourth Plenary Session of the 11th CPC Guangdong Central Committee made a strategic three-year arrangement on the implementation of industrial transformation and upgrading. Since then, in March of the same year, the Guangdong Provincial Government issued the Three-Year Action Plan for Industrial Transformation and Upgrading in Guangdong Province (2015-2017), which stated that it would take three years to initially form a modern industrial system with domestic leading and international competitiveness, and steadily realize the transformation from a large industrial province to a strong one.

The measure of economic transformation and upgrading in the eastern region is also supported by the central government. In the Government Work Report in March 2012, the then premier Wen Jiabao proposed to "actively support the eastern region in transforming its economy and participating in international competition and cooperation at a higher level". In March 2016, the Outline of the 13th Five-Year Plan adopted at the Fourth Session of the 12th National People's Congress further made it clear to support the eastern region to "accelerate the transformation to innovation-driven development and create a new highland with international influence". For this purpose, the State Council and other relevant departments have launched a series of policies and measures in recent years. In November 2011, the Ministry of Commerce, the National Development and Reform Commission and other four ministries jointly issued the Guiding Opinions on Promoting the Transformation and Upgrading of Processing Trade, which proposed to improve the overall level of processing trade, extend the industrial chain, increase added value, increase domestic income, and realize the transformation of processing trade from scale-driven growth to high quality efficiency-driven development. In October 2014, the State Council issued Several Opinions on Promoting Transformation, Upgrading, Innovation and Development of National Economic and Technological Development Zones, requiring the national economic and technological development zones in the eastern region should to take the lead in transformation development patterns and participating in international economic cooperation and competition at a higher level, and lifting their position in the global value chain and international division of labor. Since 2016, the State Council has also successively approved the Shanghai Systematic Promotion of Comprehensive Innovation and Reform Experiment to Accelerate the Construction of a Science and Technology Innovation Center with Global Influence, Experimental Plan for Systematic Promotion of Comprehensive Innovation and Reform in Beijing-Tianjin-Hebei Region, Experimental Plan for Systematic Promotion of Comprehensive Innovation and Reform in Guangdong and Beijing's Overall Plan for Strengthening the Construction of a National Science and Technology

Innovation Center, whereby to accelerate the pace of economic transformation and upgrading in the eastern region through relying on comprehensive innovation.

Driven by the policies of the central and local governments, the pace of economic transformation and upgrading in the eastern region has experienced significant acceleration in recent years, resulting in notable initial achievements. It is foreseeable that this process will propel the eastern region into a new phase of sustained and high-speed growth. At present, under the background of the rapid decline of the national economic growth rate, the eastern region has achieved medium- and high-speed growth by relying on transformation and upgrading. The growth rate of GRP in the eastern region was 8.0% in 2015 and 7.5% in 2016, both slightly higher than the average growth rate of all other regions. Among them, in 2016, the growth rate of GRP in Tianjin and Fujian exceeded 8.0%, and the other six provinces were in the medium-high speed range of 6.5%-8.0%. For the eastern region at present, the GRP per capita has exceeded US$11, 000, and it is about to enter the stage of high-income economy. It is not easy to achieve medium-and high-speed growth of over 6.5% as a whole. In 2016, the GRP achieved in the eastern region has exceeded RMB40 trillion, and every 1% increase in the total economic output is equivalent to RMB403.7 billion, which is about 10% more than the sum of the increments brought by every 1% increase in the central and western regions and northeastern region. More importantly, the transformation and upgrading strategy has significantly improved the industrial development level and innovation capability of the eastern region, and driven strategic emerging industries to develop rapidly. In 2016, the eastern region accounted for 68.5% of the total number of patent applications granted in the country, with invention patents accounting for 67.3% of the national total. Between 2012 and 2016, the number of patent applications granted in the eastern region experienced an annual growth rate of 11.3%, with invention patents growing at an annual rate of 21.9%.

4.4 The initiative for coordinated development of the Beijing-Tianjin-Hebei region

The Beijing-Tianjin-Hebei region, along with the Yangtze River Delta and Pearl River Delta regions, serves as a core economic zone in China. Despite covering less than 2.3% of the total land area, the region accounted for 8.1% of the national population and contributed 9.7% to the national GDP in 2016. With China's capital involved, the

Beijing-Tianjin-Hebei region benefits from its advantageous transportation location, dense population, developed industries and towns, as well as abundant resources in science, education, culture, information, and high-quality professionals. It has evolved into an urban agglomeration and intelligence-intensive area with global influence, playing a crucial role in supporting China's economic development. However, compared to the Pearl River Delta and Yangtze River Delta regions, this region's development is significantly imbalanced. High-quality resources, high-end factors of production, and industrial activities are heavily concentrated in the core cities of Beijing and Tianjin, resulting in a substantial development gap between Beijing-Tianjin and Hebei. In particular, the gap in GRP per capita between Beijing-Tianjin and Hebei has widened in recent years. Consequently, it is imperative to promote the coordinated development of the region, with a particular focus on that between Beijing-Tianjin and Hebei, as it represents a pressing challenge that demands urgent attention.

4.4.1   Forming a spatial structure featuring polycentric network

For a long time, due to the dual-core structure arising from administrative division and administrative region economy, there always exist many contradictions and conflicts between "twin cities" like Shenyang and Dalian in Liaoning, Jinan and Qingdao in Shandong, Guangzhou and Shenzhen in Guangdong, Chongqing and Chengdu in Chengdu-Chongqing Economic Zone, so it is quite difficult to straighten out the inter-city relations. In the Beijing-Tianjin-Hebei region, Beijing and Tianjin hold a prominent core position, and their spatial structure belongs to a typical dual-core structure. The relationship between Beijing and Tianjin has not been effectively managed, with more emphasis on competition than cooperation. For example, Beijing used to choose Tangshan instead of Tianjin as its export port, and jointly established Jingtang Port with Hebei. Most industries in Beijing were also transferred to Tangshan and other places in Hebei Province with few to Tianjin. So far, Beijing and Tianjin have not fully established a cooperative pattern that showcases industrial complementarity and a rational division of labor. In particular, both being municipalities directly under the central government, Beijing and Tianjin has not developed a sound mechanism for regional cooperation and market competition as well as for sufficient cross-regional flow of production factors due to the constraints of administrative divisions and administrative systems. Under the current new situation, therefore, in order to promote the integration of Beijing, Tianjin, and Hebei, we must correctly handle the relationship between Beijing and Tianjin, strengthen the interaction and cooperation between Beijing and Tianjin, and jointly write a "Tale of Two Cities" of Beijing and Tianjin in the new era of socialist modernization.

In 2016, the GRP per capita in the Beijing-Tianjin-Hebei region exceeded US$10,000 (specifically US$10,025), accompanied by a notable urbanization rate of 63.9%. Notably, both Beijing and Tianjin achieved a remarkable GRP per capita of over US$17,000, with an urbanization rate surpassing 80% (see Table 4-6). The Beijing-Tianjin-Hebei region as a whole has entered the late stage of industrialization and urbanization, so it is inevitable for the region to promote the formation of a spatial structure featuring polycentric network through optimal development. The term "polycentric" refers to the construction of a four-level hierarchy of "two cores, four sub-centers, multi-polarity, and multi-micro-centers". Specifically, "two cores" means the construction of Beijing and Tianjin as two main centers, forming a pattern of interaction between the two cities. As the capital, Beijing's function has been clearly defined as a political center, international exchange center, cultural center, and scientific and technological innovation center. In the future, according to the "four-center" positioning, the focus of our work is to firmly and orderly relieve its non-capital roles, optimize and upgrade its core functions of the capital, build Tongzhou (its sub-center) and Xiong'an New Area into new "two wings" for Beijing's development, and finally properly solve the problem of "big city disease". As a national comprehensive industrial base, trade center and international port city, Tianjin is required to give full play to its advantages in ports, logistics, manufacturing and commerce, strengthen the function of "Northern Economic Center", promote the overall transformation and upgrading of industries, and accelerate the construction into a national advanced manufacturing R&D base, northern international shipping core area, financial innovation operation demonstration region and pioneering region for reform and opening up. The "four sub-centers" is about building four comprehensive deputy centers of Shijiazhuang, Tangshan, Langfang, and Baoding to share some functions of Beijing and Tianjin and drive the development of the rest parts in Hebei Province through making full use of the location advantages and the existing development foundation. "Multi-polarity" means building a number of green growth poles and growth points with different characteristics, and providing strong support for the sustained medium and high-speed growth of the Beijing-Tianjin-Hebei region through giving full play to the role of Handan, Xingtai, Zhangjiakou, Chengde, Qinhuangdao, Cangzhou, Hengshui and other regional central cities as well as some new districts and new towns. The term "multi-micro-centers" means strengthening infrastructure and public services according to the standards of modern small cities, building a number of modern small towns equipped with industrial support, rich cultural atmosphere, beautiful environment, balanced occupation and residence, and complex functions, and forming a large number of professional "micro-centers" that are suitable for living and working both.

Table 4-6   Economic development levels of different parts in
the Beijing-Tianjin-Hebei region in 2016

Indicators	Actual level			Taking that in Hebei as 1	
	Beijing	Tianjin	Hebei	Beijing	Tianjin
Urbanization rate (%)	86.50	82.93	53.32	1.62	1.56
GRP per capita (RMB)	114,653	115,053	42,736	2.68	2.69
GRP per capita (USD)	17,261	17,321	6,434	2.68	2.69
Per capita disposable income (RMB)	52,530.40	34,074.50	19,725.40	2.66	1.73

Source: Calculated in accordance with *China Statistical Yearbook Abstract* (2017).

The term "network" refers to construct a number of key development axes through relying on important traffic arteries and routes so as to guide the rational agglomeration and evacuation of factors, population and industries, and to promote the formation of a network-like spatial balanced development pattern. For this purpose, current priority goes to build and cultivate a two-level axis for key development. As to the first-level, as proposed in the Guidelines for Coordinated Development of the Beijing-Tianjin-Hebei Region, it should be the three industrial development zones of Beijing-Tianjin, Beijing-Baoding-Shijiazhuang, Beijing-Tang shan-Qin huangdao, which also from an urban agglomeration axis. With superior transportation location, dense population, industry and towns, and solid development foundation, these three zones play a decisive role in optimizing and transforming the development of the Beijing-Tianjin-Hebei region. In addition, in the long run, the areas along the coastline should be taken as a new first-level axis for key development. The axis extends along the coastline to include Tianjin Port, Tangshan Port, Qinhuangdao Port and Huanghua Port and other ports. It gathers important functional areas such as Tianjin Binhai New Area, Tangshan Caofeidian New Area, Laoting New Area and Cangzhou Bohai New Area. It is an ideal place for developing open economy, port logistics, port industry and modern manufacturing industry, with great potential for future development. On this basis, a number of second-level axes for key development should be constructed to meet future needs. In this way, through the gradual extension and interweaving of the two-level axes for key development, a spatial structure featuring polycentric network is to be gradually formed, thus realizing the coordinated development and spatial balance of Beijing, Tianjin, and Hebei.

4.4.2 Relieving Beijing of functions nonessential to its role as the capital

The disorderly extension and overloaded expansion in Beijing in recent years have resulted in severe "big city diseases" such as traffic congestion, skyrocketing housing prices, resource shortages, and environmental deterioration. This situation can be attributed to two major factors. First, as the capital, Beijing assumes too many functions, leading to the excessive concentration of factors, population, and industries. This has surpassed the region's capacity in terms of resources, environment, and urban infrastructure. The population explosion in Beijing serves as a prime illustration of this phenomenon. From 2005 to 2014, the migrant resident population in Beijing experienced an annual increase of 489,000, which accounted for 74.2% of the overall increase in the permanent population. Within the permanent population, the percentage of permanent migrants steadily rose from 12.4% in 1998 to 38.1% in 2014. Since the orderly relief of Beijing's non-capital roles in 2015, the permanent population of the city has been steadily increasing, although at a slower pace. According to estimates, the actual limit of sustainable population is lower than 13 million, with a more reasonable limit being 6.67 million (Shi Minjun et al., 2013). As of 2000, the population had already reached 13.636 million, and by the end of 2016, it had grown to 21.729 million. This rapid growth has put immense pressure on the city's water resources, far surpassing their carrying capacity. Second, the city proper is home to a wide range of top-notch resources, facilities, and employment opportunities. However, this concentration has led to a significant separation between places of work and residence, resulting in lengthy commutes and exacerbating issues such as traffic congestion, skyrocketing housing prices, and environmental pollution. To illustrate, more than 60% of municipal hospitals, approximately 50% of key middle schools, and 70% of theaters are concentrated in the core area of the Capital. Moreover, job opportunities in Beijing are primarily concentrated in the main urban areas, namely Dongcheng, Xicheng, Chaoyang, Fengtai, Shijingshan, and Haidian districts. Therefore, it is imperative to actively embrace the "de-functionalization" strategy, gradually relieve Beijing of its non-capital core functions, and strategically adjust and optimize its economic and spatial structures. These measures will serve as the backbone in curing Beijing's "big city diseases".

According to the plan, Beijing would limit its population to less than 23 million by 2020, which requires a 15% reduction in the city proper. For this goal and the eradication of the "big city diseases", apart from further improving the carrying capacity of resources and environment, the key is to orderly relieve Beijing of functions nonessential to its role as the capital through exercising both regulation and control in an integrated way. On the one hand, efforts should go to strict control over the growth (in-flow of population) and active dissolution of the demographic stock. In the former case, it is necessary to set strict thresholds for the population and industrial access in accordance with the functional positioning of the capital. In the latter case, we should relieve Beijing of functions nonessential to its role as the capital, whereby to guide the relief of population, industry, and facilities, and realize the coordinated relief of functions, population, industry and facilities. At present, for the purpose of this relief, it is necessary to adopt a multi-level relief strategy combining centralization and decentralization. The term "combining" means that the sub-center of the capital (Tongzhou), Xiong'an New Area, and Tianjin Binhai New Area will be taken as centralized places to relieve Beijing's nonessential functions, and at the same time, surrounding areas are encouraged to undertake Beijing's relief of functions nonessential to its role as the capital in an orderly manner according to their own conditions. The term "multi-level" means that the nonessential functions of the city proper of Beijing will be relieved to the suburbs of Beijing, cities in Hebei Province, Tianjin and even other regions according to the characteristics of different functions. Some administrative and institutional service institutions, scientific research, education, training, medical institutions and other social public service functions should be relieved to the suburbs close to the city proper and Langfang, Baoding, Zhangjiakou, Chengde, Qinhuangdao and other areas in Hebei Province. Some manufacturing, logistics and other functions can be relieved to Tangshan, Zhangzhou, Handan and other areas far away from the central city; Some functions, such as regional enterprise headquarters, technical services, transformation of scientific research achievements and industrialization bases, can also be relieved to other regions in the northeast and west from a long distance to promote the coordinated development of regional economy.

On the other hand, we should give full play to the role of government guidance and market regulation through exercising regulation and control. According to the Guidelines for Coordinated Development of the Beijing-Tianjin-Hebei Region, the current focus is to orderly relieve four types of non-essential roles of the capital, namely, (1) developing general industries, especially high-consumption industries; (2) developing some tertiary industries such as regional logistics bases and regional specialized markets; (3) providing some social public service functions such as education, medical care, and training institutions; (4) establishing some organizations providing administrative and business services and corporate headquarters. Since these nonessential functions of the capital that need to be relieved involve different types of industries, institutions, or enterprises, and they differ much in their willingness to be relieved, needs for development and factors considered, it is necessary to formulate differentiated plans and take into account the interests of all parties. In particular, it is necessary to organically combine the government's planning with market regulation, and give full play to the decisive role of the market in resource allocation. For government agencies and institutions, universities, state-owned enterprises, etc., orderly relief can be carried out through administrative means according to the plan; for private enterprises and residents, we should give full consideration to their willingness to relocate, and mainly adopt economic means to actively guide them, instead of destroying the decisive role of market mechanism. In the process of orderly relief, we should make full use of land, price, finance, taxation, credit and other means to guide the rational flow of population and factors and promote the orderly transfer of industries.

4.4.3　Optimizing the layout of spaces for production, living, and ecological conservation

In the Beijing-Tianjin-Hebei region, there are clear constraints on resources and the environment, particularly the scarcity of water resources, severe air pollution, and ecological degradation. These issues have garnered widespread attention. The region is recognized as one of China's most water-stressed areas in terms of water resources. In 2014, the per capita water resources were only 124.7 cubic meters, only 6.2% of the national average, including 95.1 cubic meters in Beijing and 76.1 cubic meters in Tianjin, which were far lower than the internationally recognized extreme water shortage standard of 500 cubic meters per capita. Due to the long-term serious overexploitation, the groundwater level has dropped sharply, forming a large-scale groundwater funnel. From 1998 to 2014, the average buried depth of groundwater in Beijing decreased by 13.78 meters, and the reserves correspondingly decreased by 7.06 billion cubic meters (Beijing Water Authority, 2015). The region also suffers from serious air pollution. In recent years, although governments at all levels have made great efforts to comprehensively control it, it has not been effectively curbed. According to the air quality monitoring results of 74 cities in China, among the 10 cities with the worst air quality, 7 are concentrated in this region, including Baoding, Xingtai, Hengshui, Tangshan, Handan, Shijiazhuang and Langfang. In 2016, the region remained home to six out of the top 10 cities in China with the poorest air quality (Ministry of Environmental Protection of the People's Republic of China, 2016, 2017), namely Hengshui, Shijiazhuang, Baoding, Xingtai, Handan, and Tangshan. The water environment in the region is also worrisome. The Haihe River Basin, which runs through the region, has been subjected to severe, long-term pollution. Out of the 161 national monitoring sections in 2016, 41.0% were classified as Inferior V-type water quality, representing an increase of 3.1 percentage points compared to the previous year (Ministry of Environmental Protection of the People's Republic of China, 2017).

Therefore, the central government has prioritized transportation, environmental protection, and industrial transfer as the primary focus areas for achieving significant progress in the near future. Various policy measures have been implemented to establish a collaborative mechanism for preventing and controlling environmental pollution in the Beijing-Tianjin-Hebei region, which is considered an optimized development zone. In addition to joint prevention and control of environmental pollution, it is necessary to strengthen ecological protection and construction, implement both environmental governance and ecological construction, and strive to shape the Beijing-Tianjin-Hebei region into an ecological urban agglomeration with world influence and competitiveness. At present, for its high development intensity and large proportion of production space, the Beijing-Tianjin-Hebei region, especially Beijing-Tianjin and other urban areas, has insufficient living space and ecological space, with reduced biodiversity and obvious ecological degradation, which seriously affects the improvement of living environment and living standards. Therefore, to spur the coordinated development of the Beijing-Tianjin-Hebei region, we must stick to the philosophy of giving priority to green development and ecological environment, that is, we need to delineate ecological red lines scientifically, set up green isolation belts rationally, and establish a number of agricultural protection areas, ecological parks, ecological functional areas, ecological parks and towns, thus effectively protecting ecological environment and building an integrated ecological corridor and network. At the same time, it is necessary to clarify the growth boundary of each city through strictly delimiting the permanent basic farmland, and preventing each city from spreading and expanding in disorder and connecting with each other, thus becoming an uninhabitable "cement forests". County-level administrative regions will be taken as regional units in determining the rational layout of spaces for production, living, and ecological conservation, and setting the upper limit of development intensity and the bottom limit of ecological space in each region, so as to provide intensive and efficient production space, moderately livable living space and beautiful ecological space. For Beijing, Tianjin and its surrounding areas, due to the shift of development stage, it is necessary to gradually reduce the proportion of production space, appropriately increase the proportion of living space, and greatly increase the scale and proportion of ecological space. In particular, it is necessary to integrate nature reserves, scenic spots, forest parks, wetland parks and other nature reserves in Beijing, Tianjin, and Hebei, thus jointly building a national park around the capital.

In the region, agriculture not only ensures the supply and security of agricultural products, but also plays a crucial role in providing essential ecological products. Consequently, it becomes an integral component of the ecological system, serving as a significant carrier of ecological space and living space. Therefore, from the perspective of large-scale ecology, agriculture must be included in the ecological system and ecological space as well. In current period, we may carry out pilot projects of agricultural protection zones in the Beijing-Tianjin-Hebei region, and reduce the use of chemical fertilizers and pesticides on the basis of achieving their zero growth, so as to make agriculture a real green industry. At the same time, taking into account the needs of the Beijing-Tianjin-Hebei region transformation and development and market demand, we will establish a number of modern leisure farms integrating planting, breeding, leisure and vacation, craft production, catering and accommodation, product sales, and entertainment, and promote the transformation of the existing farms featured with sightseeing and picking into large-scale modern leisure farms, pursuing integration and development of the primary, secondary and tertiary industries in rural areas, and making contributions to improvement of ecological environment and quality of life in the Beijing-Tianjin-Hebei region.

Under the existing fiscal system, urban development and the construction of industrial parks are more economically beneficial compared to agricultural production and rural development. Therefore, in order to optimize the "production-living-ecological" space, it is essential to establish a comprehensive ecological compensation mechanism that encompasses vertical, horizontal, and market-oriented approaches. This mechanism should provide compensation for water conservation areas, agricultural reserves, ecological parks, and important ecological functional areas, enabling these regions to thrive and share in the fruits of reform and development even without being developed. The coordinated development of the Beijing-Tianjin-Hebei region should embody the concept of "undeveloped development", "undeveloped prosperity", or "undeveloped affluence". Currently, the region can take the lead in conducting a comprehensive assessment of ecological value and use the size and changes of this value as an important criterion for ecological compensation. In addition to increasing financial support from the central and provincial governments, it is also necessary to implement pilot projects of horizontal and market-oriented ecological compensation mechanisms in this region.

Chapter 5
Further Progress in the Large-Scale Development of the Western Region

Since the launch of the strategy for the large-scale development of the western region[1] in 1999, local governments and relevant departments have responded with a range of supportive activities and measures. With the strong backing of national policies, the progress in developing the western region has been steady and impressive: significant increase in investment, gradual acceleration of regional economic growth, and a narrowing development gap between the eastern and western regions. However, it is important to note that the western development, being a long-term strategy for the great rejuvenation of the Chinese nation, requires our sustained and unwavering efforts to ensure ultimate success. In particular, as we further implement this strategy, there remain several problems that need immediate solutions and further investigation.

5.1 Geographical scope and connotation of the western development

5.1.1 Geographical scope

The geographical scope of the western region varies in various periods. In the Seventh Five-year Plan period, the State Planning Commission classified the whole country into three major economic regions, namely the eastern coastal, central, and western regions. This classification was based on the distance from the coastline and indicators of economic development. At that time, the western region covered nine provinces: Shaanxi, Gansu, Ningxia, Qinghai, and Xinjiang in the northwest, and Sichuan (including Chongqing), Yunnan, Guizhou, and Tibet in the southwest. And this figure turned into 10 after Chongqing became a municipality directly under the central

---

[1] For the sake of conciseness, the "strategy for the large-scale development of the western region" is abbreviated as "the Strategy" in most instances throughout this chapter. —*Tr.*

government in March 1997. The zoning method and outcomes significantly influenced China's subsequent division of economic zones. In the Ninth Five-year Plan, the State Planning Commission continued with this zoning method, referring to the central region and western region collectively as the central and western regions.

Clearly, the early zoning of these three major economic regions was determined both by their respective geographical locations and levels of economic advancement. Yet this dual-standard zoning method obscures the real inter-provincial disparities within each region. For example, in 1999, the GRP per capita in Guangxi accounted for only 13.5% of that in Shanghai and 35.4% of that in Guangdong. Due to such significant disparities, the Ministry of Agriculture adopted the comprehensive development level as the basis for classifying regions when formulating policies for the development of township enterprises. Consequently, Guangxi, Hainan, and Inner Mongolia were categorized as part of the western region, while Shaanxi and Sichuan (including Chongqing) were placed in the central region. In February 1993, the State Council issued the Decision on Accelerating the Development of Township Enterprises in the Central and Western Regions, which also employed this zoning approach. However, this method compromised the geographical unity of the regions, hindering the comprehensive development of the southwest and northwest regions, particularly when Shaanxi and Sichuan (including Chongqing) were designated outside the western region.

In the academic community in China, there exists a widely embraced concept known as the Great West, which comprises ten provinces located in the southwest and northwest of China. It also includes Guangxi in the south and Inner Mongolia in the north. This concept has gained much popularity over time. Firstly, similar to the southwestern and northwestern regions, both Guangxi and Inner Mongolia are also home to diverse minority ethnic groups and face challenges for economic and social development. Secondly, due to their geographical proximity to and historical connections, Guangxi and Inner Mongolia share similarities with the southwest and northwest regions in terms of regional economy, social norms, and cultural features. Therefore, it is logical to include these two autonomous regions in the western region and integrate them into the national policy of large-scale development in the western region.

For this reason, in the early days of launching the initiative, the Western Development Office of the State Council[1] explicitly brought Guangxi and Inner

---

[1] The abbreviation of the Office of the Leading Group for Western Regional Development of the State Council, established in 2000 and abolished in 2008. Relevant functions were merged into the Western Development Department of the National Development and Reform Commission.

Mongolia into the regional scope of the western development, thus forming a strategic pattern of developing the extended western region on a large scale. Therefore, when it comes to the strategy for developing the west, the geographical scope of the western region is usually defined as comprising those 12 provinces, autonomous regions and municipalities, including Guangxi and Inner Mongolia. It spans a vast land area of 6.85 million square kilometers, constituting around 71.4% of China's total land area. In 2016, the resident population in the region reached 374 million, accounting for 27.1% of China's total population; and the regional GDP amounted to RMB15.65 trillion, representing 20.3% of the national total.

It should be pointed out that in addition to the 12 provinces, autonomous regions and municipalities mentioned above, the initiative of the western development also includes Enshi Tujia and Miao Autonomous Prefecture in Hubei Province, Xiangxi Tujia and Miao Autonomous Prefecture in Hunan Province, and Yanbian Korean Autonomous Prefecture in Jilin Province, thus forming a "10+2+3" regional pattern. During the implementation process, the State Council has also extended the favorable policy for developing the western region to certain underdeveloped or impoverished areas in the central, northeastern, and eastern regions. For example, in January 2007, the State Council made it clear that 243 counties (cities, districts) in the central region would enjoy policies similar to those for the development of the western region; In December 2010, in the Plan for Ecological Protection and Economic Transformation in Greater and Lesser Khingan Forest Area (2010-2020) approved by the State Council, it was made clear that when arranging central budget investment and other relevant central special investments in infrastructure, ecological construction, environmental protection, poverty alleviation and development, and social undertakings, Greater and Lesser Khingan Forest Area would enjoy the favorable policy for the large-scale development of the western region. In June 2012, the State Council also granted Ganzhou city the same right in its document titled Several Opinions on Supporting the Revitalization and Development of Gannan and Other Former Central Soviet Areas. Since 2014, the government has extended the application of the policy for developing the western region to include 13 former Central Soviet districts and counties in Guangdong Province. This expansion applies to the allocation of central budget investment and foreign preferential loans as well as to the subsidy provision for investments in water conservancy.

5.1.2   The background of the western development

As early as the middle and late 1980s, some Chinese scholars proposed to speed up the development of the western region (Guo Fansheng, Zhu Jianzhi, 1985; Wei Houkai, 1987). In the early 1990s, Deng Xiaoping clearly put forward the strategic thought of "Two Overall Situations", holding that when the national development reaches a certain level, conceivably when the whole country has achieved a moderately prosperity by the end of the 20th century, more efforts should be made to help the central and western regions to accelerate their development. Since 1991, the central government has begun to prioritize the coordinated development of regional economies, and has successively adopted a series of policies and measures, such as opening up border areas, regions along rivers, and interior provincial capitals to the outside world, accelerating the development of township enterprises in the central and western regions, to promote the economic development of the central and western regions.

At the turn of the century, then President Jiang Zemin emphasized from a comprehensive perspective that the western development initiative is a significant national development strategy. In August 1997, Jiang put forward in his instructions on the Investigation Report on Controlling Soil Erosion and Building Ecological Agriculture in Northern Shaanxi that "(let's) recreate a breathtaking scenery in the northwestern region of China". During his visit to Shaanxi in June 1999, he further stated that "we must expedite the development of the central and western regions without delay, with particular emphasis on intensifying our efforts to advance the large-scale development of the western region". This was the first occasion where China's top leadership has officially introduced the concept of "the large-scale development of the western region". On September 22, the Decision of the Central Committee of the Communist Party of China on Several Major Issues Concerning the Reform and Development of State-owned Enterprises adopted by the Fourth Plenary Session of the 15th CPC Central Committee formally proposed that "the state should implement the strategy for the large-scale development of the western region". On September 29, Jiang further emphasized at the Central Working Conference about Nationality Affairs that "to promote the large-scale development of the western region is a major strategic task for China's development in the next century". Afterwards, Jiang reiterated multiple times the readiness to accelerate the development of the central and western regions, especially the development of the western region. The term "readiness" here primarily pertains to the following conditions.

Firstly, China's remarkable progress in terms of national strength and living standards over the past 20 years of the reform and opening up has made it both necessary and feasible to prioritize coordinated regional development. In 1999, China's GDP reached RMB8,191.09 billion, with a per capita GDP of RMB6,534, reflecting significant growth of 5.73 times and 4.22 times respectively compared to 1978. If calculated in accordance to the current average exchange rate of renminbi to US dollar, the per capita GDP amounted to US$789, surpassing the World Bank's minimum threshold of US$761 for middle-income economies (World Bank, 1999). In the same year, the per capita disposable income of urban households in China reached RMB5,854, while that of rural households reached RMB2,210. These figures represented an increase of 2.61 times and 3.38 times respectively compared to 1978. Furthermore, the impoverished rural population in China has decreased from 250 million in 1978 to 34.12 million by the end of 1999 (using 1978 as the benchmark). With these achievements, China has possessed sufficient capability of mobilizing its efforts to address the growing development gap between the eastern and western regions.

Secondly, with its location advantages and the support of national policies, the eastern region has achieved sustained and high-speed economic growth since the reform and opening up, which has basically equipped itself with the mechanism and capacity of ensuring self-development. From 1980 to 1999, the region experienced an average annual GDP growth rate of 12.0%. Notably, between 1991 and 1999, this growth rate surged to an impressive 14.2%. This remarkable progress exemplified the establishment of a robust self-development mechanism in the eastern region, enabling it to achieve rapid economic development and foster self-reliance by the end of the 20th century. In 1999, the GRP per capita in the eastern region reached US$1,303. Thus, the eastern region has already transitioned into a middle-income economy as defined by the World Bank, and Shanghai, Shenzhen, Xiamen with GRP per capita approaching or exceeding US$4,000 at that time, was starting to cross the threshold of the upper middle-income stage. Therefore, even if the country shifts its development focus to the central and western regions, the eastern region will still be able to maintain enough momentum for relatively rapid growth through relying on its self-development mechanism.

In addition, accelerating the economic development of backward areas is also a common practice in developed market economies. The experience of those economies shows that, the spontaneous action of market forces tends to produce a kind of regional cumulative circular causal effect, which leads to the flow of production factors such as capital, technology and talents from backward areas with slow growth to prosperous areas with rapid growth. That is to say, the spontaneous power of the market tends to widen but rather than bridge the development gap between regions (Myrdal, 1957), at least in the initial and middle stages of economic development. In pursuit of balanced regional development, many governments around the world have implemented counter-market regulations since the 1930s, taking measures such as financial assistance, tax incentives, credit facilitation, technological advancements, and improved information services to actively bolstering the economic progress of underdeveloped regions, like the Tennessee River Basin and Appalachia in the United States, Hokkaido in Japan, and the economically deprived southern regions of Italy. In these countries, the central government mostly focuses the national regional policies on those "problem areas" facing many difficulties and being in urgent need of aids, especially backward low-income areas and recession areas stuck in high unemployment.

Therefore, the decision made by the central government at the turn of the century to expedite the growth of the central and western regions through implementing the strategy can be seen as an extension and enhancement of Deng Xiaoping's strategic ideas. These strategic ideas, namely "those who get rich first help and drive others to get rich later, so that common prosperity can be achieved" and "Two Overall Situations", form a significant component of the Deng Xiaoping Theory. The implementation of western development implies a significant adjustment in China's state strategy for regional development. Previously, the focus was primarily on supporting the eastern coastal region, but now the emphasis is shifting towards supporting the development of the central and western regions, with particular attention to the western regions. As a crucial state strategy in the 21st century, the development of the western region holds a priority position in China's master strategy for coordinated regional development, plays a fundamental role in the construction of a socialist harmonious society, and occupies a distinct position in sustainable development.

5.1.3　Specific meanings of the large-scale development of the western region

Despite its relatively low level of economic and social development, the western region of China has undergone significant transformation over the course of thousands of years, rendering it markedly distinct from the "westward movement" or western development that followed the American War of Independence. The western region is home to numerous ethnic minority groups and has a rich cultural heritage. In particular, the Guanzhong area, renowned as one of the birthplaces of Chinese culture, has experienced long periods of prosperity in history and exerted substantial influence on China's politics, economy, and culture. Therefore, in a new historical context, the implementation of the western development has three specific meanings.

First of all, large-scale development of the western region means redevelopment. Since the founding of the PRC, in order to change the serious imbalance in the distribution of productive forces left over from the past, the Chinese government has organized large-scale western development twice. The first occurred during the First Five-year Plan period and the second, during the "Third Front" Construction period. Especially during the latter period, the state invested hundreds of billions of yuan in the western region to build a large number of new industrial bases, large- and medium-sized SOEs and scientific research institutions, thus laying the foundation for industrialization in the western region. After over five decades of development, the western region had achieved a robust economic foundation experienced noticeable improvements in composite economic strength and living standards by the end of the 20th century. In such circumstances, the strategy proposed by the central government should not be regarded as mere "development" in the conventional sense, but rather as a form of "redevelopment", carrying the specific meaning of "further accelerating development", "redeveloping", or "deep development".

Secondly, the concept of the large-scale development of the western region demonstrates a determination towards all-round development, and its implementation goes beyond just environmental measures such as tree planting and grass seeding, as well as infrastructure development. From both domestic and international experiences, it is evident that the development of any region, including the western region as envisioned by the central government, should be approached in a comprehensive and integrated manner. The concept bears a very wide range of connotations, including not only ecological environment protection and infrastructure construction, but also the all-round development of economy, society, science and technology, and education. Therefore, it should be regarded as an overall and comprehensive concept, and some comprehensive policies and measures should be taken to speed up the comprehensive development of the western region, so as to finally realize the long-term goal of western modernization.

Finally, the concept of the large-scale development of the western region signifies a commitment to long-term development, and its execution is a daunting and challenging task that will span across centuries. Based on the current development situation in the western region, it is estimated that it will require a minimum of 40 to 50 years for the region to achieve comprehensive modernization, bridge the development gap with the eastern region, or surpass the developed areas in the east. Such progress can never be accomplished within a five-year plan or even a ten-year plan (Wang Luolin, 2002). Enhancing the protection of the ecological environment and advancing infrastructure construction are crucial prerequisites and foundations for the successful execution of the western development initiative. From a long-term development perspective, the key to effectively implementing the western development lies in accelerating the pace of industrialization and urbanization, while leveraging scientific and technological advancements and institutional innovations to invigorate the entire western region. This will facilitate the optimization and upgrading of the regional industrial structure, ultimately fostering all-round development and sustainable prosperity in the regional economy and society.

5.2   Objectives and policy measures of the large-scale development of the western region

Implementing the Strategy is an important strategic task for China's development in the 21st century. In February 2002, The Comprehensive Plan for Western Development During the 10th Five-Year Plan Period issued by the State Planning Commission and the Western Development Office of the State Council set the overall strategic objectives of the western development: After several generations of hard work, by the middle of the 21st century when the whole country basically realizes modernization, we will have fundamentally put an end to the backwardness of the western region, significantly narrowed the regional development gap, and built a new west with economic prosperity, social stability, ethnic solidarity, scenic beauty and common affluency. This plan has made a comprehensive planning on the strategic objectives, main tasks, and key areas for the development of the western region during the 10th Five-year Plan period, with particular emphasis on infrastructure development, ecological conservation, environmental protection, industrial restructuring, scientific and technological progress, education, and social programs. Subsequently, the NDRC and other relevant departments compiled the 11th, the 12th, and the 13th Five-year Plan for the large-scale development of the western region, in which the strategic objectives, key areas, and main tasks in each period were clearly defined. According to the 13th Five-year Plan, the overall objective was that, by 2020, the western region would have achieved the goal of building a moderately prosperous society in all respects in synchronization with the whole country, and at the same time, gain sufficient momentum for the region's sustained and sound economic growth.

In terms of the choice of spatial patterns and key areas for development, the Comprehensive Plan for Western Development During the 10th Five-Year Plan Period proposed to start with developing key economic zones and then extend over time to neighboring areas, and that was why the Western Lanzhou-Lianyungang and Lanzhou-Xinjiang Economic Belt, the Yangtze River Upstream Economic Belt, and the Nanning-Guiyang-Kunming Economic Region were chosen for prior development. In reality, it was indeed a challenging task to develop these "two belts and one region" when considering factors such as population, industry, and urban agglomeration. Therefore, the 11th Five-Year Plan for the Development of the Western Region decided to promote such key economic zones as Chengdu-Chongqing, Guanzhong-Tianshui, and Beibu Gulf Rim (Guangxi) to take the lead in pursuing development and then to serve as strategic highlands in driving the development of the western region. For this, the NDRC successively organized the preparation of the Development Plan for the Guangxi Beibu Gulf Economic Zone, the Development Plan for the Guanzhong-Tianshui Economic Zone, and the Regional Plan for the Chengdu-Chongqing Economic Zone. Based on the network approach to development, the 13th Five-Year Plan for the Development of the Western Region proposed to build an overall spatial pattern taking the western sections of the Land Bridge, the Beijing-Tibet Channels, the Yangtze River-Sichuan-Tibet, the Shanghai-Kunming, and the Pearl River-Xijiang River passages as five horizontal axes, Baotou-Kunming and Hohhot-Nanning passages as two vertical axes, and key border areas as the outer ring. At the same time, to avoid the poor effect of the previous Generalized System of Preferences policies, the western development plan placed more weight on classified guidance since the 11th Five-year Plan, in which key economic zones, metropolitan areas, resource-rich areas, key border port towns and areas with large ethnic minority populations were identified. Later in the 12th Five-year Plan, key areas for development were classified into key economic zones, major agricultural production areas, key ecological areas, open border areas, and areas of extreme poverty; and in the 13th Five-year Plan, into key innovation pilot areas, green development demonstration areas, inland and border open pilot areas, and areas fighting for moderate prosperity in all respects.

In order to realize the strategic objectives and complete the main tasks mentioned above, the central government formulated and implemented a series of policies and measures. For example, in October 2000, the State Council issued the Notice on Implementing Several Policies and Measures for the Large-scale Development of the Western Region; in August 2001, the Western Development Office of the State Council issued the Opinions on Implementing Several Policies and Measures for the Large-scale Development of the Western Region; in March 2004, the State Council issued Several

Opinions on Further Promoting the Large-Scale Development of the Western Region to specify the policies and measures for the development of the western region from 10 aspects; in June 2010, the CPC Central Committee and the State Council issued Several Opinions on Deeply Implementing the Strategy for the Large-Scale Development of the Western Region to clarify the overall requirements, development goals, key tasks and policy measures for further promoting the development of the western region in the second decade. Relevant departments also introduced a series of relevant policies and measures, which mainly focused on the following aspects.

5.2.1   Policy on infrastructure construction

The accelerated development of infrastructure serves as a crucial cornerstone for the western development strategy. Ever since its initiation, the Chinese government has focused on expediting the construction of water conservancy, transportation, communication, energy, and other types of infrastructure in both urban and rural areas within the region. This concerted effort aims to effectively foster the development and promote the region's openness. For example, in terms of water conservancy, the Western Development Office of the State Council, the Ministry of Water Resources and the State Planning Commission jointly issued the Outline of Water Conservancy Development Plan in the Western Region in January 2002, and the Ministry of Water Resources issued the 12th Five-Year Plan for Water Conservancy Development in the Western Region, and continued to increase investment in water conservancy infrastructure in the west in 2012. From 2000 to 2008, the central water conservancy construction investment in the region amounted to RMB106.8 billion, with an average annual rate of 21%, much higher than the 11% of the national total of the same kind in the same period; and in 2012, it allocated RMB68.2 billion, accounting for 43% of the national total. During the 2011-2016 period, total water conservancy investment completed in the region amounted to RMB911.91 billion, accounting for 34.5% of the national total. In terms of transportation, the focus was on to the construction of highways, railways, airports, natural gas trunk pipelines, and inland water transportation in the region. A number of major projects have been completed, including the west-east gas transmission, the expansion of airports, the Qinghai-Tibet railway, and the High-speed Railways of Lanzhou-Xinjiang, Shanghai-Kunming, Guiyang-Guangzhou, Nanning-Guangzhou, Lanzhou-Chongqing, and Chengdu-Chongqing, thus forming a comprehensive transportation network with high-speed railways and highways as the backbone. From 2000 to 2016, the western region gained 28,900 kilometers of new railways under operation and 1,372,900 kilometers of new highways, accounting for 43.7% and 41.0% of the national total, respectively. Notably, 1,196,900 kilometers of classified highways were completed, with 45,100 kilometers being new expressways, accounting for 39.0% and 37.9% of the national total, respectively. In addition, China also increased its investment in infrastructure in western rural areas, implementing the Construction of County-level Highway Asphalt Pavements Project, the Light up Every Township Project and the Project for Radio and TV Coverage in Each Village, and strengthening the construction of small- and medium-size facilities dealing with water supply and conservancy, roads in poor counties, power grid reconstruction and other projects. As of 2016, the state had started a total of 300 key projects for the development of the western region, with a total investment of RMB6.35 trillion (see Table 5-1). Among them, 30 new key projects were started in 2016, with a total investment of RMB743.8 billion into major infrastructure programs such as railways, highways, large-scale water conservancy hubs, and energy bases in the region.

Table 5-1   Newly launched key projects for the large-scale
development of the western region

Year	Number of projects	Investment (RMB bn)	Year	Number of projects	Investment (RMB bn)
2000	10	108.5	2009	18	468.9
2001	12	202.6	2010	23	682.2
2002	14	332.4	2011	22	207.9
2003	14	130.9	2012	22	577.8
2004	10	76.9	2013	20	326.5
2005	10	136.0	2014	33	835.3
2006	12	165.4	2015	30	768.7
2007	10	151.6	2016	30	743.8
2008	10	436.1	Total	300	6,351.5

Source: National Development and Reform Commission of the People's Republic of China.

5.2.2   Policy on ecological conservation and environmental protection

Since the implementation of the strategy, China has increased budgetary support to improve the production conditions and ecological environment in the western region by carrying out projects to return farmland to forests and grasslands ("grain for green"), to green barren hills and deserts, to prevent and control desertification, to protect virgin forests, to restore and build natural grasslands, and to exercise comprehensive control over soil erosion in a planned and step-by-step manner. The "grain for green" project launched in 1999 was one of major ecological restoration programs in China. In

September 2000, the State Council issued Several Opinions on Further Improving the Pilot Work of Turning Marginal Farmland to Forests and Grasslands, which set forth relevant requirements and regulations for the pilot "grain for green" work and defined the state-level subsidy standards. Specifically, each *mu*[1] of farmland returned in the upper reaches of the Yangtze River and in the upper and middle reaches of the Yellow River received an annual subsidy of 150kg and 100kg of grain (raw grain), respectively. In addition, there was a cash subsidy of RMB20 per *mu* and a seedling fee subsidy of RMB50 per *mu*. The duration of grain and cash subsidies was set at five years for economic forest and eight years for ecological forest. In April 2002, the State Council issued Several Opinions on Further Perfecting the Policies and Measures of Turning Marginal Farmland to Forests to broaden the geographical coverage of the subsidy policy. With the standards for cash subsidies as well as for seedlings and afforestation fees unchanged, the grain subsidy of 150kg per *mu* expanded to cover the Yangtze River Basin and its southern regions, and that of 100kg, expanded to include the Yellow River Basin and its northern regions. The duration of grain and cash subsidies for turning grass would be two years, while turning economic forests would receive subsidies for five years, and turning ecological forest would receive subsidies for eight years. By the end of 2006, a total of 139 million *mu* of uncultivated land had been reforested, while 225 million *mu* of unproductive hills and wasteland had been successfully afforested and designated for conservation purposes. In 2007, the State Council made the decision shift the emphasis of the "grain for green" project from comprehensive promotion to consolidation of achievements. This involved extending and adjusting direct subsidies to farmers who had returned farmland to forest. Additionally, the central government established a special fund to support the consolidation of achievements in this regard. From 2008 to 2011, the central government further allocated a total of RMB46.2 billion of special funds to consolidate the "grain for green" achievements. In January 2014, the CPC Central Committee and the State Council issued Several Opinions on Comprehensively Deepening Rural Reform and Accelerating Agricultural Modernization, proposing that "in 2014, our 'grain for green' project will persist, with a specific focus on regions characterized by steep-slope farmland, severely desertified farmland, and crucial water source areas". In the same year, the Overall Plan for a New-Round Turning Marginal Farmland to Forests and Grasslands approved by the State Council stated that by 2020, about 42.4 million *mu* of eligible sloping farmland and severely desertified

---

[1] *mu*, a Chinese unit of area (equal to 1/15 of a hectare or 1/6 of an acre) — *Tr.*

land would have been returned to forest and grass; the state set the task of turning 5 million *mu* of farmland to grasslands in 2014; 10 million *mu* in 2015; and 15.1 million *mu* in 2016. According to the plan, the state-level subsidy standard was set at RMB1,500 per *mu* for turning farmland to forests and RMB800 per mu for turning to grasslands. And the latter standard was raised to RMB1,000 per *mu* in December 2015. Furthermore, as part of the implementation of the western development strategy, the government has expedited the construction of nature reserves in the western region. Notably, it has approved several pilot projects, including Three-River Source National Park, Giant Panda National Park, Patatson National Park, and Qilian Mountain National Park.

5.2.3   Policy on industrial restructuring

With its abundance of energy, minerals, tourism, agriculture, and animal husbandry resources, the western region possesses significant potential for the development of distinctive and advantageous industries. As early as May 2006, the Western Development Office of the State Council, along with five other departments, jointly released the Opinions on Promoting the Development of Characteristic Industries with Advantages in the Western Region. This document identified six specific industries as key areas for development, namely the energy and chemical industry, the development and processing of important minerals, characteristic agriculture and animal husbandry and their respective processing, major equipment manufacturing, high-tech industries, and the tourism industry.

In August 2010, the State Council issued the Guiding Opinions on Undertaking Industrial Transfer in the Central and Western Regions to encourage these two regions to develop industries that are characteristic and advantageous based on their local conditions, and to offer corresponding policy support in taxation, finance, investment and land. For the same aim, the State Economic and Trade Commission[1] and other departments jointly issued the Catalogue of Advantageous Industries for Foreign Investment in the Central and Western Region in June 2000. This catalogue underwent revisions by the NDRC and the Ministry of Commerce in 2004, 2008, 2013, and 2017. In August 2014, the NDRC formulated and promulgated the Catalogue of Encouraged Industries in the Western Region to implement differentiated industrial policies. Additionally, relevant departments developed specific policies for certain industries.

---

[1] The institution was abolished in March 2003, and relevant functions were merged into the newly established Ministry of Commerce and the NDRC.

In terms of agriculture development, the Ministry of Agriculture issued two guiding documents in December 2002 and in November 2015. The former, Opinions on Accelerating the Development of Characteristic Agriculture in the Western Region, defined the significance, general approaches, key tasks, and policy measures of accelerating the development of characteristic agriculture in the western region, and the latter, Guiding Opinions on the Adjustment of Corn Structure in the "sickle bend" Area, proposed to reduce the corn planting area by more than 50 million *mu* in the "sickle bend" area[1] by 2020, including 10 million *mu* in the cold and cool areas in the northeast, 30 million *mu* in the farming-pastoral ecotone in the north, 5 million *mu* in the sandstorm arid areas in the northwest and 5 million *mu* in the rocky desertification areas in the southwest. With regard to the construction of energy bases, the focus was on the West-East Gas Transmission Project and West-East Power Transmission Project, highlighting the development, comprehensive utilization, and outward transmission of oil and gas in Shaanxi-Gansu-Ningxia, Tarim Basin, Tsaidam Basin, Sichuan-Chongqing regions, and the construction of hydropower bases in the southwest. The state also accelerated the construction of China-Kazakhstan, China-Russia, China-Mongolia and China-Myanmar and other international oil and gas pipelines with strategic significance. In terms of industrial development, at the beginning of the western development, the State Planning Commission released its Guiding Opinions on Industrial Restructuring and Development in the Western Region During the 10th Five-Year Plan Period. The State Economic and Trade Commission formulated the Guiding Opinions on the Adjustment of the Industrial Structure in the Northwest Region During the 10th Five-Year Plan Period. Furthermore, the State Planning Commission also implemented the High-tech Industrialization Special Project in the Western Region from 2000 onwards to support the development of high-tech industries in the West.

In terms of service industry development, the China National Tourism Administration and other departments jointly compiled the Investment Plan for Tourism in the Western Region (2003-2007).

5.2.4　Policy on internal and external opening

China has implemented a series of policies and measures to attract more foreign

---

[1] Its scope includes the cold and cool areas in northeast China, the ecotone between agriculture and animal husbandry in north China, the sandstorm area in northwest China, the area along Taihang Mountain and the rocky desertification area in southwest China. It is called the "sickle bend" area because it is distributed in a sickle bend from northeast to north China-southwest-northwest in the topographic map.

investment to the central and western regions. For instance, 70% of preferential loans granted by international organizations, particularly international financial institutions, were allocated to these regions. From 2001 to 2010, state-encouraged foreign-invested enterprises in the west were only required to pay 15% of the total corporate income taxes. Newly established foreign enterprises engaged in sectors such as transportation, electricity, and water conservancy in the western region might qualify for exemption from corporate income tax for the first two years of profit-making, and a 50% reduction for the following three years. Moreover, self-use equipment imported as part of the total investment by foreign-invested enterprises in encouraged and advantageous industries in the western region could be exempted from import duty and import VAT. Foreign-invested enterprises in the eastern region were also encouraged to reinvest in the central and western regions. Projects with foreign investment exceeding 25% were entitled to the same preferential treatment as foreign-invested enterprises. The West-East Gas Transmission Project was fully open to foreign investment. Furthermore, restrictions on the shareholding ratio of foreign investment in western China and the proportion of domestic banks' renminbi loans for fixed asset investment were appropriately relaxed. The requirements for operating years and registered capital for foreign investment in commercial projects in the western region were also relaxed. Following the implementation of "Income Tax Integration" [1] in 2008, foreign investments in encouraged projects in the western region continued to receive tax incentives until December 31, 2020. Additionally, in order to further promote all-round international openness, the government established 49 state-level economic and technological development zones, eight export processing zones, 16 comprehensive bonded zones, as well as the Chongqing Lianglu Cuntan Bonded Port Area and Guangxi Qinzhou Bonded Port Area in the western region. Moreover, pilot free trade zones were approved for development in Chongqing, Sichuan, and Shaanxi, while Ningxia and Guizhou were designated as inland open economy pilot zones. Furthermore, Chongqing and Chengdu were selected to develop cross-border electronic commerce comprehensive pilot zones.

In order to support the expansion and opening up of border areas, the National Ethnic Affairs Commission and other departments successively launched the Program

---

[1] The term refers to China's practice of integrating its Provisional Regulations of the People's Republic of China on Enterprises Income Tax and Income Tax Law of the People's Republic of China for Enterprises with Foreign Investment and Foreign Enterprises into one law—Enterprise Income Tax Law of the People's Republic of China, which ensured that China' domestic and foreign-invested enterprises would apply the same corporate income tax law, enjoying the same tax rate and tax incentives.

for Revitalizing Border Areas and Enriching the People During the 11th Five-year Plan Period, Action Plan to Revitalize Border Areas and Enrich the People (2011-2015), and the Program for Revitalizing Border Areas and Enriching the People During the 13th Five-year Plan. In December 2015, the State Council issued the Opinions on Several Policies and Measures to Support the Development and Opening up of Key Border Areas to adopt various measures to accelerate development and opening up of key border areas such as key development and opening-up pilot zones, border national ports, border cities, border economic cooperation zones and cross-border economic cooperation zones. Since the introduction of the border opening strategy in 1992, the State Council has successively approved several cities along the border, including Manzhouli, Erenhot, Yining, Bole, Tacheng, Wanding, Ruili, Hekou, Pingxiang, and Dongxing, to be open cities. Additionally, twelve border economic cooperation zones were established in the western region, namely Manzhouli, Erenhot, Pingxiang, Dongxing, Wanding, Hekou, Ruili, Lincang, Yining, Bole, Tacheng, and Jeminey. Furthermore, six key development and opening experimental zones have been approved in Dongxing, Pingxiang, Ruili, Mengla (Mohan), Manzhouli, and Erenhot. In addition to this, Kashgar and Khorgos Economic Development Zones were established, along with several cross-border economic cooperation zones such as China-Kazakhstan Khorgos International Border Cooperation Center, China-Laos Mohan-Moding Economic Cooperation Zone, China-Vietnam Pingxiang-Tongdeng Cross-border Economic Cooperation Zone, China-Vietnam Dongxing-Mangjie Cross-border Economic Cooperation Zone, and China-Mongolia Ebudug-Bayanhushu Cross-border Economic Cooperation Zone. These measures have significantly contributed to the successful opening up of the western region.

In terms of internal opening, the focus was on promoting regional cooperation by encouraging domestic capital, technology, talent, and intelligence to flow to the west region, and mobilizing social resources to participate in the western development. As early as May 2002, in order to attract private investment at home and abroad, the State Taxation Administration issued the Notice on Implementing Specific Implementation Opinions on Tax Policies Related to the Large-scale Development of the Western Region, offering western China specific preferential tax policies. For instance, the state-encouraged domestic enterprises in the western region were permitted to pay their enterprise income tax at a reduced rate of 15% from 2001 to 2010. Moreover, newly established domestic enterprises in such sectors as transportation, power, water conservancy, postal services, radio and television in the region were exempt from paying enterprise income tax during the initial two years of production and operation, with the tax rate being halved from the third to fifth year. To safeguard the ecological environment, the agricultural specialty income acquired from turning farmland to forest was exempt from agricultural specialty tax for a duration of 10 years, commencing from the year of income acquisition. Concurrently, in an effort to promote the transformation and industrial relocation in the western region, the State Council granted approval for the establishment of six national new areas in the region, namely Liangjiang in Chongqing, Lanzhou in Gansu, Xixian in Shaanxi, Gui'an in Guizhou, Tianfu in Sichuan, and Dianzhong in Yunnan. Furthermore, Sichuan and Xi'an were designated as two state-level comprehensive innovation and reform experimental zones. In addition, the NDRC sanctioned the establishment of state-level industrial relocation demonstration zones in the west, including Guidong in Guangxi, Chongqing along the Yangtze River, Shanxi-Shaanxi-Henan Yellow River Golden Triangle, Yinchuan-Shizuishan in Ningxia, Gansu Lanzhou-Baiyin Economic Zone in Gansu, and Guang'an in Sichuan.

5.2.5   Policy on science, education, and social development

In terms of the development of science and technology, relevant departments have implemented a range of policies and measures. The Ministry of Science and Technology has taken proactive steps by formulating guiding documents such as Several Opinions on Strengthening Science and Technology Work in the Western Region Development and Science and Technology Plan for Western Region Development During the 11th Five-year Plan Period. Additionally, the Ministry of Science and Technology, along with the State Planning Commission and the State Economic and Trade Commission, have allocated special funds for science and technology in the western region. These funds are specifically aimed at promoting the development of high-tech industries, technological innovation, and holistic governance over ecological environment. Moreover, numerous science and technology demonstration bases and high-tech incubators have been established in the western region to support projects such as agricultural industrialization, value-added transformation of resources, industrialization of traditional Chinese medicine, and the trial production of key new products. In July 2013, the NDRC and the Chinese Academy of Sciences jointly released the Action Plan for Science and Technology to Boost the Transformation and Development of the Western Region (2013-2020). Moreover, the State Council upgraded several qualified high-tech industrial development zones in the western region to national high-tech industrial development zones, aiming to promote scientific and technological innovation as well as the development of high-tech industries. Up to this point, there have been 35 state-level high-tech industrial development zones in western China, accounting for 22.4% of the national total. Since 2015, the State Council has also approved the establishment of national independent innovation demonstration zones in Chengdu High-tech Industrial Development Zone, Xi'an High-tech Industrial Development Zone, and Chongqing High-tech Industrial Development Zone. Additionally, the Ministry of Science and Technology has agreed to support the pilot construction of Guiyang Big Data Industry Technology Innovation Experimental Zone. The 13th Five-year Plan for the Development of the Western Region, released in January 2017, explicitly proposed to support the construction of pilot projects in such as Liangjiang New Area, Gui'an New Area, Zhongwei, Hohhot, and Yan'an to establish technological innovation pilot areas for the big data industry.

In terms of educational development, the steadfast increase in government support for education in the western region has propelled the education in the region to new heights. This was achieved through the implementation of the project of "Two Basics"[1] in the western region, the deepening of reforms regarding funding for rural compulsory education, as well as the implementation of initiatives such as the nutrition improvement plan, the school building safety project, the basic school conditions improvement plan for underprivileged rural schools, the special post plan for rural teachers, counterpart support, targeted enrollment, and other major measures. In order to accelerate the development of education in the western region, the Outline of the National Medium- and Long-Term Education Reform and Development Plan (2010-2020) issued by the CPC Central Committee and the State Council in 2010 proposed the implementation of the revitalization plan of higher education in the central and western regions and the counterpart support plan of eastern universities to western universities. In 2012, the Ministry of Education and the Ministry of Finance jointly launched a project to enhance the overall capabilities of universities located in the central and western regions. In provinces where there are no universities directly under the Ministry of Education, special support was provided to one top-tier university with the strongest academic resources, highest academic standards, and regional advantages in the respective area. The NDRC and the Ministry of Education also jointly initiated Basic Capacity Building

---

[1] A campaign to "basically" achieve universal coverage of the nine-year compulsory education and eradicate illiteracy among middle age and young people in the western area of China. —*Tr.*

Project of Universities in Central and Western China, focusing on supporting the development and construction of 100 local universities with characteristics and strengths in 24 provinces in the central and western regions. To ensure that the education in the central and western regions meets the standards necessary for achieving a moderately prosperous society in all respects by 2020, the Ministry of Education devised and executed the Action Plan for Accelerating the Development of Education in the Central and Western Region (2016-2020) in 2016, and the General Office of the State Council issued the Guiding Opinions on Accelerating the Development of Education in the Central and Western Regions, which outlined 150 specific projects and initiatives.

In terms of talent development, the Ten-year Plan for Talent Development in the Western Region was issued by the General Offices of the CPC Central Committee and the State Council in February 2002. This document clearly outlined the objectives, main tasks, organizational guarantees, and policy measures for talent development in the western region. Furthermore, in February 2007, the Opinions on Further Strengthening the Construction of Talent Team in the Western Region was issued, which presented nine opinions on further strengthening the construction of talent teams in the region. Additionally, relevant departments formulated and implemented corresponding policies and measures. For instance, the Notice on Implementing the Western Plan of College Students' Volunteer Service was jointly issued by the Central Committee of the Communist Youth League, the Ministry of Education, the Ministry of Finance, and the Ministry of Personnel in June 2003. This notice, effective from 2003, aimed to promote volunteer service in the western region among college graduates. The Ministry of Personnel encouraged and supported college graduates from the central and eastern regions to work in the western region, following the policy of "free to come and go". Other measures, like facilitating the exchange of cadres between the eastern and western regions, strengthening training of management experts in the western region, and encouraging eastern cities to offer assistance in personnel training for the western region also yielded positive outcomes and provided robust talent support for the development of the region.

In terms of health and culture construction, the state has increased its support for rural health infrastructure, family planning services and grass-roots cultural construction in the western region. It has organized and implemented projects such as the construction of hospitals, blood stations, family planning service networks and mobile service vehicles in poor counties, the construction of grass-roots cultural facilities, and radio and television coverage to support the development of medical, health, cultural and other social undertakings in the western region.

5.3 Evaluation on the effects of implementing the strategy

Since the initiation of the strategy for the large-scale development of the western region, the central government has significantly amplified its financial and policy assistance towards the western region. Between 2000 and 2012, the financial transfer payments from the central government to the western region reached RMB8.5 trillion and the central budget allocated over one trillion yuan for investment purposes in the western region, accounting for approximately 40% of the national total in both cases. The resolute backing of the central policy has facilitated the implementation of the strategy in a systematic and methodical manner, resulting in commendable achievements. However, certain prominent issues still persist in this process.

5.3.1 Achievements obtained in the large-scale development of the western region

Since the central government put forward the strategy for the large-scale development of the western region in 1999, the State Council and relevant departments have successively formulated and implemented a series of plans and policies and measures. With the strong support of relevant national policies, the work of developing the western region has been steadily advanced, and remarkable achievements have been made in economic and social development and ecological environment construction, which are embodied in the following aspects.

5.3.1.1 Steady increase in the proportion of fixed asset investment

From 2000 to 2016, the total investment in fixed assets in the western region grew at an average annual rate of 21.9%, which were 2.5 percentage points higher than the national average and also, 4.4 and 5.5 percentage points higher than that in the eastern and northeastern regions respectively. The implementation of the strategy for the large-scale development of the western region led to a steady increase in the growth rate of total investment in fixed assets in the western region during the first 10 years. Starting at 7.4% in 1999, it rose to 38.6% in 2009, surpassing both the national average of 30.4% and the eastern region's growth rate of 23.5% in that year, and ranking top among the four major regions. However, following this peak, the growth rate of investment in the western region exhibited a tendency to drop in light of the rapid decline in national investment growth. In 2016, the total investment in fixed assets in the western region increased by 11.9% against the previous year, a decline of 26.7 percentage points from 2009, but it remained the highest among the four major regions. Thanks to the sustained and rapid investment growth, the proportion of the total investment in fixed assets in the western region has steadily increased, rising from 18.2% in 1999 to 25.9% in 2016, which represented a growth of 7.8 percentage points over a span of 17 years (see Figure 5-1). In recent years, the joint efforts of investment and national policies have contributed much to the rapid progress in the construction of infrastructure and ecological environment in the western region, especially the transportation and communication facilities. By 2013, the forest coverage rate in the western region reached 17.49%, marking an increase of 7.17 percentage points compared to one decade ago.

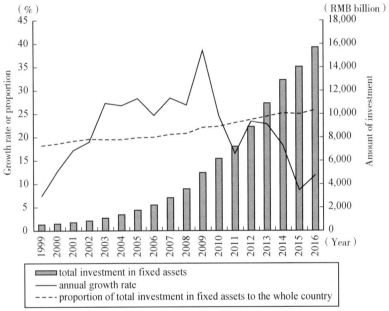

Figure 5-1   Growth rate of total investment in fixed asset in the western region and its proportion to the national total

Note: The data in this figure were calculated at current prices.

Source: Calculated according to the relevant data in *Comprehensive Statistical Data and Materials on 50 Years of New China* and the series of *China Statistical Abstract* over years.

5.3.1.2   High-speed growth of regional economy

Since the initiation of the strategy, the growth rate of the western region's GRP has consistently accelerated. It increased from 7.3% in 1999 to 14.9% in 2007. Despite being affected by the financial crisis in 2008, the growth rate slightly declined but still reached 13.1%, surpassing the national average and the eastern region by 1.1 and 1.9 percentage points, respectively. From 2009 to 2011, the region's GRP maintained a high-speed growth, with an annual growth rate exceeding 13.5%. Since 2012, as China's economy transitioned to a new normal, the region's growth rate has experienced a gradual decline, reaching 8.2% in 2016 from 12.5% in 2012. Yet the region still maintained the highest growth rate among the four major regions. From 2000 to 2016, the region's GRP grew at an average annual rate of 11.6%. Notably, between 2005 and 2011, the average growth rate reached 13.8%, making it the fastest-growing region in China. Thanks to the rapid development, the gap in growth rate between the western and eastern regions has been narrowing. By 2007, the economic growth rate in the western region had surpassed that of the eastern region by 0.3 percentage points. Since 2009, the growth rate in the western region has consistently exceeded the average level in other regions and the country as a whole. It is important to highlight that as a result of this rapid economic growth, the GRP per capita in the western region has also been increasing year by year. It rose from 59.2% in 2003 to 74.1% in 2016. Additionally, the proportion of the region's GRP in the total of all regions in China increased from 16.9% to 20.1% during the same period.

5.3.1.3　Rapid progress in regional industrialization

With strong policy support, the pace of industrialization in the western region has significantly accelerated since the initiation of the strategy. Between 1999 and 2011, the western region experienced rapid growth in the proportion of industrial added value to GRP, which increased from 32.9% to 43.0%, a rise of 10.1 percentage points. And in recent years, as China has entered the late stage of industrialization, this proportion exhibited a dramatic decline in all regions. Specifically, the eastern region reached its peak in 2006, the northeastern region in 2008, and, the central and western regions in 2011. Furthermore, the eastern, northeastern, and central regions exhibited a higher peak proportion, around 47%, compared to the western region which stood at merely 43.0%. Between 2011 and 2016, the western region witnessed a decline in this proportion from 43.0% to 33.8%. This reduction of 9.2 percentage points was second only to the northeastern region and surpassed that observed in the eastern and central regions (see Table 5-2). Up to this point, this proportion in the western region was lower than that in the eastern region and even lower than that in the central region. Evidently, the western region lagged behind in terms of economic development and its industrialization process remained incomplete. Consequently, the substantial decline in the proportion posed a challenge to the region's economic growth. Therefore, it was imperative to prevent the western region from encountering a similar scenario of "declining before becoming prosperous" that occurred in the northeastern region.

Table 5-2   Changes in the proportion of industrial
                          added value to GRP by region   Unit: %

Region	1999	2005	2006	2007	2008	2009	2010	2011	2012	2013	2014	2015	2016
Eastern	42.5	46.5	47.1	46.8	46.9	44.1	44.1	43.7	42.6	41.7	40.2	38.4	37.4
Northeast	42.9	44.0	45.1	45.8	47.3	43.5	46.2	46.8	44.4	43.4	41.5	37.1	31.6
Central	38.5	40.1	42.0	43.2	44.8	43.5	45.7	46.9	46.2	45.5	42.8	40.0	38.8
Western	32.9	35.3	37.9	39.3	41.1	39.7	42.2	43.0	42.0	41.0	38.7	35.6	33.8
Average	40.0	43.2	44.4	44.7	45.5	43.1	44.2	44.5	43.4	42.5	40.5	38.1	36.6

Source: Calculated according to the relevant data in *China Statistical Yearbook* over the years.

5.3.1.4   Significant improvement in residents' living standards

After more than a decade of development, the western region has made significant progress in its economic and social development, with a continuous enhancement of its comprehensive development capacity. From 1999 to 2016, the western region's GDP per capita increased rapidly from US$544 to US$6,299 and in relative terms (with the national average set at 100), it increased from 60.7% to 74.8%, an increase of 14.1 percentage points. Conversely, the central region only saw a 5.2 percentage point increase, while the eastern and northeastern regions experienced declines of 16.2 and 30.9 respectively. Currently, the western region's GDP per capita is steadily approaching that of the central region, and meanwhile, there has been significant income growth for both urban and rural residents in the western region. From 2014 to 2016, if calculated at current prices, the per capita disposable income of urban and rural residents in the western region increased from RMB13,890 to RMB18,407, with an average annual growth rate of 9.8%, which was 1.1, 2.1 and 1.7 percentage points higher than that in the eastern, northeastern, and central regions respectively (see Table 5-3). The relative level of per capita disposable income of urban and rural residents in the western region increased from 75.9% to 77.3%, an increase of 1.4 percentage points, while the relative level in other regions tended to decline. By 2016, the relative level of per capita disposable income of urban and rural residents in the western region had reached 85.1% and 80.2% respectively.

Table 5-3   Growth and relative level of per capita disposable
                   income of urban and rural residents by regions   Unit: %

Region	Per capita disposable income (RMB)				Annual growth rate (2014-2016)	Relative level of per capita disposable income (taking the average as 100)			
	2013	2014	2015	2016		2013	2014	2015	2016
National	18,310	20,167	21,996	23,821	9.2	100	100	100	100
Eastern	23,877	26,168	28,433	30,655	8.7	130.4	129.8	129.3	128.7
Northeast	17,893	19,600	21,010	22,352	7.7	97.7	97.2	95.5	93.8
Central	15,829	17,482	19,106	20,006	8.1	86.5	86.7	86.9	84.0
Western	13,890	15,343	16,833	18,407	9.8	75.9	76.1	76.5	77.3

Source: Calculated according to the relevant data in *China Statistical Yearbook* over the years.

5.3.1.5   Narrowed development gap between eastern and western regions

Since 2003, the sustained and rapid economic growth in the western region has led to a gradual narrowing of the relative gap in GRP per capita between the eastern and western regions, despite the ongoing expansion of the absolute gap. The GRP per capita in the western region was 63.0% lower than that in the eastern region in 2003, down to 60.7% in 2005 and 50.7% in 2010. This ratio further dropped to 43.2% in 2016, representing a significant decrease of 19.8 percentage points compared to 2003, and 17.0 percentage points compared to 1999, prior to the implementation of the Strategy. The widening of the absolute gap in GRP per capita in the eastern and western regions could be primarily attributed to the disparities in their development foundations. However, there has been a noticeable narrowing of the relative income gap in urban and rural residents between the eastern and western regions since 2007. In 2013, the per capita disposable income of urban and rural residents in the western region was 41.8% lower than that in the eastern region. This gap coefficient further decreased to 40.0% in 2016.

5.3.1.6   Noticeable enhancement in the degree of openness

Since the implementation of the strategy, the western region has witnessed rapid growth in its total export volume. Between 2001 and 2016, the region's total export volume increased at an average annual rate of 16.9%, surpassing the eastern region and the whole country by 2.7 and 2.6 percentage points respectively. Specifically, from 2001 to 2014, it gained an annual increase of 21.7%, ranking highest among the four major regions and exceeding the national average by 4.3 percentage points. However, from 2015 to 2016, amidst the overall decline in China's total export volume, the western region also experienced a decline surpassing that of the eastern and central regions. With the rapid growth of total exports, the western region's share in China's total export volume exhibited an upward trajectory, rising from 3.5% in 2004 to 6.9% in 2014, but fell back to 6.0% after 2015 (see Figure 5-2). At the same time, the actual utilization of foreign capital in the region also witnessed substantial growth, rising from US$1.941 billion in 2005 to US$11.571 billion in 2011, and maintaining a stable level of around US$10 billion ever since. This signifies a noticeable enhancement in the western region's degree of openness to the international community in recent years.

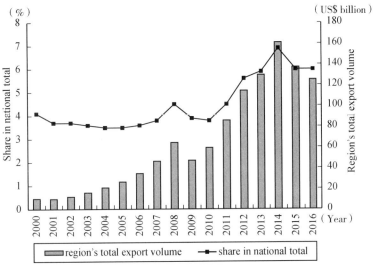

Figure 5-2   Changes in western region's total export volume and the share in national total

Source: Calculated according to the relevant data in *China Statistical Yearbook* over the year.

5.3.2   Key challenges facing the western development

However, it is worth noting that the western region is currently experiencing relatively low levels on both economic development and industrial growth. Infrastructure in the region remains relatively weak, and the ecological environment continues to deteriorate without any fundamental changes. This is particularly evident in impoverished rural areas where people still face significant challenges in their daily lives. In order to achieve the central government's vision of a modern and prosperous western region, characterized by social progress, stable livelihoods, national unity, pristine natural landscapes, and improved living standards, substantial and sustained efforts will be required in the future. Currently, the key challenges that the western development faces can be identified in the following areas.

5.3.2.1 The low level of industrial development

The western region exhibits a low level of industrial development, primarily characterized by a high proportion of mining and raw material industries, a short industrial chain, limited processing depth, and a low degree of comprehensive utilization. Moreover, the recent rapid expansion of heavy chemical industries, such as energy and raw materials, has further worsened the situation. In fact, some parts of the region have even witnessed a reversal of their industrial structure, leading to an increase in the prevalence of low-level structure. For instance, between 2001 and 2015, the proportion of resource industries in Inner Mongolia increased from 60.9% to 70.2%, representing a significant increase of 9.3 percentage points. [1] So far, specialized products with advantages in the region, such as raw coal, crude oil, natural gas, raw salt, finished sugar, coke, sulfuric acid, caustic soda, soda ash, agricultural nitrogen, phosphorus and potassium fertilizers, cement, power generation, and hydropower, are still primarily based on resources.

5.3.2.2 Investment-driven growth model

Since the initiation of the strategy, the rapid economic growth in the western region has been primarily propelled by resource exploitation and investment. Notably, the expansion of the resource-based heavy chemical industry has played a pivotal role in driving this growth. Based on the contribution of the three main drivers of economic growth in different regions, it is evident that investment played a significant role in the growth of the western region. Specifically, investment accounted for 71.6% of the region's GDP growth from 2000 to 2016. This percentage surpassed both the national average and the eastern region by 15.4 and 24.3 percentage points respectively, and it was also higher than that observed in the central and northeastern regions (see Table 5-4). This dominance of investment as the main driver of economic growth in the western region remained unchanged in any period. However, due to the limited capacity of the heavy chemical industry to absorb labor and the sluggish pace of urbanization, employment opportunities in the western region have grown at a relatively slow rate. Consequently,

---

[1] The statistical scope of resource industries includes mining industry, petroleum processing, coking and nuclear fuel processing industry, chemical raw materials and chemical products manufacturing industry, ferrous metal smelting and rolling processing industry, non-ferrous metal smelting and rolling processing industry, non-metallic mineral products industry, electricity and heat production and supply industry.

there is a severe shortage of new job opportunities, leading to a large-scale migration of surplus rural laborers to the eastern region in search of employment opportunities.

Table 5-4　　　　Contribution of three main drivers to GRP growth
by region from 2000 to 2016　　　　　Unit: %

Region	2000-2011			2012-2016			2000-2016		
	Final consumption expenditure	Gross capital formation	Net outflow of goods and services	Final consumption expenditure	Gross capital formation	Net outflow of goods and services	Final consumption expenditure	Gross capital formation	Net outflow of goods and services
Eastern	44.7	49.9	5.4	58.5	42.9	−1.4	49.9	47.3	2.9
Northeast	39.7	70.1	−9.8	130.8	2.7	−33.4	53.1	60.2	−13.3
Central	43.0	62.9	−5.9	59.7	61.6	−21.3	49.5	62.4	−11.9
Western	46.5	71.8	−18.3	61.6	71.4	−32.9	52.5	71.6	−24.1
National	44.3	58.8	−2.8	61.2	52.2	−13.4	50.6	56.2	−6.7

Source: Calculated according to the relevant data in *China Statistical Yearbook* over the years.

5.3.2.3　A big gap between urban and rural development

Since the implementation of the western development strategy, the western region has experienced a significant surge in urbanization. From 2000 to 2016, the urbanization rate in the western region rose rapidly from 28.68% to 50.20%, with an average annual increase of 1.35 percentage points, ranking second only to the central region. The urbanization gap between the western and eastern regions has begun to narrow, decreasing from 18.27 percentage points in 2010 to 15.74 percentage points in 2016. Alongside this rapid urbanization, the income gap between urban and rural areas in the western region has also begun to narrow since 2008. The ratio of per capita disposable income of urban residents to Net Income Per Capita of farmers decreased from 3.76 : 1 in 2006 to 3.32 : 1 in 2013. Furthermore, when considering per capita disposable income, the income ratio of urban and rural residents in western China declined from 2.94 : 1 in 2014 to 2.88 : 1 in 2016. However, it is worth noting that the income gap between urban and rural residents in the western region remains considerably higher than that in the eastern, central, and northeastern regions (see Table 5-5). Particularly, in 2016, the per capita disposable income ratio of urban and rural residents in Gansu, Guizhou, Yunnan, Qinghai, Tibet, and Shaanxi exceeded 3 : 1. This indicates the significant income disparity between urban and rural residents in the western region, with a prominent urban-rural dual structure that still persists.

Table 5-5   Changes in urban-rural income gap
by region from 2005 to 2016

Year	National	Eastern	Central	Western	Northeast
2005	3.22	2.83	2.98	3.69	2.58
2006	3.28	2.88	3.02	3.76	2.62
2007	3.33	2.90	3.03	3.73	2.64
2008	3.31	2.91	2.97	3.69	2.57
2009	7.73	2.93	3.00	3.72	2.63
2010	3.23	2.86	2.90	3.58	2.48
2011	3.13	2.75	2.81	3.46	2.35
2012	3.10	2.74	2.78	3.42	2.35
2013	3.03	2.69	2.71	3.32	2.31
2014	2.75	2.58	2.47	2.94	2.37
2015	2.73	2.57	2.46	2.91	2.38
2016	2.72	2.56	2.45	2.88	2.37

Note: The data from 2005 to 2013 represent the ratio of per capita disposable income of urban residents to Net Income Per Capita of farmers, and those from 2014 to 2016, the ratio of per capita disposable income of urban and rural residents.
Source: Calculated according to the relevant data in *China Statistical Yearbook* over the years.

5.3.2.4 Limited access to public service

The western region faced challenges in terms of economic development and local financial resources. In 2015, the per capita local fiscal revenue in the region only accounted for 69.2% of the national average, 52.4% of the eastern region, and 20.3% of Shanghai. This disparity in financial resources, combined with the underdeveloped infrastructure and limited public services, resulted in a low level of public service capacity at the local governments in the region, particularly those at the county and township levels. To date, the western region, especially rural areas, remote mountainous areas, and border areas, still faces challenges in terms of public service facilities such as transportation, communication, medical and health care, culture, tap water, and garbage disposal. These areas offer limited access to public services, still having a long way to go before achieving the central government's goal of equalizing access to basic public services across the country.

5.3.2.5 The prominent problem of rural poverty

As of 2016, based on the poverty line standards set in 2010, there were still 22.5 million rural individuals living in poverty in this region, accounting for 51.9% of the national impoverished rural population. Moreover, the incidence of poverty in western rural areas remained significantly higher than the national average of 4.5%, standing at 7.8%. Notably, provinces such as Guizhou, Yunnan, Guangxi, and Sichuan had a population of over 3 million living in poverty, while Gansu and Shaanxi, over 2 million. Additionally, the poverty incidence in Tibet, Xinjiang, Gansu, and Yunnan remained above 10% (see Table 5-6). The majority of persistently impoverished groups in the region reside in areas characterized by harsh natural conditions, including deep mountain regions, rocky mountain areas, alpine mountain areas, and Loess Plateau areas. These areas have limited resources and challenging natural conditions, leading to a high incidence of poverty and formidable obstacles to poverty eradication. Among the 14 contiguous poverty-stricken areas in China, the western region is home to most of them, with a high incidence of poverty. In 2016, the poverty incidence stood at 13.5% in the Wumeng Mountain area, 13.2% in Tibet, 12.7% in the areas with large Tibetan populations of Sichuan and southern Xinjiang, 12.4% in the Liupan Mountain area, 12.2% in the border mountainous area of western Yunnan, and 11.9% in the rocky desertification area of Yunnan, Guizhou, and Guangxi. All these figures exceed the average poverty level of 10.5% in all areas of the region.

Table 5-6   Impoverished rural population and poverty incidence
in the western region in 2016

Region	Poor population (thousand)	Poverty incidence (%)	Region	Poor population (thousand)	Poverty incidence (%)
National	43,350	4.5	Yunnan	3,730	10.1
Western	22,500	7.8	Tibet	340	13.2
Inner Mongolia	530	3.9	Shaanxi	2,260	8.4
Guangxi	3,410	7.9	Gansu	2,620	12.6
Chongqing	450	2.0	Qinghai	310	8.1
Sichuan	3,060	4.4	Ningxia	300	7.1
Guizhou	4,020	11.6	Xinjiang	1,470	12.8

Source: Sorted in accordance with *China Statistical Abstract* (2017) and data from National Bureau of Statistics.

5.3.2.6   Dominance of high-carbon economy

Due to the prevalence of resource-based industries, particularly energy and heavy chemical industries, the western region remained in the stage of industrialization promotion. Coupled with low levels of technology and management, this has labelled its economic development as "high consumption and high emission", that is, a high carbon economy. In 2015, the energy consumption per RMB10,000 of GDP in the western region was 0.85 tons of standard coal, which was 37.1% higher than the national average, and 70.0%, 30.8%, and 18.1% higher than that in the eastern, central, and northeastern regions respectively. Particularly in the provinces in northwest China, the energy consumption per RMB10,000 of GDP exceeded 1.0 tons of standard coal. For instance, Ningxia, Qinghai, Xinjiang, Gansu, and Inner Mongolia recorded 1.86 tons, 1.71 tons, 1.68 tons, 1.11 tons, and 1.05 tons of standard coal respectively. The discharge of "three wastes" per unit of industrial added value in the western region also surpassed the national average and that in the eastern region. The high-carbon economy in the western region was closely associated with its development stage, industrial structure, and role in the national division of labor.

5.3.2.7 High costs associated with logistics and taxes

Due to its long distance from coastal ports and major consumption markets, inadequate industrial supporting facilities, and underdeveloped productive service industry, the western region faces significant challenges with high logistics costs. These costs severely hindered the influx of private capital and impeded business development. Furthermore, the average industrial tax burden in the region has consistently exceeded that in the eastern region. In 2008, taxes paid by enterprises above designated size in the region, including product sales taxes, surcharges, and value-added tax, accounted for 7.13% of product sales revenue. This figure was 48.9% and 79.6% higher than the national and eastern averages, respectively. Although the tax burden gap has narrowed in recent years, it has not been fundamentally resolved. In 2015, taxes paid by industrial enterprises above designated size in the western region accounted for 5.0% of product sales revenue, still 21.6% and 33.7% higher than the national and eastern region averages, respectively. This situation was closely related to the concentration of foreign investment and exports benefiting from tax incentives in the eastern region. Conversely, high-tax industries were disproportionately located in the western region, and local governments in the western region enforced stricter tax collection measures. In contrast, the abundant financial resources and ample tax sources enabled the local governments in the eastern region to adopt a more lenient tax policy for a more favorable business environment.

5.4   Prospect of the large-scale development of the western region

It has been almost two decades since the introduction of the strategy in 1999. Over this period, the phrasing of this strategy in the documents released by the central government has progressed from the initial "implement the strategy for the development of the western region" to the subsequent "further implement the strategy for the large-scale development of the western region" and finally, to the recent "strengthen measures to achieve a new phase in the large-scale development of the western region", signifying the ongoing advancement and enhancement of the strategy. It is clear that the strategy plays a significant role in the national strategic framework for coordinated regional development, whether the objective is to win a decisive victory in building a moderately prosperous society in all respects or to embark on a new journey towards the second centenary goal of fully building a modern socialist country.

5.4.1   Future focuses of the western development

Implementing the strategy for the large-scale development of the western region is a challenging and long-term endeavor. As China is currently in a crucial phase of implementing this strategy, the primary objective is to ensure that the western region enters the moderately prosperous society. For that, we must unwaveringly carry out the strategy in a comprehensive and thorough manner, adhering to the principle of "prioritizing wealth creation, maintaining social stability, and pursuing high-quality development". Furthermore, we should place greater emphasis on upholding social stability, expanding employment opportunities, and improving the well-being of the people. By effectively enhancing the region's development quality, self-sufficiency, and overall competitiveness, we can expedite its journey towards sustained, stable, rapid, and healthy development.

5.4.1.1   Always prioritize the maintenance of social stability

The western region, characterized by its extensive border, is inhabited by areas with ethnic minority groups and old revolutionary base areas. The convergence of factors such as poverty creates a complex situation in the region. Therefore, when implementing the strategy, our utmost priority should always be maintaining social stability. This can be achieved by seamlessly integrating economic progress with social stability, adhering to the principle of "doing two jobs at once and attaching equal importance to each". In particular, we must attach great significance to promoting all-round development of the "areas with unique features", focusing on effectively resolving the various problems and difficulties they face, establishing a long-term mechanism for their self-sustaining growth, and making social stability and national unity in the western region. The primary objective as we strive for great prosperity through the large-scale development.

5.4.1.2 Enable the people in the West to enjoy more benefits

Since the implementation of the strategy, China has made significant efforts to initiate numerous major projects in the areas of infrastructure, ecological and environmental improvement, and industrial development. These endeavors have played a crucial role in expediting the region's progress and overcoming its previous backwardness. Moving forward, in addition to continuing the construction of those major projects, it is imperative that we prioritize enhancing public welfare in the western region. This entails addressing pressing issues in education, culture, healthcare, social security, safety, and living conditions, as they are intricately linked to the well-being of the public. By doing so, the residents in the western region can genuinely enjoy greater benefits from the large-scale development and experience substantial improvements in their income and living standards.

5.4.1.3 Spare no efforts to expand employment opportunities

To foster economic prosperity and ensure social stability in the western region, it is crucial to enable the natives to settle down and start businesses just within the region through prioritizing employment and expanding local job opportunities for the natives, instead of simply exporting cheap labor to the eastern region for labor-intensive work. Therefore, it is necessary to offer more national fiscal and policy support to attract domestic and international private investors, to encourage coastal enterprises, development zones, and processing trade to relocate in the west, and to motivate migrant workers from the region to return to their hometowns and start businesses. Particular attention should be paid to the development of new industries in the western region that combine technology-intensive and labor-intensive components for the purpose of job creation.

5.4.1.4 Effectively improve the quality and ability of western development

Currently, the economic growth in the western region heavily relies on resources and investment, and there is still a long way to go in order to achieve the shift from being driven by factors to being driven by innovation. In certain resource-based areas, economic development is mainly driven by resource-based industries. Although this model may temporarily bring about high-speed regional economic growth and increased government revenue, it is ultimately unsustainable. Therefore, our focus should be on developing superior resources, actively promoting the resource recycling industry chain, enhancing the industrial supporting system, and achieving the deepened processing and comprehensive utilization of resources. Additionally, it is essential to accelerate the regional economic transformation, vigorously foster alternative industries and strategic emerging industries, encourage moderate diversification of industries, and earnestly enhance the quality of regional economic development and capacity for sustainable development. This will lay a solid foundation for innovation-driven development.

5.4.1.5 Strive to build a green and low-carbon industrial system in the west

Green development is a crucial component of the new development philosophy. The report to 19th CPC National Congress explicitly highlights the need to "promote green development" and "promote a sound economic structure that facilitates green, low-carbon, and circular development". Given the fragile ecological environment and significant carbon emissions prevalent in the western region, it is imperative to uphold the principle of green development and swiftly establish a green and low-carbon industrial system that embodies both western characteristics and international competitiveness. Hence, it is essential to expedite the growth of distinctive and advantageous green and low-carbon industries, forge numerous green industrial parks and bases that leverage regional strengths and exhibit strong competitiveness, and devote concerted efforts to constructing a contemporary green and low-carbon industrial system in the western region. This endeavor will serve as a solid foundation for the region's development by providing robust support for green industries.

5.4.2 New initiatives for deepening the large-scale development of the western region

To further promote the large-scale development of the western region, we must adopt new initiatives. In the new period, the primary focus lies on implementing the following four core initiatives, which encompass the combination of transformation and catch-up, the cultivation of new growth poles, the synergistic interactions among four driving forces, and the development of new models for opening up.

5.4.2.1 Combining transformation and catch-up

The western region holds tremendous strategic potential in supporting China's future economic growth. However, it is also an ecologically sensitive and fragile area, particularly in the northwest and Qinghai-Tibet Plateau. The natural conditions in these regions are characterized by harsh natural environments, including a dry and rainy climate, and limited water resources. These areas serve as the source of major rivers and act as a vital ecological shield for the entire country. Consequently, there exists a prominent conflict between economic development and ecological protection in this region. In light of the concept of green development, the acceleration of economic development in the western region presents a dilemma. On the one hand, in order to bridge the development gap with the eastern region, it is necessary to implement a catch-up strategy for leap-forward development, which, however, will exert great pressure on the region's fragile ecological environment. On the other hand, as an important ecological shield in China, the western region must prioritize ecological conservation and environmental protection. To overcome this dilemma, the region must completely abandon the traditional model of extensive development and integrate leapfrog catch-up with a transformation of the development mode. This will allow for the pursuit of a green development model that minimizes energy resource consumption and avoids sacrificing the ecological environment, while achieving the organic integration of economic development and environmental protection. Essentially, the aim is to achieve green transformation while catching up, making significant strides in both green transformation and the shift in the development mode. This leapfrog approach to green development will effectively prevent the negative impacts of the "resource curse". Clearly, in order to swiftly narrow the development gap with the developed eastern regions, the western region must combine transformation and catch-up, and embrace the path of innovation-driven, leapfrog green development.

5.4.2.2 Cultivating new growth poles

In recent years, China's regional economic growth has experienced a shift from being driven by a single dominant region to being driven by multiple regions. Previously, China's rapid economic growth relied heavily on a few areas such as the Pearl River Delta and the Yangtze River Delta. However, due to changes in domestic economic conditions and the external environment, this unipolar-driven pattern has changed. Looking ahead, the future development pattern of China will be characterized by the rise of numerous city clusters in the northern coastal, central, western, and northeastern regions. City clusters such as the Shandong Peninsula, Yangtze River midstream, the Central Plains, the Northeast Harbin-Dalian Industrial Belt, the Chengdu-Chongqing, and the Guanzhong-Tianshui are expected to emerge as new leading regions and growth poles, supporting China's sustained and rapid economic growth. This will result in a diversified regional competition pattern with multiple growth poles. Given this new situation, it is crucial for China's spatial development pattern to undergo strategic transformation as soon as possible. This entails shifting from the previous point-axis development strategy to a multi-center network development strategy (Wei Houkai, 2009d, 2014).

In order to promote the formation of a multi-center network development pattern, it is of great urgency to expedite the cultivation and establishment of several new growth poles in the western region in the future. Since the implementation of the 11th Five-year Plan, the government has proposed to develop the Chengdu-Chongqing, Guanzhong-Tianshui, and Beibu Gulf Economic Zones, and has mobilized efforts to develop plans for these three key areas. Moving forward, while continuing to prioritize the planning and construction of these economic zones, we will concentrate on fostering two types of growth poles. One is national growth poles, such as the urban agglomerations of Chengdu-Chongqing, Guanzhong-Tianshui, Lanzhou-Xining, and Beibu Gulf, will be given special attention. The other is regional growth poles, including urban agglomerations like Hohhot-Baotou-Ordos-Yulin, Central Guizhou, Central Yunnan, Cities along the Yellow River in Ningxia, and Tianshan North Slope, will also be nurtured (Wei Houkai, 2016b). It is crucial to rely on the planning and construction of these two-level urban agglomerations or growth poles to guide and propel the entire process of the western development.

5.4.2.3   Promoting synergistic interactions among four driving forces

In the western region, industrialization is still in progress, while urbanization is advancing rapidly. To further implement the strategy, it is crucial to seamlessly integrate industrialization with urbanization, IT application, and agricultural modernization in the western region. This necessitates our commitment to fostering synergistic interactions among these four driving forces, with industrialization acting as the backbone, urbanization as the platform, IT application as the tool, and agricultural modernization as the foundation.

First of all, in driving the western region to embark on a path of new industrialization, characterized by resource conservation, environmental friendliness, high production efficiency, innovation orientation, full utilization of human resources, and the equitable sharing of development achievements, we should focus on establishing a contemporary industrial system featuring low consumption, low emissions, high efficiency, and competitiveness. To this end, we should devote serious energy to the construction of information infrastructure and facilitate the seamless integration of industrialization and IT application; and also, we need to implement the strategy of extending industrial chains by leveraging the potential of industrial parks and agglomeration areas. This will involve further enhancing our industrial supporting system and promoting the growth and clustering of industrial chains. By doing so, we can cultivate and establish several distinctive and advantageous industrial chains that possess a strong competitive edge. Moreover, we must also prioritize transforming the agricultural production model and expediting the pace of agricultural modernization according to the requirements in terms of economies of scale, eco-friendliness, intensification, industrialization, and specialization.

Furthermore, taking into consideration the unique circumstances and conditions prevailing in each locality, we should comprehensively enhance the quality of urbanization in the western region by pursuing a new path of urbanization that is both feasible and tailored to the region. To accomplish this, we should (1) fully unleash the driving forces and exemplary role of the central cities in the area; (2) prioritize the ongoing development of urban agglomerations in Chengdu-Chongqing, Guanzhong-Tianshui, and Beibu Gulf, while expediting the planning and construction of such six urban agglomerations as mentioned above, thereby establishing them as new growth poles in the western region; (3) accelerate the construction of small towns, bolster infrastructure and public services, prioritize industrial support, and effectively enhance their absorptive capacity; (4) reinforce participation and cooperation between small cities or towns and larger cities, promoting large cities' engagement in high-end service industries, while encouraging small cities and towns to specialize and develop their unique characteristics, thereby fostering a new paradigm featuring rational division of labor, complementary competition, and coordinated progress among cities of all sizes and small towns.

5.4.2.4 Developing new models for opening up

We must accelerate the progress of opening up the western region to both international and domestic markets. This necessitates the establishment of a new opening-up model featuring "achieving development, growth, and upgrading through opening up". Specifically, we need to enhance both the efficiency of utilizing foreign investments and the level of opening up to the outside world. Furthermore, we should actively encourage the large-scale inflow of private capital from domestic and foreign investors, thereby facilitating the all-round development and opening up of the region.

The first move is to speed up the all-round opening up of central cities and key areas. We need to take the following specific measures: (1) dedicate increased efforts towards constructing new districts, including Liangjiang in Chongqing, Xixian in Shaanxi, Lanzhou in Gansu, Gui'an in Guizhou, Tianfu in Sichuan and Dian-zhong in Yunnan; (2) deepen the reform of Pilot Free Trade Zones in Chongqing, Sichuan, and Shaanxi; (3) vigorously promote the transformation and upgrading of western high-tech industrial development zones, economic and technological development zones, and bonded port areas; (4) establish high-level and comprehensive international inland ports or dry ports by leveraging transportation hub cities like Chongqing and Xi'an; and (5) encourage the relocation of inward foreign investment, coastal industries, and processing trade to the central and western regions.

The second move is to accelerate the development and opening up of border areas through following measures: (1) continue to advance the implementation of the action plan for prospering border areas; (2) further open up the western region's external channels with the eastern, central and northeastern regions as well as the neighboring countries; (3) speed up infrastructure construction such as transportation, communication, ports, power supply and water supply, and environmental sanitation in border areas; (4) flexibly adjust the approval requirements for establishing various "special areas" in border regions, while establishing new border economic cooperation zones, mutual trade zones, and bonded zones; (5) in border port cities such as Kashgar in Xinjiang, Manzhouli in Inner Mongolia, Dongxing in Guangxi, and Ruili in Yunnan, establish special border economic zones that offer higher openness, greater flexibility, and more favorable advantages by integrating existing resources; and (6) through bold experiments on developing and opening border areas, encourage the establishment of cross-border economic cooperation zones in regions with ripe conditions, and promote resource exploitation, economic development, and social stability through opening up, based on bold experiments conducted in border areas.

Chapter 6
Revitalizing the Old Industrial Bases in the Northeast

The northeastern region is home to China's important old industrial bases as well as commodity grain production bases. Since the founding of the PRC in 1949, old industrial bases in the northeast have made critical contributions to national industrialization and food security. However, due to the rigid and outdated ways of thinking and institutional mechanisms during the transition from a planned to market economy, the northeastern economy has faced various problems and challenges since the initiation of the reform and opening up in 1978, including depleted resources in mining cities, extensive layoffs in SOEs leading to difficulties in re-employment, an excessive backlog of agricultural products, a heavy burden on local public finance, a weakened economic momentum, and a decline in industrial competitiveness. To effectively solve these problems and restore to its former glory as important industrial bases, the CPC Central Committee and the State Council decided in 2003 to launch the national strategy for revitalizing old industrial bases in the northeast and other parts of China (hereinafter referred to as Revitalization Strategy), and subsequently, relevant departments rolled out a series of policies and measures. The strong policy support has invigorated rapid economic growth in the northeastern region, demonstrating significant progress in pursuing the Revitalization Strategy. However, with the recent slowdown of national economic growth and the issue of industrial overcapacity, the region's economy now faces new challenges. In this sense, long-term and arduous efforts are still necessary to achieve the central government's strategic goal of fully revitalizing the northeast.

6.1 Background of launching the Revitalization Strategy

Since 1949, the northeastern region has been at the forefront of urbanization and industrialization in China, boasting a significantly higher level of economic development compared to the eastern, central, and western regions. In 1980, the region's

GRP per capita reached an impressive 150.8, nearly double that of the central and western regions. However, since the reform and opening up, the region's economic growth has been hindered for various reasons, resulting in sluggish industrial production and what academia refers to as the "northeast phenomenon" (Kong Weiwei, 1992; Sun Naiji, 1993). Unfortunately, this development challenge has also spread to the agricultural and other sectors. Therefore, it is imperative to leverage the region's local strengths and implement active and effective policies and measures to revitalize old industrial bases in the northeast.

6.1.1   The strategic position of the northeast

The northeast of China is an important region with a well-developed economy and efficient allocation of production factors. Its economic development aligns harmoniously with the local natural resources and greatly benefits from a well-connected transportation network. From an economic perspective, there are two concepts regarding the geographical scope of northeast China. The first concept includes Liaoning, Jilin, and Heilongjiang provinces, covering a land area of over 790,000 square kilometers (equivalent to 8.2% of the entire country). In 2016, this region supported a total population of 109.1 million and generated a GRP of RMB5,231.02 billion, accounting for 7.9% and 6.8% of the national total, respectively. The second one incorporates the aforementioned three northeastern provinces along with the four cities (league) in the eastern part of Inner Mongolia, namely Hulun Buir City, Hinggan League, Tongliao City, and Chifeng City. These four cities (league) were historically included in northeast China due to their geographical proximity, historical and economic ties, and similar economic and social characteristics. In the Northeast Revitalization Plan, approved by the State Council in August 2007, the geographical scope was further expanded to include Hulun Buir City, Hinggan League, Tongliao City, Chifeng City, and Xilingol League (the eastern region of Inner Mongolia), thus making the planned area cover 1.45 million square kilometers and a total population of 120 million. Due to limitations in statistical data, the majority of the data used in this book refers to China's three northeastern provinces, unless otherwise stated.

Historically, northeast China held a very important position in China's politics, economy and military affairs. Northeast China was occupied, could the People's Republic of China be founded. In this sense, northeast China can conceivably make or break the whole country. From the perspective of development, northeast China, as an important old industrial base in China, has great capacity and potential for development due to its sound infrastructure, strong strength in sci-tech and education, and a group of high-quality industrial workers. Therefore, under the new situation, northeast China is fully qualified and also capable of building itself into one of the most developed regions in China and becoming an important growth pole to support the sustained and rapid growth of China's economy in the future.

The region emerged as a significant center for heavy and chemical industries, establishing itself as a leading player in China's national economy during the early years of the PRC. This was made possible through substantial investment from the government, which allocated 58 out of 156 key state-sponsored projects to the region during the First Five-year Plan period. Since the founding of the PRC in 1949, the region has played a crucial, historic role in developing an independent and comprehensive economic system, contributing to China's industrialization and urbanization. Additionally, it has provided other regions with significant resources such as capital, technology, materials, equipment, and skilled professionals to support their economic growth. Prior to the implementation of the Revitalization Strategy, the region was home to many industries and products that held pivotal positions in the national economy. For example, the region accounted for 2/5 of the country's crude oil production, 2/7 of crude oil processing, 1/2 of timber supply, 1/3 of commodity grain production, 1/3 of complete sets of power station equipment, 1/3 of shipbuilding output, 1/4 of ethylene and automobile, as well as 1/8 of steel output (Wang Luolin & Wei Houkai, 2005b). Furthermore, the region boasted notable strengths in science and technology, education, the availability of technical talent, and the agro-processing industry.

In comparison with other regions, the region possesses several distinct advantages. Firstly, it boasts a well-balanced abundance of energy, minerals, water, soil, talent, and technology. Secondly, it boasts a robust infrastructure, particularly in terms of its road and railway networks. Thirdly, it possesses solid foundations for industrial development, especially in the areas of raw material and equipment manufacturing industries. Lastly, it exhibits a relatively strong presence in scientific and technological advancements and education, which has resulted in the graduation of a highly skilled workforce. However, despite those evident advantages, the region faces several challenges. Firstly, it grapples with outdated modes of thinking and ideas that stemmed from the legacy of the planned economy. This is particularly evident in misconceptions surrounding employment, a bureaucratic prioritization mindset, and arbitrary government interventions. Secondly, the region contends with rigid and inactive mechanisms, especially in the realm of business operations and administration. These mechanisms burden enterprises with heavy obligations to operate social programs, consequently impeding their development and vitality. Lastly, the region suffers from institutional lags, which have caused its various reforms on economic systems to significantly lag behind those in the southeast coastal areas. As a result, the region's overall pace of the reform and opening up lags behind by at least 10-15 years (Wang Luolin & Wei Houkai, 2005b).

6.1.2   Problems facing the northeast economy prior to the Revitalization Strategy

Overall, before the launch of the Revitalization Strategy, the economy in the northeast was mainly faced with following problems.

6.1.2.1   Slow growth with signs of relative decline

As previously mentioned, northeast China, known for its old industrial bases, played a dominant role in China's national economy as a first-generation leader. Since 1949, it has contributed greatly to China's economic development and industrialization. However, as the reform and opening up seriously lagged behind, the region's economy has faced a series of challenges since the 1980s and has even shown signs of relative decline. These challenges include the loss of its SOEs' vitality, a sluggish private economy, limited inflow of foreign investment, and a decline in competitiveness and market share in the secondary industry, particularly in the manufacturing sector. Between 1981 and 2001, the manufacturing sector in the region saw an average annual growth rate of only 7.6% (measured at current prices), while the coastal emerging industrial area (Guangdong, Fujian, Jiangsu, Zhejiang, and Shandong) achieved a growth rate of 14.8%. As a result, the region's contribution to the national manufacturing output decreased from 18.7% in 1980 and 17.8% in 1985 to 9.1% in 1997 and 8.0% in 2001, while that proportion in the coastal emerging industrial area increased from 25.4% in 1980 to 50.4% in 2001. Overall, the regions' value-added industrial output also experienced a rapid decline in the proportion in the national total, dropping from 17.8% in 1980 to 10.6% in 2002.

In general, regional economic decline can be categorized into four types: location-based decline, resource-based decline, structural decline, and disaggregation decline (Wei Houkai, 1991). The (relative) decline in industry and economy in the northeastern region since the reform and opening up can be primarily attributed to resource-based decline and structural decline. In essence, it bears some resemblance to the "depression syndrome" observed in certain depression-stricken areas of industrialized countries. Initially observed in its industrial sector during the 1980s and 1990s, the relative economic decline had gradually extended to its agricultural sector by the early 21st century, which was referred to as the "new northeast phenomenon" by the media (Chen Kaixing & Dong Jun, 2002). As the significant granary and grain reserve base of China, the region accounted for 38.0% and 28.6% of China's soybean and corn production respectively in 2002. However, due to high costs, low quality, import shocks, and limited capacity for food processing and transformation, there emerged huge stockpiles of soybeans and corn in the region. According to relevant data, the corn stockpiles in Jilin Province reached a staggering 40 million tons at that time, equivalent to the total output of the entire province for two years (Liu Gengxi, 2002). The increasing grain stockpiles resulted in both policy-related losses for grain depots and financial burdens on local governments. For instance, in Heilongjiang Province, an annual expenditure of as much as RMB4.5 billion from central and provincial fiscal funds was required to address the over-storage of grain, in addition to RMB1.38 billion for the grain risk fund. However, due to budget constraints, only approximately RMB700 million was available, leading to a shortfall of over RMB600 million (Wei Houkai, 2003a).

6.1.2.2 Massive presence of SOEs and widespread job cuts

First, a massive presence of SOEs and a unitary structure of property rights. Being home to old industrial bases, the northeastern region had a large number of SOEs, especially those under central administration, and the state-owned sector held an important position in the regional economy. In 2003, the combined output of state-owned and state-controlled industrial enterprises accounted for 67.5% of all state-owned industrial enterprises and non-state-owned industrial enterprises above designated size, surpassing the national average of 37.5%. Specifically, Liaoning accounted for 58.1%, Jilin accounted for 75.8%, and Heilongjiang accounted for 79.4% of this total. According to the Main Indicators of Centrally-Supervised Enterprises Distributed in Northeast China in 2002, the total assets, sales revenue, and total profits of industrial enterprises above national Level III, including Daqing Oilfield Limited Company, accounted for 45.3%, 72.1%, and 81.3% respectively, of the state-owned and state-controlled industrial enterprises in northeast China. Excluding Daqing Oilfield, among the 913 centrally administered SOEs in this region, 55% were wholly state-owned companies, with 70% of the employees, 67.1% of the total assets, and 52.6% of the sales revenue. However, these enterprises collectively incurred a loss of RMB6.9 billion and had a negative return on equity (ROE) of -11.9% (Planning Bureau of the State-owned Assets Supervision and Administrative Commission, 2004).

Second, heavy involvement in monopoly and foundation industries and challenges for industrial transformation. The northeastern region was faced with great challenges to its industrial transformation as a high proportion of its enterprises were involved in monopoly and foundation industries. By the end of 2002, among the 913 centrally administered SOEs (excluding Daqing Oilfield) in the northeastern region, 149 were engaged in monopoly industries, with their total assets and sales revenue accounting for 58.2% and 52.7% of the regional total respectively. However, these enterprises reported an overall loss of RMB5.2 billion and a ROE of −12.2%. Additionally, 281 SOEs were categorized under underlying industries, with their total assets and sales revenue amounting to 64.1% and 59.0% of the regional total respectively. However, these enterprises also incurred an overall loss of RMB3.9 billion and an ROE of −7.5% (Planning Bureau of the State-owned Assets Supervision and Administrative Commission, 2004). These enterprises that heavily involved in monopoly and foundation industries were characterized by their low profitability and heavy reliance on resources, thus having greatly hindered the industrial transformation of SOEs in this region.

Third, SOEs' poor performance and high asset-liability ratio. According to a survey conducted by the Central Research Group of China Democratic League (2003), among the 1,507 local state-owned and state-controlled industrial enterprises in Liaoning province, 308 were insolvent, with an average asset-liability ratio of 135%; and in Heilongjiang province, the asset-liability ratio of local SOEs was 83%, with 36.7% of them being insolvent and a distressing incidence of loss reaching 49.9%. In addition, a study carried out by the Planning Bureau of the State-owned Assets Supervision and Administrative Commission (SASAC) (2004) revealed that out of the region's centrally administered SOEs and their subsidiaries above the national Level III, 371 enterprises (excluding Daqing Oilfield) reported a loss of approximately RMB470 million in 2002, with the incidence of loss standing at 40%. Furthermore, the centrally administered SOEs in the region had accumulated huge debts in the past, with an average asset-liability ratio of 76.4%, much higher than the national average level of 64.8% for SOEs.

Fourth, the "white elephants" for the SOEs, especially the heavy burden of social programs they are required to operate. In a 2002 survey conducted by China's Ministry of Finance (MOF) on SOEs' financial reports on final accounts revealed that, it was found that SOEs in the northeastern region were responsible for running a staggering 7,183 social programs. These programs employed a total of 491,000 individuals and received RMB15.38 billion in subsidies as enterprise expenditures. Among those programs, 3,476 (equivalent to 48.4%) were operated by enterprises directly under the central government or those affiliated to other central departments, with 307,000 employees involved and RMB12.99 billion of subsidies received, accounting for 62.5% and 84.5% respectively. To illustrate the extent of these obligations, let us consider a few specific examples. Harbin Electric Corporation, for instance, was responsible for the operation of 37 social programs, receiving a total subsidy of RMB416 million and incurring renovation costs of RMB257 million. Similarly, China FAW Group Corporation dedicated nearly RMB500 million each year to fulfill its social obligations. Daqing Petroleum Administration Bureau operated 257 social institutions, employing 40,000 individuals and receiving an annual subsidy of RMB2.2 billion. Furthermore, numerous factories were mandated to run "large collectives", most of which were operating at a loss. Statistics revealed that, out of the 4, 655 factory-run large collectives in the region, 70.4% were either at a loss or had been shut down altogether. The overall loss incurred in 2002 reached a staggering RMB1.16 billion. As a result of these losses, the total assets, total liabilities, and owner's equity of these large collectives amounted to RMB81.85 billion, RMB83.6 billion, and −1.75 billion, respectively. In essence, they were insolvent due to the poor quality of their assets. Additionally, among the 1.247 million registered collective workers in these factories' large collectives, 847,000 were off-duty workers, accounting for two-thirds of the total. This situation has led to a portion of urban residents falling into extreme poverty (SASAC Planning Bureau, 2004).

Fifth, widespread job cuts and mounting pressure in employment. The lack of flexibility in their mechanisms, excessive staffing, outdated technology, and over-used equipment, mounting debts and heavy obligation to operate social programs had deprived the SOEs in the region of vitality, efficiency, and competitiveness. Consequently, there have been massive layoffs and a surge in employment pressure. According to a survey, in Liaoning Province alone, there were 1.5 million employees who left their positions in state-owned and collective enterprises and 830,000 registered unemployed persons in urban areas; in Heilongjiang Province, 1.49 million individuals were registered as unemployed in urban areas (Central Research Group of China Democratic League, 2003). This situation was even more dire in some resource-depleted mining cities. For example, Fushun Mining Group in Liaoning Province left a total of 122,500 people in need of re-employment, accounting for one-third of the city's population. In Fuxin, another city in Liaoning Province, there were 152,000 laid-offs in 2002, accounting for 20% of the urban population, and the actual unemployment rate reached as high as 30.6%.

6.1.2.3   Resource-based cities in urgent need of industrial transformation

Northeast China is home to several resource-based cities with a singular industrial structure. Due to extensive exploitation over time, most of these cities were on the brink of resource depletion. As of 2003, the recoverable reserves in Daqing Oilfield, responsible for nearly half of China's oil production, stood at a mere 745 million tons (equivalent to only 30% remaining). By 2020, the annual output could only be sustained at approximately 20 million tons. The Liaohe Oilfield had already extracted 77.1% of its proven geological reserves of crude oil, along with 82.6% of its natural gas reserves, resulting in a noticeable decline in oil and gas production. In addition, in Heilongjiang Province, the four major coal production bases (Hegang, Jixi, Shuangyashan, and Qitaihe) were either on the verge of coal exhaustion or had shut down their wells. Within the next decade, it was projected that 11 out of the 35 key state-owned coal mines in Liaoning Province would be abandoned. Major iron ore mining areas such as Anshan Mountain, Dagu Mountain, Yanqian Mountain, and Waitou Mountain had reached the final stages of mining, resulting in a decline in production capacity over time. Compounding these challenges was the fact that most of these cities had a singular industrial structure, characterized by limited industrial diversity and a lack of alternative sectors. For example, in 2002, the value-added output from non-oil industries in Daqing accounted for only 5.9% of the total value-added industrial output. Similarly, in Yichun and the Greater Hinggan Mountains, non-forest industries contributed to only about one-third of the value-added output, while non-coal industries in Hegang, Jixi, Qitaihe, and Shuangyashan accounted for a mere 32.5%. In resource-based cities in the northeast, the ratio of output value for coal, wood, and oil products to that of extended processing was only 1 : 0.69, significantly lower than the national average of 1 : 2.84. Due to their singular structure, short industrial chains, heavy reliance on energy and raw material industries, and lack of alternative sectors, these cities faced immense pressure in terms of industrial structure transformation and employment transfer.

6.1.2.4   High ratios of non-performing assets and loans, low credit rating, and great
             financing difficulties

Prior to the implementation of the Revitalization Strategy, northeast China faced challenges with regards to the high levels of non-performing assets and non-performing bank loans of its SOEs. According to the Planning Bureau of SASAC (2004), the non-performing debts of the SOEs in Liaoning Province amounted to RMB292.1 billion. Out of this, RMB189.1 billion was owed to banks, RMB90 billion to the government, and RMB13 billion to employees. The total value of non-performing assets in the region reached RMB52.53 billion. Furthermore, these enterprises had poor performance, high asset-liability ratios, significant long-standing arrears, and a prevalent practice of maliciously evading debts. These issues, combined with institutional and policy-related factors, led to high non-performing loan ratios in banks across the region, resulting in increased financial risks. Relevant data indicated that the interest collection rate (the ratio of interest actually collected to interest revenue) of financial institutions in the three northeastern provinces averaged only around 70%. By the end of 2002, the balance of uncollected interest receivable stood at RMB192.9 billion. The non-performing loan ratio was nearly 10 percentage points higher than the national average. A significant number of banks reported losses, with the net loss of all financial institutions reaching as high as RMB18 billion (Zhang Ying, 2004). As a consequence, major commercial banks in China classified these three provinces as high-credit-risk areas. Credit lines were strictly limited, and many grassroots banks were required to seek approval from their provincial branches or even head office for each loan granting. Consequently, many city- and county-level bank branches had almost been deprived of authority for granting loans, primarily serving the purpose of accepting local deposits. Even some provincial branches had restricted authority in this regard. This credit crunch hindered the financial sector from supporting local economic development, exacerbating the tensions between banks and enterprises while creating additional financial risks. Moreover, it made financing less accessible and affordable for enterprises, particularly for private SMEs.

6.1.2.5 Huge resource consumption, serious environmental pollution, and great challenges for sustainability

In the northeast, particularly in its cities that rely heavily on resources and produce raw materials, heavy and chemical industries held a significant share, leading to excessive consumption of resources and energy as well as exacerbation of environmental pollution. In 2002, the consumption of standard coal in the region was 1.81 tons per RMB10,000 of GRP, which was 28.4%, 66.1%, and 13.1% higher than the national average, the eastern region (excluding Hainan), and the central region respectively. The emission of waste gas in the northeast in 2003 was 55,200 standard cubic meters per RMB10,000 of value-added industrial output, which was 16.5% higher than the national average and 66.3% higher than the eastern region. Moreover, some resource-based cities faced severe challenges in restoring ecological balance in mine subsidence areas. For example, Liaoning Province had seven coal mining subsidence areas, and Shuangyashan City in Heilongjiang Province had eight, covering a total area of 333 square kilometers and 133 square kilometers, respectively. In Daqing, the forest coverage rate was only about 9%, and 84% of the total area suffered from grassland degradation, salinization, and desertification, posing a severe threat to regional and local ecological balance.

6.2   Goals and tasks of the Revitalization Strategy

To help the northeastern region in overcoming its developmental challenges, the Chinese government has altered its initial approach to adjust and transform old industrial bases primarily through turning around SOEs' economic performance since the 16th CPC National Congress in 2002. In line with the Revitalization Strategy, the central government formulated and implemented a new strategy to revitalize old industrial bases in the northeast and other parts of China, which took revitalizing old industrial bases in an all-round manner and rejuvenating their vitality as the ultimate goal. The Revitalization Strategy, therefore, is an integral part of China's overall strategy for regional development, and its successful implementation is a natural requirement for building a moderately prosperous society in all respects, promoting coordinated regional development, and achieving common prosperity.

6.2.1   Reflections on the previous approach to adjust and transform old industrial bases

To address the myriad challenges confronting old industrial bases in the northeast, the relevant government departments ever rendered substantial support in terms of financial assistance and policy measures. Since the 1980s, a series of policies and measures related to finance, credit, and investment have been implemented to support the transformation of old industrial bases, including the establishment of the Fund for Adjustments and Transformation of Old Industrial Bases and the identification of six key old industrial bases (Shanghai, Tianjin, Wuhan, Chongqing, Shenyang, and Harbin) for the transformation of these bases, two of which are located in the northeast. During the Eighth Five-year Plan period (1991-1995), these six old industrial bases received a total of RMB20.2 billion under the State Special Loan program, along with RMB13.4 billion provided as the special loan for old industrial bases (Wang Yiming, 1998). Additionally, four cities in the northeast, namely Qiqihar, Harbin, Changchun, and Shenyang, were among the 18 pilot cities[1] selected in August 1994 for capital structure

---

[1] The eighteen pilot cities for capital structure optimization are Shanghai, Tianjin, Qiqihar, Harbin, Changchun, Shenyang, Tangshan, Taiyuan, Qingdao, Zibo, Changzhou, Bengbu, Wuhan, Zhuzhou, Liuzhou, Chengdu, Chongqing, and Baoji.

optimization. State-level pilot projects were carried out in these cities, focusing on "capital increase, transformation, diversion, and bankruptcy". In the later stage of the Ninth Five-year Plan (1996-2000), the northeastern region received further support through China's debt-to-equity swap program and the utilization of national debt funds to boost domestic demand. The 10th Five-year Plan period (2001-2005) saw Fuxin, a resource-based city in Liaoning Province, being included in a pilot program for industrial transformation. Nevertheless, although these policies and measures have generated some positive results, the region still faces significant challenges in terms of adjusting and transforming its old industrial bases. This can be fundamentally attributed to certain misconceptions in strategic mindset:

(1) The concept of adjusting and transforming old industrial bases was narrowly confined to adjusting and transforming the secondary industry itself.

(2) The focus of industrial revitalization was solely on the turnaround of SOEs, neglecting the technological advancement and efficiency improvement in the private and foreign-invested sectors.

(3) More emphasis was placed on project investment and technological transformation, rather than on fostering a change in mindset, innovating mechanisms and systems, and improving the business environment of enterprises.

(4) The role of the government was overemphasized, resulting in a heavy reliance on government support and solutions, while the cultivation of market forces and non-governmental entities was ignored.

(5) The positive impact of opening up on regional economies was underestimated, and no significant and influential measures, such as the opening up of Guangdong and the establishment of the Pudong New Area in Shanghai, were implemented.

Based on the above analysis, the adjustments and transformation of old industrial bases go beyond merely reviving the secondary industry or just implementing SOEs' technological transformation and turnaround. To fundamentally address the various challenges faced by the northeast, the key lies in revitalizing its old industrial bases and restoring its vitality. This revitalization necessitates a comprehensive revitalization of the entire region's economy, which involves many fields such as industry, agriculture, service industry, and social security, rather than solely focusing on the secondary industry. Domestic and international experience also demonstrates that revitalizing the regional economy is the key to adjusting and transforming old industrial bases, instead of simply bailing out struggling enterprises. This is because only a fully revitalized regional economy, with continuously increasing industrial competitiveness, can ensure more employment opportunities and an enhanced capacity to handle problems. Therefore, to adjust and transform old industrial bases in the northeast, it is imperative to dispel the misconception that solely emphasizes the secondary industry and views turning around SOEs as a quick solution. Instead, the region should embark on a path of deepening reforms and expanding opening up, with a focus on institutional, systematic, and technological innovations. The emphasis should be on expanding employment, adjusting the economic structure, and enhancing industrial competitiveness, thus facilitating a comprehensive and sustainable revitalization of the regional economy.

6.2.2   Goals and tasks of revitalizing the northeast

Revitalizing old industrial bases in the northeast was an important strategic decision made by the CPC Central Committee and the State Council in the new period. As early as November 2002, the report to the 16th CPC National Congress made it clear that "We should support the northeastern region and other old industrial bases in accelerating their adjustments and transformation and support cities and areas mainly engaged in natural resources exploitation in their efforts to develop alternative industries." In March 2003, then Premier Zhu Rongji further proposed the idea of supporting old industrial bases in the northeast and other parts of China to expedite the adjustments and transformation in his Government Work Report. In October 2003, the CPC Central Committee and the State Council jointly released Several Opinions on Implementing the Revitalization Strategy of Old Industrial Bases in the Northeast and Other Parts of the Country, which stated that "the time is ripe and the conditions are right for implementing the revitalization strategy of old industrial bases, particularly those in northeast China", and clearly proposed that "after a period of unremitting efforts, old industrial bases will be adjusted and transformed into well-structured, technologically advanced, and competitive new ones that would function well and serve as new growth engines of the national economy". The core idea of the Opinions was to comprehensively revitalize the old industrial base in the northeast. Its formulation use "revitalization" instead of "adjustments and transformation", and indicate that future national support would primarily target northeast China.

The Northeast Revitalization Plan, approved by the State Council in August 2007, elaborated on the general approach, objectives, tasks, and policy measures for the revitalization, and proposed that "it will take 10 to 15 years to achieve comprehensive survival, to make the northeast into an important fast-growing economic region with sound system and mechanism for development, rational industrial structure, relatively coordinated urban-rural and regional development, sustainable resource-based cities, social harmony, and a high level of comprehensive economic development, and, to become a region that provides strong economic support to the whole country—a base for internationally competitive equipment manufacturing, a base for new raw material and energy security, a base for commodity grain and agriculture and animal husbandry production, a base for technological R&D and innovation, and at the same time, an important zone safeguarding national ecological security". This "four bases plus one safeguarding zone" was an important functional position assigned by the state to old industrial bases in the northeast.

In September 2009, after five years of implementing the Revitalization Strategy, the State Council issued Opinions on Further Implementing the Revitalization Strategy of Old Industrial Bases in the Northeast and Other Parts of China. This document enriched the meaning of the strategy and introduced 28 new policies and measures from nine different aspects. In January 2012, the State Council discussed and approved the 12th Five-year Plan for Revitalizing the Northeast. According to this plan, more emphasis should be placed on industrial transformation and upgrading, scientific and technological innovation, demand structure optimization, coordinated development, resource conservation, environmental protection, improving living standards, and deepening the reform and opening up throughout this period. The plan set "six new" goals for the revitalization of the northeast, which were to achieve a new level of economic development, enter a new phase of industrial transformation and upgrade, create a new situation for the sustainable development of resource-based cities, take new steps in ecological construction and environmental protection, achieve new results in improving public well-being, and make new breakthroughs in deepening reform and opening up. In March 2013, the State Council officially released the National Plan for Adjustments and Transformation of Old Industrial Bases (2013-2022), which was jointly prepared by the NDRC, the Ministry of Science and Technology, the Ministry of Industry and Information Technology, and the MOF. This plan proposed that "the main direction is to rebuild the new competitive advantages of industries and enhance the comprehensive functions of cities in an all-round way", and (We should) "strengthen the adjustments and transformation of old industrial bases in China, promote their comprehensive, coordinated, and sustainable development, as well as shape them into important new industrial bases for the country and important growth poles for regional economic development". Additionally, the plan encouraged different types of old industrial cities to "pursue their own unique paths of adjustments and transformation". It covered 120 old industrial cities in China, including 95 prefecture-level old industrial cities and 25 municipal districts of municipalities directly under the Central Government, cities with separate plans, and provincial capitals.

In light of the national economic slowdown, the northeastern region has experienced a diminishing rate of economic growth since 2012. This has led to operational difficulties for some industries and the emergence of deep-seated institutional and structural problems. To address this challenging situation, the State Council introduced 35 near-term policy measures from 11 aspects in August 2014 to support the revitalization of the region. In April 2016, the CPC Central Committee and the State Council issued Several Opinions on Comprehensive Revitalization of the Northeast Old Industrial Base, which clarified the overall approach, development goals, and key tasks for accelerating the implementation of the Revitalization Strategy, and emphasized the need to improve the quality and efficiency of economic development and strive to create a new development path with higher quality, better efficiency, improved structure, and full utilization of advantages. It was expected that by approximately 2030, the region would achieve a comprehensive revival, spearhead modernization across the country, become a region providing strong economic support to the whole country, and fulfil its strategic position of "four bases plus one safeguarding zone". In August of the same year, the NDRC issued the Implementation Plan for Promoting the Revitalization of Old Industrial Base in Northeast China on a Rolling Three-year Basis (2016-2018). This plan identified 137 key tasks and 127 major projects for different years, with an estimated total investment of approximately RMB1.6 trillion. In response to the downward pressure on the region's economy, the State Council issued the Opinions on Deepening the Implementation of a New Round of Northeast Revitalization Strategy and Accelerating Economic Stabilization in Northeast China in November, which outlined 14 specific tasks and measures across four aspects, providing a comprehensive plan for revitalization. During the same month, the State Council approved the Plan for the Revitalization of the Northeast during the 13th Five-year Plan Period, which proposed that by 2020, "northeast China will have made significant progress in the reform and innovation of institutional mechanisms and the shift of economic growth patterns, and achieved distinctively more balanced, coordinated and sustainable development, so as to achieve the grand goal of building a moderately prosperous society in an all-round way in line with the pace of the whole country".

6.3 Main measures to revitalize the northeast

In order to carry out the Revitalization Strategy, the State Council announced its decision to set up a leading group dedicated to revitalizing old industrial bases on December 2, 2003. This decision subsequently resulted in the establishment of the Northeast Revitalization Office of the State Council[1] in April 2004. Over the subsequent years, various departments developed and executed a range of targeted policies and measures, with a particular emphasis on the following aspects.

6.3.1 Institutional and systemic innovations

Reform of SOEs has played a crucial role in stimulating institutional and systemic innovations in old industrial bases in the northeast. As early as 2004, a pilot program was initiated to relieve three enterprises directly under the central government (PetroChina, Sinopec, and Dongfeng Motor) from their social program obligations. Under this program, 729 primary and secondary schools and 512 institutions related to public security, prosecution, and courts were separated from these enterprises, involving 23,717 retired teachers and 70,069 in-service employees. Specifically, PetroChina's subsidiaries in the three northeastern provinces spun off over 259 primary and secondary schools and institutions related to public security, prosecution, and courts, which affected 7,464 retired teachers and 22,520 in-service employees and cost a total subsidy of RMB1.3 billion from the central government. In 2005, the second round of the program was launched to relieve 74 centrally administered SOEs of their obligations of managing 1,560 primary and secondary schools as well as institutions related to public security, prosecution, and courts, with over 80,000 in-service workers and retired teachers involved. Notably, a considerable proportion of these enterprises were situated in the northeast. Furthermore, following the principle of "prioritizing key regions, making integrated planning, and implementing step by step", the central government increased its support for the policy-mandated bankruptcy of SOEs in the old industrial bases in the northeast, which facilitated the smooth exit of resource-depleted coal businesses, non-ferrous metal mines, and military enterprises. From 1999 to 2004, the central government allocated RMB17.15 billion in aid funds for bankruptcy, accounting for 23% of the national total. These funds were provided to

---

[1] The agency has now been dissolved, and its functions have been integrated into the Department of Northeast Revitalization under the National Development and Reform Commission.

67 enterprises directly under the central government or under local administration in the three northeastern provinces, resulting in the resettlement of 566,000 employees, including 207,000 retirees.

In the 1970s and 1980s, collectively owned businesses operated by SOEs were established with the aim of providing employment opportunities for educated youth returning to cities and the offspring of SOE employees. However, many of these businesses found themselves in a state of semi-shutdown or even complete shutdown as they encountered various challenges such as limited scale, redundant staff, ill-defined property rights, inactive mechanisms, poor management, and weak market competitiveness. After conducting a study on the pilot reform of collectively owned businesses operated by SOEs in the northeast in October 2005, the State Council decided to initially implement pilot reforms in select cities and centrally administered SOEs from the northeast under the principle of "pilot first, then promote". In November of the same year, the State Council approved the Guiding Opinions on the Pilot Reform of Collectively Owned Businesses Operated by SOEs in Northeast China, which was jointly submitted by the MOF, SASAC, and the Ministry of Labor and Social Security. It proposed that, based on the pilot reform, it should take approximately three years to effectively address the issues faced by collectively owned businesses operated by SOEs in the region. Subsequently, the practice would be extended nationwide in due course. The specific approaches to reform might vary. For collectively owned businesses that were eligible for reorganization and restructuring, they should be developed into market-oriented legal entities with clear property rights, independent accounting, and sole responsibility for profits and losses through appropriate measures. For those that were ineligible or were burdened with significant losses, insolvency, and inability to repay debts, they should be allowed to shut down or go bankrupt in accordance with the law.

Regarding other system reforms, since 2004, the pilot program aimed at enhancing the urban social security system has expanded its coverage from Liaoning province to also include Heilongjiang and Jilin provinces. Under this program, the state contributes 3.75%, while employers contribute 1.25% towards the individual social security accounts, which in turn provide funds for 5% of the total amount. In the same year, the central government subsidized a total of RMB4.57 billion in Heilongjiang and Jilin provinces to incorporate basic cost of living allowances into the unemployment insurance system and ensure sufficient funding for individual social security accounts. By 2005, these two provinces successfully provided adequate funding for 6% of the individual accounts for basic endowment insurance, effectively integrating the basic living security of workers laid off from state-owned enterprises into the unemployment insurance system. In April 2010, with the approval of the State Council, the Shenyang Economic Zone was officially designated as a national experimental zone for comprehensive coordinated reforms with the aim of achieving new industrialization. Furthermore, in June 2013, the State Council approved the Overall Plan for Comprehensive Coordinated Trial Reforms to Develop Modern Agriculture in the "Two Plains" of Heilongjiang Province, proposing the development of the Songnen Plain and Sanjiang Plain as the core area of China's national commodity grain base, model area for green food production, pilot area for high-efficiency ecological agriculture, and leading area for coordinating urban-rural development. In March 2016, the NDRC, the Ministry of Industry and Information Technology, the All-China Federation of Industry and Commerce, and the China Development Bank jointly issued the Guiding Opinions on Promoting the Development and Reform of Private Economy in Northeast China. This document outlines the guiding principles, main objectives, and tasks for promoting the development and reform of the private economy in the northeast during the new era.

6.3.2 Fiscal and financial support

In terms of fiscal and tax support, the policy of exempting agricultural tax was initially implemented in Jilin and Heilongjiang provinces in 2004[1] with the aim of enhancing the scope and scale of grain production subsidies in the northeast. In August of the same year, the State Council approved the Request for Instructions on Revitalizing old industrial bases in northeast China, which was submitted by the MOF and other departments. The State Council made the following decisions: (1) Starting from July 1, 2004, enterprises in eight major industries in the northeast would enjoy incremental deduction for the value-added tax included in their machinery and equipment purchases. (2) The depreciation period of fixed assets and intangible assets transferred or invested by industrial enterprises in the northeast was to be shortened by no more than 40%. (3) The pre-tax deduction standard of taxable wages for enterprises in the northeast was increased to RMB1,200 per person per month. (4) The resource tax standard for mines and low-abundance oilfields in depletion period was to be reduced by no more than 30% at the provincial level. In September of the same year, the MOF and the State Taxation Administration (STA) issued the Provisions on Several Issues Concerning

---

[1] On December 29, 2005, The 19th Session of the Standing Committee of the 10th National People's Congress adopted a decision to abolish the Agricultural Tax Regulations and cancel the agricultural tax from January 1, 2006.

Expanding the Scope of VAT Deduction in Northeast China and the Interim Measures for Expanding the Scope of VAT Deduction in Northeast China in 2004. These provisions laid out specific rules for the implementation of the expanded VAT deduction. Furthermore, in December 2006, the MOF and the STA decided to waive all types of industrial and commercial taxes and late payment fees owed by enterprises in old industrial bases in the northeast before December 31, 1997. This work was successfully completed in 2009. In January 2007, the MOF and three other departments determined that import duties and import-related value-added tax paid by domestic enterprises on 16 imported key parts for the development and manufacturing of major technical equipment, as well as for the import of raw materials that could not be produced domestically, would be refunded after collection. The refunded taxes would be considered a state investment and primarily used as state capital for enterprise's research, development, and production of new products, as well as the enhancement of capacity for independent innovation. In November 2010, the central government further strengthened its efforts in providing "four subsidies"[1] for agriculture in the northeast. Various methods, such as subsidies for interest on loans and subsidies for investment, were adopted to support the development of modern agriculture in the region. Additionally, the NDRC arranged investment from the central government budget to subsidize the preliminary work of major revitalization projects in the region and inter-provincial cooperation projects.

In terms of financial support, the Several Opinions on Implementing the Revitalization Strategy of Old Industrial Bases in the Northeast and Other Parts of the Country issued by the CPC Central Committee and the State Council in 2003 stated that "commercial banks are permitted to adopt flexible measures to handle non-performing assets, and reduce or even exempt corporate borrowers' off-balance-sheet interest in arrears independently". At the beginning of 2004, four wholly state-owned commercial banks and three policy banks were authorized to independently determine the requirements, standards, time limits, authority, and repayment methods for off-balance-sheet interest arrears of sub-prime, suspicious, and loss loans based on specific conditions. The Leading Group for Shareholding System Reform of Wholly State-owned Commercial Banks and its Office actively promoted the shareholding system reform of relevant banks. This helped address the issue of non-performing loans in old

---

[1] The term "four subsidies" refers to direct subsidies to grain producers, general subsidies for purchasing agricultural supplies, subsidies for planting superior crop varieties and subsidies for purchasing agricultural machinery and tools. —*Tr.*

industrial bases, including northeast China, by writing off lost assets and stripping suspicious loans. By the end of 2004, the local branches of Bank of China, China Construction Bank, and Bank of Communications in three northeastern provinces (including the city of Dalian) had written off RMB34 billion of lost assets and stripped off nearly RMB50 billion of suspicious loans during the shareholding system reform. In 2004, the People's Bank of China wrote off RMB60 billion of non-performing assets in the northeast. It also increased financial support for pilot rural credit cooperatives in Jilin Province, including the promotion of personal microfinance loans to laid-off workers. Sponsored by the NDRC and the Northeast Revitalization Office of the State Council, the Northeast China Small and Medium-sized Enterprises Financing Re-Guarantee Co. Ltd. was officially founded in February 2008. It received a capital injection of RMB3 billion from the MOF, Liaoning, Jilin, Heilongjiang, Inner Mongolia, and the Export-Import Bank of China. In 2009, RMB1.5 billion of non-performing loans granted to the region's equipment manufacturing industry were legally reduced or canceled. In July 2010, China Development Bank issued the Opinions on Further Supporting the Comprehensive Revitalization of the Northeast Old Industrial Base. This document clarified the general requirements, working principles, priorities, and key areas of its supporting efforts for the revitalization of the northeastern region.

6.3.3   Industrial transformation and upgrade

To promote the advancement of agriculture in the northeastern region, a vital base for grain cultivation and agricultural production in China, the government allocated RMB3.43 billion of national debt funds in 2004 to support the region's agriculture, forestry, and water conservancy. Additionally, in January 2010, the General Office of the State Council disseminated the Guiding Opinions on Accelerating the Transformation of Agricultural Development Mode in Northeast China to Develop Modern Agriculture, a joint publication by the NDRC and the Ministry of Agriculture (MOA). It was proposed that by 2015, the region's overall grain production capacity would remain stable at over 100 million metric tons, and by 2020, the region would achieve levels of agricultural land output rate, resource utilization rate, and labor productivity on par with those observed in developed nations. In June 2012, a comprehensive campaign was initiated by the Ministry of Water Resources, the MOF, and the MOA to promote water conservation and enhance grain production in Liaoning, Jilin and Heilongjiang provinces, and Inner Mongolia, planning to invest RMB38 billion within four years to build 38 million *mu* of high-efficient water-saving irrigation projects in these four regions, so as to increase the overall grain production capacity by 20 billion *Jin*[1] and the average annual income, by more than RMB16 billion. In August 2014, the State Council issued the Opinions on Several Major Policies and Measures to Support the Revitalization of Northeast China in the Near Future, which clarified the necessity to consolidate and improve the northeastern region's position as the core area of commodity grain production, and to strengthen the construction of grain storage and logistics facilities. In 2014, a national pilot program for subsoiling 100 million *mu* of farmland was primarily implemented in the northeast; investment from the central government budget reached RMB1.4 billion to support the construction of standardized grain storage facilities with capacity of 6.4 billion *Jin* and a series of bulk grain logistics facilities in the northeast; and additionally, the central government allocated RMB500 million to repair and renovate old and dangerous warehouses with storage capacity of 20 billion *Jin*. The northeastern region would also be the next primary destination of new warehouses with capacity of 100 billion *Jin*.

To support the region's industrial transformation and upgrade, especially in its advantageous fields including petrochemical, iron and steel, major technical equipment, shipbuilding, automobiles and parts, deep processing of agricultural products, and medicine, China issued special treasury bonds to promote the adjustments and transformation of the region's industrial structure, with special focus on localizing the production of major equipment. In 2003, the first 100 treasury bonds projects for revitalizing the old industrial bases in the northeast were launched. These projects received a total investment of RMB61 billion, with RMB31.7 billion sourced from bank loans and the remainder raised by enterprises themselves. The national debt funds allocated for these projects would receive a subsidy at an annual interest rate of 6% for a duration of three years, calculated based on the loan amount for each individual project. After another 197 treasury bonds projects launched in 2004, the total investment in these two batches of projects amounted to RMB108.9 billion. In 2005, 234 more such projects were launched, with investment totaling RMB60.2 billion; in 2006, another 29 projects were added with a total investment of RMB14.4 billion. By the end of 2007, there have been a total of 324 treasury bonds projects carried out in northeast China.

In addition, the NDRC launched the Special Projects for Revitalizing the High-tech Industrialization of the Northeast Old Industrial Base at the end of 2003. As part of this initiative, a total of 118 high-tech industrialization projects in northeast China were

---

[1] *Jin*, a weight unit commonly used in China, is equivalent to 0.5 kilograms. —*Tr.*

implemented before and in 2004, with state investment of RMB560 million; nineteen projects were started in 2005, with a total investment of RMB1.79 billion and national subsidies of RMB163 million. Continuing into 2012, special projects were implemented to restructure the industrial structure of the old industrial base in the region, primarily focusing on supporting the transformation and upgrade of traditional industries such as equipment manufacturing, raw materials, automobiles, and agro-processing. The Three-Year Action Plan for Cultivating and Developing Emerging Industries in Northeast China, formulated by the NDRC in August 2015, outlined an annual allocation of RMB100-RMB200 million to each province (region) in the Northeast and Inner Mongolia Autonomous Region. This funding aimed to support the development of emerging industries in the northeastern region, with the implementation period spanning from 2016 to 2018. In December 2015, the State Council approved the construction plan of Sino-German (Shenyang) High-end Equipment Manufacturing Industrial Park, and envisioned to transform the park into an international, intelligent, and green high-end equipment manufacturing park. In April 2016, the State Council granted approval to designate the Shenyang and Dalian National High-tech Industrial Development Zones as national independent innovation demonstration zones and the sci-tech innovation and entrepreneurship centers in Northeast Asia.

To accelerate transformation of the region's resource-based cities, the Northeast Revitalization Office of the State Council held a symposium on sustainable development of region's resource-based cities in Dalian (Liaoning Province) in August 2005. On the basis of carrying out a pilot project in Fuxin (Liaoning Province), more cities including Daqing, Yichun, Liaoyuan, Baishan, and Panjin were put under the pilot program of economic transformation of resource-based cities. Starting from the experience of the pilot transformation of resource-based cities in northeast China, the State Council issued Several Opinions on Promoting the Sustainable Development of Resource-Based Cities in December 2007, and rolled out such measures as setting up financial transfer payment, reforming resource tax, establishing sustainable development reserve, setting up special loans and earmarking special fund for investment from the central government budget. In March 2008, the first group of 12 cities dependent on now-depleted resources was designated, with six located in the northeast, namely Fuxin, Panjin, Yichun, Liaoyuan, Baishan, and Greater Hinggan Mountains; in March 2009, the second group of 32 cities (districts) of such type was announced, with 10 in the northeast, namely Fushun, Beipiao, Gongchangling, Yangjiazhangzi, Nanpiao, Shulan, Jiutai, Dunhua, Qitaihe, and Wudalianchi; in November 2011, the third group of 25 cities (districts, counties) were identified, with four in the northeast, namely Erdaojiang, Wangqing, Hegang, and Shuangyashan. The central government provided financial support to those cities relying on now-depleted resources through financial transfer payments. Additionally, the same policy was extended to nine county-level areas in the forest regions in the Greater and Lesser Hinggan Mountains. In 2007, RMB832 million was transferred to the first group of 12 cities; in 2008, RMB3.48 billion went to 44 such cities, and in 2013, the transfer payment reached RMB16.8 billion. In June 2009, the NDRC released the first batch of budgetary capital investment plans for employment absorption, comprehensive utilization of resources, and development of alternative industries in resource-based cities in the northeast, involving 19 projects with a total investment of RMB1.1 billion, which were expected to create about 13,000 jobs. In September 2016, the NDRC and other four departments jointly issued the Implementation Opinions on Supporting Industrial Transformation and Upgrade of Old Industrial Cities and Resource-based Cities, proposing that it would take about 10 years to establish and improve the endogenous power mechanism and platform support system to support industrial transformation and upgrade, and build a modern industrial cluster with distinctive characteristics. In January 2017, the NDRC formulated the Guiding Opinions on Strengthening Classification and Guiding the Cultivation of New Kinetic Energy for the Transformation and Development of Resource-Based Cities. In April of the same year, the NDRC and other four departments jointly issued the Notice on Supporting the Construction of the First Batch of Industrial Transformation and Upgrade Demonstration Zones in Old Industrial Cities and Resource-Based Cities, and designated 12 cities (economic zones) including central Liaoning (Shenyang-Anshan-Fushun) and central Jilin (Changchun-Jilin-Songyuan) as the first batch of demonstration zones for industrial transformation and upgrade.

6.3.4   Opening to the outside world and regional cooperation

A series of measures were taken to promote the region's opening up. As early as June 2005, the Implementation Opinions on Promoting the Further Opening to the Outside World of the Northeast Old Industrial Base was promulgated by the State Council, proposing 29 specific measures to further open up northeast China from five aspects. In September 2006, the Catalogue of Priority Industries for Foreign Investment in Liaoning Province was issued by the NDRC and the MOC. And in September 2009, the heads of China and Russia formally approved the Outline of Cooperation Plan between Northeast China of the People's Republic of China and Far East and Eastern

Siberia of the Russian Federation (2009-2018), planning to implement a number of key cooperation projects. Great efforts were also made to promote regional cooperation within the northeast. In January 2009, the Outline of China's Tumen River Regional Cooperative Development Plan—Taking Changchun-Jilin-Tumen as the Pilot Zone for Development and Opening up was approved, which framed a plan of comprehensively promoting Tumen River regional cooperative development through developing and opening up Changchun-Jilin-Tumen region as the leading zone in promoting the development of northeast China. In April 2012, the Several Opinions on Supporting the Construction of China's Tumen River Region (Hunchun) International Cooperation Demonstration Zone was issued, proposing to develop Hunchun International Cooperation Demonstration Zone into an important economic growth pole in northeast China and a bridgehead for the cooperation and development of Tumen River region. In August of the same year, the State Council approved the Outline of the Plan of Opening Northeast China to Northeast Asia (2012-2020), which set up the following six key tasks for regional cooperation: (1) strengthen the construction of border transportation network and port facilities, (2) enhance the leading role of key areas, (3) deepen cooperation in key industries, (4) expand foreign investment cooperation, (5) improve the development and level of foreign trade, and (6) strengthen cooperation in humanities and other fields. In August 2013, the State Council approved the Border Development and Opening Plan of Heilongjiang and Northeast Inner Mongolia, deciding to build Heilongjiang and Northeast Inner Mongolia into bridgeheads and hubs for China's opening to Russia and Northeast Asia. In August 2014, the State Council proposed to strengthen the connection between the revitalization of northeast China and the development of the Russian Far East, and accelerate the preparation of the Sino-Russian Regional Cooperation and Development(Investment)Fund in accordance with the plan approved by the State Council; and promote Harbin and Changchun airports to implement a 72-hour visa-free transit policy for some countries and regions; In March 2017, the General Administration of Customs put forward 22 specific support measures in its Several Measures to Support the New Round of Northeast Revitalization.

To further open the northeastern region, the State Council also approved the establishment of various economic functional zones in the region. In addition to the Shanghai Yangshan Free Trade Port Area and Tianjin Dongjiang Bonded Port Area, the State Council approved the Dalian Dayaowan Free Trade Port Area in August 2006. Covering an area of 6.88 square kilometers, this port area serves as a hub for port operations, logistics, and processing. It enjoys the same favorable policies on taxation and foreign exchange as bonded zones, export processing zones, and free trade logistics parks. Furthermore, the State Council approved the establishment of Dalian Jinpu New Area in June 2014, Harbin New Area in December 2015; and Changchun New Area in February 2016. In March 2017, the State Council also approved the Overall Plan of China (Liaoning) Pilot Free Trade Zone, covering 119.89 square kilometers and including Dalian, Shenyang, and Yingkou. In recent years, the State Council went further to approve the establishment of a number of state-level high-tech industrial development zones, economic and technological development zones, export processing zones, bonded zones, and border economic cooperation zones in northeast China. Till present, there have been 16 state-level high-tech industrial development zones, 22 state-level economic and technological development zones, four export processing zones, five (comprehensive) bonded zones and five border economic cooperation zones in northeast China (see Table 6-1).

Table 6-1   State-level economic functional zones in northeast China

Type	Number	Functional zones
State-level high-tech industrial development zone	16 (156)	Liaoning: Shenyang, Liaoyang, Dalian, Benxi, Anshan, Fuxin, Yingkou, Jinzhou; Jilin: Changchun, Changchun Jingyue, Yanji, Tonghua Medicine, Jilin; Heilongjiang: Harbin, Qiqihar, Daqing
State-level economic and technological development zone	22 (219)	Liaoning: Dalian, Yingkou, Shenyang, Dalian Changxing Island, Jinzhou, Panjin Liaobin Coast, Shenyang Huishan, Tieling, Lushun; Jilin: Changchun, Jilin, Siping Hongzui, Changchun Automobile, Songyuan; Heilongjiang: Harbin, Binxi, Hailin, Harbin Limin, Daqing, Suihua, Mudanjiang, Shuangyashan
Export processing zones	4 (63)	Shenyang (Zhangshi) Export Processing Zone, Shenyang Export Processing Zone, Hunchun Export Processing Zone, Dalian Export Processing Zone
Bonded zone	1 (12)	Dalian Free Trade Zone, Liaoning
Comprehensive bonded zone	4 (65)	Suifenhe Comprehensive Bonded Zone, Comprehensive Bonded Zone of Harbin, Shenyang Comprehensive Bonded Zone, Changchun Xinglong Comprehensive Bonded Zone
Free trade port area	1 (14)	Dalian Dayaowan Free Trade Port Area
Border economic cooperation zone	5 (17)	Dandong Border Economic Cooperation Zone, China Tumen River Region (Hunchun) International Cooperation Demonstration Zone, Heihe Border Economic Cooperation Zone, Suifenhe Border Economic Cooperation Zone, Helong Border Economic Cooperation Zone
Experimental zone for integrated, complete reform	2 (12)	National experimental zone for integrated, complete reform to achieve new industrialization (Shenyang Economic Zone); Experimental zones for integrated, complete reform to Develop Modern Agriculture in the "Two Plains" of Heilongjiang Province
State-level new area	3 (19)	Dalian Jinpu New area, Harbin New area, Changchun New area

(continued)

Type	Number	Functional zones
National innovation demonstration zone	1 (17)	Shenyang-Dalian National Independent Innovation Demonstration Area
Free trade pilot zone	1 (11)	China(Liaoning)Pilot Free Trade Zone

Note: The data in brackets represent the national totals.

Source: Sorted according to the data released by relevant agencies and online data.

In terms of regional cooperation, the State Council proposed in November 2016 in its Opinions on Deepening the Implementation of the New Round of Northeast Revitalization Strategy and Accelerating the Economic Stabilization in Northeast China that, (We will) "establish a cooperation mechanism between Liaoning, Jilin, and Heilongjiang provinces, and Jiangsu, Zhejiang, and Guangdong provinces. Additionally, Shenyang, Dalian, Changchun, and Harbin will pair up with Beijing, Shanghai, Tianjin, and Shenzhen. This will be achieved through the exchange and training of cadres for specific posts, and actively attracting projects and investments to northeast China through market-oriented cooperation". In March 2017, the General Office of the State Council issued the Work Plan for Counterpart Cooperation between Northeast China and Some Provinces and Cities in Eastern China. As part of this plan, counterpart cooperative relations were formed between the three northeastern provinces and the three eastern provinces (Liaoning and Jiangsu, Jilin and Zhejiang, Heilongjiang and Guangdong), as well as the four northeastern cities and the four eastern cities (Shenyang and Beijing, Dalian and Shanghai, Changchun and Tianjin, Harbin and Shenzhen). Furthermore, efforts were made to encourage the Inner Mongolia Autonomous Region to actively engage with eastern provinces and cities in order to explore potential cooperation mechanisms. This initiative represents an innovative approach based on the successful experience of pairing-up assistance between the eastern and western regions.

6.3.5 Ecological and environmental governance

Since the implementation of the Revitalization Strategy, China has attached great importance to the ecological construction and environmental protection in the northeast. According to the Plan for Ecological Protection and Economic Transformation of the Forest Regions in the Greater and Lesser Hinggan Mountains (2010-2020) jointly issued by the NDRC and the State Forestry Administration (SFA) in December 2010, the forest regions in the Greater and Lesser Hinggan Mountains were identified as state-level key pilot zones for establishing a sound mechanism for ecological compensation; the counties (banner[1], districts)with forest coverage rate above 70% within the Greater Hinggan Mountains Forest Ecologic Functional Zone would enjoy the same financial transfer payment policy offered to cities dependent on now-depleted resources; special funds from the central budgetary investment were earmarked to support the forest regions in Greater Hinggan Mountains to develop alternative industries that could fully absorb employment and support forest regions to substitute coal for wood; when pouring investment from the central budget and other relevant central special investment in infrastructure, ecological construction, environmental protection, poverty alleviation and development, and public undertakings, the forest regions in the Greater and Lesser Hinggan Mountains in Heilongjiang Province was allowed to enjoy the same policy for the large-scale development of the western region. Since 2014, the central government has consistently allocated an annual fiscal fund of RMB2.35 billion for the purpose of protecting natural forest resources. This financial support aimed to facilitate the implementation of a pilot project focused on halting all commercial logging activities within the key state-owned forest regions of Heilongjiang. In August 2015, the NDRC and the SFA jointly released the Ecological Protection and Economic Transformation Plan of Changbai Mountain Forest Area (2015-2024).

Treating subsidence areas and rebuilding shanty areas are the key points of environmental governance in the old industrial base in the northeast. In 2003, the Several Opinions of the CPC Central Committee and the State Council on Implementing the Revitalization Strategy of Northeast Old Industrial Base stated that the central government's subsidy ratio to the three northeastern provinces would be increased to 50% for the treatment of coal mining subsidence areas left over from the history of former state-owned key coal mines. At the same time, the state took measures to comprehensively treat the mining subsidence areas of 15 former state-owned key coal mines in northeast China first. In rebuilding shanty areas, the State Council held a symposium on the pilot work of rebuilding shanty areas of local coal mines decentralized by the central government in northeast China in Dalian on August 12, 2005. In October of the same year, the Ministry of Construction issued the Guiding Opinions on Promoting Rebuilding Shanty Areas in Northeast China. Since 2005, Liaoning Province has completed the rebuilding of contiguous shanty areas of more than 50,000 square meters within two years, and started the rebuilding of urban contiguous

---

[1] Banner (*qi*) — an administrative division in China, historically derived from the organizational structure of Mongolian tribes. It is still used today in regions such as Inner Mongolia and others. — *Tr.*

shanty areas of less than 50,000 square meters since 2007. Jilin and Heilongjiang provinces have also fully implemented the plan for rebuilding urban or dilapidated shanty areas since 2006. In November 2008, the central government allocated RMB150 million to carry out the pilot project of rebuilding shanty areas first in state-owned forest regions in Jilin, Heilongjiang, and Inner Mongolia. In August 2014, the State Council stated in its Opinions on Several Major Policies and Measures to Support the Revitalization of Northeast China in the Near Future that the central government would continue to intensify its support for rebuilding shanty areas in northeast China, earmarking more funds for investment from the central government budget to the construction of supporting infrastructure concerning rebuilding shanty areas in industrial and mining areas (including coal mines), state-owned forest regions, and state-owned reclamation areas in northeast China. In 2014, northeast China started to rebuild 700,000 shanty areas, being granted a credit line of about RMB60 billion, and striving to take the lead in basically completing the rebuilding of existing shanty areas in China within the following two or three years.

In addition, the central government decided to increase the allocation of special fund for investment from the central government budget. Starting in 2014, a total of RMB2 billion would be earmarked each year to relocate and renovate old industrial zones in urban areas as well as separated industrial and mining areas in the northeastern region. In March 2015, the NDRC formulated the Special Implementation Measures for the Relocation and Renovation of Old Industrial Zones in Northeast China, which proposed to provide support for 15 old industrial zones in urban areas in 2015, in addition to the 10 that were supported in 2014. Gradually, all eligible old industrial zones in urban areas would be included in this support program, with the ultimate goal of completing the relocation or renovation of these zones by 2020. Moreover, the NDRC would subsidize 30%-40% of the investment in fixed assets for any project meeting the evaluation criteria.

6.4   Results and dilemmas of northeast economic development

Over the past decade since the implementation of the Revitalization Strategy, the northeastern region has made smooth and orderly progress in its reform and opening up, and has achieved rapid socio-economic development, which has demonstrated that the strategy has yielded positive results. However, after a phase of rapid growth, the region's economy has encountered new challenges since 2013, including a significant decrease in investment, a sharp decline in GRP growth, and notable industrial recession, amidst the global economic slowdown and the downward pressure on China's economy. Beside the impact of macroeconomic downturn, the new predicament facing the northeast economy could be attributed to combined effects of various internal and external factors, among which, structural and institutional factors such as severe lag in industrial transformation and upgrade, ineffective or incomplete SOE reforms, underdeveloped private economy, and a lack of vitality in innovation mechanisms played a crucial role.

6.4.1   The initial results of the Revitalization Strategy

Thanks to the strong support of national policies and the active efforts of the three northeastern provinces, the northeastern region has experienced significant growth in total investment in fixed assets and rapid development of both its society and economy since the implementation of the Revitalization Strategy. When it comes to total investment in fixed assets, the region has witnessed remarkable growth since 2004, with an average annual growth rate of 28.8% from 2004 to 2012. This growth rate surpasses that of the eastern region, the entire country, as well as the central and western region (see Table 6-2). In other words, the northeastern region ranked top among the four regions in terms of investment growth over this period. More specifically, the region achieved highest investment growth rate in six out of these nine years.

The rapid growth of total investment in fixed assets led to the region's high-speed economic growth. Between 2005 and 2012, the region's GRP experienced an impressive average annual growth rate of 12.9%. This growth rate was only second to the western region's (13.6%), surpassing the national average (12.6%), as well as the central region (12.8%) and the eastern region (12.1%). Particularly noteworthy is the region's outstanding performance in 2008, with a GRP growth rate of 13.5%. This growth rate was the highest among the four major regions, surpassing the average growth rate of each region by 1.5 percentage points, and exceeding the growth rate in the eastern region by 2.3 percentage points. Such figures demonstrate that the Revitalization Strategy has achieved favorable effects and desirable results in the first decade of its implementation.

Table 6-2   Growth rates of total investment in fixed assets in
Northeast and other regions   Unit: %

Region	2004	2005	2006	2007	2008	2009	2010	2011	2012	2013	2014	2015	2016	2004-2012	2013-2016
National	26.8	26.0	23.9	24.8	25.9	30.0	23.8	12.0	20.3	19.1	14.7	9.8	7.9	23.6	12.8
Eastern	24.5	21.9	19.7	18.7	19.8	22.9	21.3	12.4	16.6	17.9	15.3	12.4	9.0	19.7	13.6
Central	32.1	28.9	29.4	32.8	32.3	35.9	26.2	12.6	22.3	22.1	17.5	15.2	11.6	27.9	16.5
Western	26.8	28.3	24.7	28.4	27.2	38.2	24.6	16.5	23.4	22.8	18.2	8.7	11.9	26.3	15.3
Northeast	32.5	37.6	37.0	32.3	34.4	26.8	29.5	6.2	25.7	13.4	−1.4	−11.1	−23.4	28.8	−6.6

Source: Calculated based on *China Statistical Yearbook* over the years.

As to the implementation effect, 11 out of the 16 main targets set in the Northeast Revitalization Plan were achieved during the 11th Five-year Plan period, leaving only five of them unachieved, namely the proportion of the output from tertiary industry in GRP, the ratio of R&D expenditure to GRP, the forest coverage rate, the number of urban basic endowment insurance participants, and the average schooling years. It is important to note that the third and fourth targets are binding targets. Notably, the average annual growth rate of GRP per capita and overall grain output in the northeast reached 13.5% and 5.5% respectively during this period. Additionally, the proportion of value added of non-public sectors increased from 36% to 54%, the urbanization rate rose from 52% to 57%, and the comprehensive utilization rate of industrial solid waste grew from 51.9% to 64%, which all exceeded the planned targets significantly.

During the 12th Five-year Plan period, most of the 25 main targets set in the 12th Five-year Plan for Revitalizing Northeast China were accomplished, with only two exceptions: the retention rate of nine-year compulsory education and the intensity of R&D investment. Over this five-year period, the urbanization rate of the permanent population in the northeastern region increased by 3.7 percentage points, the share of the value added of the tertiary industry in GDP increased by 8.6 percentage points, and grain output increased by 24.5%. Additionally, the per capita disposable income of urban and rural residents grew at an average annual rate of 8.8% and 9.6% respectively, both exceeding the regional economic growth rate. These achievements demonstrated the effective achievement of the revitalization targets as outlined in the 12th Five-year Plan. Apart from the slightly lower than planned retention rate of nine-year compulsory education, all other binding targets were successfully achieved.

6.4.2 The new predicament facing the northeast economy

In the face of the global economic downturn and the downward pressure on China's economy, coupled with the ineffective or unfulfilled institutional reforms and the lagging industrial transformation and upgrade, the northeastern region's economy has encountered new difficulties since 2013. After experiencing rapid growth, the region's economy encountered difficulties. The growth rate of GRP dropped from an 8.4% year-on-year increase in 2013 to 5.9% in 2014, 4.5% in 2015, and further declined to 2.5% in 2016. This put the region at the lowest rank among the four major regions during these four years. In comparison to 2012, the region's growth rate of GRP fell by 7.7 percentage points in 2016, while the national average fell by only 2.9 percentage points during the same period. From 2013 to 2016, the average annual growth rate of the region's GRP was only 5.3%, which was 3.0 percentage points lower than the national average, 2.9 percentage points lower than the eastern region, and 3.4 and 3.8 percentage points lower than the central and western regions respectively. In particular, the provincial GRP of Liaoning grew at a rate of only 3.0% in 2015, the lowest among all provinces (autonomous regions and municipalities) in China. Meanwhile, the growth rates in Heilongjiang and Jilin were only 5.7% and 6.5% respectively, positioning them as the third and fourth lowest in China. The situation varied in 2016. On the one hand, Liaoning witnessed a significant decline in GRP growth, with a decrease of 2.5% compared to the previous year.[1] On the other hand, Heilongjiang and Jilin experienced a slight improvement with GRP growth rates of 6.1% and 6.9% respectively, showing a marginal increase from the previous year.

The sharp slowdown in the region's GRP in recent years could primarily be attributed to the substantial decline in investment and the ongoing economic recession in the industrial sector. The investment growth rate in the northeastern region has consistently dropped since 2013, with a total drop of 49.1 percentage points in the first four years. Between 2013 and 2016, the average annual growth rate of total investment in fixed assets in northeast China was −6.6%. Specifically, in 2014, 2015, and 2016, the growth rates were recorded at −1.4%, −11.1%, and −23.4% respectively, all significantly lower than the average growth rate observed in other regions. Notably, the rapid growth of the northeast economy in the past few years was mainly driven by investment, mirroring the development pattern observed in the western region. From 2000 to 2011, 70.1% of GRP growth in the northeast was fueled by capital formation, surpassing the 49.9% in the eastern region and the national average of 58.5%. However, with a lack of weak innovation drive, the substantial decline in investment growth in the northeast in recent years has sharply declined the contribution rate of capital formation to economic growth, with the rate plummeting to an abnormal 2.7% during the 2012-2016 period.

In terms of industrial growth, the recent decline in market demand significantly reduced the prices of energy and resource products, and resulted in a severe overcapacity in heavy and chemical industries such as coal, steel, cement, and plate glass. Consequently, companies in those sectors were facing production and operational difficulties, causing industrial growth to slow down and profitability to decline sharply.

---

[1] Admittedly, the rapid decline of Liaoning's economic growth rate in previous years resulted partially from "getting rid of adulteration or exaggeration in statistics". In 2016, the GRP in Liaoning decreased by 2.5%, while the household consumption increased by 10.1%, and the per capita disposable income of urban and rural residents increased by 5.6% and 6.8% respectively.

This situation was particularly urgent in the northeastern region for the sake of its heavy reliance on heavy and chemical industries. In 2015, the total value added by industrial enterprises with annual main business revenue of at least RMB20 million in China witnessed a year-on-year increase of 6.1%. However, there was a decline of 2.3% in the northeastern region. Specifically, Liaoning experienced a decrease of 4.8%, Heilongjiang witnessed a slight increase of 0.4%, and Jilin only saw a modest growth of 5.3%. Furthermore, the total profits of these enterprises dropped by 2.3% compared to the previous year, but the northeast experienced a significant decline of 33.3% (specifically, down 38.1%, 16.4%, and 58.5% in Liaoning, Jilin, and Heilongjiang respectively). As a result of the industrial recession, the value added of the secondary industry in the northeastern region only saw a modest increase of 1.5% in 2015, followed by a decline of 1.0% in 2016 compared to the previous year. Specifically, Liaoning experienced a decrease of 0.3% and 7.7%, while Heilongjiang saw a meager increase of 1.4% and 2.6%, both significantly lower than the national average. Nevertheless, the value added of the tertiary industry in the northeastern region showed a more positive growth, with an increase of 8.4% in 2015 and 5.8% in 2016 (see Table 6-3). These figures indicate that the recent economic challenges faced by the northeastern region were primarily caused by the recession in industrial sectors, particularly in Liaoning. This recession not only affected the relative performance but also resulted in an absolute decline, resulting in decreased local fiscal and tax revenues, increased employment pressure in urban areas, and heightened social tensions. In 2015, Liaoning experienced a decrease of 33.4% in public budget revenues, while Heilongjiang saw a drop of 10.4% in public fiscal revenues, and Jilin witnessed a decline of 2.0% in full-caliber financial revenue. Furthermore, the tax revenue organized by the tax authorities of the three northeastern provinces (before deducting export tax rebates) fell by 12.1% in the same year, which is 19.3 percentage points lower than the national average growth rate.

Table 6-3   Growth rates of the three industries in the northeast and other regions   Unit: %

Region	2015				2016			
	GRP	Primary industry	Secondary industry	Tertiary industry	GRP	Primary industry	Secondary industry	Tertiary industry
Eastern	8.0	3.1	6.6	9.9	7.6	2.8	6.0	9.4
Central	8.1	4.0	7.3	10.7	8.0	3.6	7.1	10.0
Western	8.6	4.7	8.3	10.0	8.3	4.5	8.2	9.4
Northeastern	4.5	4.6	1.5	8.4	2.5	1.4	−1.0	5.8

(continued)

Region	2015				2016			
	GRP	**Primary industry**	**Secondary industry**	**Tertiary industry**	**GRP**	**Primary industry**	**Secondary industry**	**Tertiary industry**
Liaoning	3.0	3.8	−0.3	7.2	−2.5	−4.6	−7.7	2.5
Jilin	6.3	4.8	5.2	8.4	6.9	3.9	6.2	8.8
Heilongjiang	5.7	5.2	1.4	10.4	6.1	5.3	2.6	8.5

Source: Calculated based on *China Statistical Yearbook* (2016-2017).

6.4.3 Causes for the economic predicament in northeast China

The current economic predicament faced by the northeastern region could be attributed to a combination of external and internal factors. Alongside the global economic slump and China's macroeconomic decline, several structural and institutional factors played a crucial role. The structural factors included the substantial presence of SOEs, especially those under central administration, a high proportion of resource-based industries in the economy, and concentration of industries with excess capacity; the institutional factors consisted of ineffective or incomplete reforms on SOEs, an underdeveloped private sector, and a lack of innovation. These factors further exacerbated the impact of the external factors. In fact, many other resource-based areas and old industrial bases were also facing similar challenges. For instance, in 2015, Shanxi witnessed a year-on-year decrease of 2.8% in the value added of industrial enterprises with annual main business revenue of at least RMB20 million, with the total profits dropping by 131.9%. Gansu and Xinjiang experienced a 132.1% and 50.2% decrease in the total profits respectively, while other areas like Tibet, Qinghai, Inner Mongolia, and Shaanxi, saw declines of over 20%. In summary, the current economic predicament in northeast China in recent years could be attributed to following causes.

The first was the impact of increasing downward pressure on economy. Since 2011, China's economy has experienced a decline in national GDP growth, dropping from 9.5% in 2011 to 6.9% in 2015 and further to 6.7% in 2016. This slowdown of economic growth has significantly reduced the market demand for energy and raw materials, resulting in egregious overcapacity in various sectors such as coal, steel, cement, electrolytic aluminum, plate glass, and petrochemicals, a significant drop in product prices, and poor performance of enterprises nationwide. Also in the picture was northeast China, a region under great pressure from "cutting overcapacity and reducing excess inventory". According to the Cement Associations of the Three Northeastern

Provinces, the production capacity of clinker and cement in northeast China reached 119.33 million tons and 254.68 million tons respectively in 2015, while the actual sales of cement only amounted to 95.32 million tons, resulting in an excess rate of 52% and 63% for clinker and cement production respectively. Additionally, the cement industry in the northeastern region has accumulated over RMB40 billion of idle assets.[1] This severe overcapacity and declining market demand led to a 15.8% decrease in cement sales and a 26% decrease in prices in 2015. Consequently, the industry experienced its first overall loss, with both sales and prices dropping simultaneously.[2] In order to effectively cut industrial capacity and carry out policy-mandated shutdowns, Jilin Coal Industry Group planned to shut down 21 unprofitable mines featuring resource exhaustion and low safety standards from 2015 to 2018, reducing a total production capacity of 15.03 million tons. The plan aimed to relocate 17,000 employees with a budget of RMB3.8 billion, and resolve nearly RMB4 billion of non-performing assets, including bank loans. The key challenges within the ambit of "cutting industrial capacity" lie in effectively managing employee resettlement and addressing debt issues, both of which are formidable undertakings.

The second was the severe delay in industrial transformation and upgrade in the northeastern region. In terms of the three-industry structure, the tertiary industry's contribution to the region's GRP remained lower than the national average (see Table 6-4), despite a constant increase in its share, rising from 37.0% in 2010 to 49.5% in 2016. Specifically, the added value of the tertiary industry in Jilin accounted for only 41.9% in 2016, which was 9.7 percentage points lower than the national average. From 2000 to 2016, there emerged an unfavorable shift in industrial structure in this region, where witnessed a 1.4 percentage points increase in the contribution of the primary industry to GRP, yet a 13.9 percentage points decline in that of the tertiary industry, despite the uncompleted process of industrialization. In terms of internal structure of the secondary industry, traditional industries in the region held a high proportion, while high-tech industries were underdeveloped. Between 2006 and 2012, the output value or revenues from the region's high-tech industries fluctuated between 4.6% and 5.1%, far lower than the national average (Xiao Guodong, 2014). Compared to industries above the designated size, the prime operating revenue of high-tech industries in the northeast accounted for only 7.1% (specifically, 6.6% in Liaoning, 8.8% in Jilin, and 4.3% in

---

[1] [2] Reported by the Cement Associations of the Three Northeastern Provinces to the research group of the National Committee of the Chinese People's Political Consultative Conference: Report on Resolving Overcapacity, Getting Rid of Difficulties and Increasing Efficiency in the Cement Industry in Northeast China, Mar. 24, 2015.

Heilongjiang) in 2016. This not only fell short of the central region (9.2%) and the western region (10.4%), but also lagged far behind the eastern region (16.1%) and the national average (13.3%). Additionally, the industries in the region were faced with limited capacity to resist external interference. This was primarily due to various factors, such as a high proportion of energy and raw materials sectors, the presence of large-sized industries with overcapacity, a short industrial chain, insufficient depth in processing, and low technological content. The majority of incumbent industrial enterprises were concentrated in the manufacturing sector, and positioned at the lower or middle part of the industrial and value chains. However, the development of upstream key raw materials, R&D of core components, and downstream services remained underdeveloped. These circumstances indicated that, in recent years, the industrial transformation and upgrade in northeast China was relatively slow or even lagging behind, especially in comparison to the wave of accelerating transformation and upgraded witnessed across the country, particularly in the eastern region.

Table 6-4　　　　　　　Changes in the three industries structure in
Northeast China and the whole country　　　　　Unit: %

Industry and sector	Whole country					Northeast China				
	2010	2014	2015	2016	Change	2010	2014	2015	2016	Change
Primary	9.5	9.1	8.8	8.6	−0.9	10.7	11.2	11.4	12.1	1.4
Secondary	46.4	43.1	40.9	39.8	−6.6	52.3	47.3	43.0	38.4	−13.9
Tertiary	44.1	47.8	50.2	51.6	7.5	37	41.5	45.6	49.5	12.5

Source: Calculated based on *China Statistical Yearbook* over the years.

The third was the ineffective or incomplete SOE reforms. Since the implementation of the Revitalization Strategy, the relevant departments have adopted a series of policies and measures to actively promote the SOE reforms in the northeastern region, including speeding up the strategic restructuring of SOEs, relieving SOEs' obligation to operate social programs, providing greater support for policy-mandated bankruptcy, and carrying out pilot reforms on large collectives run by factories. These measures had a positive impact on boosting the vitality of SOEs in the region. However, it should be noted that the state-owned sector predominated the region's economy, characterized by low operational efficiency and the persistent burden of SOEs. In 2016, state-controlled industrial enterprises contributed 39.4% to the total operating revenues of the region's industrial enterprises with an annual main business revenue of at least RMB20 million. This figure included 44.8% in Liaoning, 40.3% in Heilongjiang, and 33.9% in Jilin, all significantly higher than the national average of 20.6%. Despite holding 53.2% of the total assets, state-controlled industrial enterprises in the northeast only generated 39.4% of the total operating revenues and 16.4% of the total profits. Notably, the "squeezing a tube of toothpaste" approach to reform failed to fundamentally alleviate the SOEs' obligations to operate social programs and support large collectives, but instead, led to constant rise in the costs of reform. For instance, an investigation conducted in March 2015 by the author and the National Committee of the Chinese People's Political Consultative Conference in Jilin Province revealed that, Jilin Coal Industry Group and Jilin Forest Industry Group still retained certain social functions, including running hospitals, supplying water, heating, and power, and offering property management service, and operating retirement institutions. The reform on collectively owned businesses operated by SOEs in Jilin Province affected a total of 3,054 enterprises and 496,000 employees. Among those enterprises, 2,532 were collectively owned businesses that were formerly controlled by the central government or operated by SOEs below the provincial level, involving 374,000 employees. To support this reform, the province was required to allocate over RMB30 billion in matching funds to provide economic compensation, subsequent endowment insurance, and medical insurance for retired employees. Additionally, Bensteel Group in Benxi of Liaoning continued to provide essential services such as water, power, and heating to over 20,000 households, as well as operate numerous vocational education and medical institutions to meet the education and healthcare needs of its staff and their family members, receiving annual subsidies exceeding RMB100 million.[1]

The fourth was the underdevelopment of private sectors in the region. Due to the inadequate or ineffective implementation of various policies, limited market access, difficulties and high costs of financing for enterprises, and the crowding-out effect caused by monopolistic SOEs, the underdeveloped private economy in the northeast has become a bottleneck in the implementation of the Revitalization Strategy. Among the three northeastern provinces, Liaoning had the highest proportion of private economy's added value to GRP, though it was still less than 67% in 2013. Jilin accounted for only 50.9% (including SMEs), while Heilongjiang had a mere 49.2% (Liu Jiajie, 2014). In 2015, the value added of the private economy in Changchun City was only 46% of its GRP, significantly lower than the national average. In terms of employment, private and individual enterprises employed 36.2% of the working population in Liaoning in 2014, and 35.4% in Jilin. These figures were much lower compared to emerging coastal

---

[1] Liu Huang, Wang Bingkun, Xin Linxia et al. "A large number of zombie companies cannot afford 'survival' or 'death'", *Economic Information Daily*, Jan. 25, 2016.

industrial zones such as 54.9% in Jiangsu, 53.1% in Zhejiang, and 40.9% in Guangdong. The region's private economy was largely underdeveloped and relatively weak in comprehensiveness due to its small economic output and low industrial level. Furthermore, local private enterprises were typically small in size, and only a few managed to grow into leading enterprises with strong driving forces. It should be noted that, unlike emerging coastal industrial zones, the northeastern region with old industrial bases was economically dominated by SOEs, especially those under central administration in some key industries. Despite the availability of private capital in some sectors, private enterprises have heavily relied on these SOEs for their production and operation, placing them at a disadvantage in the market competition. Furthermore, the outdated employment concept inherited from the planned economy era, as well as obstacles related to equitable market access, a level playing field, financial services, and law enforcement, have also impeded the healthy development of the private economy in northeast China.

The fifth was the insufficient of vitality in scientific and technological innovation. The region's economy primarily driven by investment over a long period of time, was hindered by a severe lack of funding for research and development, weak capacity for innovation, and ineffective utilization of scientific and technological achievements. In 2016, China's intensity of R&D investment (the proportion of internal expenditure on R&D to GDP) stood at 2.11%, while it was only 1.69% in Liaoning, 0.94% in Jilin, and 0.99% in Heilongjiang, all being significantly lower than the average level in the eastern region and the whole country (see Table 6-5). Among the industrial enterprises with an annual main business revenue of at least RMB20 million in the region, only 4.2% owned R&D institutions and only 10.1% engaged in R&D activities, both ranking the lowest among the four major regions. Furthermore, the internal expenditure of R&D accounted for merely 0.74% of prime operating revenues, with Jilin being as low as 0.39%, which is far below the national average. Insufficient funding for R&D resulted in a very low proportion of domestic applications for three types of patents in the northeast compared to the national total in 2016, with 3.2% of patent applications accepted and 3.3% of patent applications granted, far lower than the share of the region's GRP and population in national total. In recent years, the region's comprehensive index of technological progress also witnessed a decline in ranking with the country. From 2009 to 2014, Liaoning dropped from sixth to 11th; Heilongjiang, from 12th to 14th; and Jilin, from 14th to 19th (Development Planning Department of Ministry of Science and Technology, 2001; 2016). In addition, despite the abundant presence of esteemed universities and scientific research institutions in the region, there was a lack of close integration and active interaction between technology and economy, as well as inefficiency in the utilization of scientific and technological findings, particularly at the local level. In 2015, only 27.7% of scientific and technological findings were applied and commercialized within Changchun city. Therefore, only through sustained and persistent efforts could the region achieve a comprehensive shift from growth fueled by factors or investments to innovation-driven growth.

Table 6-5   Comparison of main scientific and technological indicators between northeast China and other regions in 2016   Unit: %

Region	Proportion of expenditure on R&D in GDP	Industrial enterprises above designated size			Domestic applications for three kinds of patents	
		Proportion of enterprises with R&D institutions	Proportion of enterprises carrying out R&D	Proportion of internal expenditure of R&D in prime operating revenues	Number of patent applications accepted	Number of patent applications granted
National	2.11 (2.03*)	16.3	23.0	0.94	100.0	100.0
Eastern	2.65*	21.8	28.3	1.11	67.4	68.5
Central	1.49*	10.4	17.1	0.74	15.5	14.0
Western	1.24*	7.5	14.8	0.66	13.2	13.3
Northeast	1.27*	4.2	10.1	0.74	3.2	3.3
Liaoning	1.69	5.1	13.4	1.10	1.6	1.5
Jilin	0.94	2.7	6.0	0.39	0.6	0.6
Heilongjiang	0.99	4.5	9.7	0.78	1.1	1.1

Note: * Calculated by aggregating the GDP of each region.

Source: Calculated in accordance with *China Statistical Yearbook* (2017) and *China Statistical Yearbook on Science and Technology* (2017).

6.5   Strategic thinking on revitalizing northeast economy

In conclusion, the recent economic predicament facing the northeastern region could be primarily attributed to the combined effects of cyclical, structural, and institutional factors, among which, the internal structural and institutional factors played a crucial role. However, there were still some misconceptions regarding the nature of the predicament. First, the external environment should take the sole blame for it. While the decline in market demand and the downward pressure on economic growth did have a more direct and obvious impact on resource-based areas and old industrial bases in the northeast, other regions facing similar macroeconomic conditions did not experience the same level of decline. This indicated that local structural and institutional factors played a more decisive role. Second, the temporary economic difficulties faced by the northeast were exaggerated, leading to a misguided perception that the Revitalization Strategy has failed.[1] In reality, the plight facing the northeastern development was quite similar to what depressed areas in developed European or American countries once experienced. According to international experience, the economic revitalization of an old industrial area trapped in a state of depression could seldom be achieved overnight. For the northeastern region, the comprehensive economic revitalization would be a long-term and arduous task, requiring gradual progress. Moreover, the first decade of implementing the strategy has witnessed rapid economic growth in the northeast, accompanied by many other notable achievements. The current economic challenges faced by the region differ greatly from those prior to the implementation of the strategy. Therefore, by no means should we ignore the effectiveness of the Revitalization Strategy based solely on the current temporary setback, nor thoroughly negate the national strategy. Evidently, the argument that the Revitalization Strategy has failed lacks substantial evidence (Zhang Keyun, 2015).

Based on international experience, following accelerated industrialization and urbanization, along with an increase in economic outputs and development levels, the economy in a region tends to slow down, shifting from high-speed growth to medium-to-high speed growth, and then to medium-to-low or even low-speed growth. However, despite the already low economic growth rate over the past few years, hovering between medium and low-speed growth, the northeastern region has not yet entered the stage of medium and low-speed growth. In 2016, the region's GRP per capita reached US$7,218, with an urbanization rate of 61.7%. Overall, the region was still in the first half stage of the late industrialization and the middle stage of urbanization, as both processes are far from being completed. Notably, during the 12th Five-year Plan period (2011-2015), the region even experienced an accelerated urbanization, with the urbanization rate growing by an average of 0.74 percentage points per annum. Although this rate was lower than that of the eastern, central, and western regions, it was significantly higher than the

---

[1] China Business Network, "Where Is the Crux of the Failure to Revitalize Northeast China?", http://www. cb.com.cn/index/show/jj/cv/cv1151649878, Aug. 4, 2014. "Media Debate: Is the Revitalization of Northeast China A Failure?" *Window of the Northeast*, 2015(7).

average growth rate of 0.58 percentage points from 2001 to 2005 and 0.49 percentage points from 2006 to 2010. Moreover, the region, boasting China's important old industrial bases, still possesses numerous advantages in various aspects. These include a solid foundation for scientific and technological advancements, a well-established educational system, and a thriving industrial sector. Additionally, the region has a large pool of highly skilled workers and serves as an important base of grain production and equipment manufacturing in China. It is evident that the region's economy is just running into temporary difficulties but has immense untapped growth potential. As long as we boldly emancipate our minds from the shackles of the outdated conceptions, rely on deepening reform, and enhancing openness on all fronts, we can successfully promote institutional restructuring, industrial transformation, and upgrade. Consequently, the northeastern region is well-prepared and capable of achieving sustainable medium-to-high speed growth in the long run. To revive its economy and achieve comprehensive revitalization under the "new normal", it is essential to move beyond solely focusing on turning around state-owned enterprises. Instead, we must prioritize finding both temporary and permanent solutions to the new predicament. This involves integrating economic bailout with transformation and upgrading as well as institutional re-engineering, and establishing a long-term mechanism that supports the comprehensive and sustained revitalization of the region.

First of all, we need to proactively address overcapacity and achieve a turnaround. The task of "cutting overcapacity" plays a significant role in promoting supply-side structural reform. To address overcapacity of SOEs engaged in the steel and coal industries and allow the so-called "zombie" enterprises to exit the market, the central government earmarked an award fund of RMB100 billion to facilitate the restructuring of industrial enterprises, which would be evenly allocated over a span of two years, with RMB50 billion specifically designated for the year 2016. The primary focus was to aid in the reemployment and training of workers who have been laid off during the restructuring process. Currently, it is essential for relevant departments to promptly devise implementation plans, as well as provide support policies and measures. This is necessary in order to assist struggling enterprises in the northeastern region, particularly those in steel, coal, cement, and other similarly challenged industries, to achieve a successful turnaround and upgrade their operations. In addition, it is crucial to eliminate outdated production capacity in accordance with the law and encourage voluntary reductions in inefficient capacity. For the coal industry, a recommended approach would be to implement the coal production capacity replacement policy, with an aim to incentivize coal enterprises in the region to gradually cease operations and close down mines grappling with issues such as resource depletion, excessive personnel, exorbitant costs, and lack of prospects for recovery. Subsequently, these enterprises could shift their focus towards exploring new coal resources in nearby areas abundant in natural resources. Furthermore, considering the difficulties posed by declining coal prices, substantial financial losses, financial strain, and a heavy tax burden, it was imperative to restore the VAT rate of 13% for coal products. For the cement industry, it is recommended that the region be included in a pilot program aimed at addressing China's cement overcapacity and providing corresponding policy support. The following measures should be considered: setting equal or reduced development goals for the industry to control overproduction; allowing cement enterprises to participate in the carbon emissions trading market, thereby promoting market access; adopting market-oriented approaches for project approvals to streamline the process; enhancing the quality standards of cement products and expediting the phase-out of P.C 32.5 cement; promoting industry self-discipline by encouraging cement enterprises in the northeastern region to sign and adhere to a self-discipline convention on staggered peak production. Breach of contract should be met with liability; assisting northeastern cement enterprises in establishing funds to reduce overcapacity, with financial support from the central government and the three provinces; granting discount loans to facilitate mergers and acquisitions within the cement industry. In addition, in view of the sharp decline in fiscal revenue growth in the region and the fiscal challenges faced by local governments, it is crucial to explore and establish an underpinning social security mechanism to ensure a safety net for livelihood in the three northeastern provinces as soon as possible.

Secondly, we need to accelerate the all-round industrial transformation and upgrade. To achieve the full revitalization of the northeast, we must clear up the misconception of solely focusing on the secondary industry and simply relying on a quick-fix solution of turning around SOEs (Wang Luolin & Wei Houkai, 2005b). That is, the revitalization efforts in the northeast should not solely concentrate on the secondary industry. The specific measures to be implemented are as follows: (1) Establishing a long-term mechanism for innovation-driven development by increasing input in innovation. This entails encouraging businesses to allocate more resources towards R&D, to establish various types of key laboratories, engineering technology research centers, postdoctoral mobile stations, to acquire overseas high-tech enterprises and sci-tech projects, and to foster strategic alliances for industrial technology innovation; promoting the integration of government, industry, university, banking, and media through taking high-tech industrial development zones and university-based science parks as the bases, through establishing a group of integrated innovation complexes as well as multi-level and multi-type sci-tech innovation platforms, and through picking up the pace in developing institutions and mechanisms for the application of sci-tech achievements in the region, including a S&T achievements conversion venture investment fund for the revitalization of the northeast. (2) Vigorously developing emerging industries of strategic importance. This includes focusing our efforts on industries such as intelligent equipment manufacturing, information technology, biomedicine, new materials, and new energy vehicles. To achieve this, we will establish Harbin, Changchun, Shenyang, and Dalian as the main hubs, with other key cities in the region serving as connecting points. By shifting our development focus from resource-based industries to emerging sectors, we aim to transform the region into a significant national center for technical research, development, and innovation. This will be achieved through enhanced collaboration between universities, banks, and local governments, as well as inter-provincial cooperation. Additionally, we will strengthen ties with the Beijing-Tianjin-Hebei region, working together to establish a thriving hub for strategic emerging industries in the central part of northeast China. (3) Accelerating the growth of emerging service industries, we should not only incentivize enterprises to establish their headquarters, operation centers, R&D centers, and design centers in the northeast, but also provide substantial support for the rapid development of sectors such as business services, modern logistics, modern finance, sci-tech services, healthcare services for the elderly, e-commerce, information and consultancy services, as well as community services. Additionally, fostering seamless integration among modern agriculture, modern manufacturing, and the service industry is crucial in order to develop new business models and create new growth poles.

Finally, a sustained long-term mechanism should be established through institutional re-engineering. The key to reviving the northeastern economy lies in institutional re-engineering, which involves building a sustained mechanism that support full revitalization through deepening reforms in following aspects. (1) There should be a vigorous development of the mixed ownership economy. This entails adopting various methods and means to embrace mixed ownership of SOEs, in order to enhance their vitality, control, influence, and ability to resist risks. The diversity of equities should extend beyond the "monopoly of state-owned assets", in accordance with the characteristics of different industries and enterprises. (2) Coordinated plans should be made to relieve SOEs from performing social functions. This can be achieved by diversifying fund channels and developing an overall plan to solve problems with a "solution package". In reference to the practice of relieving centrally administered SOEs of the burden of providing water, electricity, heating, gas, and property management services to their employees' homes, the central government can provide half of the fund needed to support SOEs in the region to transfer or strip off the social programs they previously operated. (3) Reforms on collectively owned businesses operated by SOEs should be completed as soon as possible. In the case of Jilin Province, the central government has recently announced that it will subsidize 50% and reward 30% of the funds needed to resettle employees in ailing large-scale collectively owned businesses, with an additional 16% coming from the provincial public budget. This leaves only 4% for the SOEs and local government to bear. However, there remains significant funding gap for the transfer of endowment insurance relations and the coverage of medical insurance for retired employees in those businesses. The corresponding financial support from the central government is therefore required. (4) We need to enable the private sector to develop and truly flourish. For this, it is necessary to break the monopoly of SOEs on industrial chains, further ease market access, and fully implement existing policies, so as to unlock the growth potential of private businesses in a more favorable business environment. (5) Turning around SOEs should be integrated with developing private economy. As an incentive, employment subsidies can be introduced to encourage private businesses to hire or resettle employees from SOEs. The central government and local governments can consider granting subsidies and providing income tax incentives to private enterprises that hire workers affected by the reduction of overcapacity in SOEs, the exit of "zombie" enterprises, and the reallocation of personnel in collectively owned businesses operated by SOEs. These measures should be in line with the relevant policies aimed at facilitating the reemployment of those who have lost their jobs.

Chapter 7
Strategy for the Rise of Central China

Following the strategies for encouraging the eastern region to take the lead in pursuing development, advancing the large-scale development of the western region, and revitalizing the old industrial bases in the northeast region, another strategic decision was made to promote the rise of the central region of China. The strategy for the rise of central China is a critical element of the overall national strategy for regional development. Due to its implementation since 2004 and the support of relevant policies, the central region has gained a good momentum for its socio-economic development, and gradually narrowed the relative gap with the eastern region. However, it should be noted that the central region still faces many obstacles and challenges in achieving a full-scale rise as soon as possible. In the current context of pursuing the Belt and Road Initiative and promoting innovation-driven regional coordinated development, it is imperative to take new strategic policies and measures to help the region to achieve green transition and leapfrog development through innovation, and to promote its comprehensive, coordinated, and sustainable development of economy and society.

7.1   Basic judgment on the so-called "central downfall"

The central region covers an area of 1.028 million square kilometers, that is, 10.7% of China's total land area and includes six inland provinces, namely Shanxi, Henan, Anhui, Hubei, Hunan, and Jiangxi. And at the end of 2016, the central region contained a population of 367 million, accounting for 26.6% of the national total; the GRP reached RMB16.06 trillion, accounting for 20.6% of China's GDP; and the GRP per-capita amounted to about RMB43,800, or US$6,588, which put the region in the "upper-middle income" as defined by the World Bank. Thanks to its advantages in geographic location (in the hinterland of China), transportation, population, natural, cultural, and tourism resources, industrial and agricultural foundations, and carrying capacity of resources and environment, the central region has established itself as a national grain production base, an energy raw material base, and an equipment manufacturing base. Since the founding of the PRC in 1949, the region has contributed greatly to China's industrialization and modernization.

At the beginning of the 21st century, when the central region seemed to be declining and lagging behind other parts of China, the "central downfall" problem emerged as a hot issue both in academia and on media. Quite a few scholars held that the central region was somewhat "sinking" (An Husen & Yin Guangwei, 2009; Yang Shenggang & Zhu Hong, 2007; Qin Chenglin & Tang Yong, 2006; Liu Naiquan & Zhang Xueliang, 2005; Li Yue, 2005; Li Lingling, et al., 2004; Zhou Shaosen et al., 2003), but there were others who argued that there was no sort of "sinking" in the central region. What needs to be discussed here is whether the downfall has severely hit the region since the reform and opening up. To answer this question, we should first define the term by certain criteria. The term "central downfall" may mainly refer to two situations: One is "downfall in growth", that is, the central region was locked in a low-growth trap, with the lowest economic growth rate among China's four major regions. The other is "downfall in level of development", that is, as time went by, the relative development level of the central region was on a continuous decline, well below the average level across China. Here we will discuss whether the economy in the central region has really met its downfall from these two aspects.

We can calculate the growth rate in the eastern, northeast, central, and western regions based on the GRP data and growth index of each province (autonomous region and municipality) (Wei Houkai, 2009). The results showed that over the 25 years from 1980 to 2004, only six years (1980, 1987-1988, 1991, and 2002-2003) saw the low growth rate in the central region, with its growth rate of GRP ranking lowest among the four regions. After experiencing low growth from 2002 to 2003, the GRP in the six central provinces exhibited a remarkable acceleration in 2004. The growth rate of GRP in the central region was 9.5% in 2002 and 10.6% in 2003, lower than that in the western and northeastern regions and far lower than that in the eastern region; but in 2004, the rate in the central region stood at 12.7%, higher than the average level in the northeastern region and equal to that in the western region. This shows that in most years since the reform and opening up, the central region did not experience low growth, that is, without any "downfall in growth". In contrast, the northeastern region got stuck in low growth in 14 out of the 25 years from 1980 to 2004, showing a rather serious "downfall in growth"; and the western region also experienced such downfall in five out of these 25 years.

Overall, the GRP in the central region grew at an annual average rate of 10.1% over the 1980-2004 period, lower than that in the eastern region (12.0%) and the average rate in China (10.7%), but higher than that in the northeast (9.0%) and the western region (9.6%). Specifically, from 1980 to 1999, the annual growth rate of GRP in the central region was 10.0%, higher than that in the northeast (8.6%) and the western region (9.4%); from 2000 to 2004, the growth rate of GRP in the central region was 10.1%, almost equal to that in the northeast and western regions (both were 10.2%). This shows that, the "downfall in growth" in the central region only occurred in a few years since the reform and opening up until the beginning of the 21st century, and in a quite moderate way. However, it should be pointed out that in most years during this period, the growth rate of GRP in the central region was below the national average, and much lower than that in the eastern region. As shown in Figure 7-1, before implementing the strategy for the rise of central China in 2004, the relative growth rate of GRP in the central region was mostly lower than 1.

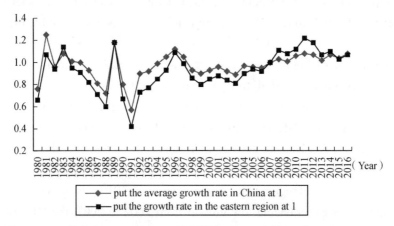

Figure 7-1   Relative growth rate of GRP in Central China from 1980 to 2016

Note: The relative growth rate in the central region is the ratio of the growth rate in the central region to the average growth rate in China or the eastern region.

Source: Calculated in accordance with the data from *China Regional Economy: A Profile of 17 Years of Reform and Opening Up* and *China Statistical Yearbook* (over the years) compiled by the National Bureau of Statistics.

Now take a look at the "downfall in level of development". Taking the average level across China as a reference, we can examine whether the development level in the central region was falling or not. Per-capita GRP is an important comprehensive index to measure the development level of a regional economy. If the average level in China is 100, the relative level of GRP per capita in the central region was 80.4 in 1983, 76.6

in 1990, 74.6 in 1997, 73.1 in 2000, and 69.7 in 2004.This shows that, overall speaking, the relative level of GRP per capita in the central region was declining continuously after the reform and opening up, that is, the "downfall in level of development" did occur and hit hardest over the two periods of 1983-1994 and 1997-2003. During the 1994-1997 period, the relative level of GRP per capita in the central region recovered, showing a rising pattern. As shown in Figure 7-2, the relative level of GRP per capita in the central region was basically consistent with the changes in the proportion of its GRP in the national total.

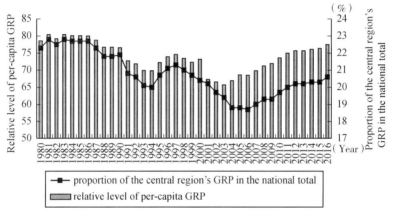

Figure 7-2   Proportion of the central region's GRP in the
national total and the relative level of GRP per capita

Source: Calculated in accordance with the data from *China Regional Economy: A Profile of 17 Years of Reform and Opening Up* and *China Statistical Yearbook* (over the years) compiled by the National Bureau of Statistics.

However, in comparison, the "downfall in level of development" in the central region was not the most serious across China. Since the reform and opening up, like in the western and northeast regions, the relative level of GRP per capita in the central region has been on a continuous decline, and only the relative level of GRP per capita in the eastern 10 provinces was increasing continuously. From 1980 to 2004, the relative level of GRP per capita declined from 78.6 to 69.7 in the central region, from 150.8 to 111.7 in the northeastern region, and from 71.2 to 58.9 in the west region, and increased from 128.7 to 155.7 only in the east region. This shows that, from the perspective of development level, both the central and western regions have fallen to varying degrees, with only the eastern region showing a rising pattern. Compared with the central region, the degree of the "downfall in level of development" in the western region was more serious. During this period, the relative level of GRP per capita in the western region decreased by 12.3 percentage points, while that in the central region only decreased by 8.9 percentage points. Although the relative level of GRP per capita in the northeast was declining sharply, it was still above the national average during this period, so it cannot be said to be a downfall.

To sum up, the "downfall in growth" in the central region was not as serious as that in the northeastern region; and the "downfall in level of development" in the central region is not as serious as that in the western region. It can be concluded that since the reform and opening up, despite the downfall to some extent, the central region was at the middle level in both of these two aspects, being away from the most serious across China. This middle level just explains why the central region has been outside of the central government's focus of attention for a long period after the reform and opening up.

Evidently, the "central downfall" is not conducive to promoting coordinated regional development and building a moderately prosperous society in all respects. And since the central region plays an indispensable strategic role in improving layout of national regional development, promoting the rise of the central region to form a new pattern of benign and interactive coordinated regional development is an objective requirement for building a moderately prosperous society in all respects and realizing the national goal of modernization, a strategic move for optimizing the national economic structure and maintaining sustained and healthy economic development, and also, an inherent requirement of socialism with Chinese characteristics.

7.2   Scientific basis for promoting the rise of central China

At the beginning of the 21st century, many scholars made explorations into how to help the central region rise in light of the "central downfall", which was regarded as the scientific basis for China to promote the rise of the central region. As was mentioned earlier, despite its existence in some way in the central region since the reform and opening up, the downfall did not justify fundamentally boosting the rise of the central region as national strategy in that in any given period, there is always one region growing at the lowest rate, and there are always some regions with development level below the national average. China decided to promote the rise of the central region mainly because there emerged some prominent regional problems and typical problem areas in that region at that time, and these areas were unable to solve the problems entirely on their own, thus giving rise to the need of corresponding policy support. Overall, the country then proposed to the strategy mainly on the three scientific bases as follows.

First of all, the central region was facing some problems that needed to be solved urgently. The first was the already low and declining level of development. In 2004, the GRP per capita in the central region was 30.3% lower than the average level of China and less than 45% of that in the eastern region. More importantly, the relative level of GRP per capita has been declining each year since 1997. The second was the enormous pressure from population transfer and employment. In 2003, the surplus rural workers in the central region amounted to over 70 million, accounting for about 40% of the rural labor force (Li Yimei et al., 2006). Due to limited employment opportunities for them, there emerged floods of migrant job-seekers each year. According to the fifth national census, there were 121 million migrants in China in 2000. Among them, 42.9% were from Anhui, Hunan, Jiangxi, Henan, and Hubei provinces (Li Xiaojian et al., 2006). The third was that the issues relating to agriculture, rural areas, and rural people were quite pronounced in the central region, one of China's major agricultural production areas, where in 2015, the rural population accounted for 33.7% of the national total; grain output, 30.1%; oil, 43.8%; and cotton, vegetables, fruits and meat, more than 25%. Therefore, the issues relating to agriculture, rural areas, and rural people in this region were extremely pronounced and also highly representative in the whole country. The fourth was about the heavy historical burden, especially that from rural public debts and arrears in accounts of grain reserves. According to the survey on Xiangyang County, Hubei Province, all 17 towns in the county were in debt, with an average public debt of RMB24.11 million at the town level; 96% of villages were in debt, with an average of RMB1.6 million per village (Han Jun, 2005). All these problems could never be solved by local governments alone without the corresponding support from the central government in terms of funds and policies.

Secondly, there were some typical secondary problem areas within the central region. The central region as a whole could not be counted as a problem area or even a complete economic region, but within it, there were some typical secondary problem areas. These areas fell into four main types: (1) Major grain-producing areas. Being located in the middle of the region and accredited as China's important commodity grain bases, Jianghan Plain, Poyang Lake Plain, Dongting Lake Plain and northern Anhui ever contributed greatly to China's food production and security, but encountered many difficulties in developing their local economy, such as the long-term disrepair of irrigation and water conservancy facilities, the slow growth of rural people's income, and the heavy burden of local public finance. (2) Impoverished areas and old revolutionary base areas. Among the key counties in the national development-oriented poverty reduction program identified by the State Council Leading Office Group office of Poverty Alleviation and Development in March 2012, 217 were in the central region, accounting for 36.7% of the 592 key impoverished counties across the country. (3) Resource-based cities with a unitary industrial structure. As China's important production base of energy and raw materials, a large number of resource-based cities in the central region were in urgent need of transformation. Among the 69 cities dependent on now-depleted resources identified by the State Council in 2008, 2009, and 2011 successively, 21 were in the central region, namely, Xiaoyi and Huozhou in Shanxi, Huaibei and Tongling in Anhui, Pingxiang, Jingdezhen, Xinyu, and Dayu in Jiangxi, Jiaozuo, Lingbao, and Puyang in Henan, Daye, Huangshi, Qianjiang, Zhongxiang, and Songzi in Hubei, Zixing, Lengshuijiang, Leiyang, Lianyuan and Changning in Hunan. (4) The old industrial base with pronounced problems. A large number of old industrial bases were established in the central region in the 1950s and the 1960s, such as Wuhan, Luoyang, and Zhuzhou, which were mainly built during the First Five-year Plan period, and Taiyuan, Zhengzhou, Huangshi, Shiyan, Xiangfan, Yichang, Xiangtan, Nanchang and Bengbu, which were mainly built during the Second Five-year Plan and "Third Front" construction periods. By the beginning of the 21st century, many cities as old industrial bases in the central region encountered great difficulties and needed urgent support from the central government. For instance, in Zhuzhou, Hunan Province, more than 50% of large- and medium-sized SOEs performed social functions, and laid-off workers totaled 120,000. It was estimated that each year, over RMB300 million would be required to cover shortfalls in pension provisions in Zhuzhou at that time.

Thirdly, to ensure fairness through compensation, it was justified for the central region to receive policy support. On the one hand, as an important base of energy raw materials as well as a major grain-producing area in China, the central region, especially its resource-based cities, commodity grain bases, and old industrial bases, ever made great contributions to and sacrifices for national economic development in the past context of long-term price control and planned economy. In this sense, certain policy support for the region should be treated as a kind of compensation. On the other hand, since the founding of the PRC in 1949, the state investment and support policies have always been weighted towards the eastern and western regions—when pursuing the efficiency goal, the eastern region with better conditions was prioritized and when focusing on the fairness goal, the western region with backward economy was valued, thus the central region in between has long been neglected. Therefore, the central region was more squeezed by market and national policies in the context of accelerating globalization and marketization. As shown in Figure 7-3, for the eastern region, its development benefited much from the coastal development strategy and opening-up policy implemented by China in the past, as well as globalization and market forces (Wei Houkai, 2005); for the western region, although its economic development was negatively influenced as market forces drove a wide variety of production factors to the eastern region, the strategy for its large-scale development undoubtedly worked well in promoting the rise of the region; and as far as the central region was concerned, neither market forces nor central regional policies were favorable to its development. In fact, the central region has seldom enjoyed preferential treatment from the central government in terms of policies for a long period of time since the reform and opening up. Worse still, the central region was unable to gain enough momentum for economic development as its talent, capital, technology and other factors were constantly flowing to the eastern region under the influence of market forces.

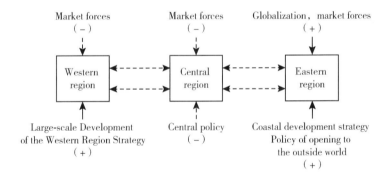

Figure 7-3　Central region under the dual squeeze of market and policies

7.3　Strategic goals and measures to promote the rise of central China

In response to the main problems existing in the development of the central region, the Central Economic Work Conference first put forward the idea of "promoting the rise of the central region" in January 2004. In March of the same year, then Premier Wen Jiabao proposed it as a major decision concerning coordinated regional development in the Government Work Report. One year later, the Fifth Plenary Session of the 16th CPC Central Committee approved the Central Committee's Proposal for Formulating the

13th Five-Year Plan for National Economic and Social Development, which clearly incorporated promoting the rise of the central region into the overall national strategy for regional development. In February 2006, then Premier Wen Jiabao chaired an executive meeting of the State Council, which deliberated on promoting the rise of the central region. In April of the same year, the CPC Central Committee and the State Council issued Several Opinions on Promoting the Rise of the Central Region, which clarified overall requirements, basic principles and main tasks of the strategy. It signified that, following the strategies for developing the western region on a large scale and the revitalizing old industrial bases in the northeast region, promoting the rise of the central region would be pursued as another national strategy. Notably, the goal of the rise of the central region would be achieved mainly through bringing the region's own strengths into full play, and the state would just "promoting", which was somewhat different from the connotations of "developing" and "revitalizing" used by the central government in the first two strategies.

7.3.1 Strategic goal and positioning of promoting the rise of central China

At the initial stage, some scholars argued that, after the strategies of developing the western region and revitalizing old industrial bases, China should no longer carry out a separate strategy to promote the rise of the central region in that from the experience of developed countries in Europe and America, the western region could be regarded as a backward region, and the northeastern region, a recession or depression region, both of which belonged to typical problem areas, but in fact, it was not the case for the central region as a whole. They confused regional development strategy with regional policy, which actually works at different levels. From the perspective of the former, it was really necessary for China to adopt an overall strategy to promote the rise of the central region, while from the perspective of the latter, it was no longer appropriate to provide regional aid in a Generalized System of Preferences approach as used before, but instead, should implement differentiated regional policies targeted at the secondary problem areas within the central region (Wei Houkai, 2006).

Generally speaking, the rise of the central region is a relative and dynamic comparative concept. To measure its success, we can roughly adopt the lowest and the highest standard. The lowest standard is that the central region achieves the rise of growth, that is, its economic growth rate exceeds the national average. In this case, the central region's total economic output holds an increasing share in that of the whole country, and the relative per capita levels of major economic indicators are on gradual increase. The highest standard means that the region achieves the rise of development level, that is, with the central region's sustained and rapid economic growth, the relative per capita levels of major economic indicators eventually approach or even exceed the national average. Only by realizing the rise of growth and development level simultaneously can the central region truly achieve the goal of an all-round rise.

It will be a long-term and arduous task to promote the all-round rise of the central region, because it is quite easier to achieve the rise of growth, but more challenging and time-demanding to achieve the rise of development level. Judging from the development of the eastern region, it is possible for the central region to gradually achieve comprehensive economic rise. Over the 25 years from 1980 to 2004, the eastern region's growth rate of GRP was 1.3 percentage points higher than the national average. Of course, the strategy for promoting the rise of the central region should not be implemented only for this sort of growth goal, which is only one of the important elements of the strategy. Sticking to the new philosophy for people-centered development, the fundamental goal of China's promoting the rise of the central region should be to make the inhabitants rich and the region prosperous, promote the region's overall economic and social development, and strive to shape the region into a modernized new one with economic prosperity, general affluence, social harmony, and a sound ecosystem by the middle of the 21st century.

In a long period after the reform and opening up, the central region experienced economic "downfall" for many reasons, but the most underlying one lay in the slow industrialization and urbanization in the region and the lack of benign interactions between these two processes. Therefore, when choosing the development path to the rise of the region, we must prioritize accelerating industrialization and urbanization, and promote the adjustment and upgrading of industrial structures, so as to create more jobs and employment opportunities in the central region and realize in-situ transfer of surplus labor force as much as possible. From the perspective of factor flow, in the past, when the state implemented the strategy for developing coastal economies, the rich labor force in the central and western regions was transferred to the coastal regions in line with the flow of capital, thus forming large-scale flows of migrant workers and aggravating the imbalance of regional development and traffic congestion; and now, when China is implementing the strategy for the rise of the central region, funds are actually transferred in line with the flow of labor force, thus drawing domestic and overseas funds to the central region to create more employment opportunities and realize in-situ transfer of rich labor force in the region. Hence, whether more employment opportunities can be created will be crucial to the success of the strategy for the rise of the central region.

Obviously, in order to realize the grand goal of building a modernized new central region, the strategic positioning of the central region should go beyond simply being a state-level energy raw material base. In fact, the previous positioning of the central region held back its development to some extent in that it was not conducive to giving full play to its comprehensive advantages. Therefore, the CPC Central Committee and the State Council released Several Opinions Concerning Boosting the Rise of the Central Region, setting the goal of "building this region into a national grain production base, an energy raw material base, a modern equipment manufacturing and high-tech industrial base, and a comprehensive transportation hub. The central region, as a bridge between the east and the west, is expected to develop by tapping local industrial strength and by coordinated and sustainable development of both economy and society". The strategic position of the central region was thus defined as "three bases plus one hub" (three kinds of production bases and a transportation hub) at that time.

In September 2009, the State Council executive meeting adopted the Plan on the Rise of Central China, which determined the overall requirements, development goals and key tasks for promoting the rise of the central region, and also, proposed a strategic layout of four economic belts and six metropolitan areas (clusters and zones), that is, accelerating the construction of economic belts along the Yangtze River, along the Lanzhou-Lianyungang, along Beijing-Guangzhou, and along Beijing-Kowloon, lines, and vigorously developing the Wuhan and the Taiyuan metropolitan areas, the Central Plains, Changsha-Zhuzhou-Xiangtan, and circum-Poyang Lake city clusters, and Wanjiang city zone. In the guidelines on implementing the strategy for promoting the rise of the central region In August 2012, the State Council further issued Several Opinions on Implementing the Strategy for Promoting the Rise of the Central Region, setting the strategic goal of promoting the rise of the central region by 2020, that is, the average annual economic growth rate in the region will continue to be faster than the national average, the proportion of the total GRP in China's GDP will be further increased, the urbanization rate will be close to the national average, the main indicators of basic public services will approach the level in the eastern region, and a comprehensive rise will be in sight.

In December 2016, the State Council approved an upgraded Plan on the Rise of Central China (2016-2025), proposing to "bring the comprehensive strength and competitiveness of the central region to a new height and open up a new prospect for an all-round rise", "strive to build the central region into an important and advanced national manufacturing center, a key region of new type of urbanization, a kernel region of modern agricultural development, a model region of ecological conservation, and a region supporting China's omni-dimensional opening up". Thus, the strategic position of the central region was renewed from the original "three bases plus one hub" to "one center plus four regions". At the same time, the Plan also proposed to create a multi-level, networked spatial development pattern by building development axial belts, developing economic growth poles, and fostering new growth drivers.

7.3.2　Policy arrangement to promote the rise of central China

To promote the rise of the central region, the General Office of the State Council has issued several documents: (1) the Notice on Implementing Opinions of the CPC Central Committee and the State Council on Promoting the Rise of the Central Region and Relevant Policies and Measures (May 2006), which decomposed 56 specific measures to promote the rise of the central region; (2) the Notice on the Scope of Following Relevant Policies for Revitalizing Old Industrial Bases Such as Northeast China and for Developing the Western Region in Six Central Provinces (January 2007), which called for following the rejuvenation policy for Northeast China and other old industrial bases in 26 cities[1] and the large-scale development policy for the western region in 243 counties (or county-level cities and districts) of the central region; and (3) the Notice on Following Relevant Policies for Revitalizing Old Industrial Bases in Northeast China and Developing the Western Region in Six Central Provinces which further refined and specified the measures for those designated cities and counties in the six provinces of the central region. Furthermore, with the approval of the State Council, an inter-ministerial joint conference system was established to boost the rise of the central region in January 2008, involving 18 departments and units such as the NDRC, the MOE, the MOF, and the Ministry of Science and Technology. In August 2010, the Guiding Opinions of the State Council on Central and Western Regions' Undertaking of Industrial Transfer was released to clarify the guidelines, basic principles, key tasks, and supporting policies for the central and western regions to orderly undertake industrial transfer. And in August 2012, the Several Opinions of the State Council on Vigorously

---

[1] Namely, Taiyuan, Datong, Yangquan, and Changzhi in Shanxi; Hefei, Ma'anshan, Bengbu, Wuhu, and Huainan in Anhui; Nanchang, Pingxiang, Jingdezhen, and Jiujiang in Jiangxi; Zhengzhou, Luoyang, Jiaozuo, Pingdingshan, and Kaifeng in Henan; Wuhan, Huangshi, Xiangfan, and Shiyan in Hubei; Changsha, Zhuzhou, Xiangtan, and Hengyang in Hunan.

Implementing the Strategy for Promoting the Rise of the Central Region was released, which formulated specific policies and measures in terms of boosting the development of major grain-producing areas, promoting conservation and intensive use of land, providing fiscal and taxation support, strengthening investment and industrial guidance, form an ecological compensation mechanism, and following national development policies in designated areas.

In response to the implementation of the strategy for the rise of the central region, China's relevant departments have rolled out a series of policies and measures. In December 2005, the General Office of the Ministry of Commerce issued the Guiding Opinions Concerning Expansion of Opening up, Improvement of Absorption of Foreign Investment and Promotion of the Rise of Central China; In February 2006, the State Intellectual Property Office issued the Decisions on Strengthening Intellectual Property Protection to Promote the Rise of the Central Region. In October 2006, the National Population and Family Planning Commission issued the Opinions on Strengthening Population and Family Planning in Central China to Promote the Rise of Central China. In April 2007, with the approval of the Office of the State Commission for Public Sector Reform, the NDRC set up the National Office for Promoting the Rise of the Central Region to focus on promoting coordination and implementation of affairs related to the rise of the central region. In May 2007, China's MOF and STA issued the Interim Measures for Expanding the Scope of Offset for Value Added Tax in the Central Region, and put some industries in 26 old industrial base cities in the central region under pilot programs of expanding scope of offset for VAT. In December 2009, the Ministry of Industry and Information Technology unveiled the Plan for Promoting the Structural Adjustment, Optimization and Upgrading of Raw Materials Industry in Central China. In May 2010, the NDRC issued the Guiding Opinions on Promoting the Development of City Clusters in Central China, proposing to "build city clusters into the core economic growth poles supporting the rise of the central region, and an important area that promotes the benign interaction among the eastern, central, and western regions and drives the sound and rapid development of the whole country". However, these relevant documents issued by various departments were more about principles than about specific policies and measures that could be directly used in practice. For instance, nearly all the documents took taxation, transfer payment, financing, and industry access as important policy tools to promote the rise of the central region, but did not work out operational rules for implementation. Most of them only roughly stipulated the supporting principles and policy directions, which were still not detailed enough and difficult to operate and implement in practice.

Meanwhile, in order to promote the rise of the central region, the State Council has successively approved a number of plans and programs for key areas in the central region, and actively promoted the construction of various types of economic functional zones. In terms of regional planning, the State Council approved the Planning of Poyang Lake Ecological Economic Zone in December 2009, the Demonstration Zone Planning for Industrial Transfer of the Wanjiang River City Belt in January 2010, the Planning of Dongting Lake Eco-Economic Zone in April 2014, the Planning for Developing City Clusters along the Middle Reaches of the Yangtze River in March 2015, the Planning for Developing the Central Plains Urban Agglomeration in December 2016, and also, the Guiding Opinions on Supporting Henan Province to Accelerate the Construction of the Central Plains Economic Zone in September 2011. These plans and opinions clarified the functional orientation and development tasks of key areas, and played an important role in giving play to regional advantages and stimulating local vitality. In terms of economic functional zones, in recent years, the State Council successively approved the establishment of Wuhan metropolitan area and Changsha-Zhuzhou-Xiangtan city cluster as national comprehensive reform pilot zones for building a resource-conserving and environment-friendly society, and approved Shanxi Province as a national comprehensive reform pilot zone for resource-based economic transformation; consented to build Wuhan Eastlake, Changsha-Zhuzhou-Xiangtan, Hefei-Wuhu-Bengbu, and Zhengzhou-Luoyang-Xinxiang National Innovation Demonstration Zones, to set up two state-level new districts—Xiangjiang New Area in Hunan and Ganjiang New Area in Jiangxi, and approved to set up free trade pilot zones in Henan and Hubei. The State Council also successively approved the establishment of 38 state-level high-tech industrial development zones, 50 state-level economic & technological development zones, eight export processing zones, and 12 comprehensive bonded zones in the central region (see Table 7-1). Among them, export processing zones included Wuhan in Hubei, Wuhu and Hefei in Anhui, Chenzhou in Hunan, Zhengzhou in Henan, Jiujiang, Nanchang and Zhangzhou in Jiangxi; comprehensive bonded zones included Zhengzhou Xinzheng and Nanyang WoLong in Henan, Wuhan Eastlake and Wuhan New Port in Hubei, Taiyuan Wusu in Shanxi, Hengyang, Xiangtan, and Yueyang Chenglingji in Hunan, Ganzhou and Nanchang in Jiangxi, Hefei and Wuhu in Anhui.

Table 7-1   State-level economic functional zones in Central China

Type	Number	Functional zones
State-level high-tech industrial development zone	38 (156)	Changzhi in Shanxi; Baotou in Inner Mongolia; Hefei, Wuhu, Bengbu, Ma'anshan Cihu, and Tongling Shizishan in Anhui; Nanchang, Xinyu, Jingdezhen, Yingtan, Fuzhou, Ganzhou, and Ji'an in Jiangxi; Yellow River Delta, Zhengzhou, Luoyang, Anyang, Nanyang, Xinxiang, Pingdingshan, and Jiaozuo in Henan; Wuhan, Xiangyang, Yichang, Xiaogan, Jingmen, Suizhou, Xiantao, Xianning, and Huanggang in Hubei; Changsha, Zhuzhou, Xiangtan, Yiyang, Hengyang, Chenzhou, and Changde in Hunan
State-level economic & technological development zone	50 (219)	Taiyuan, Datong, Jinzhong, and Jincheng in Shanxi; Wuhu, Hefei, Ma'anshan, Anqing, Tongling, Chuzhou, Chizhou, Lu'an, Huainan, Ningguo, Tongcheng, and Xuancheng in Anhui; Zhengzhou, Luohe, Hebi, Kaifeng, Xuchang, Luoyang, Xinxiang, Hongqi Canal, and Puyang in Henan; Wuhan, Huangshi, Xiangyang, Puyang, Wuhan Lingkong Port, Jingzhou, Ezhou Gedian, and Shiyan in Hubei; Changsha, Yueyang, Changde, Ningxiang, Xiangtan, Liuyang, Loudi, and Wangcheng in Hunan; Nanchang, Jiujiang, Ganzhou, Jinggangshan, Shangrao, Pingxiang, Yichun, Longnan, and Ruijin in Jiangxi
Export processing zone	8 (63)	Wuhan in Hubei; Wuhu and Hefei in Anhui; Chenzhou in Hunan; Zhengzhou in Henan; Jiujiang, Nanchang, and Ganzhou in Jiangxi
Comprehensive bonded zone	12 (65)	Zhengzhou Xinzheng and Nanyang Wolong in Henan; Wuhan Eastlake and Wuhan New Port in Hubei; Taiyuan Wusu in Shanxi; Hengyang, Xiangtan, and Yueyang Chenglingji in Hunan; Ganzhou and Nanchang in Jiangxi; Hefei and Wuhu in Anhui
National comprehensive reform pilot zone	3 (12)	Wuhan metropolitan area and Changsha-Zhuzhou-Xiangtan city cluster: national comprehensive reform pilot zones for building a resource-conserving and environment-friendly society; Shanxi Province: national comprehensive reform pilot zone for resource-based economic transformation
State-level new area	2 (19)	Xiangjiang New Area in Hunan; Ganjiang New Area in Jiangxi
National Innovation Demonstration Zone	4 (17)	Wuhan Eastlake, Changsha-Zhuzhou-Xiangtan, Hefei-Wuhu-Bengbu, and Zhengzhou-Luoyang-Xinxiang
Free trade pilot zone	2 (11)	China (He'nan) Pilot Free Trade Zone; China (Hubei) Pilot Free Trade Zone

Note: Figures in brackets are national totals.

Source: Sorted out according to the data posted on the relevant official websites.

7.4   Progress in promoting the rise of the central China

With the strong support of national policies, the central region has, since the inception of the strategy for promoting the rise of the central region in 2004, made remarkable progress in absorbing investment on a large scale, promoting industrial transformation and upgrading, accelerating industrialization and urbanization, increasing incomes of urban and rural residents, and narrowing the development gap with the eastern region. Especially, with industrial transfer from the coastal regions getting faster, the central region has increasingly become a main destination for industrial relocation since the 2008 financial crisis. This indicates that the strategy has achieved remarkable achievements in recent years.

7.4.1   The rapid expansion of investment

The strategy for promoting the rise of the central region has effectively driven the rapid expansion of investment into the central region. In 2004, the total investment in fixed assets into the region amounted to RMB1,252.91 billion and experienced a rapid expansion to RMB15,970.56 billion in 2016, representing an impressive increase of 11.7 times. Thus, the total investment in fixed assets into the region during this period grew at an average annual rate of 24.3%, 4.1 percentage points higher than the national average growth rate and 6.5, 7.5 and 1.5 percentage points higher than that of the eastern, northeastern and western regions respectively. Specifically, the total investment in fixed assets into the central region increased by 27.9% annually from 2004 to 2012, second only to 28.8% in the northeastern region and higher than that in the eastern and western regions; increased by 16.5% annually from 2013 to 2016, ranking highest among the four major regions. With sustained and rapid increase in investment, the total investment in fixed assets into the central region held a continuously increasing share in the national total, from 17.8% in 2004 to 26.3% in 2016, up 8.5 percentage points, which was the largest increase among the four major regions (down by 11.4 and 2.7 percentage points in the eastern and northeastern regions respectively, up only by 6.4 percentage points in the western region). Obviously, the rapid expansion of investment in fixed assets has driven the rapid growth of the central economy and greatly supported the rise of the central region.

7.4.2   The rapid economic growth

The rapid expansion of investment helped the central region gain powerful momentum for economic growth in recent years. Before the implementation of the strategy, the economic growth rate in the central region was lower than the national average growth rate, and even lower than that in the eastern region. From 1980 to 2003, the central region's GRP grew at an average annual rate of 10.4%, 0.7 percentage points lower than the national average growth rate and 2.0 percentage points lower than that in the eastern region. From 1998 to 2003, the region's GRP increased by 9.2% annually, 0.8 and 1.8 percentage points lower than the national average and that of the eastern region respectively. With the implementation of the strategy, the region achieved rapid economic growth, with the growth rate exceeding the national average and that of the eastern region for nine consecutive years since 2008 (see Figure 7-1). From 2004 to 2016, the region's GRP grew at an average annual rate of 11.5%, 0.2 and 0.5 percentage points higher than the national average and that of the eastern region respectively. In the period of 2008-2016, the GRP of the region grew at an average annual rate of 10.7%, 0.5 and 1.0 percentage points higher than the national average and that of the eastern region respectively. In contrast, however, the economy of the central region experienced a slightly lower growth rate compared to the western region, with a difference of 0.7 percentage points in the period of 2004-2016. Despite this, the central region has made significant progress in bolstering its position within China's economy, thanks to its rapid economic development. In 2006, the region's GDP accounted for 18.7% of the national total, the lowest share since the reform and opening up. However, by 2016, this proportion had increased to 20.6%, marking a noteworthy rise of 1.9 percentage points from the 2006 level, demonstrating the notable economic success of the national strategy for promoting the rise of the central region.

7.4.3   The narrowing development gap with the eastern region

With sustained and rapid economic growth, the development gap between the central region and the country as a whole, especially the eastern region has been progressively narrowing. If we put the national average at 100, the relative level of per capita GDP in central China in 2003 was 65.7, which was the lowest since the reform and opening up. With a steady increase since then, the region's relative level of per capita GDP amounted to 77.4 in 2016, significantly higher than that in 2003 (see Figure 7-2). During this period, the central region gradually narrowed its development gap with the eastern region. In 2003, the per capita GDP of the central region was 58.9% lower than that of the eastern region. In 2014, this relative gap coefficient reduced to 43.0%, yet slightly up to 43.5% in 2016.In terms of the regional income gap between urban and rural residents, the central region was also rapidly narrowing its gap with the eastern region and the country as a whole since the implementation of the strategy for the rise of central China. In 2005, the per capita disposable income of urban residents in the central region was RMB8,809, and the Net Income Per Capita of rural residents was RMB2,957, 34.1% and 37.4% lower than those in the eastern region respectively; by

2015, the per capita disposable income of urban residents and that of rural residents in the central region amounted to RMB26,810 and RMB10,919, only 26.9% and 23.6% lower than those in the eastern region respectively. However, in 2016, the income gap between the central and the eastern region widened slightly because both the growth rate of per capita disposable income of urban residents and that of rural residents in the central region were lower than those in the eastern region.

7.4.4   The gradual acceleration of industrial transformation and upgrading

The implementation of the strategy has accelerated industrialization and optimized industrial structure in the central region. From 2004 to 2016, apart from a steady increase in the proportion of the added value of the secondary and tertiary industries, the region witnessed 7.4 percentage points decline from 17.8% to 10.4% in the proportion of the added value of the primary industry in its GRP, far exceeding the national average decline in the same period. And during this period, the proportion of industrial added value in its GRP followed an inverted U-shaped pattern, which was roughly consistent with the change pattern in the western region. In 2003, when the strategy was yet to implement, the proportion of industrial added value in the central region was only 38.8%, far lower than that in eastern and northeastern regions; by 2011, this proportion had rapidly risen to 46.9%, surpassing the northeastern region and leaving the eastern and western regions far behind. After that, as China's economy entered a "new normal" stage and the real economy remained in the doldrums, the proportion of industrial added value in the central region dropped drastically, and dropped to 38.8% by 2016, which was in line with that in 2003. However, the proportion of the added value of the tertiary industry in the central region rose rapidly from 34.1% in 2011 to 44.1% in 2016.With the rapid advancement of industrialization, all parts of the central region have intensified efforts in developing high-tech and strategic emerging industries, which has significantly accelerated the supererogation of industrial structure. From 2006 to 2015, the region's high-tech industrial enterprises and their employees increased by 10.9% and 14.5% each year respectively, and, the nominal annual growth rates of their prime operating revenue, total profit, and export delivery value reached 30.5%, 32.7%, and 39.1% respectively, all much higher than the national average (see Table 7-2). The central region ranked top among the four major regions in terms of the four of these five indicators except export delivery value. Strategic emerging industries in the central region were also rapidly growing. For instance, in 2016, the added value of strategic emerging industries achieved a YoY increase of 16.4%

in Anhui; and in Jiangxi, it amounted to RMB116.60 billion, accounting for 14.9% of the industries above designated size, an increase of 10.7%, or up 1.9 percentage points over the previous year.

Table 7-2   Average annual growth rate of main indicators of
high-tech industries by region (2006-2015)   Unit: %

Region	Number of businesses	Average number of employees	Prime operating revenue	Total profit	Export delivery value
National	5.4	7.4	15.2	20.2	11.2
Eastern	4.2	6.3	12.8	18.0	9.2
Central	10.9	14.5	30.5	32.7	39.1
Western	7.7	9.1	26.8	29.5	40.9
Northeast	2.3	3.4	14.9	25.4	1.6

Note: Prime operating revenue, total profit, and export delivery value are nominal growth rates calculated at prices of that year.

Source: Calculated based on *China High-Tech Statistical Yearbook* (*2016*).

7.4.5   The accelerated urbanization

Since the urbanization rate rose over 30 percent by the end of the 10th Five-year Plan period, the central region has entered the accelerating stage of urbanization. During the 1979-2000 and 2001-2005 periods, the region's urbanization rate increased only at an average annual rate of 0.72 and 1.35 percentage points respectively; but from 2005 to 2016, the rate grew from 36.55% to 52.77%, an average annual increase of 1.47 percentage points, which was higher than the national average and that of other three regions. Specifically, from 2006 to 2010, the rate rose by an annual average of 1.41 percentage points, second only to that in the eastern region; from 2011 to 2016, the rate increased by an annual average of 1.53 percentage points, the highest among the four regions. This indicated that the gap in urbanization rate between central region and the eastern and northeastern regions has been narrowing since the implementation of the strategy.

The increasing urbanization promoted the rapid emergence and integration of city clusters in the central region, which in turn, continuously optimized the region's spatial pattern of urbanization. At present in the central region, a development-oriented urbanization pattern with local characteristics has taken initial shape, which takes Beijing-Kowloon and Beijing-Guangzhou railway lines as the vertical axes, and Yangtze River and Lanzhou-Lianyungang railway line as the horizontal axes, and is based on one city belt of Wanjiang, two metropolitan areas of Wuhan and Taiyuan, three city clusters of Central Plains, Changsha-Zhuzhou-Xiangtan, and circum-Poyang Lake and also dotted with other cities and small towns.With only 31% of the region's land area, these six clusters supported 49% of the population, and produced 61% of the GRP in the central region in 2012 (Duan Xiaowei et al., 2016). With increasing population and economic agglomeration, these six clusters have become the region's kernel growth poles as well as the mainstay of promoting urbanization and absorbing new urban population in the central region.

7.4.6   Steady growth of urban and rural personal incomes

Since the implementation of the strategy, the urban and rural personal incomes in central region have been steadily increased. In terms of urban residents' income growth, from 2006 to 2016, the per capita disposable income in the region increased by 11.4% annually, 0.2 and 1.0 percentage points higher than that in the national average and the eastern region respectively. In terms of rural residents' income growth, from 2006 to 2013, the Net Income Per Capita in the central region increased by 13.9% annually, which was 0.5 and 1.5 percentage points higher than the national average and that in the eastern region respectively. When it comes to disposable income, from 2014 to 2016, the per capita disposable income of rural residents in the region increased by 9.5% annually in nominal terms, slightly higher than the national average and that in the eastern region, but lower than that in the western region (see Table 7-3). With the continuous growth of residents' income, Engel coefficient of urban and rural households in the central region dropped rapidly from 2004 to 2015, with the former down from 38.5% to 30.6%, a decrease of 7.9 percentage points more than the 7.1 percentage points of the national decrease and the latter down 50.2% to 31.5%, a decrease of 18.7 percentage points more than the 14.2 percentage points of the national level.

Table 7-3   Average nominal growth rate of per capita income of
urban and rural residents by region   Unit: %

Indicators	National	Eastern	Central	Western	Northeast
Average annual growth rate of per capita disposable income of urban and rural residents from 2014 to 2016	9.2	9.0	9.4	9.8	7.7
Average annual growth rate of per capita disposable income of urban residents from 2006 to 2016	11.2	10.4	11.4	11.3	11.5

(continued)

Indicators	National	Eastern	Central	Western	Northeast
Average annual growth rate of Net Income Per Capita of rural residents from 2006 to 2013	13.4	12.4	13.9	14.1	14.4
Average annual growth rate of per capita disposable income of rural residents from 2014 to 2016	9.4	9.3	9.5	10.1	7.9

Source: Calculated in accordance with the relevant data from *China Statistical Yearbook* over the years.

7.5   State aid policy to promote the rise of central China

China's 13th Five-year Plan highlighted the necessity of "forcefully implementing the overall strategy for regional development to promote the large-scale development of the western region, the revitalization of the northeastern region, the rise of the central region, and the trailblazing of the eastern region". The report to the 19th CPC National Congress further made it clear to "help the central region rise by tapping into local strengths". Given the drawbacks brought on by the past Generalized System of Preferences aid policies targeted at the western region and old industrial bases such as northeast China (Wang Luolin & Wei Houkai, 2005), there is neither reason nor necessity to implement the same sort of aid policy again for central China in the future. To some extent, the central region will have to rely more on itself for the rise; therefore, with focus on building an endogenous mechanism of self-development, the state should tailor its aid policies to local conditions and provide category-specific guidance, so as to give better support in developing the region into a major grain-producing area and an energy raw material base and facilitating the industrial transformation and upgrading of resource-based cities, the adjustment and transformation of old industrial bases, and development of old revolutionary base areas in the central region by widening funding channels, adopting preferential policies and launching major projects. Specifically, this sort of differentiated aid policy for promoting the rise of central region mainly serves such purposes.

7.5.1   Developing major grain-producing areas and processing local agricultural products

The central region is an important national grain production base as well as an agricultural production base. Except Shanxi, the other five central provinces belong to

13 major grain producing provinces across the country. In 2016, the region's grain output accounted for 29.7% of the national total, among which, rice accounted for 39.9%; wheat, 43.2%; oil crops, 42.5% (with peanuts, rapeseeds, and sesame seeds accounting for 43.4%, 49.7%, and 86.1%, respectively); and hemp, 34.4% (with kenaf accounting for 77.4%; and tea, 30.0%). To ensure national food security and increase farmers' income and affluence, it is of great significance to accelerate the construction of major grain-producing areas and the development of modern and efficient agriculture in the central region. Corresponding measures may include: (1) expand investment in irrigation and water conservancy facilities, projects to upgrade rural power grids, water source projects, county and township roads, agricultural science and technology promotion and technical training, selection and cultivation of improved varieties, pest and disease control, and eco-environment protection in central rural areas, especially in major grain-producing areas, so as to effectively improve rural production and living conditions and enhance the ability of agriculture to resist natural disasters; (2) provide greater financial support to the major grain-producing areas in the region, increase financial transfer payments to major grain-growing provinces and counties, to help them solve problems left over from history and reduce the burden on local public finance; (3) effectively improve the efficiency and effectiveness of agricultural subsidies by further improving the agricultural subsidy policy and adjusting agricultural subsidy methods for higher directivity and accuracy; and (4) make more efforts to develop various types of grain whole sale markets to improve grain circulation infrastructure in major producing areas, and vigorously develop the intensive processing industry of agricultural products to speed up the processing and transformation of grain and other agricultural products.

7.5.2 Speeding up structural adjustment and industrial transformation of resource-based cities

At present, various structural contradictions further highlight in the central region as some resource-based cities, such as Datong, Linfen, Jiaozuo, Hebi, Pingxiang, Zhongxiang, and Linxiang, have exhausted local resources and many others have been on the verge of exhaustion. In response, it is necessary for the resource-based cities in the region to speed up structural adjustment and industrial transformation by actively cultivating alternative industries, continuously extending industrial chains, and determinedly participating in more value-added processing and manufacturing. And it is also necessary for the government to provide more national support of fiscal and other relevant policies by establishing and improving the withdrawal mechanism of declining industries. In addition, efforts will be intensified for the comprehensive treatment and ecological restoration of mine subsidence areas. From 2004 to 2010, China launched a treatment program for coal mining subsidence areas in key state-owned coal mines, which covered 9 mining areas (about 1,049 square kilometers of coal mining subsidence areas) in Datong, Yangquan, Fenxi, Wanbailin, Gujiao, Huozhou, Lu'an, Jincheng, and Xuangang in Shanxi Province, and resettled more than 180,000 affected residents, benefiting more than 600,000 people. In 2014, Shanxi Province started a new round of treatment of coal mining subsidence areas to resettle 655,000 people from 1,352 villages and repair or reinforce more than 1.1 million unsafe houses. Since 2017, the NDRC has earmarked special funds for comprehensive treatment of coal mining subsidence areas in the central government budget, which targeted the first group of 17 key coal mining subsidence areas. Among them, there were five in the central region, namely, Zezhou County and Yuanping City in Shanxi, Suixi County in Anhui, Baofeng County in Henan, and Yongxing County in Hunan. Comprehensive treatment of coal mining subsidence area is a huge systematic project, involving residents' risk-avoiding relocation, infrastructure and public service facilities, ecological restoration and environmental remediation, and the development of alternative industries. Therefore, it is necessary to pursue green development, and establish a sustainable long-term compensation mechanism through incorporating the treatment of subsidence areas into coal production costs under the Polluter-Pays Principle.

7.5.3 Adjusting, transforming and revitalizing the old industrial bases

In central China, a number of old industrial bases were established in the 1950s and the 1960s, many of which are facing many difficulties and need corresponding policy support from the central government. As early as 2007, the State Council determined to follow the revitalization policy for old industrial bases such as northeast China in 26 cities in the central region. In 2013, the National Plan for the Adjustment and Transformation of Old Industrial Bases (2013-2022) approved by the State Council put 34 prefecture-level cities and municipal districts of six provincial capitals in central region under the program. Therefore, it is necessary to organize relevant agencies to classify and comprehensively evaluate the previous policies and measures for the revitalization of old industrial bases such as northeast China, and gradually follow then in the central and western regions. The newly formulated policies and measures for old industrial bases shall treat the northeastern region and the central and western regions equally where conditions permit. At the same time, we should conscientiously implement and refine various fiscal and taxation policies, financing policies, and land policies put forward in the plan, and support the old industrial bases in the central region to speed up adjustment, transformation and upgrading. In particular, we should give full play to the region's comprehensive advantages in terms of location, resources, factors, and industries, and intensify efforts to support the transformation and upgrading of energy and raw materials industry and equipment manufacturing industry in the old industrial bases in the region. We also need to keep extending the industrial chain, vigorously develop strategic emerging industries such as high-end equipment manufacturing, new materials, new energy, energy conservation and environmental protection, biotechnology, and new generation information technology, so as to promote the deep integration of manufacturing and modern service industries, and build a number of advanced manufacturing clusters with strong influence and competitiveness. In short, industrial transformation and upgrading is the prerequisite for the overall revitalization of old industrial bases in central region.

7.5.4 Increasing support for the development of impoverished areas and old revolutionary base areas

In central China, the rural poor were relatively concentrated in the past. From 2010 to 2016, the proportion of its rural poor population in national total increased from 30.8% to 33.9% despite a drop from 50.96 million to 14.68 million. In 2016, there were six provinces with more than 3 million rural poor across the country, two provinces among which were in the central region, with 3.71 million in Henan and 3.43 million in Hunan. They were mainly located in Lvliang Mountain area, where the incidence of poverty remained as high as 13.4% in 2016. Therefore, in the fight against poverty, priority should be given to helping locals rise out of poverty and live in prosperity, thus creating effective interactions between poverty alleviation and rural revitalization with targeted measures in light of local conditions. At the same time, more than half of China's old revolutionary base areas are in the central region, and most of them are located in mountainous areas. Residents there are still living an extremely hard life because of inconvenient transportation, backward infrastructure, and underdeveloped economy. Therefore, the central government should attach great importance to the development of these areas, increasing its fiscal transfer to them and providing strong support in red tourism and ecological industries development, infrastructure construction, rural revitalization, talent cultivation, and employment training.

7.5.5 Encourage the relocation of industries and enterprises from the coastal to the central and western regions

Since the beginning of the 21st century, with the rising cost of land, labor, and other factors in the eastern region, as well as the shortage of energy and resources, the carrying capacity of resources and environment in some eastern regions like the Pearl River Delta and the Yangtze River Delta has been fading, making some resources-based and labor-intensive industries begin to speed up their transfer to surrounding areas, and the central region proved to be an ideal destination for such large-scale industrial transfers. To support the central and western regions to undertake industrial transfer, China set up a number of state-level demonstration zones for industrial relocation in the central and western regions in recent years. Admittedly, these demonstration areas are mainly awarded a title, without many substantive policy measures. Therefore, we should learn from the experience of the UK, France, and other countries and adopt a "carrot and stick" approach to encouraging the relocation of industries and enterprises from the coastal to the central and western regions. The so-called "carrot" means that the government should "induce" coastal enterprises to invest in the central and western regions with preferential policies, such as those for ensuring an appropriate supply of land or providing financial and tax incentives. In particular, strong policy support should be given to coastal enterprises that undertake investments in state-level demonstration zones for industrial relocation in the central and western regions. The so-called "stick" means to adopt a stricter market access standard and impose certain restrictions on the expansion of resource-based and labor-intensive industries in the Pearl River Delta, the Yangtze River Delta, and other places, so as to encourage coastal regions to accelerate industrial transformation and upgrading, and make room for the development of similar industries in the central and western regions.

Chapter 8
Economic and Social Development
in Ethnic Minority Areas

For China, a unified multi-ethnic country, ethnic affairs are a major issue that must be well addressed in building socialism with Chinese characteristics. With a series of special preferential policies and measures based on the actual situation in ethnic minority areas, the Chinese government has, since the reform and opening up, helped those areas to accelerate the economic development and achieved remarkable results. To intensify efforts to support the accelerated development and synchronized prosperity in ethnic minority areas is a major element in China's coordinated regional development strategy and one of the fundamental requirements for the road to coordinated regional development with Chinese characteristics.

8.1 Basic characteristics of ethnic minority areas

"Ethnic minority areas" is a shortened term for areas with large ethnic minority populations, specifically referring to ethnic autonomous areas. In China, there are five autonomous regions, 30 autonomous prefectures, and 120 autonomous counties (banners), accounting for 63.9% of China's total land area. The ethnic autonomous areas are widely distributed across 20 of China's 31 provinces, autonomous regions, and municipalities directly under the central government (excluding Hong Kong, Macao, and Taiwan Region), as each of China's ethnic group is characterized by either living in homogeneous communities of their own or living together with and mixing with other groups. Notably, the western region serves as the primary residential area for ethnic minority groups, accommodating 71.3% of the national ethnic minority population from over 40 ethnic minority groups (based on the 2010 census data, excluding unidentified ethnic groups). Out of China's 155 ethnic autonomous areas, 5 autonomous regions, 27 autonomous prefectures, and 83 autonomous counties (banners) are located in the western region. In 2016, the region supported 90.7% of the total 216 million people of China's ethnic autonomous areas, with the ethnic minority population accounting for 43.9%. For statistical convenience, some literatures define large ethnic minority areas as the eight ethnic minority concentrated provinces (autonomous regions) with large ethnic minority populations, that is, five autonomous regions plus three multi-ethnic provinces of Yunnan, Qinghai and Guizhou. Generally speaking, ethnic minority areas have the following basic characteristics.

8.1.1 Rich in natural resources, but poor in environmental conditions

Being productive and rich in minerals, ethnic minority areas are China's important bases for energy and raw material, part of which are indispensable to national economy and public welfare. In 2015, the grassland area in ethnic autonomous areas accounted for 72.8% of the national total; the forest area, 43.5%; the forest volume, 42.9%; and the total amount of water resources, 40.7%. The basic reserves of major mineral resources also occupied a large proportion in nation total, among which manganese ore accounted for 76.7%; zinc ore, 66.4%; chromium ore, 65.2%; kaolin, 64.2%; bauxite ore, 63.5%; lead ore, 63.5%; copper ore, 45.7%; coal, 35.4%; pyrite, 25.2%, and the remaining technically recoverable reserves of oil and natural gas, 22.5% and 38.6% respectively. In particular, Inner Mongolia, Guangxi, Xinjiang and Tibet are important storage places for China's energy resources including coal, oil, natural gas, manganese, bauxite, and chromium as well as mineral resources including ferrous metals, non-ferrous metals, and non-metallic minerals. By the end of 2015, the ensured reserves of 17 kinds of resources in Inner Mongolia ranked first in China, of which the measured reserves of rare earth ranked first in the world, and coal reserves accounted for 26.24% of the national total; the reserves of 12 kinds of minerals in Guangxi ranked first in China, especially the non-ferrous metals such as aluminum and tin; the reserves of five kinds of minerals in Xinjiang ranked first in China, among which, the predicted oil resources accounted for 30% of the national onshore oil resources, the predicted natural gas accounted for 34% of the national onshore natural gas resources, and the predicted coal reserves accounted for 40% of the national total; and the chrome ore reserves in Tibet accounted for 37.1% of the national total, ranking first in China.

At the same time, ethnic autonomous areas are mainly in mountainous areas in the southwest, northwest, central and southern regions, barren plateaus, deserts, or karst areas, where both transportation and communications are underdeveloped, and contact with the outside world is quite difficult because of their remote geographical location—being on the edge of provinces and far away from core cities. In some autonomous regions, prefectures, and counties, people find it difficult to stabilize their production and improve their livelihood due to such factors as complex geological structure, fragile eco-environment, cold and arid climate, sparse vegetation, raging sandstorms, frequent natural disasters, and lack of oxygen, soil, water, and other living conditions.

8.1.2   Economic and social underdevelopment

Compared to other regions, the relatively low level of economic development in ethnic autonomous areas could be attributed to the following factors. In 2016 and compared to the national total, the population of ethnic autonomous areas accounted for 15.6%, but their GDP accounted for only 9.4%; the total investment in fixed assets, 11.6%; the total retail sales of social consumer goods, 7.5%; and the export value, only 2.6%, all lower than the population share of ethnic autonomous areas, revealing their relatively low level of development. At the per capital level of main indicators for economic development, if the national average is 100, the relative level of GDP and investment in fixed assets in ethnic autonomous areas in 2016 was 73.7 and 74.5, while the relative levels of total retail sales of consumer goods, public budgetary revenue, and export value were only 47.9, 28.6, and 16.7, respectively.

Judging from the per capita GDP, the gap between ethnic minority areas and the national average remained significant. In 1995, the per capita GDP of ethnic autonomous areas was RMB3,055, only equivalent to 60.0% of the national per capita GDP. By 2000, the proportion had dropped to 56.0% (see Table 8-1). Over the 10th Five-year Plan period, when ethnic autonomous areas achieved rapid economic development, the GRP per capita increased from RMB4,451 in 2000 to RMB8,991 in 2005, and the relative gap with the national average began to narrow. Since then, the relative gap between per capita GDP in ethnic autonomous areas and per capita GDP nationwide has obviously narrowed. By 2010, the relative level of per capita GDP in ethnic autonomous areas had rapidly risen to 71.4, and further increased to 77.2 in 2012. However, since 2012, due to the gradual slowdown of the national economic growth, the gap in GRP per capita between ethnic autonomous areas and the national average has widened slightly, and this situation persisted until 2016. Notably, the absolute gap between the GRP per capita in ethnic autonomous areas and the national average has been constantly widening, from RMB2,036 in 1995 to RMB5,377 in 2005 and further to RMB14,184 in 2016.

Table 8-1   Comparison of per capita GDP between ethnic autonomous areas and the whole country

Year	Per capita GRP in ethnic autonomous areas (RMB)	National per capita GDP (RMB)	Absolute gap (RMB)	Relative level (100 in the whole country)
1995	3,055	5,091	−2,036	60.0
2000	4,451	7,942	−3,491	56.0
2005	8,991	14,368	−5,377	62.6
2010	22,060	30,876	−8,816	71.4
2011	27,401	36,403	−9,002	75.3
2012	30,871	40,007	−9,136	77.2
2013	33,732	43,852	−10,120	76.9
2014	34,320	47,203	−12,883	72.7
2015	35,181	50,251	−15,070	70.0
2016	39,796	53,980	−14,184	73.7

Source: Calculated based on *China Statistical Yearbook* over the years.

The economic underdevelopment in ethnic minority areas has seriously affected social development and restricted the improvement of the local living standards. At present, the problems of social underdevelopment and low living standards still remains widespread in ethnic minority areas. In 2015, the per capita disposable income of urban residents in ethnic autonomous areas was RMB26,083.1, and the Net Income Per Capita of rural residents was RMB8,889.3, which were 18.0% and 17.5% lower than the national average respectively. Therefore, it has become one of the important elements of securing a decisive victory in building a moderately prosperous society in all respects to effectively solve problems relating to ethnic minority groups, accelerate the development in ethnic minority areas and promote the coordinated development of regional economy.

8.1.3   Low openness to the outside world

Since the reform and opening up, a series of preferential policies for domestic and foreign trade such as border trade, pairing assistance, preferential treatment for private trade enterprises has helped to continuously boost the economic openness in ethnic minority areas. However, compared to the national average, the comprehensive opening and the development level of export-oriented economy was still low in ethnic minority areas. In terms of actual utilization of foreign capital, the amount of foreign capital actually utilized in ethnic autonomous areas in 2015 was only US$6.794 billion, accounting for only 5.4% of the national total; the per capita amount was only US$36.5, only 39.7% of the national average. In terms of import and export, ethnic autonomous areas were low not only in total import and export volume, but also in per capita exports as well as the ratio of dependence foreign trade. In 2015, the total export volume of ethnic autonomous areas stood at US$64.678 billion, accounting for only 2.8% of China's total; the per capita export value was US$347.4, only 21.0% of the national average. The ratio of dependence on foreign trade, an important indicator reflecting export-oriented economy, is the ratio of total amount of import and export to GDP (GRP). In 2015, this ratio of dependence on foreign trade in ethnic autonomous areas was 10.3%, including 3.8% on imports and 6.5% on exports, while the national indicators were 38.3%, 16.3% and 22.0% respectively in the same period. It can be seen that ethnic autonomous areas had low economic openness and apparently followed an inward-oriented development.

8.1.4　Rapid growth of population, and great pressure on resources and environment

In comparison, the population in ethnic minority areas has increased rapidly since the reform and opening up. From 1991 to 2016, the population in ethnic autonomous areas grew at the rate of 13 ‰, far higher than the national average rate of 7.3 ‰ in the same period. Judging only from the population density, ethnic minority areas can be described as "vast and sparsely populated". However, due to the poor natural conditions in most of those areas, such as frigid or drought environment, and desert or mountainous regions, there are still quite a few areas that are currently uninhabitable and depopulated, where local resources and environment have limited carrying capacity and eco-environment conservation is a really challenging task. Tong Yufen (2009), who studied the population bearing pressure in northwest China, held that the population there would be overloaded by 2030, with the maximum overload rate reaching 24%. With the rapid growth of population, in some ethnic minority areas with poor natural conditions, the pressure on resources and environment is growing inexorably. Therefore, how to take various measures including eco-migration to promote the coordinated development of population, economy, resources, and environment in ethnic minority areas, and to alleviate poverty and build a moderately prosperous society as soon as possible will be an arduous task for us.

8.1.5　Year-on-year increase in expenditure on basic public services, yet with large demand gap

Basic public services cover such areas as compulsory education, public health, basic scientific research, public welfare cultural undertakings, and basic social security.

In ethnic autonomous areas, both the public budgetary revenue and the public budgetary expenditure have grown rapidly since the 1990s. If calculated at constant prices of that year, the annual growth rate reached 15.5% and 18.2% on average from 1991 to 2016 respectively, showing a rapid year-on-year increase. As the public budgetary expenditure grew faster than the revenue, ethnic autonomous areas witnessed a widening gap between them, up from 45.2% in 1990 to 69.8% in 2016 (see Figure 8-1). This huge gap was mainly filled by central government transfer payments. The gap ratio mentioned here refers to the ratio of the public budgetary deficit (expenditure minus revenue) to the public budgetary expenditure. With the rapid growth of the public budgetary expenditure, the per capita public budgetary expenditure in ethnic autonomous areas was also increasing each year, from RMB199 in 1990 to RMB10,925 in 2016, an increase of nearly 54 times. However, compared to the national average, the per capita public budgetary expenditure in ethnic autonomous areas was still low, 5.8% lower than the per capita expenditure in the national general public budget in 2016. Judging from the facts that ethnic minority areas were still underdeveloped, with public facilities stuck in such common problems as low availability, uneven distribution in urban and rural areas, and high costs for construction and maintenance, and a large amount of special

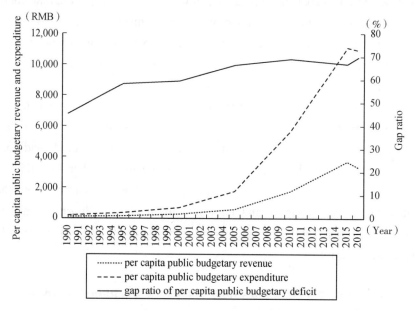

Figure 8-1   Per capita public budgetary revenue and expenditure and the gap
ratio in ethnic autonomous areas

Source: Calculated based on *China Statistical Yearbook (2017)*.

expenditures crowding out the expenditures for basic public services, the national input to the basic public services in ethnic minority areas was still insufficient, thus leaving a large demand gap in expenditure in basic public services.

8.2 Central policies for supporting the development of ethnic minority areas

Based on China's reality as a unified multi-ethnic country with long-standing problems relating to ethnic minority groups, the central government has implemented special assistance policies for ethnic minority areas, and has established and improved a system of central policies for supporting the development of ethnic minority areas with rich content and diverse types since the founding of the PRC. The central policies for supporting the development of ethnic minority areas here is a term used to generalize a wide-ranging variety of policies, measures and means adopted by the central government to support the development of those areas. The discussion will focus on the following six aspects.

8.2.1 Fiscal policy

Through measures such as increasing funds transfers and allocating development fund, the central government has intensified financial support to ethnic minority areas, so as to promote the socio-economic development, the development-driven poverty alleviation, and the eco-environment construction of those areas.

8.2.1.1 Financial transfer payment

For a long period of time, the central government and local governments at all levels have attached great importance to increasing funds transfers to ethnic minority areas. After the founding of the PRC, the central government implemented preferential policies such as "exercising centralized control over total revenues and expenditures and providing subsidies when deficiency arises" and raising the proportion of budget reserves for ethnic minority areas (two percentage points higher than that in other areas). From 1980 to 1988, the central government implemented a fixed subsidy mechanism with an annual increase of 10% for China's eight ethnic minority concentrated provinces and autonomous regions. In 1994, the central government implemented policy-based transfer payments to ethnic minority areas. Since 2000, apart from general and special transfer payments, the central government arranged transfer payments to ethnic minority areas to support China's eight ethnic minority concentrated provinces and autonomous regions and eight ethnic autonomous prefectures located in other provinces. The sources of funds are as follows: (1) policy-related transfer payments to ethnic minority areas gained a special increase of RMB1 billion in 2000, and then increased each year at the rate equivalent to the growth rate of the VAT revenue shared by the central government in the previous year; (2) for the eight ethnic minority concentrated provinces and autonomous regions and eight ethnic autonomous prefectures in other provinces (autonomous regions), 80% of the annual increase in VAT revenue over the previous year was transferred to ethnic minority areas. Since 2006, the State Council has brought the ethnic autonomous counties under the jurisdiction of non-ethnic minority provinces and non-ethnic autonomous prefectures under the program of financial transfer payment, thereby achieving full coverage of all areas with large ethnic minority populations. During the 2000-2015 period, transfer payments from the central government to ethnic minority areas totaled RMB395.5 billion, with RMB58.2 billion in 2015; and in 2016, RMB2.385 billion of special funds was allocated to support the cultural development in areas with large ethnic minority populations. Such increase in transfer payments showed that the central government attached great importance to the development of ethnic minority areas.

8.2.1.2   Fund for Ethnic Minorities Development

Fund for Ethnic Minorities Development refers to the special fund launched by the central government to support the development of areas with large ethnic minority populations. It was called "New Development Fund" at its inception in 1992, when a total amount of RMB60 million was allocated in accordance with the Notice of the State Council on Several Issues Concerning Further Implementing the "Law on Regional Ethnic Autonomy of the People's Republic of China". Until 1998, the fund was used with compensation and primarily to assist the socio-economic development at the grass-roots level in ethnic minority areas. In 1998, it was changed to free use as required by the fiscal reform, and renamed the Fund for Ethnic Minorities Development, the size of which reached RMB300 million in that year. By 2004, the total fund has amounted to RMB450 million, and the scope of application has expanded to 27 provinces, from 16 provinces in 1992; in 2016, the total size amounted to RMB4.6 billion, up 15% over the previous year. In addition, to support the development of 22 ethnic minority groups with small populations, in 2002 and from the fund, the National Ethnic Affairs Commission and the MOF allocated RMB33 million to construct 246 projects in the areas where such groups live in compact communities. This move benefited 982,000 local people, 35.1% of whom (345,000 people) belong to ethnic minority groups with small populations. In December 2016, the State Council issued the Program for Developing Ethnic Minority Areas and Ethnic Groups with Small Populations During the 13th Five-Year Plan Period and proposed to establish and improve a long-term investment mechanism for governments at all levels to support the development of ethnic minority groups, and decided to leverage the existing fund to prioritize the poverty alleviation in impoverished areas with large ethnic minority populations, the development of ethnic minority groups with small populations, the revitalization of border areas, and the improvement of ethnic minority groups' livelihood. According to the program, in 2017, the NDRC would increase the central budgetary investment to RMB800 million in a bid to support the development of ethnic minority groups with small populations, that is, to support the construction (mainly in such four aspect: infrastructure, basic public service facilities, the eco-environment protection and improvement of human settlements, and ethnic cultural inheritance) of the administrative villages in areas where ethnic minority groups with small populations live in compact communities in Liaoning, Inner Mongolia and other 11 provinces and autonomous regions as well as Xinjiang Production and Construction Corps.

8.2.2　Taxation policy

The central government has implemented tax policies to support the development of ethnic minority areas, focusing on investment, ethnic trade, and enterprises. Firstly, there are preferential tax policies for investments. Since 1992, the central government has implemented measures to reduce or exempt the fixed asset investment regulation tax in ethnic minority areas. Initially, there was a reduction or exemption of the fixed asset investment regulation tax (although this tax has been suspended and abolished since 2000). Secondly, there are preferential tax policies for ethnic trade. Starting from 1994, the state has imposed a reduced rate of 10% tax on special agricultural products on enterprises that purchase raw materials for border-selling tea, and has exempted the state-designated producers and distributors from VAT on border-selling tea exclusively sold to ethnic minority groups. From 2001 to 2005, the state first levied and then refunded 50% of actually paid VAT on goods sold by state-owned ethnic trade enterprises and supply and marketing cooperatives at the county level, and exempted VAT on goods sold by state-owned ethnic trade enterprises below the county level (excluding counties) and grass-roots supply and marketing cooperatives. From 2006 to 2008, the state exempted VAT on goods (except oil and tobacco) sold within ethnic trading counties by ethnic trade enterprises and supply and marketing cooperative enterprises at or below the county level. According to surveys and calculations, during the 10th Five-year Plan period, China's ethnic trade enterprises at the county level or above enjoyed 50% of VAT, with a discount of about RMB1.2 billion; those below the county level were exempted from VAT of about RMB1 billion; and border tea production and distribution enterprises were exempted from VAT of about RMB50 million.[1] Thirdly, there are preferential tax policies for enterprises. From 1994 to 1997, the state stipulated that the newly established enterprises in the old revolutionary base areas, areas with large ethnic minority populations, border areas, and impoverished areas would be exempted from income tax for three years. From 2001 to 2010, the state reduced or exempted corporate income tax on enterprises in areas with large ethnic minority populations in the western region.

8.2.3 Opening-up policy

To promote the socio-economic development in ethnic minority areas, China has, since the 1990s, implemented a series of opening-up policies, which mainly include: (1) in 1992, the state successively opened inland provincial capitals (autonomous region capitals), implemented the strategy for opening up border areas, established 13 open border cities and 241 Category-1 ports, and designated 14 border economic and technological cooperation zones; (2) in 1994, the National Ethnic Affairs Commission and the State Commission for Restructuring the Economic Systems approved the establishment of the first batch of pilot zones for the reform and opening up in ethnic autonomous areas, including Hulun Buir and Wuhai in Inner Mongolia, Yanbian in Jilin, Qiandongnan in Guizhou and Yili in Xinjiang; (3) in 1996, the State Council issued the Notice on Relevant Issues Concerning Border Trade, which put forward the administration and policy measures to promote border trade and economic cooperation; (4) in 2010, the central work conference on Xinjiang proposed to establish economic development zones in Kashgar and Khorgos of Xinjiang by implementing special

---

[1] Speech by Yang Jianqiang, Deputy Director of the State Ethnic Affairs Commission, at the National Conference on Ethnic Trade and Production of Ethnic Commodities with Special Needs, in *China's Ethnic Statistical Yearbook* (*2007*), Beijing: The Ethnic Publishing House, 2008.

policies; (5) in 2011, the State Council successively issued the Opinions on Supporting Yunnan Province to Speed up Shaping Itself into an Important Bridgehead Opening to the Southwest and the Opinions on Supporting the Construction of Kashgar and Khorgos Economic Development Zones; and (6) after 2012, the State Council successively approved the establishment of Ningxia and Guizhou inland open economic pilot zones. Those policies have accelerated the opening up and socio-economic development in areas with large ethnic minority populations.

Since the Belt and Road Initiative was launched, various policies and measures have been adopted to actively promote the deep integration of ethnic minority areas into the initiative. In December 2015, the State Council issued the Opinions on Several Policies and Measures to Support the Development and Opening up of Key Border Areas to open up border ethnic minority areas in an all-round way and make it take the lead in pursuing the Initiative. These key border areas, including five key development and opening-up pilot zones, 72 state-level border ports, 28 border cities, 17 border economic cooperation zones, and one cross-border economic cooperation zone, are mostly concentrated in ethnic minority areas.

8.2.4   Industrial policies

In terms of infrastructure construction, China prioritized its support to ethnic minority areas. For instance, the central government allocated a relatively higher proportion of its financial construction fund, other special construction funds, and policy-based bank loans to build infrastructure in ethnic minority areas minority populations; and at the same time, allowed local governments in ethnic minority areas to provide those infrastructure projects' matching funds (if necessary) at a relatively reduced proportion. During the 11th Five-year Plan period, the central government's investment in water conservancy in ethnic minority areas grew at an annual rate of 42.4%, which was above the national average. During the 13th Five-year Plan period, the state implemented major projects such as comprehensive transportation infrastructure construction, tourism transportation facilities construction, key water conservancy projects construction, information networking construction, urban and rural infrastructure construction in ethnic minority areas, where the infrastructure was further improved.

Regarding the development of township and village enterprises, the State Council approved and transmitted the Report of the Ministry of Agriculture on Promoting the Sustainable and Healthy Development of Township and Village Enterprises in March 1992, proposing that governments at all levels and relevant agencies should give more support in terms of policies and funds to further promote the development of township and village enterprises in impoverished areas and areas with large ethnic minority populations. In the same month, the State Council assented to arrange special discount loans for those enterprises in areas with large ethnic minority populations, requiring the Agricultural Bank of China to increase its special loan by RMB100 million each year during the Eighth Five-year Plan period to support township enterprises in areas with large ethnic minority populations. Subsequently, the Bank formulated and implemented the interim measures for managing discount interest loans for township and village enterprises in areas with large ethnic minority populations, and later, the MOF, the National Ethnic Affairs Commission, and the MOA jointly issued the Interim Measures for Discounted Interest Loans for Township and Township Enterprises in Areas with Large Ethnic Minority Populations.

In terms of the development of specialty industries, in order to promote faster development of mineral resources in ethnic minority areas, in 1994, the state adjusted the distribution ratio of mineral resources compensation fees between the central government and autonomous regions to 4 : 6, and that for other provinces and municipalities stood at 5:5. In 1995, the Eighth National People's Congress passed the Electricity Law of the People's Republic of China, which stipulated that the state shall help and support the development of electricity in areas with large ethnic minority populations. During the 13th Five-year Plan period, the state established demonstration bases for mineral functional materials and for food and agricultural products export in ethnic minority areas, implemented the project of "foster one thousand and strengthening one hundred of enterprises dealing with ethnic trade and ethnic products", promoted the protection and development of traditional handicrafts of ethnic minority groups, and boosted the development of specialty industries with characteristics such as medicine and halal food in areas with large ethnic minority populations.

In terms of trade policy, the state has adopted preferential policies favoring ethnic trade enterprises regrading profit retention, self-owned funds and price subsidies since 1963. After 1991 and based on new situations, the preferential policies were renewed to provide designated producers of ethnic trade and ethnic special-needed commodities with preferential interest rates for working capital loans, financial interest subsidies for technical transformation loans and preferential tax relief. During the Eighth Five-year Plan period (1991-1995), the state introduced a preferential policy of 2.4‰ lower monthly interest rate for normal working capital loans of designated producers, and the interest gap would be filled directly with government subsidies; reduced or exempted product tax, value-added tax and income tax of designated producers; and from 1992 to 1994, banks arranged loans of RMB40 million each year to support the construction of grass-roots ethnic trade outlets and the technological transformation of designated producers, with the central and local governments each bearing half of the interest. From the Ninth to 12th Five-year Plan period (1996-2015), the state continued to implement the renewed policies for designated producers of products for ethnic trade and use. Among them, discount loans for technological transformation were adjusted to RMB100 million each year since 2000, with an increase of RMB500 million and RMB1 billion each year during the 11th and the 12th Five-year Plan period respectively.

8.2.5 Poverty alleviation policies

Rural poverty is the key problem hindering the development of ethnic minority areas. Since the reform and opening up, China has formulated and implemented a series of poverty alleviation policies for ethnic minority areas.

The first is to give priority support. In 1983, the State Council convened a national conference on production and living in areas with large ethnic minority populations, and proposed to basically solve the problems of adequate food and clothing, access to safe housing and drinking water for some people in a relatively short period of time. In 1987, 27 impoverished counties in pastoral areas were identified as key national support, and special discount loans for poverty alleviation in pastoral areas were established. In 1990, the state established the Food and Clothing Fund for Impoverished Areas with Large Ethnic Minority Populations in 1990, focusing on supporting 141 impoverished counties with large ethnic minority populations. In 1994, in implementing the Priority Poverty Alleviation Program (1994-2000)[1], 116 more such poor counties in areas with large ethnic minority populations were made accessible to preferential policies due to the relaxation of poverty standards. In 2001, another 10 counties in ethnic minority areas were identified as national key counties for poverty alleviation, and Tibet was included into the key support program as a special area as a whole. In 2005, the state prioritized the inclusion of impoverished villages with large ethnic minority populations in the plan for whole-village development-oriented poverty alleviation. In 2009, the state adopted new poverty standards with expanded coverage to fully implement poverty alleviation policies for low-income rural people in ethnic minority areas. The state also granted

---

[1] The Priority Poverty Alleviation Program (1994-2000), China's first ever national poverty alleviation program with definite goals, targets, measures and deadlines, committed to ensuring that the basic needs of 80 million impoverished rural residents would be met in the seven years from 1994 to 2000. —*Tr.*

poverty alleviation loans for ethnic minority groups at preferential interest rates, the term of which was normally 1-3 years, and for long-term projects with good economic and social benefits, could be extended to 5 years. The Outline for Development-oriented Poverty Reduction for China's Rural Areas (2011-2020) maps out 14 contiguous impoverished areas, 11 of which are in ethnic autonomous areas, and among 592 national key counties for poverty alleviation, 263 are in ethnic autonomous areas; among 30,000 impoverished villages identified in the 12th Five-year Plan for whole-village development-oriented poverty alleviation, 13,158 are in ethnic autonomous areas (The State Council Information Office, 2016a).

The second is to launch pairing assistance. Since 1995, poverty alleviation assistance has been directed to designated targets in ethnic minority areas. In 1996, the central government[1] arranged for economically developed areas and economically underdeveloped areas to try to cooperate for poverty alleviation, pairing off Beijing with Inner Mongolia, Tianjin with Gansu, Shanghai with Yunnan, Guangdong with Guangxi, Shandong with Xinjiang, Liaoning with Qinghai, Fujian with Ningxia, and Dalian, Qingdao, Shenzhen, Ningbo with Guizhou, while continuing to mobilize the central and local departments, combining their own advantages, to help impoverished areas eradicate poverty and achieve prosperity in terms of technical training, undertaking projects and non-reimbursable assistance, thus promoting East-West cooperation for poverty alleviation. In the same year, the National Ethnic Affairs Commission implemented a four-level ethnic affairs committee responsibility system for targeted poverty alleviation: the state, autonomous region, prefecture (city), and county (banner). On the basis of summing up the past experience of supporting Tibet, the state decided in 2010 to pair off 19 provinces to support Xinjiang. On February 4, 2013, the General Office of the State Council issued the Guiding Opinions on Pairing Assistance to Guizhou, calling on eight cities in six provinces, namely, Liaoning, Shanghai, Jiangsu, Zhejiang, Shandong and Guangdong to provide pairing assistance to pair with eight cities (prefectures) in Guizhou, specifically, Shanghai, Dalian, Suzhou, Qingdao and Shenzhen with cities of Zunyi, Liupanshui, Tongren, Anshun and Bijie, respectively; and Hangzhou, Guangzhou, and Ningbo with prefectures of Qiandongnan, Qiannan, and Qianxinan, respectively. On July 20, 2016, General Secretary Xi Jinping presided over

---

[1] In 1996, the central government held the National Conference on Development-driven Poverty Alleviation, further clarifying the steadfast commitment to the goal of being able to provide adequate food and clothing for the impoverished people by the end of the 20th century and confirming the shift from relief-based poverty alleviation to development-driven poverty alleviation. —*Tr.*

a symposium on poverty alleviation cooperation between the eastern and western regions in Yinchuan of Ningxia, to deploy east-west cooperation for poverty alleviation in the new era.

The third is to carry out actions to help border areas prosper and enrich the lives of local residents. In 1999, the state implemented an action aimed at revitalizing border areas and enriching the lives of those living there. One year later, the National Ethnic Affairs Commission and the Ministry of Finance jointly launched a pilot campaign of this kind whereby 17 pilot border counties were identified across the country, and RMB51 million of special funds were allocated by the central government each year. The central government poured a total of RMB368 million into the action to develop border areas and enriching the people living there from 2000 to 2005; and RMB111 million of the Fund for Ethnic Minorities Development to further promote the Action in key support counties in 2006.[1] In June 2007, the State Council issued the Program for Revitalizing Border Areas and Enriching the People During the 11th Five-Year Plan Period. In 2009, the National Ethnic Affairs Commission expanded the pilot areas of the action to all 136 border counties and 58 border farms of Xinjiang Production and Construction Corps; the central government earmarked a total of RMB484 million from the Fund for Ethnic Minorities Development as subsidy funds for the action. From 2012 to 2015, it allocated RMB14.59 billion of the Fund for Ethnic Minorities Development to specially support the action, support the development of ethnic minority groups with small populations, and carry out the protection and development of ethnic minority characteristic villages and traditional handicrafts; the state arranged an investment of RMB550 million in the central budget to help infrastructure construction, improvement of people's production and living conditions and development of social undertakings in border areas and ethnic minority areas with small populations (The State Council Information Office, 2016a).

The fourth is to support the development of ethnic groups with small populations. In the 1990s, the National Ethnic Affairs Commission began to attach importance to supporting the development of ethnic minority groups with small populations. In 2001, the State Council requested relevant regions and departments to offer special policy support to them. The central government allocated subsidies for their development from the Fund for Ethnic Minorities Development: a total of RMB117 million from 2002 to

[1] *Tutorial Reader on Learning the Guiding Principles from the Central Ethnic Work Conference*, Beijing: The Ethnic Publishing House, 2005.

2004, and RMB112 million each year since 2005. In 2005, the State Council approved to launch the Plan for Supporting the Development of Ethnic Minority Groups with Small Populations (2005-2010), giving priority support to 640 administrative villages inhabited by 22 ethnic groups with a total population of less than 100,000. During these six years, a total of RMB3.751 billion of various funds was invested and 11,168 projects were constructed. In 2011, the State Council renewed the plan (2011-2015), proposing that by 2015, administrative villages inhabited by ethnic minority groups with small populations would basically ensure that those villages are equipped with five infrastructure conditions and local residents have access to ten types of necessities or facilities[1], and areas inhabited by ethnic minority groups with small populations will basically achieve "one reduction, two reaches and three improvements"[2]. On this basis, the State Council issued the Plan for Promoting the Development of Areas with Large Ethnic Minority Populations and Ethnic Minority Groups with Small Population Over the 13th Five-year at the end of 2016 to further support the development of areas and ethnic minority groups with small populations.

8.2.6   Regional support policy

To support the development of ethnic minority areas, all of China's five autonomous regions, 30 autonomous prefectures, and 120 autonomous counties nationwide are either covered by the large-scale development of the western region, or enjoy the same preferential policies as the western regions. In September 2007, the Several Opinions on Further Promoting Economic and Social Development in Xinjiang was promulgated, which made comprehensive arrangements for accelerating Xinjiang's economic and social development and further improving the living standards of all ethnic minority groups in Xinjiang. Since 2008, the State Council has successively formulated and issued guiding opinions on promoting socio-economic development of areas with large Tibetan

---

[1] Villages inhabited by ethnic minority groups with small populations have been equipped with oil roads, electricity, radio and television, information (telephone, broadband), and biogas (clean energy); and the villagers living there have access to safe drinking water, affordable housing, sanitary toilets, basic farmland with high and stable yield (grassland, forest land with economic returns, water surface for aquaculture) or income-increasing industries, preschool education, clinic service, rooms for cultural activities including reading, venues for sports fitness and ethnic cultural activities, office for village affairs, farmer's supermarket (convenience store) and agricultural resources store.

[2] In areas with small ethnic minority populations, the number of poor people has been reduced by half or more; the Net Income Per Capita of farmers and herdsmen has reached the local average or above; the Net Income Per Capita of farmers and herdsmen of about 1/2 ethnic groups has reached the national average or above; and the security level of infrastructure, people's well-being, and self-development ability has been greatly improved.

populations in Tibet, Ningxia, and Qinghai as well as of Guangxi, Yunnan, Inner Mongolia, and Guizhou, thus the special national policy to support the development of ethnic minority areas has covered the three provinces with large ethnic minority populations and five autonomous regions. In August 2014, the General Office of the State Council issued the Notice on the Work Plan of Developed Provinces (Municipalities) to Offer Pairing Assistance to the Economic and Social Development of Areas with Large Tibetan Populations in Sichuan, Yunnan and Gansu Provinces, which determined the principle of pairing off one province (municipality) with one prefecture during 2014-2020 period, specifically, Tianjin with Gannan Tibetan Autonomous Prefecture and Tianzhu Tibetan Autonomous County, Shanghai with Diqing Tibetan Autonomous Prefecture, Zhejiang with Aba Tibetan and Qiang Autonomous Prefecture and Muli Tibetan Autonomous County, and Guangdong (including Shenzhen) with Ganzi Tibetan Autonomous Prefecture. The implementation of these regional support policies has effectively promoted the development of ethnic minority areas.

8.3   Progress of socio-economic development in ethnic minority areas

With the strong support of the CPC Central Committee and the State Council's policies, ethnic minority areas have achieved rapid economic growth in recent years, together with continuously improved infrastructure and public services, steadily advanced various social undertakings, greatly improved living standards, and remarkable results in rural poverty alleviation through development. This demonstrates that under the framework of the coordinated regional development strategy, the policies implemented by the central to support the development of ethnic minority areas have achieved remarkable progress.

8.3.1   Rapid growth of fixed assets investment in ethnic minority areas

Since the reform and opening up, the central government has convened four central conferences on ethnic affairs in 1992, 1999, 2005, and 2014, which have served as a platform for launching a series of major engineering programs and infrastructure construction projects to boost investment in ethnic minority areas. Additionally, six central working conferences on Tibet have been held, wherein the government has encouraged more prosperous provinces and municipalities to extend their support to

Tibet through participating in various construction initiatives. For instance, during the fourth central working conference on Tibet convened in 2001, the central government, along with relevant provinces and municipalities, allocated resources and funding to support Tibet through 117 projects and 70 projects, respectively. The total investment for these projects exceeded RMB40 billion. With the strong support of national policy, the fixed asset investment in ethnic minority areas has grown rapidly since the reform and opening up. If calculated at current prices of that year, the total investment in fixed assets reached RMB7,044.99 billion in 2016, 104.3 times that in 1992 and 28.4 times that in 2000; since 1997, it has been growing faster than the nation as a whole, except in 2012, 2014, and 2016; from 1997 to 2016, it grew at an annual average rate of 20.8%, 3.0 percentage points higher than the national average; specifically, from 2001 to 2016, its average annual growth rate stood at 23.3%, 3.3 percentage points higher than the national average. This demonstrates that, the total investment in fixed assets in ethnic minority areas has achieved a sustained and rapid growth in recent years.

8.3.2 Good economic development momentum in ethnic minority areas

The economy in ethnic minority areas experienced significant fluctuations and slow growth in its early stages of the reform and opening up, partially due to unfavorable natural conditions and weak economic foundations. However, at the beginning of the 21st century, the central government implemented a range of policies and measures to enhance support for these areas. With the strong support of national policies, the economy of ethnic minority areas has gained rapid growth momentum in recent years, with growth rate continuously exceeding the national average. From 1993 to 2016, the GRP of ethnic autonomous areas achieved an average annual growth rate of 11.3%, roughly the same as the average national growth rate of 11.4%. However, different stages had different pictures. From 1993 to 2003, an average annual growth rate the GRP of ethnic autonomous areas was 10.0%, about 1.5 percentage points lower than the national average, while since 2004, the growth rate of ethnic autonomous areas has been higher than the national average (see Figure 8-2). From 2004 to 2016, the average annual growth rate reached 12.3%, 2.3 percentage points higher than that in the previous stage and 1.0 percentage points higher than the national average. Specifically, from 2011 to 2016, the GRP of ethnic autonomous areas grew at an average annual rate of 10.1%, 0.9 percentage points higher than the national average. This shows that from the perspective of economic growth, the national policy for supporting economic development in ethnic minority areas has achieved good results in recent years. With the rapid economic growth, ethnic minority areas have been holding an increasing share in China's GDP, and the development gap has gradually narrowed between ethnic minority areas and other regions. In 2000, the GRP of ethnic autonomous areas accounted for only 7.70% of the national total, and by 2015, the proportion had increased to 9.71%. In addition, ethnic minority areas have developed a number of advantageous industries with their own characteristics and market competitiveness and have continuously optimized the industrial structure, with the added value composition of three industries in ethnic autonomous areas changed from 37.7 : 34.4 : 27.9 to 15.0 : 42.4 : 42.6 from 1992 to 2016.

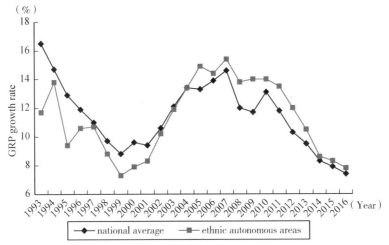

Figure 8-2   Comparison of GRP growth rate between ethnic
autonomous areas and the whole country

Note: The term "national average" here is based on the aggregate of 31 provinces, autonomous regions, and municipalities (excluding Hong Kong, Macao, and Taiwan region), which is generally higher than the national GDP growth rate.

Source: Calculated based on *China Statistical Yearbook* (*2017*) and *China Ethnic Statistical Yearbook* (*2016*).

8.3.3   The vigorous development of culture, education, and health undertakings of ethnic minority groups

To promote the development of ethnic minority literary and artistic talent, the state and relevant departments have taken various measures including the establishment of ethnic minority literary and art groups, art colleges, cultural centers, and mass art galleries. These efforts aim to foster a thriving environment for ethnic minority cultural and artistic creations, as well as contribute to the overall development of ethnic cultural and artistic undertakings. From 1979 to 2015, the number of art institutions in ethnic autonomous areas increased from 645 to 1,321, of which the numbers of art performance troupes and venues increased from 589 to 1,063 and from 56 to 157 respectively; the numbers of cultural centers and cultural stations increased from 544 to 795, from 2,024 to 8,665 respectively; and libraries increased from 331 in 1981 to 758 in 2015. Thus, the cultural heritage of ethnic minorities has been well protected and carried forward, and a large number of precious oral and intangible cultural heritages have been rescued, excavated and sorted out. The Minorities Art Festival of China, which has become a national statutory activity and held for five times till now, has gained much popularity and further carried forward the excellent traditional culture of ethnic minorities. Great progress has been made in ethnic press and publication, radio, film and television and particularly, through implementing Project for Radio and TV Coverage in Each Village, "Tibet and Xinjiang Project"[1] and "2131 Project"[2], there emerged 603 radio stations, television stations and radio and television stations in ethnic autonomous areas in 2015, with a comprehensive coverage rate of 97.62% for television and 95.56% for broadcasting.

The quality of education for ethnic minority groups has been rapidly restored and improved, and a large number of minority educational institutions at all levels have been established one after another. At present, China has already created an ethnic education system including ethnic minority primary schools, middle schools, vocational colleges and higher education institutions. Before the PRC was founded in 1949, the illiteracy rate of ethnic minority groups in China was above 95%, and there was only one higher education institution for ethnic minority groups. In the early days of the PRC, there were only 1,300 ethnic minority students in institutions of higher learning across the country, accounting for only 1.4 % of all students. By 2015, there had been 32 different types of ethnic minority colleges and universities, and 2,142,900 junior college and college students from ethnic minority groups, accounting for 8.16% of the national total. There were more than 10,000 schools in 13 provinces and autonomous regions that provided bilingual education or taught in ethnic languages. From 2012 to 2015, under the Program for Training High Caliber Core Personnel for Ethnic Minority Groups, China enrolled and trained 16,000 master's degree candidates and 4,000 doctoral candidates, thus making all of China's 55 ethnic minority groups have graduate students (The State Council Information Office, 2016b).

---

[1] It refers to the project of extending radio and television coverage to areas with large ethnic minority populations like Tibet, Xinjiang and other border areas, which was officially launched in September 2000.

[2] In 1998, the Ministry of Culture and the State Administration of Radio, Film and Television put forward the goal of showing movies in rural areas, which was called "2131 Project", that is, at the beginning of the 21st century, showing one movie in one village in one month in the vast rural areas.

Ethnic minority areas have witnessed great progress in its healthcare sector, effective control of endemic and infectious diseases, and significant improvement in local residents' health quality and social security. From 1978 to 2015, the number of medical institutions in ethnic autonomous areas increased from 23,934 to 52,646, an increase of 120%. The number of beds in medical and healthcare institutions and medical workers per 10,000 people increased from 22.37 to 46.84 and from 25 to 51, increasing by 109.4% and 107.1%, respectively. Social security in ethnic minority areas has obviously improved, especially the standards of subsistence allowances for urban and rural residents have been raised above the national average. In 2015, the annual subsistence allowances for urban and rural residents in ethnic autonomous areas reached RMB6,654 and RMB2,878 per capita, 75.1% and 62.9% higher than the national average, respectively. In addition, ethnic traditional sports have flourished. The National Ethnic Traditional Sports Meeting has been held for ten times, which has greatly enriched the sports and cultural life of the people of all ethnic groups.

8.3.4   Significant improvement in living standards in ethnic minority areas

Since the reform and opening up, with the strong support of national policies and other regions, the economy in ethnic minority areas has kept a momentum of rapid development. Both the living standards of urban and rural households and the production and living conditions in rural areas have improved significantly. From 1978 to 2015, the per capita disposable income of urban residents in ethnic autonomous areas increased from RMB307 to RMB26,083.11, an increase of 84 times; the Net Income Per Capita of rural residents increased from RMB138 to RMB8,889.25, an increase of 63.4 times [1]. Especially, since 2006, the growth rate of per capita income of urban and rural residents in ethnic autonomous areas has been higher than the national average, and the income gap between ethnic minority areas and other areas has been gradually narrowing. If calculated at current prices of that year, the per capita disposable income of urban residents and the Net Income Per Capita of rural residents in ethnic autonomous areas have increased by 12.1% and 15.1% in nominal terms, 0.5 and 2.1 percentage points higher than the national average in the same period, respectively. If the national average is put at 100, from 2006 to 2015, the relative level of per capita disposable income of urban residents and that of Net Income Per Capita of rural residents in ethnic autonomous areas increased from 79.1 to 82.0 and from 70.2 to 82.5, respectively. The

---

[1] The data for 1978 comes from the State Council Information Office (2009).

living conditions of urban and rural residents in ethnic minority areas have also been significantly improved. From 2000 to 2015, the per capita housing area of urban residents and rural residents in ethnic autonomous areas increased from 16.5 square meters to 35.8 square meters and from 22.6 square meters to 36.6 square meters, respectively. The rapid development of economy and society in ethnic minority areas has laid a solid material foundation for promoting the prosperity and development of all ethnic groups. Taking Xinjiang as an example, the mortality rate decreased from 20.82 ‰ in 1949 to 4.26 ‰ in 2016, the average life expectancy increased from 30 to 72.35 years, and by the end of 2016, the incidence of poverty had dropped to 10 percent or less (The State Council Information Office, 2017).

8.3.5 Notable progress in fighting poverty through development in ethnic minority areas

For the low level of development and a large poor population, ethnic minority areas tended to have a high incidence of poverty. Based on China's 1978 poverty standard, ethnic minority areas had more than 40 million impoverished people in 1985 (The State Council Information Office, 2009), nearly one third of China's total rural poor population in that year. After joint efforts from all sectors of society, ethnic minority areas have made notable progress in fighting poverty through development. From 2001 to 2015, the impoverished population in ethnic autonomous areas reduced from 38.81 million to 18.05 million, and the incidence of poverty down from 30.4% to 13.8%, based on the 2010 poverty standard. During the same period, the incidence of poverty in rural areas decreased from 12.7% to 5.7%, and the gap between the incidence of poverty in ethnic autonomous areas and the whole country was narrowing each year (see Table 8-2); the poor population in three provinces with large ethnic minority populations and five autonomous regions decreased from 39.17 million to 18.13 million, a decrease of 21.04 million or 53.7%; the incidence of poverty decreased from 27.2% to 12.4%, down 14.8 percentage points (The State Council Information Office, 2016a). In view of the difficult natural conditions, it was an amazing achievement in itself to keep the pace of poverty alleviation in ethnic minority areas basically synchronized with that of the whole country since the reform and opening up. In this sense, ethnic minority areas played a key and determining role in ensuring that by the year 2020, all rural residents living below the current poverty line had been lifted out of poverty, and poverty was eliminated in all poor counties and regions.

Table 8-2   Poor population and incidence of poverty: ethnic
autonomous areas vs. the whole country (2011–2015)

Indicators		2011	2012	2013	2014	2015
Poor population	Ethnic autonomous areas (10 thousand)	3,881	3,159	2,613	2,236	1,805
	Rural China (10 thousand)	12,238	9,899	8,249	7,017	5,575
	Proportion (%)	31.7	31.9	31.7	31.9	32.4
Incidence of poverty	Ethnic autonomous areas (%)	30.4	24.6	20.7	17.7	13.8
	Rural China (%)	12.7	10.2	8.5	7.2	5.7
	Higher (percentage points)	17.7	14.4	12.2	10.5	8.1

Source: Household Survey Office of National Bureau of Statistics, *Poverty Monitoring Report of Rural China* (*2016*), Beijing: China Statistics Publishing House, 2016.

8.4   Problems in the central policies for supporting ethnic minority areas

With the strong backing of government policies, ethnic minority areas have made significant strides in socio-economic development in recent years. However, due to their weak economic foundations as well as inadequate production and living conditions, these areas still lag behind the more developed regions in the east. In order to address these challenges and achieve sustainable development, comprehensive support from national policies is still required. It is worth noting that the current central policies in this area still have some room for improvement, as outlined below (Wei Houkai et al., 2012).

8.4.1   Incompleteness of the policy system to support the development of ethnic minority areas

Since the founding of the PRC, especially the launch of the reform and opening up, a host of policies and measures have been formulated and implemented in terms of fiscal and tax incentives, industrial support, poverty alleviation through development, opening up to the outside world, and pairing assistance, with the aim to promote the development of ethnic minority areas. However, as most of them were included in other related policies in a scattered way, a complete policy system for supporting ethnic minority areas has not been developed, which has, to some certain extent, offset the implementation effect. For this reason, it is necessary to intensify the ethnic policy system integration and strengthen the overall function, improving the effectiveness and efficiency of dealing with ethnic affairs (Yu Zidong, 2001).

Meanwhile, the existing policy support is more like simply injecting help into ethnic minority areas than enabling those areas to help themselves, that is, such policies fail to provide enough stimulus or incentive to develop themselves. This is one of the important reasons for the low self-development capability of ethnic minority areas. Some scholars argue that simply offering help may lead to a locked state with backwardness lingering on, and that only through empowering them to develop themselves can the advantages of backwardness be ultimately exploited (Zheng Changde, 2017). Fundamentally, the prosperity of ethnic minority areas hinges on self-development capability; it can never be achieved through relying solely on policy assistance. Therefore, the central leadership's policies for supporting the development of ethnic minority areas should focus more on providing economic stimuli and motivating local governments, so as to fully mobilize the enthusiasm of local governments, enterprises, and residents to develop a sound self-development mechanism and enhance self-development capability of ethnic minority areas.

8.4.2   Poor continuity and stability of existing supporting policies

To develop the economy and get rid of the poverty and backwardness of areas with large ethnic minority populations, China has formulated and implemented a series of policies to support the development of those areas since the founding of the PRC. But in general, those economic policies exhibit low stability and continuity in implementation due to frequent changes and adjustments. Relevant studies show that the average stability index of economic policies in china for areas with large ethnic minority populations stand at 63.41%, while the policies on preferential taxation, financial subsidies, and industrial development have a relatively lower stability, and that the stability index of ethnic trade policies, which are particularly important for ethnic economy, is only 20% (Wen Jun, 2004).Obviously, most of the current policies and measures are introduced as a quick fix to solve the problems in ethnic minority areas, and a long-term, effective mechanism has not been developed that can ensure the normal implementation and proper functions as expected. Furthermore, even if a long-term mechanism for sustainable development has been established in those areas, the continuity and effects of policies are still uncertain. In addition, with the comprehensive introduction of the socialist market economy system, most of the ethnic economic policies rolled out in the planned economy era are losing their performability, thus demanding urgent consolidation, adjustment, improvement, and refinement due to the serious impacts and challenges in recent years.

8.4.3 Failure to fully reflect particularity of ethnic minority areas

The difference between ethnic minority areas and other areas lies in ethnicity, which is mainly reflected in ethnic culture. Therefore, the central government shall take ethnicity into full account and respect ethnic culture when formulating and implementing ethnic economic policies for ethnic minority areas. Policies that respect ethnicity will facilitate the active participation of ethnic minority groups, thereby boosting economy and realizing common prosperity for all ethnic groups. Since China's various ethnic minority areas and ethnic groups vary greatly in development level and characteristics, the formulation and implementation of ethnic economic policies need to be based on local conditions, targeted on specific ethnic groups, and adapted to actual circumstances (Zhang Lijun et al., 2010). However, most of China's policies to support ethnic minority areas were introduced in the form of regional economic policies and intended to drive the economy of ethnic minorities through the economic progress of regions inhabited by ethnic minority groups. However, due to differences in ability, quality, language and other factors, various social groups within the same region may experience disparities in their access to economic opportunities, preferential policies, and benefits of economic progress. Some out-of-the-way areas are economically backward and culturally disadvantaged; minority residents there tend to encounter more obstacles in performing economic activities. And meanwhile, it is quite difficult for regional economic policies with industrialization and modernization as primary goals to pay due attention to the economic activities characterized with tradition, especially with ethnic tradition. In this sense, regional economic policies may not necessarily lead to the economic development of ethnic minority groups, thus causing some sort of deviation from original policy goals.

8.4.4 Deviation between existing supporting policies and their objectives

In some way, policies for supporting the development of ethnic minority areas serve as affirmative actions under the basic framework of China's regional economic policies to help those areas get more access to development opportunities according to the principle of "giving priority to ethnic minority areas under the same conditions", but few of them are specifically targeted to ethnic minority areas and most are the extended versions of general regional economic policies, although there exist some policies to support ethnic groups with small populations and facilitating ethnic trade. Such an incomplete policy system often causes deviations between existing supporting policies and their original goals, and demands more efforts to intensify their coupling effect. For instance, in ethnic minority areas, fiscal policy should take improving public services and ensuring equitable access to basic public services as the primary goal, but actually, the structurally unsound, low-proportioned fiscal transfer payment has to a great extent hindered the central government's capacity of providing equitable basic public services (Lei Zhenyang & Cheng Aihua, 2010). The goal of tax policy benefiting the western region and ethnic minority areas is to reduce tax burden, but as a matter of fact, the tax burden in those areas is heavier than that in the eastern and other areas (Wei Houkai & Yuan Xiaomeng, 2010). The credit support policy intends to provide low-interest loans for ethnic minority areas, but some ethnic residents still have no access to them. Preferential loan policies for ethnic trade and products also have some problems in implementation (Wu Xiaoping, 2015). As policies on resource exploitation, especially on resource pricing, are far from being perfect, some superior resources in ethnic minority areas have been exploited but failed to play its due role in boosting economic development, which may have a negative impact on ethnic relations. In implementing other policies, including those on poverty alleviation, for the development of ethnic minority groups with small populations, and on ecological compensation, there also exist problems like goal deviation and content distortion.

8.4.5 Insufficient consideration of long-term deficiencies and special factors in ethnic minority areas

As China has entered a new stage of fully implementing the regional coordinated development strategies, existing support policies are playing a more and more obvious role in balancing the development gap between ethnic minority areas and other areas: the equalization efforts have been bridging the gap in basic public services. In ethnic minority areas, however, the same amount of input can only produce limited equalization effect because of long-term deficiencies and low quality in basic public services, which inhibits the improvement of local living standards. Studies show that, in seven out of three provinces with large ethnic minority populations and five autonomous regions (except Inner Mongolia), "high birth rate coexists low consumption level of rural residents" (Wang Yanzhong, 2017). At the same time, huge special expenditures in ethnic minority areas have driven up the cost of basic public services. From a natural geography perspective, the natural conditions in which China's ethnic minority groups reside are often challenging. These impact communities are typically found in remote regions characterized by plateaus, mountains, intermountain basins, deserts, and the Gobi. Due to their sparse population and the challenge of achieving economies of scale, ethnic minority areas face the burden of marginally increasing costs in providing equitable basic public services for residents. In those areas, a long list of special fiscal expenditures—such as unique expenditures on ethnic and religious affairs, on border construction, on ecological conservation and environmental protection, and on administrative power—will inevitably squeeze out the expenditures on basic public services when fiscal capacity is given and limited. Further, ethnic minority areas also undertake some proxy affairs, such as regional security, border security, ethnic culture protection, anti-secession, which benefit beyond the administrative subjects in ethnic minority areas (Wu Wenzhong et al., 2016). Therefore, in formulating national public policies, it is of necessity to fully consider the long-term deficiencies and special factors in ethnic minority areas and enhance the supply capacity of basic public services in those areas, so as to equalize access to basic public services among different regions.

8.5   Adjustment directions of policies for developing ethnic minority areas

Accelerating the development of ethnic minority areas is of great significance for promoting coordinated regional development and building a moderately prosperous society in all respects. In the new era, central policies for supporting the development of ethnic minority areas will be adjusted by taking the general approaches as follows: (1) increase financial and tax support to accelerate the development of ethnic minority areas; (2) actively improve self-development capability of ethnic minority through supporting the industrial development, speeding up the opening up both externally and internally, and establishing and improving mechanisms of regional ecological compensation and self-development; and (3) based on the particularity of ethnic minority areas, further improve special supporting policies, and pairing assistance policies to help those areas accelerate their development (Wei Houkai et al., 2012).

8.5.1   Increase financial transfer payments to ethnic minority areas

First of all, we should increase general transfer payments. The financial transfer payment system takes balancing disparities in financial resources between regions and ensuring equitable access to basic public services as its important goals, which, however, are far from being achieved at present because the financial resources in ethnic minority areas are still highly limited. To further enhance the development capacity of ethnic minority areas and improve their public services, it is necessary to increase general transfer payments, use "factor method" more in calculating transfer payments, so that transfer payments can be further distributed to border areas, and areas in the central and western regions, thus playing a better role in allocating public financial resources and ensuring equitable access to public services.

Secondly, we should further improve the transfer payment system in ethnic minority areas. In order to couple with the strategy for the large-scale development of the western region and to support the development of ethnic minority areas, the central government has started to transfer payments to ethnic minority areas since 2000. Transferring payments to ethnic autonomous counties under the jurisdiction of non-ethnic provinces and non-ethnic autonomous prefectures, the central government has covered all areas with large ethnic minority populations into its transfer payment system since 2006. In 2010, the Ministry of Finance issued the Measures for Transfer Payments from the Central Government to Local Areas with Large Ethnic Minority Populations and established a steady increase mechanism for transfer payments to those areas; in 2017, factors reflecting ethnic characteristics, such as the proportion of ethnic population, the number of aboriginal ethnic minority groups, and the types of ethnic minority groups with small populations, were introduced to strengthen support for ethnic minority areas, with many types of ethnic minority groups, and with wide distribution of ethnic minority groups with small populations. The central government's transfer payments to ethnic minority areas increased rapidly from RMB2.55 billion in 2000 to RMB70.4 billion in 2017. To help accelerate the development of ethnic minority areas, we should transfer more payments with better methods in the future, and effectively improve the utilization efficiency of funds transferred from the central government.

Lastly, in comparison to their counterparts in other regions, governments in ethnic autonomous areas are mandated to exert additional administrative authority, which involves conducting public awareness campaigns and educational initiatives regarding ethnic and religious policies, mediating ethnic interests, resolving disputes arising from ethnic and religious differences, and taking action against separatism and sabotage activities. Besides, more public institutions and staff are needed for those governments, which follow that the state should, when calculating and determining the size of fiscal dependents in ethnic minority areas, take into full account the local realities and allow for an appropriate expansion. Therefore, the obviously higher administrative costs for governments in ethnic autonomous areas than in other regions make it justifiably necessary to direct more financial transfer payments towards ethnic minority areas, so as to meet the needs of socio-economic development of those areas, ensure local governments' role in providing equitable basic public services, and maintain stability of ethnic minority areas and border peace.

8.5.2　Accelerate resource tax reform

Being rich in mineral resources, especially coal, oil, gas and other energy sources and some important mineral resources, is one of the few outstanding advantages in ethnic minority areas, which provides favorable conditions for the development of resource-based industries. But in stark contrast to the abundance of resources, some places have fallen into pollution and poverty after having developed their resources. There exist many problems in developing resources in ethnic minority areas, such as disordered exploitation and irrational benefit sharing, which has given rise to the prominent phenomenon of "affluent poverty" and made it difficult to meet the needs of economic development in ethnic minority areas. Actually, an important cause for the above situation lies in the large defects in the current resource tax system. Therefore, it is imperative to speed up resource tax reform.

The current resource tax system was initially adopted in 1993. Although the tax rate has been raised many times since 2004, it is still too low when compared to the actual resource price. On June 1, 2010, the state launched the pilot reform of resource tax in Xinjiang, and ad valorem collection has been implemented resources tax for crude oil and natural gas in Xinjiang at a rate of 5%, but this tax rate was still far below the global average of 10%. Since December 1, 2014, ad valorem taxation for coal resources tax has been applied to the whole country, with the tax rate being determined by the provincial government in the range of 2%-10%. On May 10, 2016, the MOF and the STA jointly issued the Notice on Comprehensively Promoting Resource Tax Reform. As of July 1, 2016, the resource tax reform characterized by ad valorem collection, ambit expansion and rights decentralization, and optimization of collection was comprehensively promoted. This resource tax reform not only delegated to local governments the right to determine the tax rate of coal and other resources, but also improved the share ratio of local governments in resource exploitation by way of ad valorem taxation and tax rate increase (Xie Mei'e & Gu Shuzhong, 2017).

No reform is allowed to damage the interests of the public. From a realistic point of view, the resource tax reform is a multi-stakeholder game. To ensure public benefits from the reform, the key is to further adjust the existing benefit sharing pattern. Many parts of China, especially ethnic minority areas, rely heavily on territorial resources to achieve economic growth. Local public have to bear the total cost arising from rapid deterioration of local environment and serious loss and waste of land and water resources in the process of resource exploitation. State-owned monopolies, such as oil companies, have been responsible for environmental pollution and ecological imbalances in local areas. However, they prioritize profit accumulation without shouldering corresponding responsibilities. Areas like Xinjiang and Inner Mongolia have served as significant exporters of natural resources, including natural gas and coal. Unfortunately, they have received inadequate compensation for the benefits derived from these resources. Therefore, in the new round of resource tax reform, it is necessary to further increase the proportion of benefit distributed to local areas, especially to ethnic minority areas. The state shall stipulate the proportion of tax paid by central enterprises to the mining areas. All mineral resources mining enterprises, regardless of where they belong, shall register at the mining areas and pay income tax locally.

8.5.3 Effectively reduce the tax burden of enterprises in ethnic minority areas

In ethnic minority areas, the specific geographical environment determines the profitability of businesses operating there. In order to stimulate ethnic economy and actively attract enterprises and private capital, it is necessary to implement preferential tax policies at present, effectively reducing the tax burden while improving the profitability of enterprises in ethnic minority areas. Specific measures include: First, adjust the allowable cost and pre-tax deduction standard, allow the inclusion of expenditures on scientific and technological innovation to cost, implement accelerated depreciation, encourage enterprises to speed up technological transformation for higher technological content of products. Second, apply the policy for the large-scale development of the western region to all ethnic minority areas and for the income from investment and operation of public infrastructure projects supported by the state in ethnic minority areas, as well as the income from the enterprise's engaging in the approved project of environmental protection, energy conservation and water saving and products with ethnic characteristics, the enterprise income tax shall be exempted from the tax year when such project has obtained the first income from putting into the commercial production and operation to the third year, and be half exempted in the following three years. In case its investment returns are still invested in ethnic minority areas, the enterprise shall be exempted from income tax. Third, under the principle of "differentiated treatment and rationalized burden", value-added tax in areas with large ethnic minority populations can be collected at reduced rate of 10% or 13%.

8.5.4　Actively support the industrial development in ethnic minority areas

Agriculture and animal husbandry policies in ethnic minority areas should be market-oriented and preferential for those areas to identify leading industries and then develop specialty and competitive products based on local endemic resources. Governments should offer major grain producing areas in the western ethnic minority areas more policy support, including setting up special funds for major agricultural development; provide tax incentives and loan support to the construction of characteristic agricultural bases, which should be closely linked with the formation of leading industries to promote specialized production and intensive management, and expand the scale of bases. Departments of agriculture, education and scientific research should actively train all kinds of technical personnel based on the reality of agricultural industrialization, launch the campaign of taking technology to the countryside to promote scientific farming. The financial transfer payment system should be improved to strengthen the cultivation and support of the entities of animal husbandry industrialization, speed up the regulation of grassland managerial rights, transform the management mode of animal husbandry, increase investment in animal husbandry infrastructure, and perfect the scientific and technological support system in pastoral areas. More efforts will be made to promote the industrialization of agriculture and animal husbandry, and to combine characteristic agriculture with green and brand agriculture. Micro-loan programs launched by the People's Bank of China and the Agricultural Bank of China will provide timely fund support for smallholder farmers and herdsmen.

As to industrial development in ethnic minority areas, we should vigorously develop industries with distinctive advantages and transform their resource advantages to economic advantages by continuously extending the industrial chain and speeding up the comprehensive utilization and deep processing of resources. We will give priority to expansion or new construction of a number of hydropower stations, thus accelerating the development of hydropower resources in the main tributaries of the upper reaches of the Yangtze River, the upper and middle reaches of the Yellow River, the Hongshui River and the Lancang River. We will speed up the programs as follows: the construction of pithead thermal power plants to make use of high-quality coal resources in Inner Mongolia and Guizhou; the development of oil and gas in Tarim and Junggar in Xinjiang; the construction of large- and medium-sized coal production bases and supporting coal preparation plants in Inner Mongolia and Guizhou; the vigorous development of potassium, sodium, magnesium and other series of chemical fertilizer industries by focusing on developing phosphorus and potassium resources in Guizhou and Qinghai; the development of pharmaceutical industries in Yunnan, Guizhou, Inner Mongolia, and Tibet, especially the industries engaged in manufacturing traditional Tibetan herb, Mongolian herb, and traditional Chinese medicines; vigorous development of advanced manufacturing industries and the construction of a number of bases of advanced manufacturing industries and emerging industries of strategic importance. At the same time, we should encourage the development of labor-intensive industries in order to create more jobs.

The government should provide policy support in terms of public finance, taxation, investment, and financing. For instance, the central government can offer corresponding assistance, such as implementing financial interest subsidies and reducing the depreciation period of fixed assets and amortization period of intangible assets for enterprises involved in major infrastructure projects, industrial projects with significant advantages, and projects catering to the specific needs of ethnic groups.

8.5.5 Further accelerate the pace of opening up ethnic minority areas

Ethnic minority areas are the core areas and important support for pursuing the Belt and Road Initiative (Zheng Changde, 2017). It is necessary to promote the deep integration of ethnic minority areas into the Belt and Road cooperation to build a new open economic system. In terms of ethnic trade, we should continue to improve the policies on ethnic trade and ethnic goods, and take flexible measures to give preferential treatment and convenience to the trade between border towns and border towns of neighboring countries and the border civilian trade. The value-added tax and enterprise income tax of ethnic trade enterprises shall be reduced or exempted in an appropriate way, and their export duties shall be refunded; we will continue to implement policies such as preferential interest rates for working capital loans, interest subsidies for technological transformation loans and preferential taxes for ethnic trade enterprise outlets and designated enterprises of producing commodities to meet special ethnic needs.

In terms of opening up, we must continue to implement action plans for boosting development and improving living standards in border areas, trying to achieve better progress in developing border trade and constructing infrastructure such as transportation, communications, ports, power and water supply, environment, and health care in ethnic minority areas; we will set up a number of new special customs regulation areas in ethnic minority areas, including cross-border or border economic cooperation zones, mutual trade zones, bonded zones, export processing zones, etc., to upgrade qualified economic and technological development zones to state-level economic and technological development zones; keep a continuous focus on investment promotion and facilitation in ethnic minority areas. While doing a good job in constructing Kashgar and Khorgos Economic Development Zones in Xinjiang, we will steadily develop cross-border economic cooperation zones such as China-Kazakhstan Khorgos International Border Cooperation Center and China-Laos Mohan-Moding Economic Cooperation Zone, and accelerate the construction of key development and opening pilot zones such as Dongxing in Guangxi, Mengla (Mohan) and Ruili in Yunnan, Erenhot and Manzhouli in Inner Mongolia. By further opening up to the outside world, a new opening pattern in ethnic minority areas will be gradually formed to promote development, prosperity and stability through opening up.

In terms of regional cooperation, we should further encourage coastal enterprises, processing trade and development zones to "go west" while supporting ethnic minority areas in developing infrastructure and effectively improving investment environment. To build important platforms for ethnic minority areas to open up to the outside world and promote regional cooperation, we will promote the role of those areas as destinations of industrial relocation, and establish state-level industrial relocation demonstration zones in parts where conditions permit. We will ensure the success of Silk Road International Expo & ITFCEW, Western China International Fair, China-ASEAN Expo, China-Eurasia Expo, China-Arab States Expo, China-South Asia Expo, China-Mongolia Expo, and China Xizang Tourism Culture International Expo.

8.5.6 Establish and improve the regional ecological compensation mechanism

Most of the rivers in China originate from ethnic minority areas, and the preservation of the environment in these upper reaches directly impacts the ecological health downstream. It is crucial to advocate for a combination of direct compensation, such as investments and project support, and indirect compensation, including additional taxes and funds for tax collection. This will facilitate the establishment of a stable platform and mechanism for compensation, enabling ethnic minority areas to enhance their capacity for sustainable development in a harmonious and environmentally friendly manner. Ethnic minority areas are often characterized by underdevelopment, lagging behind in terms of industrialization. Simultaneously, they face the challenge of resource exportation and ecological vulnerability. In the pursuit of industrialization and resource development, it becomes imperative to prevent environmental destruction and achieve green prosperity through the integration of economic growth and environmental protection. This necessity extends not only to ethnic minority areas but also to the entire country. Consequently, the state should provide special policy support. Therefore, it is essential to increase the transfer payments for ecological protection in ethnic minority areas, effectively compensating the local population's interests. Encouraging and assisting them in safeguarding the environment, fostering the development of green industries, and improving their living standards should be prioritized.

The state shall accelerate the establishment of an ecological compensation mechanism. It shall, according to the principle that "developers make payments, beneficiaries offer indemnities and destroyers make compensations", give rational indemnities to the ethnic autonomous areas, which have made contributions in the protection of ecological environment such as the protection of wild animals and plants and the construction of natural reserves, by way of public finance transfer payment or project support at the levels of state, region, and industry. It is also necessary to actively explore the introduction of eco-compensation tax[1], reasonably determine the share ratio between the central government and local governments according to the actual situation of cross-regional ecological compensation, and use all the central ecological compensation tax for transfer payments to restricted development zones and prohibited development zones.

It is recommended that specific and operational measures be introduced as soon as possible to implement Article 66 of the *Law of the People's Republic of China on Regional Ethnic Autonomy*[2], that is, where ethnic autonomous areas make contribution to the ecological balance and environmental protection of the state, the state shall give them due benefit compensation. In establishing an eco-compensation mechanism, governments should fully consider the actual situation in ethnic minority areas and make

---

[1] According to the *Environmental Protection Tax Law of the People's Republic of China*, which was adopted at the 12th National People's Congress of the People's Republic of China and came into force on January 1, 2018, the term used in China is "environmental protection tax", instead of "eco-compensation tax". —*Tr.*

[2] The law was amended in accordance with the *Decision on the Amending the Law of the People's Republic of China on Regional Ethnic Autonomy* made at the 20th Session of the Standing Committee of the Ninth National People's Congress on February 28, 2001.—*Tr.*

overall arrangements, instead of making up for it all at once. A workable management mechanism and a fixed source of funds are needed to ensure the success of projects concerning the overall and long-term ecological interests of the country, such as the Three-North Shelter Forest Program (TNSFP) and the program for soil and water conservation in the middle and upper reaches of the Yangtze River. Governments should encourage innovation and exploration in ecological and environmental policies such as levying environmental protection tax, establishing and improving the eco-compensation mechanism, leveraging resources like assets, operating resources in a market-based way, and sewage trading system.

8.5.7   Further improve the paired-up assistance policy

The paired-up assistance between the economically developed areas and the less-developed minority areas, organized and encouraged by China since the reform and opening up, has played an important role in promoting the socio-economic development of ethnic minority areas. This policy should be further consolidated and improved in the future. Firstly, more assistance providers are needed. In the pairing up in 1979, Beijing was decided to assist Inner Mongolia, Hebei to Guizhou, Jiangsu to Guangxi and Xinjiang, Shandong to Qinghai, Shanghai to Yunnan and Ningxia, and the whole country to Tibet. In 1996, the State Council determined that 15 developed eastern provinces and cities would assist 11 western provinces and autonomous regions. In 2010, 19 provinces and cities across the country were identified to provide paired support to Xinjiang. In 2013, eight cities in six provinces (municipalities), including Liaoning, Shanghai, Jiangsu, Zhejiang, Shandong and Guangdong, were designated to help eight cities (prefectures) in Guizhou. The practice has proved that this one-to-one or one-to-many kind of paired-up assistance can no longer meet the needs of the development of ethnic minority areas. We suggest an adjustment that several provinces and cities provide support to a province with large ethnic minority populations or autonomous region, so as to intensify the efforts in this regard. While continuing to advocate paired assistance at provincial administrative units, we can identify affluent provinces (cities), especially those in coastal areas as the main bodies providing pairing support to areas with large ethnic minority populations and helping the latter develop economy and improve public services. Secondly, it is crucial to expand the coverage of assistance recipients. Apart from the three provinces with large ethnic minority populations and five autonomous regions, there are also eight ethnic autonomous prefectures and 52 ethnic autonomous counties scattered in other provinces and cities in China. These areas, mostly characterized by economic underdevelopment, are in dire need of paired-up assistance from more developed areas. It is imperative that the assistance to these ethnic autonomous areas be primarily organized and implemented by the provinces and cities in which they are located. Finally, when organizing paired-up assistance, it is essential to integrate efforts in economic development with improvements in public services. Assistance providers should leverage their capital, technology, talent, management expertise, and reputation to undertake practical initiatives on an annual basis in ethnic minority areas. This will assist in establishing a self-development mechanism and enhancing their capacity for sustainable progress. Simultaneously, it is crucial to establish an incentive mechanism that encourages donations from various sectors and attracts assistance from the international community. This will pave the way for enhancing public services in areas with large ethnic minority populations.

Bibliography

[1] An Husen, Yin Guangwei, "Central Region Falling: Phenomenon and the Conjecture of Its Internal Mechanism", *Journal of Zhongnan University of Economics and Law*, 2009(1).

[2] An Shuwei, "Impact of the Silk Road Economic Belt and Maritime Silk Road for China's Regional Economic Development", *On Economic Problems*, 2015 (4).

[3] Beijing Water Authority. *Beijing Water Resources Bulletin* (2014), Aug., 2015.

[4] Bo Yibo, *Review of Some Major Decisions and Events*, Beijing: Party School of the CPC Central Committee Publishing House, 1991.

[5] Cai Fang, Wang Dewen and Du Yang, "The Institutional Factors in the 'Conditional Convergence' of China's Economic Growth: The Impact of the Distortions in Labor Market on Regional Disparities", *Social Sciences in China*, 2001 (2).

[6] Caselli, F., W. J. Coleman II, "The U.S. Structural Transformation and Regional Convergence: A Reinterpretation", *Journal of Political Economy*, 2001 (3).

[7] Chen Dongsheng, *Regional Economics*, Zhengzhou: Henan University Press, 1993.

[8] Chen Dongsheng, *Theory and Practice of Economic Layout*, Shenyang: Liaoning University Press, 1989.

[9] Chen Jianxun, *Analysis of Regional Exports and Economic Growth in the Chinese Mainland*, Taipei: Chung-Hua Institute for Economic Research, 1992.

[10] Chen Kaixing, Dong Jun, "What the 'New Northeast Phenomenon' Tells China's Agriculture", *Development Herald*, Feb. 5, 2002.

[11] Cui Qiyuan, "Problems in Measuring China's Inter-Provincial Disparities", in Liu Shucheng, Li Qiang, and Xue Tiandong, *Research on China's Regional Economic Development*, Beijing: China Statistics Press, 1994.

[12] Demurger, S., "Infrastructure Development and Economic Growth: An

Explanation for Regional Disparities in China?" *Journal of Comparative Economics*, 2001(1).

[13] Deng Xiaoping, *Selected Works of Deng Xiaoping* (Vol. Ⅲ), Beijing: People's Publishing House, 1993.

[14] Department of Development Planning, Ministry of Science and Technology, "Statistical monitoring results of scientific and technological progress in China and regions in 2015", http://www.sts.org.cn/, Jun. 30, 2016.

[15] Department of Development Planning, Ministry of Science and Technology, "Statistical monitoring results of scientific and technological progress in China and regions in 2010", *Statistical Data of Chinese S&T Papers* (Issues 1-2), Jan. 31, 2011.

[16] Dong Min, Guo Fei. "Inverted U-shaped Trend and Countermeasures of Urban-Rural Income Gap in the Process of Urbanization", *Contemporary Economic Research*, 2011(8).

[17] Duan Xiaowei, Li Lulu, Miao Changhong and Hu Zhiqiang, "Evaluation of Industry Transfer Comprehensive Undertaking Ability of Six Major Urban Agglomerations in the Central Region", *Scientia Geographica Sinica* (Vol. 36), 2016(3).

[18] Fan Jianyong, "Industrial Structure Imbalance, Spatial Agglomeration and Changes in Regional Disparities in China", *Shanghai Economic Research*, 2008(2).

[19] Fan Jianyong, Zhu Guolin, "Evolution of China's Regional Gap and Its Structural Decomposition", *Journal of Management World*, 2002(7).

[20] Fang Chuanglin, Mao Qizhi and Ni Pengfei, "Discussion on the scientific selection and development of China's urban agglomerations", *Acta Geographica Sinica*, 2015(4).

[21] Fang Chuanglin, Yao Shimou, Liu Shenghe et al., *China Urban Agglomeration Development Report 2010*, Beijing: Science Press, 2011.

[22] Feng Changchun, Zeng Zanrong and Cui Nana, "The economic disparities and their spatio-temporal evolution in China since 2000", *Geographical Research*, 2015(2).

[23] Gao Chunde, "Theory and Practice of Regional Economic Development in China", *Research on Liaoning Economic Plan*, 1989(6).

[24] Gao Lianshui, "Which Kinds of Factors in What Extent Have Decided the Residential Income Inequality", *The Journal of Quantitative and Technical Economics*, 2011(1).

[25] Guo Fansheng, Zhu Jianzhi, "Western Development and 'Western Theory'", *Scientific Management Research*, 1985(6).

[26] Han Jun, "Public Financial Crisis and Rural Development: Case Studies of Xiangyang County in Hubei Province, Yanling County in Henan Province, and Taihe County in Jiangxi Province", in Hiroyuki Kato, Guo Xiaoming, *Proceedings on Globalization and Economic Development in China's Inland Regions*, Chengdu: Sichuan Publishing Group, Sichuan People's Publishing House, 2005.

[27] Household Survey Office, National Bureau of Statistics, *China Rural Poverty Monitoring Report 2016*, Beijing: China Statistics Press, 2016.

[28] Hu Angang, Xiong Yizhi, "An Analysis of Area Gaps in China's Knowledge Development: Their Characteristics, Roots Thereof and Our Policies", *Journal of Management World*, 2000(3).

[29] Karl Marx, Friedrich Engels, *The Complete Works of Marx and Engels* (Vol. 20), Beijing: People's Publishing House, 1979.

[30] Kong Weiwei, "Double Drives of Deepening Reform and Promoting Scientific & Technological Progress: A Brief Discussion on Getting Rid of the 'Northeast Phenomenon'", *Academic Exchange*, 1992(2).

[31] Lei Zhenyang, Cheng Aihua, *Performance Evaluation and System Innovation of Financial Transfer Payment in Ethnic Minority Areas*, Beijing: People's Publishing House, 2010.

[32] Lenin, *Selected Works of Lenin* (Vol. 2), Beijing: People's Publishing House, 1972.

[33] Li Fangyi, Liu Weidong, "Impacts of Energy Intensity Targets in 12 FYP on Regional Economic Development of China", *China Soft Science*, 2014(2).

[34] Li Lingling, Wei Xiao and Chen Wei, "'Central Downfall' and Hunan Economy Rise", *Economic Geography*, 2004(6).

[35] Li Peilin, Wei Houkai, *Annual Report on Poverty Reduction of China* (2016), Beijing: Social Sciences Academic Press (China), 2016.

[36] Li Xiaojian, Gao Genghe and Li Erling, "The Disparity of Public Policy Supply and the Central China's Development", in Zhou Shaosen, Chen Dongsheng, *The Rise of the Central Region*, Beijing: Economic Science Press, 2006.

[37] Li Xibao, "A Case Study on the Changes in the Innovation Capability of China's Regions: A Concept Based on the Innovation System", *Journal of Management World*, 2007(12).

[38] Li Yimei, Zhang Wen, Yin Jidong, "The Rural Labor Transfer and Human Resource Development in the Central Region", in Zhou Shaosen, Chen Dongsheng, *The*

Rise of the Central Region, Beijing: Economic Science Press, 2005.

[39] Li Yue, "The Duality of 'Central Collapse' and the Strategic Orientation of 'Central Rise'", *China Economic Times*, Apr. 2005.

[40] Liang Bin, Jiang Tao, "Natural Resources, Regional Economic Growth and Industrial Structure: Theoretical and Empirical Analysis Based on DSGE Model", *Research on Financial and Economic Issues*, 2016(4).

[41] Liu Gengxi, "Where is the Northeast Grain Outlet?", *China Animal Husbandry Bulletin*, 2002(4).

[42] Liu Jiajie, "The Development Status and Reform Path of the Private Economy in Northeast China", in Ma Ke, Huang Wenyi, *Report on the Development of Northeast China* (2014), Beijing: Social Sciences Academic Press (China), 2014.

[43] Liu Naiquan, Zhang Xueliang, "Mutual Influences of Economic Growth in Eastern, Central and Western Areas", *Contemporary Economic Management*, 2005(1).

[44] Liu Shenglong, Hu Angang, "Transportation Infrastructure and Economic Growth: The Perspective of China's Regional Disparity", *China Industrial Economics*, 2010 (4).

[45] Liu Shucheng et al., "Calculation, Analysis and Policy Suggestions of Income Differences among Different Regions in China", in Liu Shucheng, Li Qiang and Xue Tiandong, *Research on Regional Economic Development in China*, Beijing: China Statistics Press, 1994.

[46] Liu Yong, "The Course, Problems and Trends of Urbanization Development in China", *Economic and Management Research*, 2011(3).

[47] Lu Dadao, Xue Xuanfeng et al., *China Regional Development Report 1997*, Beijing: The Commercial Press, 1997.

[48] Luo Zhigang, "National Urban System, Main Functional Area and National Space System", *Urban Planning Forum*, 2008(3).

[49] Ma Shuanyou, "Central Financial Transfer Payment and Regional Economic Convergence", Wang Luolin, Wei Houkai, *China's Western Development Policy,* Beijing: Economy and Management Publishing House, 2003.

[50] Mao Zedong, *On the Ten Major Relationships*, Beijing: People's Publishing House, 1976.

[51] Mao Zedong, *Selected Works of Mao Zedong* (Vol. V), Beijing: People's Publishing House, 1977.

[52] Ministry of Environmental Protection of the People's Republic of China,

"Bulletin on the State of the Environment in China 2016", May 2017.

[53] Ministry of Environmental Protection of the People's Republic of China, "Bulletin on the State of the Environment in China 2015", May 2016.

[54] Myrdal, G., *Economic Theory and Underdeveloped Regions*, London: Duckworth, 1957.

[55] National Ethnic Affairs Commission of the People's Republic of China, *Tutorial Reader on Learning the Guiding Principles from the Central Ethnic Work Conference*, Beijing: The Ethnic Publishing House, 2005.

[56] Pei Changhong, Zheng Wen, "Basic Objectives and Main Features of China's New Open Economy System", *Economic Perspectives*, 2014(4).

[57] Peng Guohua. "The Matching of Skills to Tasks, Labor Migration and Chinese Regional Income Disparity", *Economic Research Journal*, 2015(1).

[58] Planning Bureau of the State-owned Assets Supervision and Administration Commission, "Research on Several Major Issues of Accelerating the Adjustment and Transformation of Central Enterprises in Northeastern Region", Nov. 2004.

[59] Qin Chenglin, Tang Yong, "Study on the Collapse Characteristics of the Overall Level of Economic Development in Central China", *Regional Research and Development*, 2006(5).

[60] Ren Yuan, Tai Xiujun, "Regional Difference and Decomposition of the Incomes in Rural Area in China on Gini Coefficients", *Reform on Economic System*, 2016(1).

[61] Rozelle, S., "Rural Industrialization and Increasing Inequality: Emerging Patterns in China's Reforming Economy", *Journal of Comparative Economics*, 1994(3).

[62] Schwarze, J., "How Income Inequality Changed in Germany Following Reunification: An Empirical Analysis Using Decomposable Inequality Measures", *Review of Income and Wealth*, 1996(1).

[63] Sha Mo, "On the Relationship between Coastal Industry and Inland Industry", *People's Daily*, Nov. 24, 1956.

[64] Shao Shuai, Qi Zhongying, "Energy Development and Economic Growth in Western China: An Empirical Analysis Based on the Resource Curse Hypothesis", *Economic Research Journal*, 2008(4).

[65] She Xiuyan, "Relationship between Urbanization and Income Gap between Urban and Rural Areas: Inverted 'U' Law and Its Applicability to China", *Social Scientist*, 2013(10).

[66] She Zidong, "The System and Integration of Chinese Ethnic Policy", *Journal of Minzu University of China* (Philosophy and Social Sciences), 2011(6).

[67] Shen Haixiong, Hu Zuohua, "Decrypting the Investment Distribution Map of Zheshang", *Economic Information Daily*, Jun. 12, 2006.

[68] Shi Minjun, Zhang Zhuoying and Zhou Dingyang, "Study on Water Resources Carrying Capacity of Beijing and Tianjin-Based on Water Footprint Perspective", in Wei Kui, Zhu Erjuan et al., *Beijing-Tianjin-Hebei Development Report* (2013): *Carrying Capacity Measurement and Countermeasures*, Beijing: Social Sciences Academic Press (China), 2013.

[69] Shorrocks, A. F., "The Class of Additively Decomposable Inequality Measures", *Econometrica: Journal of the Econometric Society*, 1980(3).

[70] Shorrocks, A., Wan, G., "Spatial Decomposition of Inequality", *Journal of Economic Geography*, 2005(1).

[71] Sun Naiji, "Advantages and Dilemma of Northeast China Economy: Thoughts on 'Northeast Phenomenon'", *Northeast Asia Forum*, 1993(4).

[72] Sun Sheng Han, "Infrastructure Improvement and Regional Development: A Case Study of China,1985-94", *Regional Development Studies* 3 (Winter), UNCRD, 1997.

[73] Sun Tieshan, Liu Xiaoquan, Li Guoping, "Evolution of China's Spatial Economy and Regional Industrial Shift: Empirical Analysis of Changes in Economic Shares of Chinese Provinces from 1952 to 2010", *Scientia Geographica Sinica*, 2015(1).

[74] Sun Yongqiang, Wan Yulin, "Financial Development, Opening-Up and the Income Gap between Urban and Rural Residents: An Empirical Analysis Based on Inter-provincial Panel Data from 1978 to 2008", *Journal of Financial Research*, 2011(1).

[75] Sun, H., *Foreign Investment and Economic Development in China*, 1979-1996, London: Ashgate Publishing Limited, 1998.

[76] Taylor, Alan M., Jeffrey G. Williamson, "Convergence in the Age of Mass Migration", *NBER Working Paper* 4711, Apr. 1994.

[77] The Central Research Group of China Democratic League, "Policy Suggestions on Accelerating the Reform of State-Owned Enterprises in Northeast China and Revitalizing Old Northeast Industrial Bases", Nov. 26, 2003.

[78] The Research Office of the Secretariat of the CPC Central Committee and the Literature Research Office of the CPC Central Committee, *Insisting on Reform, Opening Up, and Invigorating the Economy: Excerpts from Relevant Important*

Documents since the Third Plenary Session of the 13th CPC Central Committee, Beijing: People's Publishing House, 1987.

[79] The State Council Information Office, *China's Ethnic Policy and Common Prosperity and Development of All Ethnic Groups* (White Book), Sep., 2009.

[80] The State Council Information Office, *China's Progress in Poverty Reduction and Human Rights* (White Book), Oct., 2016(a).

[81] The State Council Information Office, *Human Rights in Xinjiang-Development and Progress* (White Book), Jun., 2017.

[82] The State Council Information Office, *The Right to Development: China's Philosophy, Practice and Contribution* (White Book), Dec., 2016(b).

[83] Theil, H., *Economics and Information Theory*, Amsterdam: North-Holland, 1967.

[84] Tian Yinong, Xiang Huaicheng, and Zhu Fulin, *On China's Financial System Reform and Macro-Control*, Beijing: China Financial and Economic Publishing House, 1988.

[85] Tong Yufen, "Analysis of Population Carrying Capacity and Carrying Pressure in Northwest China", *Population and Economy*, 2009(6).

[86] Tsui, K. Y., "Decomposition of China's Regional Inequalities", *Journal of Comparative Economics*, 1993 (3).

[87] Wan Guanghua, "An Empirical Analysis of Income Differences and Changes among Rural Residents in China", *Economic Research Journal*, 1998(5).

[88] Wan Guanghua, Lu Ming and Chen Zhao, "Globalization, and Regional Inequality: Chinese Evidence", *Social Sciences in China*, 2005(3).

[89] Wang Chengqi, Zhang Jianhua and An Hui. "Foreign Direct Investment, Regional Difference and China's Economic Growth", *The Journal of World Economy*, 2002(4).

[90] Wang Fei, Li Shantong, Evolution Trend and Influencing Factors of Regional Disparity in China, *Modern Economic Research*, 2016(12).

[91] Wang Haibo, *The History of Industrial Economy of China* (*1949.10-1957*), Beijing: Economy and Management Publishing House, 1994.

[92] Wang Haibo, *The History of Industrial Economy of China*, Beijing: Economy and Management Publishing House, 1986.

[93] Wang Luolin, *The Next 50 Years: China's Western Development Strategy*, Beijing: Beijing Press, 2002.

[94] Wang Luolin, Wei Houkai, "Main Policy and Measures for Revitalizing the Industrial Base of Northeast China", *China Economic Times*, Jul. 18, 2005(a).

[95] Wang Luolin, Wei Houkai, *Strategy and Policy for Revitalizing Northeast China*, Beijing: Social Sciences Academic Press (China), 2005(b).

[96] Wang Yanzhong, *China Social Security Development Report* (2017), Beijing: Social Sciences Academic Press (China), 2017.

[97] Wang Yeqiang, Wei Houkai, "Analysis on the Time and Space Characteristics of Industrial Geographic Concentration", *Statistical Research*, 2006(6).

[98] Wang Yeqiang, Wei Houkai, "The Adjustment and Responses to the National Strategy of Regional Development During the Period of the National 13th Five-Year Plan", *China Soft Science*, 2015(5).

[99] Wang Yiming, *Research on Regional Economic Policy in China*, Beijing: China Planning Press, 1998.

[100] Wei Hao, Zhao Chunming, "An Empirical Analysis of the Influence of Foreign Trade on the Income Gap between Urban and Rural Areas in China", *Finance and Trade Economy*, 2012(1).

[101] Wei Houkai, "A Brief Discussion on the Problem of Regional Economic Recession", *Research on Financial and Economic Issues*, 1991(4).

[102] Wei Houkai, "A New Strategy of China's Land Development in the New Period", *Green Leaf*, 2009(d)(9).

[103] Wei Houkai, "Analysis of the Difference between GRP and GDP Growth Rate in China", *Academic Journal of Zhongzhou*, 2009(a) (2).

[104] Wei Houkai, "China's Regional Economic Growth and Its Convergence", *China Industrial Economics*, 1997(a)(3).

[105] Wei Houkai, "Coastal industrial clusters are at risk of recession", *Decision-Making*, 2009(c) (2).

[106] Wei Houkai, "Cracking the Northeast Phenomenon and Revitalizing the Economy of the Three Provinces", *China Economic Information*, 2003(a) (20).

[107] Wei Houkai, "Development of Township Enterprises and Regional Differences in China", *Chinese Rural Economy*, 1997(b) (5).

[108] Wei Houkai, "Difficulties and Solutions for Coastal Economy", *China Development Observation*, 2009(b) (7).

[109] Wei Houkai, "Effects of Foreign Direct Investment on Regional Economic Growth in China", *Economic Research Journal*, 2002(4).

[110] Wei Houkai, "New Development View of Regional Economy", *China Industrial Economics*, 2010(4).

[111] Wei Houkai, "Objectives, Models and Policies for the Development of Western China", *Productivity Research*, 1987(6).

[112] Wei Houkai, "On the Coordinated Development Strategy of China's Regional Economy", *New Horizons from Tianfu*, 1994(3).

[113] Wei Houkai, "Regional Development Strategy and Regional Policy", in Lu Dadao et al., *Theory and Practice of Regional Development in China*, Beijing: Science Press, 2003(b).

[114] Wei Houkai, "Some Theoretical Thoughts on City-Based Society", *Urban Studies*, 2013(5).

[115] Wei Houkai, "The Developmental Difference of China's Regional Infrastructure and Manufacturing Industry", *Journal of Management World*, 2001(b) (6).

[116] Wei Houkai, "The New Dilemma of the Northeast Economy and the Strategic Thinking of Revitalization", *Social Science Journal*, 2017(1).

[117] Wei Houkai, "The Scientific Foundation and State Assistance Policy for Promoting the Rise of Economy in Central China", *Economic Survey*, 2006(1).

[118] Wei Houkai, *A New Road to Urbanization with Chinese Characteristics*, Beijing: Social Sciences Academic Press (China), 2014.

[119] Wei Houkai, Cheng Aihua and Zhang Dongmei, "Research on the Central Leadership's Policies for Supporting the Development of Ethnic Minority Areas", *Journal of South-Central University for Nationalities* (Humanities and Social Sciences), 2012(1).

[120] Wei Houkai et al., *Industrial Agglomeration and Cluster Strategy in China*, Beijing: Economy and Management Publishing House, 2008.

[121] Wei Houkai et al., *Regional Policy in China: Review and Outlook*, Beijing: Economy and Management Publishing House, 2011.

[122] Wei Houkai et al., *Research on China's Industrial Layout Adjustment*, Institute of Industrial Economics of CASS, Dec., 2005.

[123] Wei Houkai et al., *Study on China's Regional Coordinated Development*, Beijing: China Social Sciences Press, 2012.

[124] Wei Houkai, *General Idea about the Western Development in the 13th Five-Year Plan*, Beijing: Economy and Management Publishing House, 2016(b).

[125] Wei Houkai, "Globalization, National Strategy and Regional Difference of

China", *Journal of Jiaxing University*, 2005(1).

[126] Wei Houkai, "Income Inequality of Residents among Regions in China and Its Decomposition", *Economic Research Journal*, 1996(11).

[127] Wei Houkai, *Modern Regional Economics*, Beijing: Economy and Management Publishing House, 2011.

[128] Wei Houkai, *New Pattern of Regional Economic Development*, Kunming: Yunnan People's Publishing House, 1995.

[129] Wei Houkai, *Regional Economic Theory and Policy*, Beijing: China Social Sciences Press, 2016(a).

[130] Wei Houkai, *Towards Sustainable and Coordinated Development*, Guangzhou: Guangdong Economy Publishing House, 2001(a).

[131] Wei Houkai, Yuan Xiaomeng, "On the Evaluation and Directional Adjustment of Tax Policies of Western Development in China", *Taxation Research*, 2010(2).

[132] Wen Jun, "Assessment of the Stability of China's Ethnic Minority Economic Policy (1949-2002)" (Part One, Part Two), *Research on Development*, 2004(3) (4).

[133] Williamson, J. G., "Regional Inequality and the Process of National Development: A Description of the Patterns", *Economic Development and Cultural Change*, Vol. XIII, No. 4, Part II, 1965.

[134] World Bank, *World Development Report* 1999/2000: *Entering the* 21st *Century*, Oxford: Oxford University Press, 1999.

[135] World Bank, *World Development Report* 2014: *Risk and Opportunity— Managing Risk for Development*, Washington, DC: World Bank, 2013.

[136] Wu Lixue, "Institutional Change, Economic Growth and Regional Differences", Chinese Academy of Social Sciences, 2004.

[137] Wu Wenzhong, Tang Fei and Li Qin, "Research on the Optimization Path of the Implementation Mechanism of Basic Public Services in Ethnic Minority Areas", *China State Finance*, 2016(16).

[138] Wu Xiaoping, "The Preferential Loans for Civil Trade and Consumer Goods to Be Implemented", *China Finance*, 2015(17).

[139] Xi Jinping, *Secure a Decisive Victory in Building a Moderately Prosperous Society in All Respects and Strive for the Great Success of Socialism with Chinese Characteristics for a New Era,* Beijing: People's Publishing House, 2017.

[140] Xiao Guodong, "Analysis of New Trends in Industrial Structure Adjustment in Three Northeastern Provinces", in Ma Ke, Huang Wenyi, *Development Report of*

Northeast China (2014). Beijing: Social Sciences Academic Press (China), 2014.

[141] Xiao Jincheng, Yuan Zhu et al., *Top Ten Urban Agglomerations in China*, Beijing: Economic Science Press, 2009.

[142] Xie Mei'e, Gu Shuzhong, "Evaluation of Resource Tax Reform and Design Thinking in China's New Period of Economic Development", *Natural Resource Economics of China*, 2017(3).

[143] Xie Shenxiang, Wang Xiaosong, "Trade Openness, FDI and Regional Income Inequality in China: An Empirical Study Based on Provincial Panel Data", *Economic Management*, 2011(4).

[144] Xu Kangning, Han Jian, "'Resource Curse' Effect on Regional Economy in China: Another Explanation to Regional Discrepancy", *The Economist*, 2005(6).

[145] Xu Yiping, "Nearly 4 Trillion 'Zhejiang Capital' Swarms Outside the Province", *Oriental Morning Post*, Jan. 5, 2011.

[146] Xu Zhaoyuan, Li Shantong, "The Effects of Inter-Regional Migration on Economic Growth and Regional Disparities", *The Journal of Quantitative and Technical Economics*, 2008(2).

[147] Y. G. Saushkin, *Economic Geography*, Beijing: The Commercial Press, 1995.

[148] Yan Chengliang, "Industrial Structure Change, Economic Growth, and Regional Development Gap", *Comparative Economic and Social Systems*, 2016(4).

[149] Yang Dali, "Changes in China's Intra-Provincial Regional Differences since the Reform", *China Industrial Economics*, 1995(1).

[150] Yang Shenggang, Zhu Hong, "Central Sinking, Financial Weakening and Studies on Realizing the Central Rising by Financial Support", *Economic Research Journal*, 2007(3).

[151] Yang Weimin et al., "Implementing functional area zoning strategy and building an efficient, coordinated, sustainable, and beautiful home: A general report on functional zoning strategy", *Journal of Management World*, 2012(10).

[152] Yao Shimou, Chen Zhenguang, Zhu Yingming et al., *China's Urban Agglomerations*, Hefei: University of Science and Technology of China Press, 2006.

[153] Yao Yuchun, Fan Xinzhang and Shu Ting, "Resource-rich Regions: Resource Endowment and Regional Economic Growth", *Journal of Management World*, 2014(7).

[154] Yao Zhizhong, Zhou Sufang, "Labor Mobility and Regional Gap", *The Journal of World Economy*, 2003(4).

[155] Yu Yongze, "Research on Dynamic Spatial Convergence of Inter-Provincial

Total Factor Productivity in China", *The Journal of World Economy*, 2015(10).

[156] Yuan Dongmei, Wei Houkai and Yang Huan, "Trade Openness, Improvement of Trade Commodity Composition and Urban-Rural Income Inequality: An Empirical Study Based on Provincial Panel Data in China", *China Soft Science*, 2011(6).

[157] Zhang Keyun, "Operation Problems and Solutions of Main Functional Areas", *China Development Observation*, 2007(3).

[158] Zhang Keyun, "View of Failure Is Untenable: How to Position the New Round of Northeast Revitalization Precisely", *People's Tribune*, 2015(21).

[159] Zhang Keyun, *Regional Economic Policies*, Beijing: The Commercial Press, 2005.

[160] Zhang Lijun, Han Xiaoyan and Wang Fei, "A Review and Evaluation of Chinese Ethnic Economic Policy", *Ethno-National Studies*, 2010(4).

[161] Zhang Ping, "Income Distribution Among Residents in Rural China", *Economic Research Journal*, 1992(2).

[162] Zhang Ping, "Income Distribution of Residents Among Rural Areas", in Zhao Renwei, Griffin Keith, *The Distribution of Income in China*, Beijing: China Social Sciences Press, 1994.

[163] Zhang Qi, "Analysis on the Gap of Economic Development in China", *Journal of Management World*, 2001(1).

[164] Zhang Xueliang, "Has Transport Infrastructure Promoted Regional Economic Growth? With an Analysis of the Spatial Spillover Effects of Transport Infrastructure", *Social Sciences in China*, 2012(3).

[165] Zhang Yan, Wei Houkai, "'U-Shaped' Change on the Degree of Regional Coordinated Development and Its Stability in China", *Jianghai Academic Journal*, 2012(2).

[166] Zhang Ying, "Financial Policy Suggestions for Revitalizing Old Northeast Industrial Bases", Gainful Investment Group, Jul. 15, 2004.

[167] Zhao Wei, Li Fen, "The Influence of Heterogeneous Labor Force Mobility on Regional Income Gaps: An Expansion of New Economic Geography Model", *Chinese Journal of Population Science*, 2007(1).

[168] Zhao Ziyang, "Report on the Sixth Five-Year Plan", *People's Daily*, Dec. 14, 1982.

[169] Zheng Changde, "The 'Five Developments' Concept and Research on the Comprehensive Economic and Social Development of Ethnic Minority Areas", *Journal*

of Ethnic Studies, 2017(1).

[170] Zhou Shaosen, Wang Zhiguo and Hu Delong, "'The Central Downfall' and the Rise of the Central Region", *Journal of Nanchang University* (*Humanities and Social Sciences*), 2003(6).

[171] Zhou Taihe, *Historical Experience of China's Economic System Reform*, Beijing: People's Publishing House, 1983.

[172] Zhou Yixing, *Urban Geography*, Beijing: The Commercial Press, 1995.

[173] Zhu Ziyun, "Double-Level Excavating Analysis of China's Inter-Provincial Gaps of Economic Development", *The Journal of Quantitative and Technical Economics*, 2015(1).

Postscript

China's regional economic development after the founding of the People's Republic of China in 1949 can be roughly divided into two stages by the year of 1978. During the first stage (before 1978), China faced a seriously unbalanced distribution of productivity and a challenging international situation. Driven by the desire for quick success, China adopted a balanced development strategy with the primary objective of addressing the imbalances in productivity distribution and narrowing regional gaps. And also, China initiated a large-scale program called the "Third Front" Construction in its interior regions to strengthen national defense. Despite its positive role in promoting the industrialization in the central and western regions, this strategy did not achieve the desired results due to its neglect of tapping into local strengths in coastal areas. Not only did it fail to effectively halt the expansion of regional gaps, but it also resulted in relatively poor macro-and micro-economic performance.

The second stage started from 1978, when the reform and opening-up policy was launched. Since then, China has, after drawing on domestic and foreign experience and lessons and taking into account its own national conditions, embarked on a strategic path towards coordinated regional development by promoting unbalanced development or gradient advancement, and has rather smoothly achieved the strategic shift from the initial unbalanced development to the subsequent coordinated regional development. This long-term historic shift finally paid off in the sense that it not only ensured high-speed growth of China's economy for more than three decades, but also boosted the general economic development of all regions through narrowing regional disparities in an all-round way. It can be said that after long-term unremitting and proactive efforts, China has gradually paved a distinctively Chinese path to coordinated regional development.

To sum up, this characteristic strategy aims at achieving multi-level coordinated regional development in a progressive manner, and it bears three fundamental characteristics. The first is the presence of a top-level design, which ensures the correct direction of regional development. The two well-known concepts proposed by Deng Xiaoping — "Those who get rich first help and drive others to get rich later, so that common prosperity can be achieved" and "Two Overall Situations"—serve as the guiding top-level design for China's regional economic development. The essence of these two concepts lies in the pursuit of unbalanced yet coordinated development, surpassing the traditional theoretical frameworks of balanced development theory and unbalanced development theory.

The second is the pursuit of multi-level regional development. Coordinated development of regional economies is jointly promoted at multiple levels. This includes the master strategy for regional development, which encompasses the large-scale development of the western region, the revitalization of the northeastern region, the rise of the central region, and the trailblazing of the eastern region. In addition, there are the coordinated development of the Beijing-Tianjin-Hebei region, the development of the Yangtze River Economic Belt, and the Belt and Road Initiative. Furthermore, China has implemented its land development strategies, such as functional zoning and multi-center networking, are also part of this multi-level pursuit.

The third is the implementation of differentiated regional policies through category-based management. Different policies have been adopted in different economic function zones, functional zones, and special type zones under classified management. This not only embodies the principle of "providing differential treatment and classified guidance", but also helps enhance the effectiveness of policy implementation.

From China's remarkable success in pursuing coordinated regional development since reform and opening up, some lessons can be derived from the following aspects. Firstly, the Communist Party of China and the Chinese government consistently prioritize coordinated regional development and consider it as a long-term fundamental policy to ensure continuity and stability. Secondly, the institutional and political advantages of socialism with Chinese characteristics provide a strong organizational guarantee for regional coordinated development. This is done through mobilizing and allocating resources of the whole Party, country, and society, and launching programs such as "pairing assistance" and poverty alleviation. Thirdly, the synergy of fiscal, financial, industrial, and regional economic policies actively promotes the rational flow and balanced allocation of production factors between regions. This facilitates the rational division of labor and coordinated development of regional economies. Fourthly, China has gradually shifted its regional policy goal from emphasizing high efficiency to prioritizing fairness. This is done by increasing transfer payments to old revolutionary base areas, areas with large ethnic minority populations, border areas, resource-exhausted cities, key ecologically functional areas, and so on. Lastly, by formulating and implementing targeted regional plans, various types of economically functional zones have been established. These zones allow local governments to take the initiative and actively cultivate new development momentum and growth poles.

This book was written and published upon the invitation of research fellow Lyu Zheng, and it is based on my previous research. I initially thought that with a good foundation, it would be an easy task. However, that has not been the case. I dedicated over a year, starting at the end of 2016 and continuing until the final draft. Throughout this process, I would like to express my gratitude to Wang Songji, Han Zhenyu, Xu-Li Luyi, Xuan Huiyong, and Cao Yipeng for their assistance in data collection and information collation. Chapter 8 has been updated based on the research results from my cooperation with Cheng Aihua and Zhang Dongmei.

In summary, China has dedicated nearly 70 years to the long-term, arduous exploration in coordinated development of regional economies, resulting in a wealth of experience and valuable lessons. Creating a comprehensive, scientific, and systematic summary is not an easy task. Therefore, this book merely offers some of my personal thoughts with the hope of promoting further development in the research and practice of regional economic theory.

Wei Houkai

Beijing

August 21, 2018